W9-BFI-463

SOLUTIONS TO BLACK EXERCISES

ROXY WILSON

Volume 1 for Chem 110

To Accompany *Chemistry: The Central Science*
Brown / LeMay / Bursten / Murphy

Taken from:

Solutions to Black Exercises
by Roxy Wilson to accompany
Chemistry: The Central Science, Eleventh Edition
by Theodore L. Brown, H. Eugene LeMay, Jr., Bruce E. Bursten, and
Catherine J. Murphy

Custom Publishing

New York   Boston   San Francisco
London   Toronto   Sydney   Tokyo   Singapore   Madrid
Mexico City   Munich   Paris   Cape Town   Hong Kong   Montreal

Taken from:

Solutions to Black Exercises
by Roxy Wilson to accompany
Chemistry: The Central Science, Eleventh Edition
by Theodore L. Brown, H. Eugene LeMay, Jr., Bruce E. Bursten, and Catherine J. Murphy
Copyright © 2009, 2006, 2003, 2000, 1997, 1994, 1991, 1988, 1985, 1981, 1977 by Pearson Education, Inc.
Published by Prentice Hall
Upper Saddle River, New Jersey 07458

All rights reserved. No part of this book may be reproduced, in any form or by any means, without permission in writing from the publisher.

This special edition published in cooperation with Pearson Custom Publishing.

All trademarks, service marks, registered trademarks, and registered service marks are the property of their respective owners and are used herein for identification purposes only.

Printed in the United States of America

10 9 8 7 6 5 4 3 2 1

2009180293

JK

**Pearson
Custom Publishing**
is a division of

www.pearsonhighered.com

ISBN 10: 0-558-37824-2
ISBN 13: 978-0-558-37824-0

CONTENTS

Chapter 1   Introduction: Matter and Measurement............................1

Chapter 2   Atoms, Molecules, and Ions.................................11

Chapter 3   Stoichiometry: Calculations with
Chemical Formulas and Equations............................23

Chapter 4   Aqueous Reactions and Solution Stoichiometry................44

Chapter 5   Thermochemistry.................................58

Chapter 6   Electronic Structure of Atoms 76

Chapter 7   Periodic Properties of the Elements 92

Chapter 8   Basic Concepts of Chemical Bonding......................108

Chapter 9   Molecular Geometry and Bonding Theories.................130

Chapter 10   Gases 154

Chapter 11   Intermolecular Forces, Liquids, and Solids 172

Chapter 13   Properties of Solutions 202

Chapter 15   Chemical Equilibrium................................237

Chapter 18   Chemistry of the Environment 298

Chapter 25   The Chemistry of Life: Organic and Biological Chemistry.......403

1 Introduction: Matter and Measurement

Visualizing Concepts

1.2 After a *physical change*, the identities of the substances involved are the same as their identity before the change. That is, molecules retain their original composition. During a *chemical change*, at least one new substance is produced; rearrangement of atoms into new molecules occurs.

The diagram represents a **chemical change**, because the molecules after the change are different than the molecules before the change.

1.3 (a) time (b) density (c) length (d) area (e) temperature

(f) volume (g) temperature

1.5 Measurements (darts) that are close to each other are *precise*. Measurements that are close to the "true value" (the bull's eye) are *accurate*.

(a) Figure ii represents data that are both accurate and precise. The darts are close to the bull's eye and each other.

(b) Figure i represents data that are precise but inaccurate. The darts are near each other but their center point (average value) is far from the bull's eye.

(c) Figure iii represents data that are imprecise but their average value is accurate. The darts are far from each other, but their average value, or geometric center point, is close to the bull's eye.

1.7 The determined age of the artifact, 1,900 years, has two significant figures. There is uncertainty in the hundreds place, indicating that the minimum uncertainty in age is 100 years. The 20-year period since the age was determined is not significant relative to the determined age.

1.9 In order to cancel units, the conversion factor must have the unit being canceled opposite the starting position. For example, if the unit cm starts in the numerator, then the conversion factor must have cm in its denominator. However, if the unit cm starts in the denominator, the conversion factor must have cm in the numerator. Ideally, this will lead to the desired units in the appropriate location, numerator or denominator. However, the inverse of the answer can be taken when necessary.

1.10 Given: mi/hr Find: km/s

$$\boxed{\begin{array}{c}\text{Given}\\ \text{mi/hr}\end{array}} \xrightarrow{\text{use } \frac{1\,\text{km}}{0.62\,\text{mi}}} \boxed{\text{km/hr}} \xrightarrow{\text{use } \frac{1\,\text{hr}}{60\,\text{min}}} \boxed{\text{km/min}} \xrightarrow{\text{use } \frac{1\,\text{hr}}{60\,\text{min}}} \boxed{\begin{array}{c}\text{Find}\\ \text{km/s}\end{array}}$$

1

Classification and Properties of Matter

1.12   (a)   homogeneous mixture

      (b)   heterogeneous mixture (particles in liquid)

      (c)   pure substance

      (d)   heterogeneous mixture

1.14   (a)   C   (b) N   (c) Br   (d) Zn   (e) Fe (f) phosphorus

      (g)   calcium   (h) helium (i) lead (j) silver

1.16   Before modern instrumentation, the classification of a pure substance as an element was determined by whether it could be broken down into component elements. Scientists subjected the substance to all known chemical means of decomposition, and if the results were negative, the substance was an element. Classification by negative results was somewhat ambiguous, since an effective decomposition technique might exist but not yet have been discovered.

1.18   *Physical properties*: silver-grey (color); melting point = 420°C; hardness = 2.5 Mohs; density = 7.13 g/cm^3 at 25°C. *Chemical properties*: metal; reacts with sulfuric acid to produce hydrogen gas; reacts slowly with oxygen at elevated temperatures to produce ZnO.

1.20   (a)   chemical

      (b)   physical

      (c)   physical (The production of H_2O is a chemical change, but its **condensation** is a physical change.)

      (d)   physical (The production of soot is a chemical change, but its **deposition** is a physical change.)

1.22   Take advantage of differences in physical properties to separate the components of a mixture. First heat the liquid to 100°C to evaporate the water. This is conveniently done in a distillation apparatus (Figure 1.13) so that the water can be collected. After the water is completely evaporated and if there is a residue, measure the physical properties of the residue such as color, density, and melting point. Compare the observed properties of the residue to those of table salt, NaCl. If the properties match, the colorless liquid contained table salt. If the properties don't match, the liquid contained a different dissolved solid. If there is no residue, no dissolved solid is present.

Units and Measurement

1.24   (a) $6.35 \times 10^{-2}\,L \ \times \ \dfrac{1\,mL}{1 \times 10^{-3}\,L} = 63.5\,mL$

      (b) $6.5 \times 10^{-6}\,s \ \times \ \dfrac{1\,\mu s}{1 \times 10^{-6}\,s} = 6.5\,\mu s$

      (c) $9.5 \times 10^{-4}\,m \ \times \ \dfrac{1\,mm}{1 \times 10^{-3}\,m} = 0.95\,mm$

(d) $4.23 \times 10^{-9} \text{ m}^3 \times \dfrac{1^3 \text{ mm}^3}{(1 \times 10^{-3})^3 \text{ m}^3} = 4.23 \text{ mm}^3$

     $4.23 \text{ mm}^3 \times \dfrac{(10^{-1})^3 \text{ cm}^3}{1^3 \text{ mm}^3} \times \dfrac{1 \text{ mL}}{1 \text{ cm}^3} \times \dfrac{1 \times 10^{-3} \text{ L}}{1 \text{ mL}} \times \dfrac{1 \text{ μL}}{1 \times 10^{-6} \text{ L}} = 4.23 \text{ μL}$

(e) $12.5 \times 10^{-8} \text{ kg} \times \dfrac{1 \times 10^3 \text{ g}}{1 \text{ kg}} \times \dfrac{1 \text{ mg}}{1 \times 10^{-3} \text{ g}} = 0.125 \text{ mg} \, (125 \, \text{μg})$

(f) $3.5 \times 10^{-10} \text{ g} \times \dfrac{1 \text{ ng}}{1 \times 10^{-9} \text{ g}} = 0.35 \text{ ng}$

(g) $6.54 \times 10^9 \text{ fs} \times \dfrac{1 \times 10^{-15} \text{ s}}{1 \text{ fs}} \times \dfrac{1 \text{ μs}}{1 \times 10^{-6} \text{ s}} = 6.54 \text{ μs}$

1.26   (a)   °C = 5/9 (87°F – 32°) = 31°C

        (b)   K = 25°C + 273 = 298 K; °F = 9/5 (25°C) + 32 = 77°F

        (c)   °C = 5/9 (175°F – 32°) = 79.444 = 79.4°C

            K = °C + 273.15 = 79.444°C + 273.15 = 352.6 K

        (d)   °F = 9/5 (755°C) + 32 = 1391°F; K = 755°C + 273.15 = 1028 K

            (It could be argued that the result of 9/5 (755) has 3 sig figs, so the final Fahrenheit temperature should have 3 sig figs, 1390°F.)

        (e)   melting point = –248.6°C + 273.15 = 24.6 K
            boiling point = –246.1°C + 273.15 = 27.1 K

1.28   (a)   volume = length³ (cm³); density = mass/volume (g/cm³)

            volume = (1.500)³ cm³ = 3.375 cm³

            $\text{density} = \dfrac{76.31 \text{ g}}{3.375 \text{ cm}^3} = 22.61 \text{ g/cm}^3 \text{ osmium}$

        (b) $125.0 \text{ mL} \times \dfrac{1 \text{ cm}^3}{1 \text{ mL}} \times \dfrac{4.51 \text{ g}}{1 \text{ cm}^3} = 563.75 = 564 \text{ g titanium}$

        (c) $0.1500 \text{ L} \times \dfrac{1 \text{ mL}}{1 \times 10^{-3} \text{ L}} \times \dfrac{0.8787 \text{ g}}{1 \text{ mL}} = 131.8 \text{ g benzene}$

1.30   (a) $\dfrac{21.95 \text{ g}}{25.0 \text{ mL}} = 0.878 \text{ g/mL}$

            The tabulated value has four significant figures, while the experimental value has three. The tabulated value rounded to three figures is 0.879. The values agree within one in the last significant figure of the experimental value; the two results agree. The liquid could be benzene.

(b) $15.0\,g \times \dfrac{1\,mL}{0.7781\,g} = 19.3\,mL$ cyclohexane

(c) $r = d/2 = 5.0\,cm/2 = 2.5\,cm$

$V = 4/3\,\pi\,r^3 = 4/3 \times \pi \times (2.5)^3\,cm^3 = 65\,cm^3$

$65.4498\,cm^3 \times \dfrac{11.34\,g}{cm^3} = 7.4 \times 10^2\,g$

(The answer has two significant figures because the diameter had only two figures.)

Note: This is the first exercise where "intermediate rounding" occurs. In this manual, when a solution is given in steps, the intermediate result will be rounded to the correct number of significant figures. However, the **unrounded** number will be used in subsequent calculations. The final answer will appear with the correct number of significant figures. That is, calculators need not be cleared and new numbers entered in the middle of a calculation sequence. This may result in a small discrepancy in the last significant digit between student-calculated answers and those given in the manual. These variations occur in any analysis of numerical data.

For example, in this exercise the volume of the sphere, $65.4498\,cm^3$, is rounded to $65\,cm^3$, but 65.4498 is retained in the subsequent calculation of mass, 7.4×10^2 g. In this case, $65\,cm^3 \times 11.34\,g/cm^3$ also yields 7.4×10^2 g. In other exercises, the correctly rounded results of the two methods may not be identical.

1.32   Calculate the volume of the rod:

$2.17\,kg \times \dfrac{1000\,g}{1\,kg} \times \dfrac{1\,cm^3}{2.33\,g} = 931.3 = 931\,cm^3$

$V = \pi\,r^2 h;\, d = 2r, r = d/2;\quad V = \pi\left(\dfrac{d}{2}\right)^2 h;\quad d^2 = \dfrac{4\,V}{\pi\,h};\, d = \left(\dfrac{4\,V}{\pi\,h}\right)^{1/2}$

$d = \left(\dfrac{4\,(931.3)\,cm^3}{\pi\,(16.8)\,cm}\right)^{1/2} = 8.401 = 8.40\,cm$

Uncertainty in Measurement

1.34   Exact: (b), (e) (The number of students is exact on any given day.)

1.36   (a) 4   (b) 3   (c) 4   (d) 5   (e) 6

1.38   (a) 7.93×10^3 mi   (b) 4.001×10^4 km

1.40   (a) $[320.5 - 6104.5/2.3] = -2.3 \times 10^3$ (The intermediate result has two significant figures, so only the thousand and hundred places in the answer are significant.)

(b) $[285.3 \times 10^5 - 0.01200 \times 10^5] \times 2.8954 = 8.260 \times 10^7$ (Since subtraction depends on decimal places, both numbers must have the same exponent to determine decimal places/sig figs. The intermediate result has 1 decimal place and 4 sig figs, so the answer has 4 sig figs.)

(c) $(0.0045 \times 20{,}000.0)$ + (2813×12) $= 3.4 \times 10^4$

       2 sig figs / 0 dec pl   2 sig figs / first 2 digits

(d)   863 $\times$ [1255   – (3.45×108)] $= 7.62 \times 10^5$

                                          (3 sig figs / 0 dec pl)

     3 sig figs $\times$ [0 dec pl / 3 sig figs]   = 3 sig figs

Dimensional Analysis

1.42   In each conversion factor, the old unit appears in the denominator, so it cancels, and the new unit appears in the numerator.

(a) $\mu m \to mm$: $\dfrac{1 \times 10^{-6}\ m}{1\ \mu m} \times \dfrac{1\ mm}{1 \times 10^{-3}\ m} = 1 \times 10^{-3}\ mm\,/\,\mu m$

(b) $ms \to ns$: $\dfrac{1 \times 10^{-3}\ s}{1\ ms} \times \dfrac{1\ ns}{1 \times 10^{-9}\ s} = 1 \times 10^{6}\ ns\,/\,ms$

(c) $mi \to km$:   1.6093 km/mi

(d) $ft^3 \to L$: $\dfrac{(12)^3\ in^3}{1\ ft^3} \times \dfrac{(2.54)^3\ cm^3}{1\ in^3} \times \dfrac{1\ L}{1000\ cm^3} = 28.3\ L/ft^3$

1.44   (a) $\dfrac{2.998 \times 10^8\ m}{s} \times \dfrac{1\ km}{1000\ m} \times \dfrac{60\ s}{1\ min} \times \dfrac{60\ min}{1\ hr} = 1.079 \times 10^9\ km/hr$

(b) $1454\ ft \times \dfrac{1\ yd}{3\ ft} \times \dfrac{1\ m}{1.0936\ yd} = 443.18 = 443.2\ m$

(c) $3{,}666{,}500\ m^3 \times \dfrac{1^3\ dm^3}{(1 \times 10^{-1})^3\ m^3} \times \dfrac{1\ L}{1\ dm^3} = 3.6665 \times 10^9\ L$

(d) $\dfrac{232\ mg\ cholesterol}{100\ mL\ blood} \times \dfrac{1\ mL}{1 \times 10^{-3}\ L} \times 5.2\ L \times \dfrac{1 \times 10^{-3}\ g}{1\ mg} = 12\ g\ cholesterol$

1.46   (a) $0.105\ in \times \dfrac{2.54\ cm}{in} \times \dfrac{1 \times 10^{-2}\ m}{cm} \times \dfrac{1\ mm}{1 \times 10^{-3}\ m} = 2.667 = 2.67\ mm$

(b) $0.650\ qt \times \dfrac{1\ L}{1.057\ qt} \times \dfrac{1\ mL}{1 \times 10^{-3}\ L} = 614.94 = 615\ mL$

(c) $\dfrac{8.75\ \mu m}{s} \times \dfrac{1 \times 10^{-6}\ m}{1\ \mu m} \times \dfrac{1\ km}{1 \times 10^3\ m} \times \dfrac{60\ s}{1\ min} \times \dfrac{60\ min}{1\ hr} = 3.15 \times 10^{-5}\ km/hr$

(d) $1.955\ m^3 \times \dfrac{(1.0936)^3\ yd^3}{1\ m^3} = 2.55695 = 2.557\ yd^3$

(e) $\dfrac{\$3.99}{lb} \times \dfrac{2.205\ lb}{1\ kg} = 8.798 = \$8.80/kg$

(f) $\dfrac{8.75\,lb}{ft^3} \times \dfrac{453.59\,g}{1\,lb} \times \dfrac{1\,ft^3}{12^3\,in^3} \times \dfrac{1\,in^3}{2.54^3\,cm^3} \times \dfrac{1\,cm^3}{1\,mL} = 0.140\,g/mL$

1.48   (a) $1486\,mi \times \dfrac{1\,km}{0.62137\,mi} \times \dfrac{charge}{225\,km} = 10.6\,charges$

         Since charges are integral events, 11 charges are required.

         (b) $\dfrac{14\,m}{s} \times \dfrac{1\,km}{1 \times 10^3\,m} \times \dfrac{1\,mi}{1.6093\,km} \times \dfrac{60\,s}{1\,min} \times \dfrac{60\,min}{1\,hr} = 31\,mi/hr$

         (c) $450\,in^3 \times \dfrac{(2.54)^3\,cm^3}{1\,in^3} \times \dfrac{1\,mL}{1\,cm^3} \times \dfrac{1 \times 10^{-3}\,L}{1\,mL} = 7.37\,L$

         (d) $2.4 \times 10^5\,barrels \times \dfrac{42\,gal}{1\,barrel} \times \dfrac{4\,qt}{1\,gal} \times \dfrac{1\,L}{1.057\,qt} = 3.8 \times 10^7\,L$

1.50 $9.0\,ft \times 14.5\,ft \times 18.8\,ft = 2453.4 = 2.5 \times 10^3\,ft^3$

         $2453.4\,ft^3 \times \dfrac{(1\,yd)^3}{(3\,ft)^3} \times \dfrac{(1\,m)^3}{(1.094\,yd)^3} \times \dfrac{48\,\mu g\,CO}{1\,m^3} \times \dfrac{1 \times 10^{-6}\,g}{1\,\mu g} = 3.3 \times 10^{-3}\,g\;CO$

1.52   Select a common unit for comparison, in this case the kg.

         $1\,kg > 2\,lb,\ 1\,L \approx 1\,qt$

         5 lb potatoes < 2.5 kg

         5 kg sugar = 5 kg

         $1\,gal = 4\,qt \approx 4\,L.\ 1\,mL\,H_2O = 1\,g\,H_2O.\ 1\,L = 1000\,g,\ 4\,L = 4000\,g = 4\,kg$

         The order of mass from lightest to heaviest is 5 lb potatoes < 1 gal water < 5 kg sugar.

1.54   A wire is a very long, thin cylinder of volume, $V = \pi\,r^2\,h$, where h is the length of the wire and $\pi\,r^2$ is the cross-sectional area of the wire.

         Strategy: 1) Calculate total volume of copper in cm^3 from mass and density

                  2) $h\ (length\ in\ cm) = \dfrac{V}{\pi\,r^2}$

                  3) Change $cm \rightarrow ft$

         $150\,lb\,Cu \times \dfrac{453.6\,g}{1\,lb\,Cu} \times \dfrac{1\,cm^3}{8.94\,g} = 7610.7 = 7.61 \times 10^3\,cm^3$

         $r = d/2 = 8.25\,mm \times \dfrac{1\,cm}{10\,mm} \times \dfrac{1}{2} = 0.4125 = 0.413\,cm$

         $h = \dfrac{V}{\pi r^2} = \dfrac{7610.7\,cm^3}{\pi(0.4125)^2\,cm^2} = 1.4237 \times 10^4 = 1.42 \times 10^4\,cm$

         $1.4237 \times 10^4\,cm \times \dfrac{1\,in}{2.54\,cm} \times \dfrac{1\,ft}{12\,in} = 467\,ft$

         (too difficult to estimate)

Additional Exercises

1.56 **(a)** A gold coin is probably a *solid solution*. Pure gold (element 79) is too soft and too valuable to be used for coinage, so other metals are added. However, the simple term "gold coin" does not give a specific indication of the other metals in the mixture.

A cup of coffee is a *solution* if there are no suspended solids (coffee grounds). It is a heterogeneous mixture if there are grounds. If cream or sugar is added, the homogeneity of the mixture depends on how thoroughly the components are mixed.

A wood plank is a *heterogeneous mixture* of various cellulose components. The different domains in the mixture are visible as wood grain or knots.

(b) The ambiguity in each of these examples is that the name of the substance does not provide a complete description of the material. We must rely on mental images, and these vary from person to person.

1.57 **(a)** A *hypothesis* is a possible explanation for certain phenomena based on preliminary experimental data. A *theory* may be more general, and has a significant body of experimental evidence to support it; a theory has withstood the test of experimentation.

(b) A scientific *law* is a summary or statement of natural behavior; it tells how matter behaves. A *theory* is an explanation of natural behavior; it attempts to explain why matter behaves the way it does.

1.59 **(a)** I. $(22.52 + 22.48 + 22.54)/3 = 22.51$

II. $(22.64 + 22.58 + 22.62)/3 = 22.61$

Based on the average, set I is more accurate. That is, it is closer to the true value of 22.52%.

(b) Average deviation $= \Sigma \,|\, \text{value} - \text{average} \,|\,/3$

I. $|\, 22.52 - 22.51 \,| + |\, 22.48 - 22.51 \,| + |\, 22.54 - 22.51 \,|/3 = 0.02$

II. $|\, 22.64 - 22.61 \,| + |\, 22.58 - 22.61 \,| + |\, 22.62 - 22.61 \,|/3 = 0.02$

The two sets display the same precision, even though set I is more accurate.

1.60 **(a)** Inappropriate. The circulation of a widely-read publication like *National Geographic* would vary over a year's time, and could simply not be counted to the nearest single subscriber. Probably about four significant figures would be appropriate.

(b) Inappropriate. In a county with 5 million people, the population fluctuates with moves, births, and deaths. The population cannot be known precisely to the nearest person, even over the course of a day. There would be uncertainty in at least the tens, probably the hundreds place in the population.

(c) Appropriate. The percentage has three significant figures. In a population as large as the United States, the number of people named Brown can surely be counted by census data or otherwise to a precision of three significant figures.

1.62   (a) $\dfrac{m}{s^2}$ (b) $\dfrac{kg-m}{s^2}$ (c) $\dfrac{kg-m}{s^2} \times m = \dfrac{kg-m^2}{s^2}$

      (d) $\dfrac{kg-m}{s^2} \times \dfrac{1}{m^2} = \dfrac{kg}{m-s^2}$ (e) $\dfrac{kg-m^2}{s^2} \times \dfrac{1}{s} = \dfrac{kg-m^2}{s^3}$

1.63   (a) $2.4 \times 10^5 \text{ mi} \times \dfrac{1.609 \text{ km}}{1 \text{ mi}} \times \dfrac{1000 \text{ m}}{1 \text{ km}} = 3.9 \times 10^8 \text{ m}$

      (b) $2.4 \times 10^5 \text{ mi} \times \dfrac{1.609 \text{ km}}{1 \text{ mi}} \times \dfrac{1 \text{ hr}}{350 \text{ km}} \times \dfrac{60 \text{ min}}{1 \text{ hr}} \times \dfrac{60 \text{ s}}{1 \text{ min}} = 4.0 \times 10^6 \text{ s}$

1.65   (a) $\dfrac{\$1950}{acre-ft} \times \dfrac{1 \text{ acre}}{4840 \text{ yd}^2} \times \dfrac{3 \text{ ft}}{1 \text{ yd}} \times \dfrac{(1.094 \text{ yd})^3}{(1 \text{ m})^3} \times \dfrac{(1 \text{ m})^3}{(10 \text{ dm})^3} \times \dfrac{(1 \text{ dm})^3}{1 \text{ L}} =$

       $\$1.583 \times 10^{-3}/L$ or 0.1583 ¢/L $(0.158$ ¢/L to 3 sig figs)

      (b) $\dfrac{\$1950}{acre-ft} \times \dfrac{1 \text{ acre-ft}}{2 \text{ households-year}} \times \dfrac{1 \text{ year}}{365 \text{ days}} \times 1 \text{ household} = \dfrac{\$2.671}{day} = \dfrac{\$2.67}{day}$

1.66   There are 209.1 degrees between the freezing and boiling points on the Celsius (C) scale and 100 degrees on the glycol (G) scale. Also, $-11.5°C = 0°G$. By analogy with °F and °C,

     $°G = \dfrac{100}{209.1}(°C + 11.5)$ or $°C = \dfrac{209.1}{100}(°G) - 11.5$

These equations correctly relate the freezing point (and boiling point) of ethylene glycol on the two scales.

     f.p. of H_2O: $°G = \dfrac{100}{209.1}(0°C + 11.5) = 5.50°G$

1.68   Density is the ratio of mass and volume. For substances with different densities, the greater the density the smaller the volume of substance that will contain a certain mass. Since volume is directly related to diameter ($V = 4/3 \pi r^3 = 1/6 \pi d^3$), the more dense the substance, the smaller the diameter of a ball that contains a certain mass. The order of the sphere sizes (diameters) is the reverse order of densities: Pb < Ag < Al.

1.69   The mass of water in the bottle does not change with temperature, but the density (ratio of mass to volume) does. That is, the amount of volume occupied by a certain mass of water changes with temperature. Calculate the mass of water in the bottle at 25°C, and then the volume occupied by this mass at $-10°C$.

     (a)   25°C: $1.50 \text{ L } H_2O \times \dfrac{1000 \text{ cm}^3}{1 \text{ L}} \times \dfrac{0.997 \text{ g } H_2O}{1 \text{ cm}^3} = 1.4955 \times 10^3 = 1.50 \times 10^3 \text{ g } H_2O$

       $-10°C$: $1.4955 \times 10^3 \text{ g } H_2O \times \dfrac{1 \text{ cm}^3}{0.917 \text{ g } H_2O} \times \dfrac{1 \text{ L}}{1000 \text{ cm}^3} = 1.6309 = 1.63 \text{ L}$

     (b)   If the soft-drink bottle is completely filled with 1.50 L of water, the 1.63 L of ice **cannot** be contained in the bottle. The extra volume of ice will push through any opening in the bottle, or crack the bottle to create an opening.

1.71   (a)   density = (35.66 g – 14.23 g)/4.59 cm^3 = 4.67 g/cm^3

        (b) $34.5 \text{ kg} \times \dfrac{1000 \text{ g}}{1 \text{ kg}} \times \dfrac{1 \text{ mL}}{13.6 \text{ g}} \times \dfrac{1 \text{ L}}{1000 \text{ mL}} = 2.54 \text{ L}$

        (c) $V = 4/3 \, \pi \, r^3 = 4/3 \, \pi \, (28.9 \text{ cm})^3 = 1.0111 \times 10^5 = 1.01 \times 10^5 = 1.01 \times 10^5 \text{ cm}^3$

               $1.011 \times 10^5 \text{ cm}^3 \times \dfrac{19.3 \text{ g}}{\text{cm}^3} = 1.95 \times 10^6 \text{ g}$

        The sphere weighs 1950 kg or 4300 pounds. The student is unlikely to be able to carry the sphere.

1.72 $0.500 \text{ L battery acid} \times \dfrac{1000 \text{ mL}}{\text{L}} \times \dfrac{1.28 \text{ g}}{\text{mL}} = 640 \text{ g battery acid}$

        $640 \text{ g battery acid} \times \dfrac{38.1 \text{ g sulfuric acid}}{100 \text{ g battery acid}} = 243.84 = 244 \text{ g sulfuric acid}$

1.74   (a)   Calculate the volume of the coin. It is a cylinder,

               $V = \pi \, r^2 h, \quad r = \dfrac{d}{2}, \quad V = \pi \left(\dfrac{d}{2}\right)^2 h = \dfrac{\pi d^2 h}{4}$

        Then use density of pure gold to calculate mass.

               $V = \pi \times \dfrac{(2.2)^2 \text{ cm}^2}{4} \times 3.0 \text{ mm} \times \dfrac{1 \text{ cm}}{10 \text{ mm}} = 1.140 = 1.1 \text{ cm}^3$

               $1.140 \text{ cm}^3 \times \dfrac{19.3 \text{ g gold}}{1 \text{ cm}^3} = 22.01 = 22 \text{ g pure gold}$

        (b) $22.01 \text{ g gold} \times \dfrac{1 \text{ tr oz}}{31.1 \text{ g}} \times \dfrac{\$640}{\text{tr oz}} = \$452.93 = 4.5 \times 10^2 \ (\$450)$

1.75 $8.0 \text{ oz} \times \dfrac{1 \text{ lb}}{16 \text{ oz}} \times \dfrac{453.6 \text{ g}}{\text{lb}} \times \dfrac{1 \text{ cm}^3}{2.70 \text{ g}} = 84.00 = 84 \text{ cm}^3$

        $\dfrac{84 \text{ cm}^3}{50 \text{ ft}^2} \times \dfrac{1^2 \text{ ft}^2}{12^2 \text{ in}^2} \times \dfrac{1^2 \text{ in}^2}{2.54^2 \text{ cm}^2} \times \dfrac{10 \text{ mm}}{1 \text{ cm}} = 0.018 \text{ mm}$

1.77   (a)   Let x = mass of Au in jewelry

               9.85 - x = mass of Ag in jewelry

               The total volume of jewelry = volume of Au + volume of Ag

               $0.675 \text{ cm}^3 = x \text{ g} \times \dfrac{1 \text{ cm}^3}{19.3 \text{ g}} + (9.85 - x) \text{g} \times \dfrac{1 \text{ cm}^3}{10.5 \text{ g}}$

               $0.675 = \dfrac{x}{19.3} + \dfrac{9.85 - x}{10.5}$ (To solve, multiply both sides by (19.3)(10.5))

$$0.675\,(19.3)(10.5) = 10.5\,x + (9.85 - x)(19.3)$$

$$136.79 = 10.5\,x + 190.105 - 19.3\,x$$

$$-53.315 = -8.8\,x$$

$$x = 6.06 \text{ g Au; } 9.85 \text{ g total} - 6.06 \text{ g Au} = 3.79 \text{ g Ag}$$

$$\text{mass \% Au} = \frac{6.06 \text{ g Au}}{9.85 \text{ g jewelry}} \times 100 = 61.5\% \text{ Au}$$

(b)   24 carats $\times$ 0.615 = 15 carat gold

1.78   A solution can be separated into components by physical means, so separation would be attempted. If the liquid is a solution, the solute could be a solid or a liquid; these two kinds of solutions would be separated differently. Therefore, divide the liquid into several samples and do different tests on each. Try evaporating the solvent from one sample. If a solid remains, the liquid is a solution and the solute is a solid. If the result is negative, try distilling a sample to see if two or more liquids with different boiling points are present. If this result is negative, the liquid is probably a pure substance, but negative results are never entirely conclusive. We might not have tried the appropriate separation technique.

1.80   The densities are:

carbon tetrachloride (methane, tetrachloro) – 1.5940 g/cm^3

hexane – 0.6603 g/cm^3

benzene – 0.87654 g/cm^3

methylene iodide (methane, diiodo) – 3.3254 g/cm^3

Only methylene iodide will separate the two granular solids. The undesirable solid (2.04 g/cm^3) is less dense than methylene iodide and will float; the desired material is more dense than methylene iodide and will sink. The other three liquids are less dense than both solids and will not produce separation.

1.82   Study (a) is likely to be both precise and accurate, because the errors are carefully controlled. The secondary weight standard will be resistant to chemical and physical changes, the balance is carefully calibrated, and weighings are likely to be made by the same person. The relatively large number of measurements is likely to minimize the effect of random errors on the average value. The accuracy and precision of study (b) depend on the veracity of the participants' responses, which cannot be carefully controlled. It also depends on the definition of "comparable lifestyle." The percentages are not precise, because the broad definition of lifestyle leads to a range of results (scatter). The relatively large number of participants improves the precision and accuracy. In general, controlling errors and maximizing the number of data points in a study improves precision and accuracy.

2 Atoms, Molecules, and Ions

Visualizing Concepts

2.2   (a)   % abundance = $\dfrac{\text{# of mass number} \times \text{particles}}{\text{total number of particles}} \times 100$

12 red ^{293}Nv particles

8 blue ^{295}Nv particles

20 total particles

% abundance ^{293}Nv $= \dfrac{12}{20} \times 100 = 60\%$

% abundance ^{295}Nv $= \dfrac{8}{20} \times 100 = 40\%$

   (b)   Atomic weight (AW) is the same as average atomic mass.

Atomic weight (average atomic mass) = $\sum$ fractional abundance $\times$ mass of isotope

AW of Nv = 0.60(293.15) + 0.40(295.15) = 293.95

(Since % abundance was calculated by counting exact numbers of particles, assume % abundance is an exact number. Then, the number of significant figures in the AW is determined by the number of sig figs in the masses of the isotopes.)

2.3   In general, metals occupy the left side of the chart, and nonmetals the right side.

metals: red and green   *nonmetals*: blue and yellow

alkaline earth metal: red   *noble gas*: yellow

2.5   In a solid, particles are close together and their relative positions are fixed. In a liquid, particles are close but moving relative to each other. In a gas, particles are far apart and moving. All ionic compounds are solids because of the strong forces among charged particles. Molecular compounds can exist in any state: solid, liquid, or gas.

Since the molecules in *ii* are far apart, *ii* must be a molecular compound. The particles in *i* are near each other and exist in a regular, ordered arrangement, so *i* is likely to be an ionic compound.

2.7   See Figure 2.22. yellow box: 1+ (group 1A); blue box: 2+ (group 2A)

black box: 3+ (a metal in Group 3A); orange box: 2– (a nonmetal in group 6A);

green box: 1– (a nonmetal in group 7A)

2.8   Cations (red spheres) have positive charges; anions (blue spheres) have negative charges. There are twice as many anions as cations, so the formula has the general form CA_2. Only $Ca(NO_3)_2$, calcium nitrate, is consistent with the diagram.

Atomic Theory and the Discovery of Atomic Structure

2.10   (a)   6.500 g compound – 0.384 g hydrogen = 6.116 g sulfur

(b)   *Conservation of mass*

(c)   According to postulate 3 of the atomic theory, atoms are neither created nor destroyed during a chemical reaction. If 0.384 g of H are recovered from a compound that contains only H and S, the remaining mass must be sulfur.

2.12   (a)   1: $\dfrac{3.56\,\text{g fluorine}}{4.75\,\text{g iodine}} = 0.749\,\text{g fluorine/1 g iodine}$

2: $\dfrac{3.43\,\text{g fluorine}}{7.64\,\text{g iodine}} = 0.449\,\text{g fluorine/1 g iodine}$

3: $\dfrac{9.86\,\text{g fluorine}}{9.41\,\text{g iodine}} = 1.05\,\text{g fluorine/1 g iodine}$

(b)   To look for integer relationships among these values, divide each one by the smallest.

If the quotients aren't all integers, multiply by a common factor to obtain all integers.

1: 0.749/0.449 = 1.67; 1.67 × 3 = 5

2: 0.449/0.449 = 1.00; 1.00 × 3 = 3

3: 1.05/0.449 = 2.34; 2.34 × 3 = 7

The ratio of g fluorine to g iodine in the three compounds is 5:3:7. These are in the ratio of small whole numbers and, therefore, obey the *law of multiple proportions*. This integer ratio indicates that the combining fluorine "units" (atoms) are indivisible entities.

2.14   Since the unknown particle is deflected in the opposite direction from that of a negatively charged beta (β) particle, it is attracted to the (–) plate and repelled by the (+) plate. The unknown particle is positively charged. The magnitude of the deflection is less than that of the β particle, or electron, so the unknown particle has greater mass than the electron. The unknown is a positively charged particle of greater mass than the electron.

2.16   (a)   The droplets carry different total charges because there may be 1, 2, 3, or more electrons on the droplet.

(b)   The electronic charge is likely to be the lowest common factor in all the observed charges.

(c)   Assuming this is so, we calculate the apparent electronic charge from each drop as follows:

   A: $1.60 \times 10^{-19} / 1 = 1.60 \times 10^{-19}$ C

   B: $3.15 \times 10^{-19} / 2 = 1.58 \times 10^{-19}$ C

   C: $4.81 \times 10^{-19} / 3 = 1.60 \times 10^{-19}$ C

   D: $6.31 \times 10^{-19} / 4 = 1.58 \times 10^{-19}$ C

The reported value is the average of these four values. Since each calculated charge has three significant figures, the average will also have three significant figures.

$(1.60 \times 10^{-19}$ C $+ 1.58 \times 10^{-19}$ C $+ 1.60 \times 10^{-19}$ C $+ 1.58 \times 10^{-19}$ C$) / 4 = 1.59 \times 10^{-19}$ C

Modern View of Atomic Structure; Atomic Weights

2.18   (a) $r = d/2; r = \dfrac{2.8 \times 10^{-8} \text{ cm}}{2} \times \dfrac{1 \text{ Å}}{1 \times 10^{-8} \text{ cm}} = 1.4 \text{ Å}$

   $r = \dfrac{2.8 \times 10^{-8} \text{ cm}}{2} \times \dfrac{1 \text{ m}}{100 \text{ cm}} = 1.4 \times 10^{-10} \text{ m}$

(b)   Aligned Sn atoms have **diameters** touching. $d = 2.8 \times 10^{-8}$ cm $= 2.8 \times 10^{-10}$ m

   $6.0 \, \mu\text{m} \times \dfrac{1 \times 10^{-6} \text{ m}}{1 \, \mu\text{m}} \times \dfrac{1 \text{ Sn atom}}{2.8 \times 10^{-10} \text{ m}} = 2.1 \times 10^{4}$ Sn atoms

(c) $V = 4/3 \, \pi \, r^3; r = 1.4 \times 10^{-10}$ m

   $V = (4/3)[(\pi(1.4 \times 10^{-10})^3] \text{ m}^3 = 1.149 \times 10^{-29} = 1.1 \times 10^{-29} \text{ m}^3$

2.20   (a)   The nucleus has most of the mass **but occupies very little** of the volume of an atom.

(b)   True

(c)   The number of electrons in an atom is equal to the number of **protons** in the atom.

(d)   True

2.22   (a) $^{31}_{16}$X and $^{32}_{16}$X are isotopes of the same element, because they have identical atomic numbers.

(b)   These are isotopes of the element sulfur, S, atomic number = 16.

2.24   (a) ^{32}P has 15 p, 17 n   (b) ^{51}Cr has 24 p, 27 n

(c) ^{60}Co has 27 p, 33 n   (d) ^{99}Tc has 43 p, 56 n

(e) ^{131}I has 53 p, 78 n   (f) ^{201}Tl has 81 p, 120 n

2.26

Symbol	^{65}Zn	^{101}Ru	^{87}Sr	^{108}Ag	^{235}U
Protons	30	44	38	47	92
Neutrons	35	57	49	61	143
Electrons	30	44	38	47	92
Mass No.	65	101	87	108	235

2.28   Since the two nuclides are atoms of the same element, by definition they have the same number of protons, 54. They differ in mass number (and mass) because they have different numbers of neutrons. ^{129}Xe has 75 neutrons and ^{130}Xe has 76 neutrons.

2.30   (a)   12 amu

(b)   The atomic weight of carbon reported on the front-inside cover of the text is the abundance-weighted average of the atomic masses of the two naturally occurring isotopes of carbon, ^{12}C, and ^{13}C. The mass of a ^{12}C atom is exactly 12 amu, but the atomic weight of 12.011 takes into account the presence of some ^{13}C atoms in every natural sample of the element.

2.32   Atomic weight (average atomic mass) = Σ fractional abundance $\times$ mass of isotope

Atomic weight = 0.7215(84.9118) + 0.2785(86.9092) = 85.4681 = 85.47

(The result has 2 decimal places and 4 sig figs because each term in the sum has 4 sig figs and 2 decimal places.)

2.34   (a)   The purpose of the magnet in the mass spectrometer is to change the path of the moving ions. The magnitude of the deflection is inversely related to mass, which is the basis of the discrimination by mass.

(b)   The atomic weight of Cl, 35.5, is an average atomic mass. It is the average of the masses of two naturally occurring isotopes, weighted by their abundances.

(c)   The single peak at mass 31 in the mass spectrum of phosphorus indicates that the sample contains a single isotope of P, and the mass of this isotope is 31 amu.

2.36   (a)   Three peaks: ^{1}H – ^{1}H, ^{1}H – ^{2}H, ^{2}H – ^{2}H

(b) ^{1}H – ^{1}H = 2(1.00783) = 2.01566 amu

^{1}H – ^{2}H = 1.00783 + 2.01410 = 3.02193 amu

^{2}H – ^{2}H = 2(2.01410) = 4.02820 amu

The mass ratios are 1 : 1.49923 : 1.99845 or 1 : 1.5 : 2.

(c) ^{1}H – ^{1}H is largest, because there is the greatest chance that two atoms of the more abundant isotope will combine.

^{2}H – ^{2}H is the smallest, because there is the least chance that two atoms of the less abundant isotope will combine.

The Periodic Table; Molecules and Ions

2.38   (a)   calcium (metal)   (b) titanium (metal)   (c) gallium (metal)

      (d)   thorium (metal)   (e) platinum (metal)   (f) selenium (nonmetal)

      (g)   krypton (nonmetal)

2.40   C, carbon, nonmetal; Si, silicon, metalloid; Ge, germanium, metalloid; Sn, tin, metal;

Pb, lead, metal

2.42   Compounds with the same empirical but different molecular formulas differ by the integer number of empirical formula units in the respective molecules. Thus, they can have very different molecular structure, size, and mass, resulting in very different physical properties.

2.44   A molecular formula contains all atoms in a molecule. An empirical formula shows the simplest ratio of atoms in a molecule or elements in a compound.

      (a)   molecular formula: C_6H_6; empirical formula: CH

      (b)   molecular formula: $SiCl_4$; empirical formula: $SiCl_4$ (1:4 is the simplest ratio)

      (c)   molecular: B_2H_6; empirical: BH_3

      (d)   molecular: $C_6H_{12}O_6$; empirical: CH_2O

2.46   (a)   4   (b) 8   (c) 9

2.48   (a) C_2H_6O

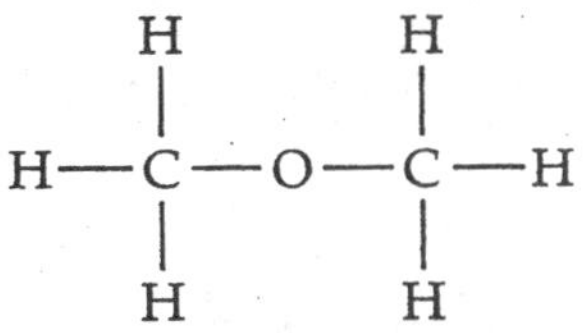

(b) C_2H_6O

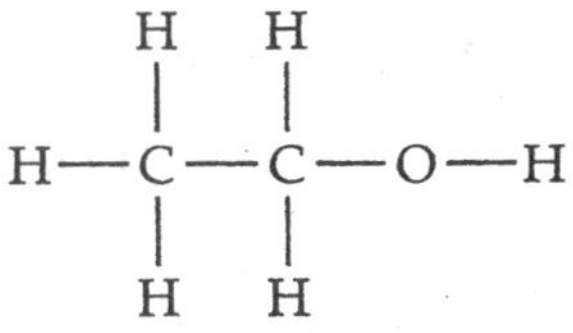

(c) CH_4O

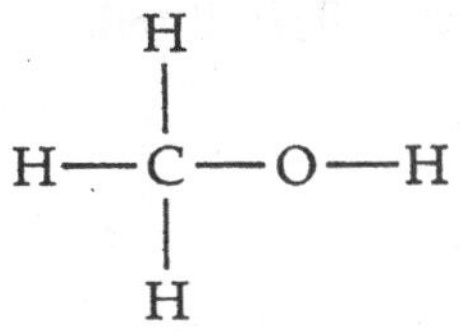

(d) PF_3

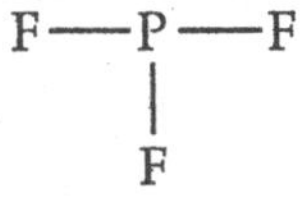

2.50

Symbol	$^{31}P^{3-}$	$^{80}Br^-$	$^{115}In^{3+}$	$^{197}Au^{3+}$
Protons	15	35	49	79
Neutrons	16	45	66	118
Electrons	18	36	46	76
Net Charge	3–	1–	3+	3+

2.52   (a) Ga^{3+} (b) Sr^{2+} (c) As^{3-} (d) Br^- (e) Se^{2-}

2.54   (a)   AgI   (b) Ag_2S (c)   AgF

2.56   (a) $CuBr_2$ (b) Fe_2O_3 (c) Hg_2CO_3 (d) $Ca_3(AsO_4)_2$ (e) $(NH_4)_2CO_3$

2.58

Ion	Na^+	Ca^{2+}	Fe^{2+}	Al^{3+}
O^{2-}	Na_2O	CaO	FeO	Al_2O_3
NO_3^-	$NaNO_3$	$Ca(NO_3)_2$	$Fe(NO_3)_2$	$Al(NO_3)_3$
SO_4^{2-}	Na_2SO_4	$CaSO_4$	$FeSO_4$	$Al_2(SO_4)_3$
AsO_4^{2-}	Na_3AsO_4	$Ca_3(AsO_4)_2$	$Fe_3(AsO_4)_2$	$AlAsO_4$

2.60   Molecular (all elements are nonmetals):

   (a) PF_5 (c)   SCl   (h) N_2O_4

   Ionic (formed from ions, usually contains a metal cation):

   (b)   NaI   (d) $Ca(NO_3)_2$ (e) $FeCl_3$ (f)   LaP   (g) $CoCO_3$

Naming Inorganic Compounds; Organic Molecules

2.62   (a)   selenate   (b)   selenide   (c)   hydrogen selenide (biselenide)

   (d)   hydrogen selenite (biselenite)

2.64   (a)   copper, 2+; sulfide, 2–   (b)   silver, 1+; sulfate, 2–

   (c)   aluminum, 3+; chlorate, 1–   (d)   cobalt, 2+; hydroxide, 1–

   (e)   lead, 2+; carbonate, 2–

2.66   (a)   potassium oxide   (b)   sodium chlorite

   (c)   strontium cyanide   (d)   cobalt(II) hydroxide (cobaltous hydroxide)

   (e)   iron(III) carbonate (ferric carbonate)

   (f)   chromium(III) nitrate (chromic nitrate)

   (g)   ammonium sulfite   (h)   sodium dihydrogen phosphate

   (i)   potassium permanganate   (j)   silver dichromate

2.68   (a) Na_3PO_4 (b) $Zn(NO_3)_2$ (c) $Ba(BrO_3)_2$ (d) $Fe(ClO_4)_2$

   (e) $Co(HCO_3)_2$ (f) $Cr(CH_3COO^-)_3$ (g) $K_2Cr_2O_7$

2.70   (a)   HBr   (b) H_2S (c) HNO_2

   (d)   carbonic acid   (e)   chloric acid   (f)   acetic acid

2.72   (a)   dinitrogen monoxide   (b)   nitrogen monoxide   (c)   nitrogen dioxide

          (d)   dinitrogen pentoxide   (e)   dinitrogen tetroxide

2.74   (a) $NaHCO_3$ (b) $Ca(ClO)_2$ (c) HCN

          (d) $Mg(OH)_2$ (e) SnF (f) CdS, H_2SO_4, H_2S

2.76   (a)   *-ane*

          (b)   Hexane has 6 carbons in its chain.

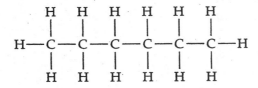

              molecular: C_6H_{14}

              empirical: C_3H_7

2.78   (a)   They both have two carbon atoms in their molecular backbone, or chain.

          (b)   In 1-propanol one of the H atoms on an outer (terminal) C atom has been replaced by an $-OH$ group.

Additional Exercises

2.80   (a)   Most of the volume of an atom is empty space in which electrons move. Most alpha particles passed through this space. The path of the massive alpha particle would not be significantly altered by interaction with a "puny" electron.

          (b)   Most of the mass of an atom is contained in a very small, dense area called the nucleus. The few alpha particles that hit the massive, positively charged gold nuclei were strongly repelled and essentially deflected back in the direction they came from.

          (c)   The Be nuclei have a much smaller volume and positive charge than the Au nuclei; the charge repulsion between the alpha particles and the Be nuclei will be less, and there will be fewer direct hits because the Be nuclei have an even smaller volume than the Au nuclei. Fewer alpha particles will be scattered in general and fewer will be strongly back scattered.

2.81   (a)   Droplet D would fall most slowly. It carries the most negative charge, so it would be most strongly attracted to the upper (+) plate and most strongly repelled by the lower (–) plate. These electrostatic forces would provide the greatest opposition to gravity.

          (b)   Calculate the lowest common factor.

              A: 3.84×10^{-8} / 2.88×10^{-8} = 1.33; $1.33 \times 3 = 4$

              B: 4.80×10^{-8} / 2.88×10^{-8} = 1.67; $1.67 \times 3 = 5$

C: $2.88 \times 10^{-8} / 2.88 \times 10^{-8} = 1.00; 1.00 \times 3 = 3$

D: $8.64 \times 10^{-8} / 2.88 \times 10^{-8} = 3.00; 3.00 \times 3 = 9$

The total charge on the drops is in the ratio of 4:5:3:9. Divide the total charge on each drop by the appropriate integer and average the four values to get the charge of an electron in warmombs.

A: $3.84 \times 10^{-8} / 4 = 9.60 \times 10^{-9}$ wa

B: $4.80 \times 10^{-8} / 5 = 9.60 \times 10^{-9}$ wa

C: $2.88 \times 10^{-8} / 3 = 9.60 \times 10^{-9}$ wa

D: $8.64 \times 10^{-8} / 9 = 9.60 \times 10^{-9}$ wa

The charge on an electron is 9.60×10^{-9} wa

(c)   The number of electrons on each drop are the integers calculated in part (b). A has 4 e⁻, B has 5 e⁻, C has 3 e⁻ and D has 9 e⁻.

(d) $\dfrac{9.60 \times 10^{-9} \text{ wa}}{1e^{-}} \times \dfrac{1e^{-}}{1.60 \times 10^{-16} \text{ C}} = 6.00 \times 10^{7}$ wa/C

2.83   (a)   2 protons and 2 neutrons

(b)   the nuclear strong force

(c)   The charge of an α particle is twice the magnitude of the charge of an electron, with the opposite sign. That is, $2 (+1.6022 \times 10^{-19})$ C = $+3.2044 \times 10^{-19}$ C.

(d) $\dfrac{3.2044 \times 10^{-19} \text{ C}}{4.8224 \times 10^{4} \text{ g/C}} = 6.6448 \times 10^{-24}$ g

6.6448×10^{-24} g $\times \dfrac{1 \text{ amu}}{1.66054 \times 10^{-24} \text{ g}} = 4.0016$ amu

(e)   The sum of the particle masses in an α particle is 2(1.0073) amu and 2(1.0087) amu = 4.0320 amu. The actual particle mass, 4.0016 amu, is less than the sum of the masses of the components. The difference is the nuclear binding energy, the energy released when protons and neutrons combine to form a nucleus. Mass and energy are interchangeable according to the Einstein relationship $E = mc^2$.

2.84   (a)   Calculate the mass of a single gold atom, then divide the mass of the cube by the mass of the gold atom.

$\dfrac{197.0 \text{ amu}}{\text{gold atom}} \times \dfrac{1 \text{ g}}{6.022 \times 10^{23} \text{ amu}} = 3.2713 \times 10^{-22} = 3.271 \times 10^{-22}$ g/gold atom

$\dfrac{19.3 \text{ g}}{\text{cube}} \times \dfrac{1 \text{ gold atom}}{3.271 \times 10^{-22} \text{ g}} = 5.90 \times 10^{22}$ Au atoms in the cube

(b)   The shape of atoms is spherical; spheres cannot be arranged into a cube so that there is no empty space. The question is, how much empty space is there? We can calculate the two limiting cases, no empty space and maximum empty space. The true diameter will be somewhere in this range.

No empty space: volume cube/number of atoms = volume of one atom

$V = 4/3\pi r^3; r = (3\pi V/4)^{1/3}; d = 2r$

$$\text{vol. of cube} = (1.0 \times 1.0 \times 1.0) = \frac{1.0\,cm^3}{5.90 \times 10^{22}\,Au\,atoms} = 1.695 \times 10^{-23}$$
$$= 1.7 \times 10^{-23}\,cm^3$$

$r = [\pi (1.695 \times 10^{-23}\,cm^3)/4]^{1/3} = 3.4 \times 10^{-8}\,cm; d = 2r = 6.8 \times 10^{-8}\,cm$

Maximum empty space: assume atoms are arranged in rows in all three directions so they are touching across their diameters. That is, each atom occupies the volume of a cube, with the atomic diameter as the length of the side of the cube. The number of atoms along one edge of the gold cube is then

$(5.90 \times 10^{22})^{1/3} = 3.893 \times 10^7 = 3.89 \times 10^7$ atoms/1.0 cm.

The diameter of a single atom is 1.0 cm/3.89×10^7 atoms = 2.569×10^{-8}
$$= 2.6 \times 10^{-8}\,cm.$$

The diameter of a gold atom is between 2.6×10^{-8} cm and 6.8×10^{-8} cm (2.6 – 6.8 Å).

(c) Some atomic arrangement must be assumed, since none is specified. The solid state is characterized by an orderly arrangement of particles, so it isn't surprising that atomic arrangement is required to calculate the density of a solid. A more detailed discussion of solid-state structure and density appears in Chapter 11.

2.86 (a) diameter of nucleus = 1×10^{-4} Å; diameter of atom = 1 Å

$V = 4/3\pi r^3; r = d/2; r_n = 0.5 \times 10^{-4}$ Å; $r_a = 0.5$ Å

volume of nucleus = $4/3\pi (0.5 \times 10^{-4})^3$ Å^3

volume of atom = $4/3\pi (0.5)^3$ Å^3

$$\text{volume fraction of nucleus} = \frac{\text{volume of nucleus}}{\text{volume of atom}} = \frac{4/3\pi (0.5 \times 10^{-4})^3\,Å^3}{4/3\pi (0.5)^3\,Å^3} = 1 \times 10^{-12}$$

diameter of atom = 5 Å, $r_a = 2.5$ Å

$$\text{volume fraction of nucleus} = \frac{4/3\pi (0.5 \times 10^{-4})^3\,Å^3}{4/3\pi (2.5)^3\,Å^3} = 8 \times 10^{-15}$$

Depending on the radius of the atom, the volume fraction of the nucleus is between 1×10^{-12} and 8×10^{-15}, that is, between 1 part in 10^{12} and 8 parts in 10^{15}.

(b) mass of proton = 1.0073 amu

1.0073 amu $\times 1.66054 \times 10^{-24}$ g/amu = 1.6727×10^{-24} g

diameter = 1.0×10^{-15} m, radius = 0.50×10^{-15} m $\times \dfrac{100\,cm}{1\,m} = 5.0 \times 10^{-14}$ cm

Assuming a proton is a sphere, $V = 4/3 \pi r^3$.

$$\text{density} = \frac{g}{cm^3} = \frac{1.6727 \times 10^{-24} \, g}{4/3 \pi (5.0 \times 10^{-14})^3 \, cm^3} = 3.2 \times 10^{15} \, g/cm^3$$

2.87   The integer on the lower left of a nuclide is the atomic number; it is the number of protons in any atom of the element and gives the element's identity. The number of neutrons is the mass number (upper left) minus atomic number.

(a)   As, 33 protons, 41 neutrons

(b)   I, 53 protons, 74 neutrons

(c)   Eu, 63 protons, 89 neutrons

(d)   Bi, 83 protons, 126 neutrons

2.89 $F = k Q_1 Q_2 / d^2$; $k = 9.0 \times 10^9 \, N \, m^2/C^2$; $d = 0.53 \times 10^{-10} \, m$;

$Q \text{ (electron)} = -1.6 \times 10^{-19} \, C$; $Q \text{ (proton)} = -Q \text{ (electron)} = 1.6 \times 10^{-19} \, C$

$$F = \frac{\dfrac{9.0 \times 10^9 \, N \, m^2}{C^2} \times -1.6 \times 10^{-19} \, C \times 1.6 \times 10^{-19} \, C}{(0.53 \times 10^{-10})^2 \, m^2} = 8.202 \times 10^{-8} = 8.2 \times 10^{-8} \, N$$

2.90   Atomic weight (average atomic mass) = Σ fractional abundance $\times$ mass of isotope

Atomic weight = 0.014(203.97302) + 0.241(205.97444) + 0.221(206.97587) +

0.524(207.97663) = 207.22 = 207 amu

(The result has 0 decimal places and 3 sig figs because the fourth term in the sum has 3 sig figs and 0 decimal places.)

2.92   (a)   There are 24 known isotopes of Ni, from ^{51}Ni to ^{74}Ni.

(b)   The five most abundant isotopes are

^{58}Ni, 57.935346 amu, 68.077%

^{60}Ni, 59.930788 amu, 26.223%

^{62}Ni, 61.928346 amu, 3.634%

^{61}Ni, 60.931058 amu, 1.140%

^{64}Ni, 63.927968 amu, 0.926%

Data from *Handbook of Chemistry and Physics*, 74th Ed. [Data may differ slightly in other editions.]

2.93   (a)   A Br_2 molecule could consist of two atoms of the same isotope or one atom of each of the two different isotopes. This second possibility is twice as likely as the first. Therefore, the second peak (twice as large as peaks 1 and 3) represents a Br_2 molecule containing different isotopes. The mass numbers of the two isotopes are determined from the masses of the two smaller peaks. Since 157.836 $\approx$ 158, the first peak represents a ^{79}Br $-$ ^{79}Br molecule. Peak 3, 161.832 $\approx$ 162, represents a ^{81}Br $-$ ^{81}Br molecule. Peak 2 then contains one atom of each isotope, ^{79}Br $-$ ^{81}Br, with an approximate mass of 160 amu.

(b)   The mass of the lighter isotope is 157.836 amu/2 atoms, or 78.918 amu/atom. For the heavier one, 161.832 amu/2 atoms = 80.916 amu/atom.

(c)   The relative size of the three peaks in the mass spectrum of Br_2 indicates their relative abundance. The average mass of a Br_2 molecule is

0.2569(157.836) + 0.4999(159.834) + 0.2431(161.832) = 159.79 amu.

(Each product has four significant figures and two decimal places, so the answer has two decimal places.)

(d) $\dfrac{159.79\text{ amu}}{\text{avg. } Br_2 \text{ molecule}} \times \dfrac{1\,Br_2 \text{ molecule}}{2\,Br \text{ atoms}} = 79.895 \text{ amu}$

(e)   Let x = the abundance of ^{79}Br, 1 – x = abundance of ^{81}Br. From (b), the masses of the two isotopes are 78.918 amu and 80.916 amu, respectively. From (d), the mass of an average Br atom is 79.895 amu.

x(78.918) + (1 – x)(80.916) = 79.895, x = 0.5110

^{79}Br = 51.10%, ^{81}Br = 48.90%

2.95   (a)   an alkali metal: K   (b) an alkaline earth metal: Ca   (c) a noble gas: Ar

        (d)   a halogen: Br   (e) a metalloid: Ge   (f) a nonmetal in 1A: H

        (g)   a metal that forms a 3+ ion: Al   (h) a nonmetal that forms a 2– ion: O

        (i)   an element that resembles Al: Ga

2.96   (a) $^{266}_{106}Sg$ has 106 protons, 160 neutrons and 106 electrons

        (b)   Sg is in Group 6B (or 6) and immediately below tungsten, W. We expect the chemical properties of Sg to most closely resemble those of W.

2.97   (a)   chlorine gas, Cl_2: ii   (b) propane, C_3H_8: v   (c) nitrate ion, NO_3^- : i

        (d)   sulfur trioxide, SO_3: iii   (e) methylchloride, CH_3Cl: iv

2.99   (a) IO_3^- (b) IO_4^- (c) IO   (d) HIO   (e) HIO_4 or (H_5IO_6)

2.100   (a)   perbromate ion   (b) selenite ion

        (c) AsO_4^{3-} (d) $HTeO_4^-$

2.101   Carbonic acid: H_2CO_3; the cation is H^+ because it is an acid; the anion is carbonate because the acid reacts with lithium hydroxide to form lithium carbonate.
Lithium hydroxide: LiOH; lithium carbonate: Li_2CO_3

2.103   (a)   potassium nitrate   (b) sodium carbonate   (c) calcium oxide

        (d)   hydrochloric acid   (e) magnesium sulfate   (f) magnesium hydroxide

2.105   (a)   In an alkane, all C atoms have 4 single bonds, so each C in the partial structure needs 2 more bonds. All alkanes are hydrocarbons, so 2 H atoms will bind to each C atom in the ring.

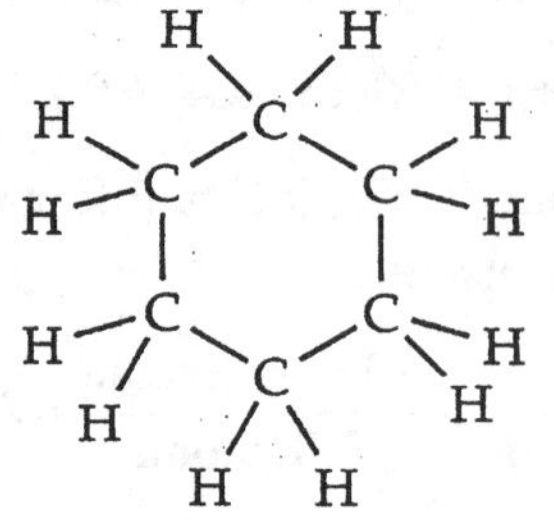

    (b)   The molecular formula of cyclohexane is C_6H_{12}; the molecular formula of *n*-hexane is C_6H_{14} (see Solution 2.64(d)). Cyclohexane can be thought of as *n*-hexane in which the two outer (terminal) C atoms are joined to each other. In order to form this C−C bond, each outer C atom must lose 1 H atom. The number of C atoms is unchanged, and each C atom still has 4 single bonds. The resulting molecular formula is $C_6H_{14-2} = C_6H_{12}$.

    (c)   On the structure in part (a), replace 1 H atom with an OH group.

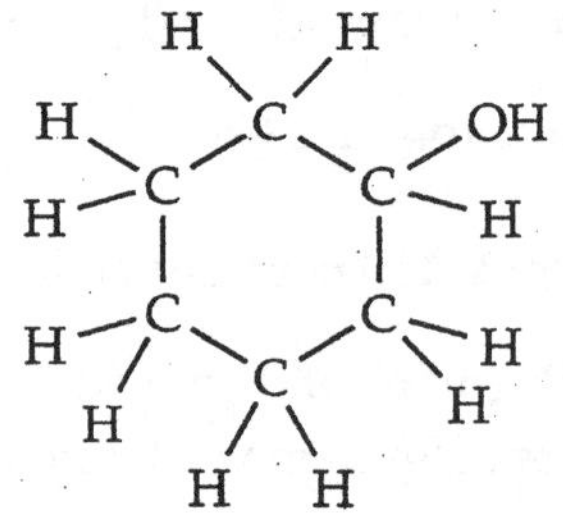

2.106   Elements are arranged in the periodic table by increasing atomic number and so that elements with similar chemical and physical properties form a vertical column or group. By its position in the periodic chart, we know whether an element is a metal, nonmetal, or metalloid, and the common charge of its ion. Members of a group have the same common ionic charge and combine in similar ways with other elements.

3 Stoichiometry: Calculations with Chemical Formulas and Equations

Visualizing Concepts

3.2

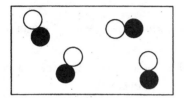

Write the balanced equation for the reaction.

$$2H_2 + CO \rightarrow CH_3OH$$

The combining ratio of H_2: CO is 2:1. If we have 8 H_2 molecules, 4 CO molecules are required for complete reaction. Alternatively, you could examine the atom ratios in the formula of CH_3OH, but the balanced equation is most direct.

3.4 The box contains 4 C atoms and 16 H atoms, so the empirical formula of the hydrocarbon is CH_4.

3.6 *Analyze.* Given: 4.0 mol CH_4. Find: mol CO and mol H_2

Plan. Examine the boxes to determine the CH_4:CO mol ratio and CH_4:H_2O mole ratio.

Solve. There are 2 CH_4 molecules in the reactant box and 2 CO molecules in the product box. The mole ratio is 2:2 or 1:1. Therefore, 4.0 mol CH_4 can produce 4.0 mol CO. There are 2 CH_4 molecules in the reactant box and 6 H_2 molecules in the product box. The mole ratio is 2:6 or 1:3. So, 4.0 mol CH_4 can produce 12:0 mol H_2.

Check. Use proportions. 2 mol CH_4/2 mol CO = 4 mol CH_4/4 mol CO;
2 mol CH_4/6 mol H_2 = 4 mol CH_4/12 mol H_2.

3.8　　(a)　$2NO + O_2 \rightarrow 2NO_2$,　$O_2 =$ 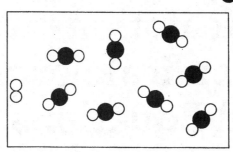,　$NO_2 =$

Each NO molecule reacts with 1 O atom (1/2 of an O_2 molecule) to produce 1 NO_2 molecule. Eight NO molecules react with 8 O atoms (4 O_2 molecules) to produce 8 NO_2 molecules. One O_2 molecule doesn't react (is in excess). NO is the limiting reactant.

(b)　$\% \text{ yield} = \dfrac{\text{actual yield}}{\text{theoretical yield}} \times 100$;　$\text{actual yield} = \dfrac{\% \text{ yield}}{100} \times \text{theoretical yield}$

The theoretical yield from part (a) is 8 NO_2 molecules. If the percent yield is 75%, then 0.75(8) = 6 NO_2 would appear in the products box.

Balancing Chemical Equations

3.10　　(a)　In a CO molecule, there is one O atom bound to C. 2CO indicates that there are **two CO molecules**, each of which contains one C and one O atom. Adding a subscript 2 to CO to form CO_2 means that there are **two O atoms** bound to one C in a CO_2 molecule. The composition of the different molecules, CO_2 and CO, is different and the physical and chemical properties of the two compounds they constitute are very different. The subscript 2 changes molecular composition and thus properties of the compound. The prefix 2 indicates how many molecules (or moles) of the original compound are under consideration.

(b)　Yes. There are the same number and kinds of atoms on the reactants side and the products side of the equation.

3.12　　(a)　$6Li(s) + N_2(g) \rightarrow 2Li_3N(s)$

(b)　$La_2O_3(s) + 3H_2O(l) \rightarrow 2La(OH)_3(aq)$

(c)　$2NH_4NO_3(s) \rightarrow 2N_2(g) + O_2(g) + 4H_2O(g)$

(d)　$Ca_3P_2(s) + 6H_2O(l) \rightarrow 3Ca(OH)_2(aq) + 2PH_3(g)$

(e)　$3Ca(OH)_2(aq) + 2H_3PO_4(aq) \rightarrow Ca_3(PO_4)_2(s) + 6H_2O(l)$

(f)　$2AgNO_3(aq) + Na_2SO_4(aq) \rightarrow Ag_2SO_4(s) + 2NaNO_3(aq)$

(g)　$4CH_3NH_2(g) + 9O_2(g) \rightarrow 4CO_2(g) + 10H_2O(g) + 2N_2(g)$

3.14　　(a)　$SO_3(g) + H_2O(l) \rightarrow H_2SO_4(aq)$

(b)　$B_2S_3(s) + 6H_2O(l) \rightarrow 2H_3BO_3(aq) + 3H_2S(g)$

(c) $Pb(NO_3)_2(aq) + 2\,NaI(aq) \rightarrow 2\,NaNO_3(aq) + PbI_2(s)$

(d) $2Hg(NO_3)_2(s) \overset{\Delta}{\rightarrow} 2HgO(s) + 4NO_2(g) + O_2(g)$

(e) $Cu(s) + 2H_2SO_4(aq) \rightarrow CuSO_4(aq) + SO_2(g) + 2H_2O(l)$

Patterns of Chemical Reactivity

3.16   (a)   Neutral Ca atom loses $2e^-$ to form Ca^{2+}. Neutral O_2 molecule gains $4e^-$ to form $2O^{2-}$. The formula of the product will be CaO, because the cationic and anionic charges are opposite and equal. $2Ca(s) + O_2(g) \rightarrow 2CaO$

(b)   The products are $CO_2(g)$ and $H_2O(l)$. $C_3H_6O(l) + 4O_2(g) \rightarrow 3CO_2(g) + 3H_2O(l)$

3.18   (a) $2Al(s) + 3O_2(g) \rightarrow Al_2O_3(s)$

(b) $Cu(OH)_2(s) \overset{\Delta}{\rightarrow} CuO(s) + H_2O(g)$

(c) $C_7H_{16}(l) + 11O_2(g) \rightarrow 7CO_2(g) + 8H_2O(l)$

(d) $2C_5H_{12}O(l) + 15O_2(g) \rightarrow 10CO_2(g) + 12H_2O(l)$

3.20   (a) $2C_3H_6(g) + 9O_2(g) \rightarrow 6CO_2(g) + 6H_2O(l)$ combustion

(b) $NH_4NO_3(s) \rightarrow N_2O(g) + 2H_2O(l)$ decomposition

(c) $C_5H_6O(l) + 6O_2(g) \rightarrow 5CO_2(g) + 3H_2O(l)$ combustion

(d) $N_2(g) + 3H_2(g) \rightarrow 2NH_3(g)$ combination

(e) $K_2O(s) + H_2O(l) \rightarrow 2KOH(aq)$ combination

Formula Weights

3.22   Formula weight in amu to 1 decimal place.

(a) N_2O: FW = $2(14.0) + 1(16.0) = 44.0$ amu

(b) $HC_7H_5O_2$: $7(12.0) + 6(1.0) + 2(16.0) = 122.0$ amu

(c) $Mg(OH)_2$: $1(24.3) + 2(16.0) + 2(1.0) = 58.3$ amu

(d) $(NH_2)_2CO$: $2(14.0) + 4(1.0) + 1(12.0) + 1(16.0) = 60.0$ amu

(e) $CH_3CO_2C_5H_{11}$: $7(12.0) + 14(1.0) + 2(16.0) = 130.0$ amu

3.24   (a) C_2H_2: FW = $2(12.0) + 2(1.0) = 26.0$ amu

$$\% C = \frac{2(12.0)\,amu}{26.0\,amu} \times 100 = 92.3\%$$

(b) $HC_6H_7O_6$: FW = $6(12.0) + 8(1.0) + 6(16.0) = 176.0$ amu

$$\% H = \frac{8(1.0)\,amu}{176.0\,amu} \times 100 = 4.5\%$$

(c) $(NH_4)_2SO_4$: FW $= 2(14.0) + 8(1.0) + 1(32.1) + 4(16.0) = 132.1$ amu

$$\% \, H = \frac{8(1.0)\,amu}{132.1\,amu} \times 100 = 6.1\%$$

(d) $PtCl_2(NH_3)_2$: FW $= 1(195.1) + 2(35.5) + 2(14.0) + 6(1.0) = 300.1$ amu

$$\% \, Pt = \frac{1(195.1)\,amu}{300.1\,amu} \times 100 = 65.01\%$$

(e) $C_{18}H_{24}O_2$: FW $= 18(12.0) + 24(1.0) + 2(16.0) = 272.0$ amu

$$\% \, O = \frac{2(16.0)\,amu}{272.0\,amu} \times 100 = 11.8\%$$

(f) $C_{18}H_{27}NO_3$: FW $= 18(12.0) + 27(1.0) + 1(14.0) + 3(16.0) = 305.0$ amu

$$\% \, C = \frac{18(12.0)\,amu}{305.0\,amu} \times 100 = 70.8\%$$

3.26   (a) CO_2: FW $= 1(12.0) + 2(16.0) = 44.0$ amu

$$\% \, C = \frac{12.0\,amu}{44.0\,amu} \times 100 = 27.3\%$$

(b) CH_3OH: FW $= 1(12.0) + 4(1.0) + 1(16.0) = 32.0$ amu

$$\% \, C = \frac{12.0\,amu}{32.0\,amu} \times 100 = 37.5\%$$

(c) C_2H_6: FW $= 2(12.0) + 6(1.0) = 30.0$ amu

$$\% \, C = \frac{2(12.0)\,amu}{30.0\,amu} \times 100 = 80.0\%$$

(d) $CS(NH_2)_2$: FW $= 1(12.0) + 1(32.1) + 2(14.0) + 4(1.0) = 76.1$ amu

$$\% \, C = \frac{12.0\,amu}{76.1\,amu} \times 100 = 15.8\%$$

Avogadro's Number and the Mole

3.28   (a)   <u>exactly</u> 12 g   (b) 6.0221421×10^{23}, Avogadro's number

3.30 3.0×10^{23} H_2O_2 molecules contains (4 atoms $\times$ 0.5 mol) = 2 mol atoms

32 g O_2 contains (2 atoms $\times$ 1 mol) = 2 mol atoms

2.0 mol CH_4 contains (5 atoms $\times$ 2 mol) = 10 mol atoms

3.32   300 million $= 300 \times 10^6 = 3.00 \times 10^8$ or 3×10^8 people

(The number 300 million has an ambiguous number of sig figs.)

$$\frac{6.022 \times 10^{23}\,\cancel{c}}{3.00 \times 10^8\,people} \times \frac{\$1}{100\,\cancel{c}} = \frac{\$6.022 \times 10^{21}}{3.00 \times 10^8\,people} = 2.007 \times 10^{13} = \$2.01 \times 10^{13}/person$$

$$\$13.5\,trillion = \$1.35 \times 10^{13} \qquad \frac{\$2.007 \times 10^{13}}{\$1.35 \times 10^{13}} = 1.487 = 1.49\,or\,1$$

Each person would receive an amount that is 1.49 (or 1) times the dollar amount of the national debt.

3.34   (a)   molar mass = 1(112.41) + 1(32.07) = 144.48 g

$$5.76 \times 10^{-3} \text{ mol CdS} \times \frac{144.48 \text{ g}}{1 \text{ mol}} = 0.832 \text{ g CdS}$$

   (b)   molar mass = 1(14.01) + 4(1.008) + 1(35.45) = 53.49 g/mol

$$112.6 \text{ g NH}_4\text{Cl} \times \frac{1 \text{ mol}}{53.49 \text{ g}} = 2.1051 = 2.11 \text{ mol NH}_4\text{Cl}$$

   (c) $1.305 \times 10^{-2} \text{ mol C}_6\text{H}_6 \times \dfrac{6.02214 \times 10^{23} \text{ molecules}}{1 \text{ mol}} = 7.859 \times 10^{21} \text{ C}_6\text{H}_6 \text{ molecules}$

   (d) $4.88 \times 10^{-3} \text{ mol Al(NO}_3)_3 \times \dfrac{9 \text{ mol O}}{1 \text{ mol Al(NO}_3)_3} \times \dfrac{6.022 \times 10^{23} \text{ O atoms}}{1 \text{ mol}}$

$$= 2.64 \times 10^{22} \text{ O atoms}$$

3.36   (a) $\text{Fe}_2(\text{SO}_4)_3$ molar mass = 2(55.845) + 3(32.07) + 12(16.00) = 399.900 = 399.9 g/mol

$$0.0714 \text{ mol Fe}_2(\text{SO}_4)_3 \times \frac{399.9 \text{ g Fe}_2(\text{SO}_4)_3}{1 \text{ mol}} = 28.553 = 28.6 \text{ g Fe}_2(\text{SO}_4)_3$$

   (b) $(\text{NH}_4)_2\text{CO}_3$ molar mass = 2(14.007) + 8(1.008) + 12.011 + 3(15.9994) = 96.0872

$$= 96.087 \text{ g/mol}$$

$$8.776 \text{ g (NH}_4)_2\text{CO}_3 \times \frac{1 \text{ mol}}{96.087 \text{ g (NH}_4)_2\text{CO}_3} \times \frac{2 \text{ mol NH}_4^+}{1 \text{ mol (NH}_4)_2\text{CO}_3} = 0.1827 \text{ mol NH}$$

   (c) $\text{C}_9\text{H}_8\text{O}_4$ molar mass = 9(12.01) + 8(1.008) + 4(16.00) = 180.154 = 180.2 g/mol

$$6.52 \times 10^{21} \text{ molecules} \times \frac{1 \text{ mol}}{6.022 \times 10^{23} \text{ molecules}} \times \frac{180.2 \text{ g C}_9\text{H}_8\text{O}_4}{1 \text{ mol aspirin}} = 1.95 \text{ g C}_9\text{H}_8\text{O}_4$$

   (d) $\dfrac{15.86 \text{ g Valium}}{0.05570 \text{ mol}} = 284.7 \text{ g Valium/mol}$

3.38   (a) $\text{C}_{14}\text{H}_{18}\text{N}_2\text{O}_5$ molar mass = 14(12.01) + 18(1.008) + 2(14.01) + 5(16.00)

$$= 294.30 \text{ g/mol}$$

   (b) $1.00 \text{ mg aspartame} \times \dfrac{1 \times 10^{-3} \text{ g}}{1 \text{ mg}} \times \dfrac{1 \text{ mol}}{294.3 \text{ g}} = 3.398 \times 10^{-6} = 3.40 \times 10^{-6} \text{ mol aspartame}$

   (c) $3.398 \times 10^{-6} \text{ mol aspartame} \times \dfrac{6.022 \times 10^{23} \text{ molecules}}{1 \text{ mol}} = 2.046 \times 10^{18}$

$$= 2.05 \times 10^{18} \text{ aspartame molecules}$$

   (d) $2.046 \times 10^{18} \text{ aspartame molecules} \times \dfrac{18 \text{ H atoms}}{1 \text{ aspartame molecule}} = 3.68 \times 10^{19} \text{ H atoms}$

3.40   (a) 7.08×10^{20} H atoms $\times \dfrac{19\,\text{C atoms}}{28\,\text{H atoms}} = 4.80 \times 10^{20}$ C atoms

      (b) 7.08×10^{20} H atoms $\times \dfrac{1\,\text{C}_{19}\text{H}_{28}\text{O}_2\,\text{molecule}}{28\,\text{H atoms}} = 2.529 \times 10^{19}$

                                         $= 2.53 \times 10^{19}$ $\text{C}_{19}\text{H}_{28}\text{O}_2$ molecules

      (c) 2.529×10^{19} $\text{C}_{19}\text{H}_{28}\text{O}_2$ molecules $\times \dfrac{1\,\text{mol}}{6.022 \times 10^{23}\,\text{molecules}} = 4.199 \times 10^{-5}$

                                         $= 4.20 \times 10^{-5}$ mol $\text{C}_{19}\text{H}_{28}\text{O}_2$

      (d) $\text{C}_{19}\text{H}_{28}\text{O}_2$ molar mass $= 19(12.01) + 28(1.008) + 2(16.00) = 288.41 = 288.4$ g/mol

          4.199×10^{-5} mol $\text{C}_{19}\text{H}_{28}\text{O}_2 \times \dfrac{288.4\,\text{g C}_{19}\text{H}_{28}\text{O}_2}{1\,\text{mol}} = 0.0121$ g $\text{C}_{19}\text{H}_{28}\text{O}_2$

3.42 25×10^{-6} g $\text{C}_{21}\text{H}_{30}\text{O}_2 \times \dfrac{1\,\text{mol C}_{21}\text{H}_{30}\text{O}_2}{314.5\,\text{g C}_{21}\text{H}_{30}\text{O}_2} = 7.95 \times 10^{-8} = 8.0 \times 10^{-8}$ mol $\text{C}_{21}\text{H}_{30}\text{O}_2$

       7.95×10^{-8} mol $\text{C}_{21}\text{H}_{30}\text{O}_2 \times \dfrac{6.022 \times 10^{23}\,\text{molecules}}{1\,\text{mol}} = 4.8 \times 10^{16}$ $\text{C}_{21}\text{H}_{30}\text{O}_2$ molecules

Empirical Formulas

3.44   (a)   Calculate the simplest ratio of moles.

          0.104 mol K / 0.052 = 2

          0.052 mol C / 0.052 = 1

          0.156 mol O / 0.052 = 3

          The empirical formula is K_2CO_3.

      (b)   Calculate moles of each element present, then the simplest ratio of moles.

          5.28 g Sn $\times \dfrac{1\,\text{mol Sn}}{118.7\,\text{g Sn}} = 0.04448$ mol Sn; $0.04448 / 0.04448 = 1$

          3.37 g F $\times \dfrac{1\,\text{mol F}}{19.00\,\text{g FSn}} = 0.1774$ mol F; $0.1774 / 0.04448 \approx 4$

          The integer ratio is 1 Sn : 4 F; the empirical formula is SnF_4.

      (c)   Assume 100 g sample, calculate moles of each element, find the simplest ratio of moles.

          87.5% N $= 87.5$ g N $\times \dfrac{1\,\text{mol N}}{14.01\,\text{g}} = 6.25$ mol N; $6.25 / 6.25 = 1$

          12.5% H $= 12.5$ g H $\times \dfrac{1\,\text{mol}}{1.008\,\text{g}} = 12.4$ mol H; $12.4 / 6.25 \approx 2$

          The empirical formula is NH_2.

3.46   See Solution 3.45 for stepwise problem-solving approach.

       (a) $55.3 \text{ g K} \times \dfrac{1 \text{ mol K}}{39.10 \text{ g K}} = 1.414 \text{ mol K}; \; 1.414/0.4714 \approx 3$

            $14.6 \text{ g P} \times \dfrac{1 \text{ mol P}}{30.97 \text{ g P}} = 0.4714 \text{ mol P}; \; 0.4714/0.4714 = 1$

            $30.1 \text{ g O} \times \dfrac{1 \text{ mol O}}{16.00 \text{ g O}} = 1.881 \text{ mol O}; \; 1.881/0.4714 \approx 4$

            The empirical formula is K_3PO_4.

       (b) $24.5 \text{ g Na} \times \dfrac{1 \text{ mol Na}}{22.99 \text{ g Na}} = 1.066 \text{ mol Na}; \; 1.066/0.5304 \approx 2$

            $14.9 \text{ g Si} \times \dfrac{1 \text{ mol Si}}{28.09 \text{ Si}} = 0.5304 \text{ mol si}; \; 0.5304/0.5304 = 1$

            $60.6 \text{ g F} \times \dfrac{1 \text{ mol F}}{19.00 \text{ g F}} = 3.189 \text{ mol F}; \; 3.189/0.5304 \approx 6$

            The empirical formula is Na_2SiF_6.

       (c) $62.1 \text{ g C} \times \dfrac{1 \text{ mol C}}{12.01 \text{ g C}} = 5.17 \text{ mol C}; \; 5.17/0.864 \approx 6$

            $5.21 \text{ g H} \times \dfrac{1 \text{ mol H}}{1.008 \text{ g H}} = 5.17 \text{ mol O}; \; 5.17/0.864 \approx 6$

            $12.1 \text{ g N} \times \dfrac{1 \text{ mol N}}{14.01 \text{ g N}} = 0.864 \text{ mol N}; \; 0.864/0.864 = 1$

            $20.7 \text{ g O} \times \dfrac{1 \text{ mol O}}{16.00 \text{ g O}} = 1.29 \text{ mol O}; \; 1.29/0.864 \approx 1.5$

            Multiplying by two, the empirical formula is $C_{12}H_{12}N_2O_3$.

3.48   (a) $\text{FW HCHO}_2 = 12.01 + 1.008 + 2(16.00) = 45.0 \quad \dfrac{\text{MM}}{\text{FW}} = \dfrac{90.0}{45.0} = 2$

            The molecular formula is $H_2C_2O_4$.

       (b) $\text{FW C}_2\text{H}_4\text{O} = 2(12) + 4(1) + 16 = 44. \quad \dfrac{\text{MM}}{\text{FW}} = \dfrac{88}{44} = 2$

            The molecular formula is $C_4H_8O_2$.

3.50   Assume 100 g in the following problems.

       (a) $75.69 \text{ g C} \times \dfrac{1 \text{ mol C}}{12.01 \text{ g C}} = 6.30 \text{ mol C}; \; 6.30/0.969 = 6.5$

            $8.80 \text{ g H} \times \dfrac{1 \text{ mol H}}{1.008 \text{ g H}} = 8.73 \text{ mol H}; \; 8.73/0.969 = 9.0$

            $15.51 \text{ g O} \times \dfrac{1 \text{ mol O}}{16.00 \text{ g O}} = 0.969 \text{ mol O}; \; 0.969/0.969 = 1$

Multiply by 2 to obtain the integer ratio 13:18:2. The empirical formula is $C_{13}H_{18}O_2$, FW = 206 g. Since the empirical formula weight and the molar mass are equal (206 g), the empirical and molecular formulas are $C_{13}H_{18}O_2$.

(b) $58.55 \text{ g C} \times \dfrac{1 \text{ mol C}}{12.01 \text{ g C}} = 4.875 \text{ mol C}; \quad 4.875/1.956 \approx 2.5$

$13.81 \text{ g H} \times \dfrac{1 \text{ mol H}}{1.008 \text{ g H}} = 13.700 \text{ mol H}; \quad 13.700/1.956 \approx 7.0$

$27.40 \text{ g N} \times \dfrac{1 \text{ mol N}}{14.01 \text{ g N}} = 1.956 \text{ mol N}; \quad 1.956/1.956 = 1.0$

Multiply by 2 to obtain the integer ratio 5:14:2. The empirical formula is $C_5H_{14}N_2$; FW = 102. Since the empirical formula weight and the molar mass are equal

(102 g), the empirical and molecular formulas are $C_5H_{14}N_2$.

(c) $59.0 \text{ g C} \times \dfrac{1 \text{ mol C}}{12.01 \text{ g C}} = 4.91 \text{ mol C}; \quad 4.91/0.550 \approx 9$

$7.1 \text{ g H} \times \dfrac{1 \text{ mol H}}{1.008 \text{ g H}} = 7.04 \text{ mol H}; \quad 7.04/0.550 \approx 13$

$26.2 \text{ g O} \times \dfrac{1 \text{ mol O}}{16.00 \text{ g O}} = 1.64 \text{ mol O}; \quad 1.64/0.550 \approx 3$

$7.7 \text{ g N} \times \dfrac{1 \text{ mol N}}{14.01 \text{ g N}} = 0.550 \text{ mol N}; \quad 0.550/0.550 = 1$

The empirical formula is $C_9H_{13}O_3N$, FW = 183 amu (or g). Since the molecular weight is approximately 180 amu, the empirical formula and molecular formula are the same, $C_9H_{13}O_3N$.

3.52   (a)   *Plan.* Calculate mol C and mol H, then g C and g H; get g O by subtraction.

Solve.

$6.32 \times 10^{-3} \text{ g CO}_2 \times \dfrac{1 \text{ mol CO}_2}{44.01 \text{ g CO}_2} \times \dfrac{1 \text{ mol C}}{1 \text{ mol CO}_2} = 1.436 \times 10^{-4} = 1.44 \times 10^{-4} \text{ mol C}$

$2.58 \times 10^{-3} \text{ g H}_2\text{O} \times \dfrac{1 \text{ mol H}_2\text{O}}{18.02 \text{ g H}_2\text{O}} \times \dfrac{2 \text{ mol H}}{1 \text{ mol H}_2\text{O}} = 2.863 \times 10^{-4} = 2.86 \times 10^{-4} \text{ mol H}$

$1.436 \times 10^{-4} \text{ mol C} \times \dfrac{12.01 \text{ g C}}{1 \text{ mol C}} = 1.725 \times 10^{-3} \text{ g C} = 1.73 \text{ mg C}$

$2.863 \times 10^{-4} \text{ mol H} \times \dfrac{1.008 \text{ g H}}{1 \text{ mol H}} = 2.886 \times 10^{-4} \text{ g H} = 0.289 \text{ mg H}$

mass of O = 2.78 mg sample − (1.725 mg C + 0.289 mg H) = 0.77 mg O

$0.77 \times 10^{-3} \text{ g O} \times \dfrac{1 \text{ mol O}}{16.00 \text{ g O}} = 4.81 \times 10^{-5} \text{ mol O}.$ Divide moles by 4.81×10^{-5}.

$$C: \frac{1.44 \times 10^{-4}}{4.81 \times 10^{-5}} \approx 3; \quad H: \frac{2.86 \times 10^{-4}}{4.81 \times 10^{-5}} \approx 6; \quad O: \frac{4.81 \times 10^{-5}}{4.81 \times 10^{-5}} = 1$$

The empirical formula is C_3H_6O.

(b) *Plan.* Calculate mol C and mol H, then g C and g H. In this case, get N by subtraction. *Solve.*

$$14.242 \times 10^{-3} \, g \, CO_2 \times \frac{1 \, mol \, CO_2}{44.01 \, g \, CO_2} \times \frac{1 \, mol \, C}{1 \, mol \, CO_2} = 3.2361 \times 10^{-4} \, mol \, C$$

$$4.083 \times 10^{-3} \, g \, H_2O \times \frac{1 \, mol \, H_2O}{18.02 \, g \, H_2O} \times \frac{2 \, mol \, H}{1 \, mol \, H_2O} = 4.5136 \times 10^{-4} = 4.532 \times 10^{-4} \, mol \, H$$

$$3.2361 \times 10^{-4} \, g \, mol \, C \times \frac{12.01 \, g \, C}{1 \, mol \, H} = 3.8866 \times 10^{-3} \, g \, C = 3.8866 \, mg \, C$$

$$4.532 \times 10^{-4} \, mol \, H \times \frac{1.008 \, g \, H}{1 \, mol \, H} = 0.45683 \times 10^{-3} \, g \, H = 0.4568 \, mg \, H$$

mass of N = 5.250 mg sample − (3.8866 mg C + 0.4568 mg H) = 0.9066

$$= 0.907 \, mg \, N$$

$$0.9066 \times 10^{-3} \, g \, N \times \frac{1 \, mol \, N}{14.01 \, g \, N} = 6.47 \times 10^{-5} \, mol \, N. \text{ Divide moles by } 6.47 \times 10^{-5}.$$

$$C: \frac{3.24 \times 10^{-4}}{6.47 \times 10^{-5}} \approx 5; \quad H: \frac{4.53 \times 10^{-4}}{6.47 \times 10^{-5}} \approx 7; \quad N: \frac{6.47 \times 10^{-5}}{6.47 \times 10^{-5}} = 1$$

The empirical formula is C_5H_7N, FW = 81. A molar mass of 160 ± 5 indicates a factor of 2 and a molecular formula of $C_{10}H_{14}N_2$.

3.54   The reaction involved is $MgSO_4 \cdot xH_2O(s) \rightarrow MgSO_4(s) + xH_2O(g)$. First, calculate the number of moles of product $MgSO_4$; this is the same as the number of moles of starting hydrate.

$$2.472 \, g \, MgSO_4 \times \frac{1 \, mol \, MgSO_4}{120.4 \, g \, MgSO_4} \times \frac{1 \, mol \, MgSO_4 \cdot xH_2O}{1 \, mol \, MgSO_4} = 0.02053 \, mol \, MgSO_4 \cdot xH_2O$$

Thus, $\dfrac{5.061 \, g \, MgSO_4 \cdot xH_2O}{0.02053} = 246.5 \, g/mol = FW \text{ of } MgSO_4 \cdot xH_2O$

FW of $MgSO_4 \cdot xH_2O$ = FW of $MgSO_4$ + x(FW of H_2O).

246.5 = 120.4 + x(18.02). x = 6.998. The hydrate formula is $MgSO_4 \cdot \underline{7}H_2O$.

Alternatively, we could calculate the number of moles of water represented by weight loss: (5.061 − 2.472) = 2.589 g H_2O lost.

$$2.589 \, g \, H_2O \times \frac{1 \, mol \, H_2O}{18.02 \, g \, H_2O} = 0.1437 \, mol \, H_2O; \quad \frac{mol \, H_2O}{mol \, MgSO_4} = \frac{0.1437}{0.02053} = 7.000$$

Again the correct formula is $MgSO_4 \cdot \underline{7}H_2O$.

Calculations Based on Chemical Equations

3.56   The **integer coefficients** immediately preceding each molecular formula in a chemical equation give information about relative numbers of moles of reactants and products involved in a reaction.

3.58 $C_6H_{12}O_6(aq) \rightarrow 2C_2H_5OH(aq) + 2CO_2(g)$

(a) $0.400 \text{ mol } C_6H_{12}O_6 \times \dfrac{2 \text{ mol } CO_2}{1 \text{ mol } C_6H_{12}O_6} = 0.800 \text{ mol } CO_2$

(b) $7.50 \text{ g } C_2H_5OH \times \dfrac{1 \text{ mol } C_2H_5OH}{46.07 \text{ g } C_2H_5OH} \times \dfrac{1 \text{ mol } C_6H_{12}O_6}{2 \text{ mol } C_2H_5OH} \times \dfrac{180.2 \text{ g } C_6H_{12}O_6}{1 \text{ mol } C_6H_{12}O_6}$

$$= 14.7 \text{ g } C_6H_{12}O_6$$

(c) $7.50 \text{ g } C_2H_5OH \times \dfrac{1 \text{ mol } C_2H_5OH}{46.07 \text{ g } C_2H_5OH} \times \dfrac{2 \text{ mol } CO_2}{2 \text{ mol } C_2H_5OH} \times \dfrac{44.01 \text{ g } CO_2}{1 \text{ mol } CO_2} = 7.16 \text{ g } CO_2$

3.60   (a) $Fe_2O_3(s) + 3CO(g) \rightarrow 2Fe(s) + 3CO_2(g)$

(b) $0.150 \text{ kg } Fe_2O_3 \times \dfrac{1000 \text{ g}}{1 \text{ kg}} \times \dfrac{1 \text{ mol } Fe_2O_3}{159.688 \text{ g } Fe_2O_3} = 0.9393 = 0.939 \text{ mol } Fe_2O_3$

$0.9393 \text{ mol } Fe_2O_3 \times \dfrac{3 \text{ mol } CO}{1 \text{ mol } Fe_2O_3} \times \dfrac{28.01 \text{ g } CO}{1 \text{ mol } CO} = 78.929 = 78.9 \text{ g } CO$

(c) $0.9393 \text{ mol } Fe_2O_3 \times \dfrac{2 \text{ mol } Fe}{1 \text{ mol } Fe_2O_3} \times \dfrac{55.845 \text{ g } Fe}{1 \text{ mol } Fe} = 104.914 = 105 \text{ g } Fe$

$0.9393 \text{ mol } Fe_2O_3 \times \dfrac{3 \text{ mol } CO_2}{1 \text{ mol } Fe_2O_3} \times \dfrac{44.01 \text{ g } CO_2}{1 \text{ mol } CO_2} = 124.015 = 124 \text{ g } CO_2$

(d)   reactants: $150 \text{ g } Fe_2O_3 + 78.9 \text{ g } CO = 228.9 = 229 \text{ g}$

products: $104.9 \text{ g } Fe + 124.0 \text{ g } CO_2 = 228.9 = 229 \text{ g}$

Mass is conserved.

3.62   (a) $CaH_2(s) + 2H_2O(l) \rightarrow Ca(OH)_2(aq) + 2H_2(g)$

(b) $8.500 \text{ g } H_2 \times \dfrac{1 \text{ mol } H_2}{2.016 \text{ g } H_2} \times \dfrac{1 \text{ mol } CaH_2}{2 \text{ mol } H_2} \times \dfrac{42.10 \text{ g } CaH_2}{1 \text{ mol } CaH_2} = 88.75 \text{ g } CaH_2$

3.64 $2C_8H_{18}(l) + 25O_2(g) \rightarrow 16CO_2(g) + 18H_2O(l)$

(a) $1.25 \text{ mol } C_8H_{18} \times \dfrac{25 \text{ mol } O_2}{2 \text{ mol } C_8H_{18}} = 15.625 = 15.6 \text{ mol } O_2$

(b) $10.0 \text{ g } C_8H_{18} \times \dfrac{1 \text{ mol } C_8H_{18}}{114.2 \text{ g } C_8H_{18}} \times \dfrac{25 \text{ mol } O_2}{2 \text{ mol } C_8H_{18}} \times \dfrac{32.00 \text{ g } O_2}{1 \text{ mol } O_2} = 35.0 \text{ g } O_2$

(c) $1.00 \text{ gal } C_8H_{18} \times \dfrac{3.7854 \text{ L}}{1 \text{ gal}} \times \dfrac{1000 \text{ mL}}{1 \text{ L}} \times \dfrac{0.692 \text{ g}}{1 \text{ mL}} = 2619.5 = 2.62 \times 10^3 \text{ g } C_8H_{18}$

$$2.6195 \times 10^3 \text{ g C}_8\text{H}_{18} \times \frac{1 \text{ mol C}_8\text{H}_{18}}{114.2 \text{ g C}_8\text{H}_{18}} \times \frac{25 \text{ mol O}_2}{2 \text{ mol C}_8\text{H}_{18}} \times \frac{32.00 \text{ g O}_2}{1 \text{ mol O}_2} = 9{,}175.1 \text{ g}$$

$$= 9.18 \times 10^3 \text{ g O}_2$$

3.66   (a)   *Plan.* Calculate a "mole ratio" between nitroglycerine and total moles of gas produced. $(12 + 6 + 1 + 10) = 29$ mol gas; 4 mol nitro: 29 total mol gas.   *Solve.*

$$2.00 \text{ mL nitro} \times \frac{1.592 \text{ g}}{\text{mL}} \times \frac{1 \text{ mol nitro}}{227.1 \text{ g nitro}} \times \frac{29 \text{ mol gas}}{4 \text{ mol nitro}} = 0.10165 = 0.102 \text{ mol gas}$$

      (b) $0.10165 \text{ mol gas} \times \dfrac{55 \text{ L}}{\text{mol}} = 5.5906 = 5.6 \text{ L}$

      (c) $2.00 \text{ mL nitro} \times \dfrac{1.592 \text{ g}}{\text{mL}} \times \dfrac{1 \text{ mol nitro}}{227.1 \text{ g nitro}} \times \dfrac{6 \text{ mol N}_2}{4 \text{ mol nitro}} \times \dfrac{28.01 \text{ g N}_2}{1 \text{ mol N}_2} = 0.589 \text{ g N}_2$

Limiting Reactants; Theoretical Yields

3.68   (a)   *Theoretical yield* is the maximum amount of product possible, as predicted by stoichiometry, assuming that the limiting reactant is converted entirely to product.

             Actual yield is the amount of product actually obtained, less than or equal to the theoretical yield. *Percent yield* is the ratio of (actual yield to theoretical yield) × 100.

      (b)   No reaction is perfect. Not all reactant molecules come together effectively to form products; alternative reaction pathways may produce secondary products and reduce the amount of desired product actually obtained, or it might not be possible to completely isolate the desired product from the reaction mixture. In any case, these factors reduce the actual yield of a reaction.

      (c)   No, 110% actual yield is not possible. Theoretical yield is the maximum possible amount of pure product, assuming all available limiting reactant is converted to product, and that all product is isolated. If an actual yield of 110% if obtained, the product must contain impurities which increase the experimental mass.

3.70   (a) $40{,}875 \text{ L beverage} \times \dfrac{1 \text{ bottle}}{0.355 \text{ L}} = 115{,}140.85 = 1.15 \times 10^5$ portions of beverage

             (The uncertainty in 355 mL limits the precision of the number of portions we can reasonably expect to deliver to three significant figures.)

             121,515 bottles; 122,500 caps; 1.15×10^5 bottles can be filled and capped.

      (b)   122,500 caps – 115,141 portions = 7,359 = 7×10^3 caps remain

             121,515 empty bottles – 115,141 portions = 6374 = 6×10^3 bottles remain

             (Uncertainty in the number of portions delivered limits the results to 1 sig fig.)

      (c)   The volume of beverage limits production.

3.72 $0.500 \text{ mol Al(OH)}_3 \times \dfrac{3 \text{ mol H}_2\text{SO}_4}{2 \text{ mol Al(OH)}_3} = 0.750 \text{ mol H}_2\text{SO}_4$ needed for complete reaction

Only 0.500 mol H_2SO_4 available, so H_2SO_4 limits.

$$0.500 \text{ mol } H_2SO_4 \times \frac{1 \text{ mol } Al_2(SO_4)_3}{3 \text{ mol } H_2SO_4} = 0.1667 = 0.167 \text{ mol } Al_2(SO_4)_3 \text{ can form}$$

$$0.500 \text{ mol } H_2SO_4 \times \frac{2 \text{ mol } Al(OH)_3}{3 \text{ mol } H_2SO_4} = 0.3333 = 0.333 \text{ mol } Al(OH)_3 \text{ react}$$

0.500 mol $Al(OH)_3$ initial – 0.333 mol react = 0.167 mol $Al(OH)_3$ remain

3.74 $4NH_3(g) + 5O_2(g) \rightarrow 4NO(g) + 6H_2O(g)$

(a)   Follow the approach in Sample Exercise 3.19.

$$1.50 \text{ g } NH_3 \times \frac{1 \text{ mol } NH_3}{17.03 \text{ g } NH_3} = 0.08808 = 0.0881 \text{ mol } NH_3$$

$$2.75 \text{ g } O_2 \times \frac{1 \text{ mol } O_2}{32.00 \text{ g } O_2} = 0.08594 = 0.0859 \text{ mol } O_2$$

$$0.08594 \text{ mol } O_2 \times \frac{4 \text{ mol } NH_3}{5 \text{ mol } O_2} = 0.06875 = 0.0688 \text{ mol } NH_3 \text{ required}$$

More than 0.0688 mol NH_3 is available, so O_2 is the limiting reactant.

(b) $$0.08594 \text{ mol } O_2 \times \frac{4 \text{ mol } NO}{5 \text{ mol } O_2} \times \frac{30.01 \text{ g } NO}{1 \text{ mol } NO} = 2.063 = 2.06 \text{ g } NO \text{ produced}$$

$$0.08594 \text{ mol } O_2 \times \frac{6 \text{ mol } H_2O}{5 \text{ mol } O_2} \times \frac{18.02 \text{ g } H_2O}{1 \text{ mol } H_2O} = 1.8583 = 1.86 \text{ g } H_2O \text{ produced}$$

(c) 0.08808 mol NH_3 – 0.06875 mol NH_3 reacted = $0.01933 = 0.0193$ mol NH_3 remain

$$0.01933 \text{ mol } NH_3 \times \frac{17.03 \text{ g } NH_3}{1 \text{ mol } NH_3} = 0.32919 = 0.329 \text{ g } NH_3 \text{ remain}$$

(d)   mass products = 2.06 g NO + 1.86 g H_2O + 0.329 g NH_3 remaining = 4.25 g products

mass reactants = 1.50 g NH_3 + 2.75 g O_2 = 4.25 g reactants

(For comparison purposes, the mass of excess reactant can be either added to the products, as above, or subtracted from reactants.)

3.76   *Plan.* Write balanced equation; determine limiting reactant; calculate amounts of excess reactant remaining and products, based on limiting reactant.

Solve. $H_2SO_4(aq) + Pb(C_2H_3O_2)_2(aq) \rightarrow PbSO_4(s) + 2HC_2H_3O_2(aq)$

$$7.50 \text{ g } H_2SO_4 \times \frac{1 \text{ mol } H_2SO_4}{98.09 \text{ g } H_2SO_4} = 0.07646 = 0.0765 \text{ mol } H_2SO_4$$

$$7.50 \text{ g } Pb(C_2H_3O_2)_2 \times \frac{1 \text{ mol } Pb(C_2H_3O_2)_2}{325.3 \text{ g } Pb(C_2H_3O_2)_2} = 0.023056 = 0.0231 \text{ mol } Pb(C_2H_3O_2)_2$$

1 mol H_2SO_4:1 mol $Pb(C_2H_3O_2)_2$, so $Pb(C_2H_3O_2)_2$ is the limiting reactant.

0 mol $Pb(C_2H_3O_2)_2$, $(0.07646 - 0.023056) = 0.0534$ mol H_2SO_4, 0.0231 mol $PbSO_4$,

$(0.023056 \times 2) = 0.0461$ mol $HC_2H_3O_2$ are present after reaction

0.053405 mol $H_2SO_4 \times 98.09$ g/mol $= 5.2385 = 5.24$ g H_2SO_4

0.023056 mol $PbSO_4 \times 303.3$ g/mol $= 6.9928 = 6.99$ g $PbSO_4$

0.046111 mol $HC_2H_3O_2 \times 60.05$ g/mol $= 2.7690 = 2.77$ g $HC_2H_3O_2$

Check. The initial mass of reactants was 15.00 g; and the final mass of excess reactant and products is 15.00 g; mass is conserved.

3.78   (a) $C_2H_6 + Cl_2 \rightarrow C_2H_5Cl + HCl$

$$125 \text{ g } C_2H_6 \times \frac{1 \text{ mol } C_2H_6}{30.07 \text{ g } C_2H_6} = 4.157 = 4.16 \text{ mol } C_2H_6$$

$$255 \text{ g } Cl_2 \times \frac{1 \text{ mol } Cl_2}{70.91 \text{ g } Cl_2} = 3.596 = 3.60 \text{ mol } Cl_2$$

Since the reactants combine in a 1:1 mole ratio, Cl_2 is the limiting reactant. The theoretical yield is:

$$3.596 \text{ mol } Cl_2 \times \frac{1 \text{ mol } C_2H_5Cl}{1 \text{ mol } Cl_2} \times \frac{64.51 \text{ g } C_2H_5Cl}{1 \text{ mol } C_2H_5Cl} = 231.98 = 232 \text{ g } C_2H_5Cl$$

     (b)   % yield $= \dfrac{206 \text{ g } C_2H_5Cl \text{ actual}}{232 \text{ g } C_2H_5Cl \text{ theoretical}} \times 100 = 88.8\%$

3.80 $H_2S(g) + 2NaOH(aq) \rightarrow Na_2S(aq) + 2H_2O(l)$

$$1.50 \text{ g } H_2S \times \frac{1 \text{ mol } H_2S}{34.08 \text{ g } H_2S} = 0.04401 = 0.0440 \text{ mol } H_2S$$

$$2.00 \text{ g } NaOH \times \frac{1 \text{ mol } NaOH}{40.00 \text{ g } NaOH} = 0.0500 \text{ mol } NaOH$$

By inspection, twice as many mol NaOH as H_2S are needed for exact reaction, but mol NaOH given is less than twice mol H_2S, so NaOH limits.

$$0.0500 \text{ mol } NaOH \times \frac{1 \text{ mol } Na_2S}{2 \text{ mol } NaOH} \times \frac{78.05 \text{ g } Na_2S}{1 \text{ mol } Na_2S} = 1.95125 = 1.95 \text{ g } Na_2S \text{ theoretical}$$

$$\frac{92.0\%}{100} \times 1.95125 \text{ g } Na_2S \text{ theoretical} = 1.7951 = 1.80 \text{ g } Na_2S \text{ actual}$$

Additional Exercises

3.82   The formulas of the fertilizers are NH_3, NH_4NO_3, $(NH_4)_2SO_4$ and $(NH_2)_2CO$. Qualitatively, the more heavy, non-nitrogen atoms in a molecule, the smaller the mass % of N. By inspection, the mass of NH_3 is dominated by N, so it will have the greatest % N, $(NH_4)_2SO_4$ will have the least. In order of increasing % N:

$(NH_4)_2SO_4 < NH_4NO_3 < (NH_2)_2CO < NH_3$.

Check by calculation:

$(NH_4)_2SO_4$: FW = $2(14.0) + 8(1.0) + 1(32.1) + 4(16.0) = 132.1$ amu

% N = $[2(14.0)/132.1] \times 100 = 21.2\%$

NH_4NO_3: FW = $2(14.0) + 4(1.0) + 3(16.0) = 80.0$ amu

% N = $[2(14.0)/80.0] \times 100 = 35.0\%$

$(NH_2)_2CO$: FW = $2(14.0) + 4(1.0) = 1(12.0) + 1(16.0) = 60.0$ amu

% N = $[2(14.0)/60.0] \times 100 = 46.7\%$ N

NH_3: FW = $1(14.0) + 3(1.0) = 17.0$

% N = $[14.0/17.0] \times 100 = 82.4$ % N

3.83   (a) $1.25 \text{ carat} \times \dfrac{0.200 \text{ g}}{1 \text{ carat}} \times \dfrac{1 \text{ mol C}}{12.01 \text{ g C}} = 0.020816 = 0.0208 \text{ mol C}$

$0.020816 \text{ mol C} \times \dfrac{6.022 \times 10^{23} \text{ C atoms}}{1 \text{ mol C}} = 1.25 \times 10^{22} \text{ C atoms}$

(b) $0.500 \text{ g C}_9\text{H}_8\text{O}_4 \times \dfrac{1 \text{ mol C}_9\text{H}_8\text{O}_4}{180.2 \text{ g C}_9\text{H}_8\text{O}_4} = 2.7747 \times 10^{-3} = 2.77 \times 10^{-3} \text{ mol HC}_9\text{H}_7\text{O}_4$

$0.0027747 \text{ mol C}_9\text{H}_8\text{O}_4 \times \dfrac{6.022 \times 10^{23} \text{ molecules}}{1 \text{ mol}} = 1.67 \times 10^{21} \text{ HC}_9\text{H}_7\text{O}_4 \text{ molecules}$

3.84   (a) $\dfrac{5.342 \times 10^{-21} \text{ g}}{1 \text{ molecule penicillin G}} \times \dfrac{6.0221 \times 10^{23} \text{ molecules}}{1 \text{ mol}} = 3217 \text{ g/mol penicillin G}$

(b)   1.00 g hemoglobin (hem) contains 3.40×10^{-3} g Fe.

$\dfrac{1.00 \text{ g hem}}{3.40 \times 10^{-3} \text{ g Fe}} \times \dfrac{55.85 \text{ g Fe}}{1 \text{ mol Fe}} \times \dfrac{4 \text{ mol Fe}}{1 \text{ mol hem}} = 6.57 \times 10^4 \text{ g/mol hemoglobin}$

3.86   *Plan.* Assume 100 g, calculate mole ratios, empirical formula, then molecular formula from molar mass.   *Solve.*

$68.2 \text{ g C} \times \dfrac{1 \text{ mol C}}{12.01 \text{ g C}} = 5.68 \text{ mol C}; \ 5.68/0.568 \approx 10$

$6.86 \text{ g H} \times \dfrac{1 \text{ mol H}}{1.008 \text{ g H}} = 6.81 \text{ mol H}; \ 6.81/0.568 \approx 12$

$15.9 \text{ g N} \times \dfrac{1 \text{ mol N}}{14.01 \text{ g N}} = 1.13 \text{ mol N}; \ 1.13/0.568 \approx 2$

$9.08 \text{ g O} \times \dfrac{1 \text{ mol O}}{16.00 \text{ g O}} = 0.568 \text{ mol O}; \ 0.568/0.568 = 1$

The empirical formula is $C_{10}H_{12}N_2O$, FW = 176 amu (or g). Since the molar mass is 176, the empirical and molecular formula are the same, $C_{10}H_{12}N_2O$.

3.87   *Plan.* Assume 1.000 g and get mass O by subtraction.   *Solve.*

(a) $0.7787 \, g \, C \times \dfrac{1 \, mol \, C}{12.01 \, g \, C} = 0.06484 \, mol \, C$

$0.1176 \, g \, H \times \dfrac{1 \, mol \, H}{1.008 \, g \, H} = 0.1167 \, mol \, H$

$0.1037 \, g \, O \times \dfrac{1 \, mol \, C}{16.00 \, g \, O} = 0.006481 \, mol \, O$

Dividing through by the smallest of these values we obtain $C_{10}H_{18}O$.

(b)   The formula weight of $C_{10}H_{18}O$ is 154. Thus, the empirical formula is also the molecular formula.

3.88   Since all the C in the vanillin must be present in the CO_2 produced, get g C from g CO_2.

$2.43 \, g \, CO_2 \times \dfrac{1 \, mol \, CO_2}{44.01 \, g \, CO_2} \times \dfrac{12.01 \, g \, C}{1 \, mol \, C} = 0.6631 = 0.663 \, g \, C$

Since all the H in vanillin must be present in the H_2O produced, get g H from g H_2O.

$0.50 \, g \, H_2O \times \dfrac{1 \, mol \, H_2O}{18.02 \, g \, H_2O} \times \dfrac{2 \, mol \, H}{1 \, mol \, H_2O} \times \dfrac{1.008 \, g \, H}{1 \, mol \, H} = 0.0559 = 0.056 \, g \, H$

Get g O by subtraction. (Since the analysis was performed by combustion, an unspecified amount of O_2 was a reactant, and thus not all the O in the CO_2 and H_2O produced came from vanillin.) 1.05 g vanillin – 0.663 g C – 0.056 g H = 0.331 g O

$0.6631 \, g \, C \times \dfrac{1 \, mol \, C}{12.01 \, g \, C} = 0.0552 \, mol \, C; \, 0.0552 \, / \, 0.0207 = 2.67$

$0.0559 \, g \, H \times \dfrac{1 \, mol \, H}{1.008 \, g \, H} = 0.0555 \, mol \, C; \, 0.0555 \, / \, 0.0207 = 2.68$

$0.331 \, g \, O \times \dfrac{1 \, mol \, O}{16.00 \, g \, O} = 0.0207 \, mol \, O; \, 0.0207 \, / \, 0.0207 = 1.00$

Multiplying the numbers above by **3** to obtain an integer ratio of moles, the empirical formula of vanillin is $C_8H_8O_3$.

3.90   The mass percentage is determined by the relative number of atoms of the element times the atomic weight, divided by the total formula mass. Thus, the mass percent of bromine in $KBrO_x$ is given by $0.5292 = \dfrac{79.91}{39.10 + 79.91 + x(16.00)}$. Solving for x, we obtain x = 2.00. Thus, the formula is $KBrO_2$.

3.91   (a)   Let AW = the atomic weight of X.

According to the chemical reaction, moles XI_3 reacted = moles XCl_3 produced

$$0.5000 \text{ g } XI_3 \times 1 \text{ mol } XI_3 / (AW + 380.71) \text{ g } XI_3$$

$$= 0.2360 \text{ g } XCl_3 \times \frac{1 \text{ mol } XCl_3}{(AW + 106.36) \text{ g } XCl_3}$$

$$0.5000 (AW + 106.36) = 0.2360 (AW + 380.71)$$

$$0.5000 \text{ AW} + 53.180 = 0.2360 \text{ AW} + 89.848$$

$$0.2640 \text{ AW} = 36.67; \text{ AW} = 138.9 \text{ g}$$

(b)   X is lanthanum, La, atomic number 57.

3.92 $C_2H_5OH(l) + 3O_2(g) \rightarrow 2CO_2(g) + 3H_2O(g)$

$C_3H_8(g) + 5O_2(g) \rightarrow 3CO_2(g) + 4H_2O(g)$

$CH_3CH_2COCH_3(l) + 11/2 \, O_2(g) \rightarrow 4CO_2(g) + 4H_2O(l)$

In a combustion reaction, all H in the fuel is transformed to H_2O in the products. The reactant with most mol H/mol fuel will produce the most H_2O. C_3H_8 and $CH_3CH_2COCH_3$ (C_4H_8O) both have 8 mol H/mol fuel, so 1.5 mol of either fuel will produce the same amount of H_2O. 1.5 mol C_2H_5OH will produce less H_2O.

3.94 $2NaCl(aq) + 2H_2O(l) \rightarrow 2NaOH(aq) + H_2(g) + Cl_2(g)$

Calculate mol Cl_2 and relate to mol H_2, mol NaOH.

$$1.5 \times 10^6 \text{ kg} \times \frac{1000 \text{ g}}{1 \text{ kg}} \times \frac{1 \text{ mol } Cl_2}{70.91 \text{ g } Cl_2} = 2.115 \times 10^7 = 2.1 \times 10^7 \text{ mol } Cl_2$$

$$2.115 \times 10^7 \text{ mol } Cl_2 \times \frac{1 \text{ mol } H_2}{1 \text{ mol } Cl_2} \times \frac{2.016 \text{ g } H_2}{1 \text{ mol } H_2} = 4.26 \times 10^7 \text{ g } H_2 = 4.3 \times 10^4 \text{ kg } H_2$$

$$4.3 \times 10^7 \text{ g} \times \frac{1 \text{ metric ton}}{1 \times 10^6 \text{ g } (1 \text{ Mg})} = 43 \text{ metric tons } H_2$$

$$2.115 \times 10^7 \text{ mol } Cl_2 \times \frac{2 \text{ mol NaOH}}{1 \text{ mol } Cl_2} \times \frac{40.0 \text{ g NaOH}}{1 \text{ mol NaOH}} = 1.69 \times 10^9 = 1.7 \times 10^9 \text{ g NaOH}$$

1.7×10^9 g NaOH = 1.7×10^6 kg NaOH = 1.7×10^3 metric tons NaOH

3.95 $2C_{57}H_{110}O_6 + 163O_2 \rightarrow 114CO_2 + 110H_2O$

molar mass of fat = 57(12.01) + 110(1.008) + 6(16.00) = 891.5

$$1.0 \text{ kg fat} \times \frac{1000 \text{ g}}{1 \text{ kg}} \times \frac{1 \text{ mol fat}}{891.5 \text{ g fat}} \times \frac{110 \text{ mol } H_2O}{2 \text{ mol fat}} \times \frac{18.02 \text{ g } H_2O}{1 \text{ mol } H_2O} \times \frac{1 \text{ kg}}{1000 \text{ g}} = 1.1 \text{ kg } H_2O$$

3.96   (a)   *Plan.* Calculate the total mass of C from g CO and g CO_2. Calculate the mass of H from g H_2O. Calculate mole ratios and the empirical formula.   *Solve.*

$$0.467 \text{ g CO} \times \frac{1 \text{ mol CO}}{28.01 \text{ g CO}} \times \frac{1 \text{ mol C}}{1 \text{ mol CO}} \times 12.01 \text{ g C} = 0.200 \text{ g C}$$

$$0.733 \text{ g } CO_2 \times \frac{1 \text{ mol } CO_2}{44.01 \text{ g } CO_2} \times \frac{1 \text{ mol C}}{1 \text{ mol } CO_2} \times 12.01 \text{ g C} = 0.200 \text{ g C}$$

Total mass C is 0.200 g + 0.200 g = 0.400 g C.

$$0.450 \text{ g H}_2\text{O} \times \frac{1 \text{ mol H}_2\text{O}}{18.02 \text{ g H}_2\text{O}} \times \frac{2 \text{ mol H}}{1 \text{ mol H}_2\text{O}} \times \frac{1.008 \text{ g H}}{1 \text{ mol H}} = 0.0503 \text{ g H}$$

(Since hydrocarbons contain only the elements C and H, g H can also be obtained by subtraction: 0.450 g sample – 0.400 g C = 0.050 g H.)

$$0.400 \text{ g C} \times \frac{1 \text{ mol C}}{12.01 \text{ g C}} = 0.0333 \text{ mol C}; \quad 0.0333 / 0.0333 = 1.0$$

$$0.0503 \text{ g H} \times \frac{1 \text{ mol H}}{1.008 \text{ g H}} = 0.0499 \text{ mol H}; \quad 0.0499 / 0.0333 = 1.5$$

Multiplying by a factor of 2, the empirical formula is C_2H_3.

(b) Mass is conserved. Total mass products – mass sample = mass O_2 consumed.

0.467 g CO + 0.733 g CO_2 + 0.450 g H_2O – 0.450 g sample = 1.200 g O_2 consumed

(c) For complete combustion, 0.467 g CO must be converted to CO_2.

$2CO(g) + O_2(g) \rightarrow 2CO_2(g)$

$$0.467 \text{ g CO} \times \frac{1 \text{ mol CO}}{28.01 \text{ g C}} \times \frac{1 \text{ mol O}_2}{2 \text{ mol CO}} \times \frac{32.00 \text{ g O}_2}{1 \text{ mol O}_2} = 0.267 \text{ g O}_2$$

The total mass of O_2 required for complete combustion is

1.200 g + 0.267 g = 1.467 g O_2.

3.98　All of the O_2 is produced from $KClO_3$; get g $KClO_3$ from g O_2. All of the H_2O is produced from $KHCO_3$; get g $KHCO_3$ from g H_2O. The g H_2O produced also reveals the g CO_2 from the decomposition of $NaHCO_3$. The remaining CO_2 (13.2 g CO_2– g CO_2 from $NaHCO_3$) is due to K_2CO_3 and g K_2CO_3 can be derived from it.

$$4.00 \text{ g O}_2 \times \frac{1 \text{ mol O}_2}{32.00 \text{ g O}_2} \times \frac{2 \text{ mol KClO}_3}{3 \text{ mol O}_2} \times \frac{122.6 \text{ g KClO}_3}{1 \text{ mol KClO}_3} = 10.22 = 10.2 \text{ g KClO}_3$$

$$1.80 \text{ g H}_2\text{O} \times \frac{1 \text{ mol H}_2\text{O}}{18.02 \text{ g H}_2\text{O}} \times \frac{2 \text{ mol KHCO}_3}{1 \text{ mol H}_2\text{O}} \times \frac{100.1 \text{ g KHCO}_3}{1 \text{ mol KHCO}_3} = 20.00 = 20.0 \text{ g KHCO}_3$$

$$1.80 \text{ g H}_2\text{O} \times \frac{1 \text{ mol H}_2\text{O}}{18.02 \text{ g H}_2\text{O}} \times \frac{2 \text{ mol CO}_2}{1 \text{ mol H}_2\text{O}} \times \frac{44.01 \text{ g CO}_2}{1 \text{ mol CO}_2} = 8.792 = 8.79 \text{ g CO}_2 \text{ from KHCO}_3$$

13.20 g CO_2 total – 8.792 CO_2 from $KHCO_3$ = 4.408 = 4.41 g CO_2 from K_2CO_3

$$4.408 \text{ g CO}_2 \times \frac{1 \text{ mol CO}_2}{44.01 \text{ g CO}_2} \times \frac{1 \text{ mol K}_2\text{CO}_3}{1 \text{ mol CO}_2} \times \frac{138.2 \text{ g K}_2\text{CO}_3}{1 \text{ mol K}_2\text{CO}_3} = 13.84 = 13.8 \text{ g K}_2\text{CO}_3$$

100.0 g mixture – 10.22 g $KClO_3$ – 20.00 g $KHCO_3$ – 13.84 g K_2CO_3 = 56.0 g KCl

3.99　(a)　$2C_2H_2(g) + 5O_2(g) \rightarrow 4CO_2(g) + 2H_2O(g)$

　　　(b)　Following the approach in Sample Exercise 3.18,

$$10.0 \, g \, C_2H_2 \times \frac{1 \, mol \, C_2H_2}{26.04 \, g \, C_2H_2} \times \frac{5 \, mol \, O_2}{2 \, mol \, C_2H_2} \times \frac{32.00 \, g \, O_2}{1 \, mol \, O_2} = 30.7 \, g \, O_2 \text{ required}$$

Only 10.0 g O_2 are available, so O_2 limits.

(c)   Since O_2 limits, 0.0 g O_2 remain.

Next, calculate the g C_2H_2 consumed and the amounts of CO_2 and H_2O produced by reaction of 10.0 g O_2.

$$10.0 \, g \, O_2 \times \frac{1 \, mol \, O_2}{32.00 \, g \, O_2} \times \frac{2 \, mol \, C_2H_2}{5 \, mol \, O_2} \times \frac{26.04 \, g \, C_2H_2}{1 \, mol \, C_2H_2} = 3.26 \, g \, C_2H_2 \text{ consumed}$$

10.0 g C_2H_2 initial – 3.26 g consumed = 6.74 = 6.7 g C_2H_2 remain

$$10.0 \, g \, O_2 \times \frac{1 \, mol \, O_2}{32.00 \, g \, O_2} \times \frac{4 \, mol \, CO_2}{5 \, mol \, O_2} \times \frac{44.01 \, g \, CO_2}{1 \, mol \, CO_2} = 11.0 \, g \, CO_2 \text{ produced}$$

$$10.0 \, g \, O_2 \times \frac{1 \, mol \, O_2}{32.00 \, g \, O_2} \times \frac{2 \, mol \, H_2O}{5 \, mol \, O_2} \times \frac{18.02 \, g \, H_2O}{1 \, mol \, H_2O} = 2.25 \, g \, H_2O \text{ produced}$$

3.100   (a) $1.5 \times 10^5 \, g \, C_9H_8O_4 \times \dfrac{1 \, mol \, C_9H_8O_4}{180.2 \, g \, C_9H_8O_4} \times \dfrac{1 \, mol \, C_7H_6O_3}{1 \, mol \, C_9H_8O_4} \times \dfrac{138.1 \, g \, C_7H_6O_3}{1 \, mol \, C_7H_6O_3}$

$$= 1.1496 \times 10^5 \, g = 1.1 \times 10^2 \, kg \, C_7H_6O_3$$

(b)   If only 80 percent of the acid reacts, then we need 1/0.80 = 1.25 times as much to obtain the same mass of product: $1.25 \times 1.15 \times 10^2 \, kg = 1.4 \times 10^2 \, kg \, C_7H_6O_3$

(c)   Calculate the number of moles of each reactant:

$$1.25 \times 10^5 \, g \, C_4H_6O_3 \times \frac{1 \, mol \, C_4H_6O_3}{102.1 \, g \, C_4H_6O_3} = 1.224 \times 10^3 = 1.22 \times 10^3 \, mol \, C_4H_6O_3$$

We see that $C_4H_6O_3$ limits, because equal numbers of moles of the two reactants are consumed in the reaction.

$$1.224 \times 10^3 \, mol \, C_4H_6O_3 \times \frac{1 \, mol \, C_9H_8O_4}{1 \, mol \, C_7H_6O_3} \times \frac{180.2 \, g \, C_9H_8O_4}{1 \, mol \, C_9H_8O_4} = 2.206 \times 10^5$$

$$= 2.21 \times 10^5 \, g \, C_9H_8O_4$$

(d)   percent yield $= \dfrac{1.82 \times 10^5 \, g}{2.206 \times 10^5 \, g} \times 100 = 82.5\%$

Integrative Exercises

3.102   (a)   *Plan.* volume of Ag cube $\xrightarrow{\text{density}}$ mass of Ag → mol Ag → Ag atoms

Solve. $(1.000)^3 \, cm^3 \, Ag \times \dfrac{10.5 \, g \, Ag}{1 \, cm^3 \, Ag} \times \dfrac{1 \, mol \, Ag}{107.87 \, g \, Ag} \times \dfrac{6.022 \times 10^{23} \, atoms}{1 \, mol}$

$$= 5.8618 \times 10^{22} = 5.86 \times 10^{22} \, Ag \text{ atoms}$$

(b)   1.000 cm^3 cube volume, 74% is occupied by Ag atoms

0.74 cm^3 = volume of 5.86×10^{22} Ag atoms

$$\frac{0.7400 \text{ cm}^3}{5.8618 \times 10^{22} \text{ Ag atoms}} = 1.2624 \times 10^{-23} = 1.3 \times 10^{-23} \text{ cm}^3 / \text{Ag atom}$$

Since atomic dimensions are usually given in Å, we will show this conversion.

$$1.2624 \times 10^{-23} \text{ cm}^3 \times \frac{(1 \times 10^{-2})^3 \text{ m}^3}{1 \text{ cm}^3} \times \frac{1 \text{ Å}^3}{(1 \times 10^{-10})^3 \text{ m}^3} = 12.62 = 13 \text{ Å}^3 / \text{Ag atom}$$

(c) $V = 4/3 \, \pi \, r^3; \; r^3 = 3V/4\pi; \; r = (3V/4\pi)^{1/3}$

$r_A = (3 \times 12.62 \text{ Å}^3 / 4\pi)^{1/3} = 1.444 = 1.4 \text{ Å}$

3.103   (a)   *Analyze.* Given: gasoline = C_8H_{18}, density = 0.69 g/mL, 20.5 mi/gal, 225 mi.

Find: kg CO_2.

Plan. Write and balance the equation for the combustion of octane. Change mi → gal octane → mL → g octane. Use stoichiometry to calculate g and kg CO_2 from g octane.

Solve. $2C_8H_{18}(l) + 25O_2(g) \rightarrow 16CO_2(g) + 18H_2O(l)$

$$225 \text{ mi} \times \frac{1 \text{ gal}}{20.5 \text{ mi}} \times \frac{3.7854 \text{ L}}{1 \text{ gal}} \times \frac{1 \text{ mL}}{1 \times 10^{-3} \text{ L}} \times \frac{0.69 \text{ g octane}}{1 \text{ mL}} = 2.8667 \times 10^4 \text{ g}$$

$$= 29 \text{ kg octane}$$

$$2.8667 \times 10^4 \text{ g } C_8H_{18} \times \frac{1 \text{ mol } C_8H_{18}}{114.2 \text{ g } C_8H_{18}} \times \frac{16 \text{ mol } CO_2}{2 \text{ mol } C_8H_{18}} \times \frac{44.01 \text{ g } CO_2}{1 \text{ mol } CO_2} = 8.8382 \times 10^4 \text{ g}$$

$$= 88 \text{ kg } CO_2$$

Check. $\left(\dfrac{225 \times 4 \times 0.7}{20} \right) \times 10^3 = (45 \times 0.7) \times 10^3 = 30 \times 10^3 \text{ g} = 30 \text{ kg octane}$

$\dfrac{44}{114} \approx \dfrac{1}{3}; \; \dfrac{30 \text{ kg} \times 8}{3} \approx 80 \text{ kg } CO_2$

(b)   *Plan.* Use the same strategy as part (a). *Solve.*

$$225 \text{ mi} \times \frac{1 \text{ gal}}{5 \text{ mi}} \times \frac{3.7854 \text{ L}}{1 \text{ gal}} \times \frac{1 \text{ mL}}{1 \times 10^{-3} \text{ L}} \times \frac{0.69 \text{ g octane}}{1 \text{ mL}} = 1.1754 \times 10^5$$

$$= 1 \times 10^2 \text{ kg octane}$$

$$1.1754 \times 10^5 \text{ g } C_8H_{18} \times \frac{1 \text{ mol } C_8H_{18}}{114.2 \text{ g } C_8H_{18}} \times \frac{16 \text{ mol } CO_2}{2 \text{ mol } C_8H_{18}} \times \frac{44.01 \text{ g } CO_2}{1 \text{ mol } CO_2} = 3.624 \times 10^5 \text{ g}$$

$$= 4 \times 10^2 \text{ kg } CO_2$$

Check. Mileage of 5 mi/gal requires ~4 times as much gasoline as mileage of 20.5 mi/gal, so it should produce ~4 times as much CO_2. 90 kg CO_2 [from (a)] × 4 = 360 = 4×10^2 kg CO_2 [from (b)].

3.104   *Plan.* We can proceed by writing the ratio of masses of Ag to $AgNO_3$, where y is the atomic mass of nitrogen.   *Solve.*

$$\frac{Ag}{AgNO_3} = 0.634985 = \frac{107.8682}{107.8682 + 3(15.9994) + y}$$

Solve for y to obtain y = 14.0088. This is to be compared with the currently accepted value of 14.0067.

3.106   *Analyze.* Given: 2.0 in × 3.0 in boards, 5000 boards, 0.65 mm thick Cu; 8.96 g/cm^3 Cu; 85% Cu removed; 97% yield for reaction. Find: mass $Cu(NH_3)_4Cl_2$, mass NH_3.

Plan. vol Cu/board × density → mass Cu/board → 5000 boards × 85% = total Cu removed = actual yield; actual yield/0.97 = theoretical yield Cu.

mass Cu → mol Cu → mol $Cu(NH_3)_4$ Cl or NH_3 → desired masses.

Solve. $2.0 \, in \times 3.0 \, in \times \frac{(2.54)^2 \, cm^2}{in^2} \times 0.65 \, mm \times \frac{1 \, cm}{10 \, mm} = 2.516 = 2.5 \, cm^3 \, Cu/board$

$\frac{2.516 \, cm^3 \, Cu}{board} \times \frac{8.96 \, g}{cm^3} \times 5000 \, boards \times 0.85 \, removed = 95,814 \, g = 96 \, kg \, Cu \, removed$

$\frac{95,814 \, g \, Cu \, actual \, yield}{0.97} = 98,777 \, g = 99 \, kg \, Cu \, theoretical$

$98,777 \, g \, Cu \times \frac{1 \, mol \, Cu}{63.546 \, g \, Cu} \times \frac{1 \, mol \, Cu(NH_3)_4Cl_2}{1 \, mol \, Cu} \times \frac{202.575 \, g}{1 \, mol \, Cu(NH_3)_4Cl_2} = 314,887 \, g$

$$= 3.1 \times 10^2 \, kg \, Cu(NH_3)_4Cl_2$$

$98,777 \, g \, Cu \times \frac{1 \, mol \, Cu}{63.546 \, g \, Cu} \times \frac{4 \, mol \, NH_3}{1 \, mol \, Cu} \times \frac{17.03 \, g \, NH_3}{mol \, NH_3} = 105,891 \, g = 1.1 \times 10^2 \, kg \, NH_3$

3.107   (a)   *Plan.* Calculate the kg of air in the room and then the mass of HCN required to produce a dose of 300 mg HCN/kg air.   *Solve.*

12 ft × 15 ft × 8.0 ft = 1440 = $1.4 \times 10^3 \, ft^3$ of air in the room

$1440 \, ft^3 \, air \times \frac{(12 \, in)^3}{1 \, ft^3} \times \frac{(2.54 \, cm)^3}{1 \, in^3} \times \frac{0.00118 \, g \, air}{1 \, cm^3 \, air} \times \frac{1 \, kg}{1000 \, g} = 48.12 = 48 \, kg \, air$

$48.12 \, kg \, air \times \frac{300 \, mg \, HCN}{1 \, kg \, air} \times \frac{1 \, g}{1000 \, mg} = 14.43 = 14 \, g \, HCN$

(b) $2NaCN(s) + H_2SO_4(aq) \rightarrow Na_2SO_4(aq) + 2HCN(g)$

The question can be restated as: What mass of NaCN is required to produce 14 g of HCN according to the above reaction?

$14.43 \, g \, HCN \times \frac{1 \, mol \, HCN}{27.03 \, g \, HCN} \times \frac{2 \, mol \, NaCN}{2 \, mol \, HCN} \times \frac{49.01 \, g \, NaCN}{1 \, mol \, NaCN} = 26.2 = 26 \, g \, NaCN$

(c) $12 \, ft \times 15 \, ft \times \frac{1 \, yd^2}{9 \, ft^2} \times \frac{30 \, oz}{1 \, yd^2} \times \frac{1 \, lb}{16 \, oz} \times \frac{454 \, g}{1 \, lb} = 17,025$

$$= 1.7 \times 10^4 \, g \, acrilan \, in \, the \, room$$

50% of the carpet burns, so the starting amount of CH_2CHCN is 0.50(17,025)

$= 8,513 = 8.5 \times 10^3$ g

$$8,513 \, g \, CH_2CHCN \times \frac{50.9 \, g \, HCN}{100 \, g \, CH_2CHCH} = 4333 = 4.3 \times 10^3 \, g \, HCN \text{ possible}$$

If the actual yield of combustion is 20%, actual g HCN = 4,333(0.20) = 866.6 $= 8.7 \times 10^2$ g HCN produced. From part (a), 14 g of HCN is a lethal dose. The fire produces much more than a lethal dose of HCN.

3.108   (a) $N_2(g) + O_2(g) \rightarrow 2NO(g)$; $2NO(g) + O_2(g) \rightarrow 2NO_2(g)$

       (b)   1 million $= 1 \times 10^6$

$$19 \times 10^6 \text{ tons } NO_2 \times \frac{2000 \, lb}{1 \, ton} \times \frac{453.6 \, g}{1 \, lb} = 1.724 \times 10^{13} = 1.7 \times 10^{13} \, g \, NO$$

       (c)   *Plan.* Calculate g O_2 needed to burn 500 g octane. This is 85% of total O_2 in the engine. 15% of total O_2 is used to produce NO_2, according to the second equation in part (a).

Solve. $2C_8H_{18}(l) + 25O_2(g) \rightarrow 16CO_2(g) + 18H_2O(l)$

$$500 \, g \, C_8H_{18} \times \frac{1 \, mol \, C_8H_{18}}{114.2 \, g \, C_8H_{18}} \times \frac{25 \, mol \, O_2}{2 \, mol \, C_8H_{18}} \times \frac{32.00 \, g \, O_2}{mol \, O_2} = 1751 = 1.75 \times 10^3 \, g \, O_2$$

$$\frac{1751 \, g \, O_2}{total \, g \, O_2} = 0.85; \quad 2060 = 2.1 \times 10^3 \, g \, O_2 \text{ total in engine}$$

2060 g O_2 total $\times$ 0.15 = 309.1 = 3.1×10^9 g O_2 used to produce NO_2. One mol O_2 produces 2 mol NO. Then 2 mol NO react with a second mol O_2 to produce 2 mol NO_2. Two mol O_2 are required to produce 2 mol NO_2; one mol O_2 per mol NO_2.

4 Aqueous Reactions and Solution Stoichiometry

Visualizing Concepts

4.2   Although CH_3OH and HCl are both molecular compounds, HCl is an acid and strong electrolyte. Strong electrolytes exist in solution almost completely as ions, so an aqueous HCl solution conducts electricity. CH_3OH is a nonelectrolyte that exists as neutral molecules in aqueous solution. Since there are no charge carriers, aqueous solutions of nonelectrolytes such as CH_3OH do not conduct electricity.

4.4   The brightness of the bulb in Figure 4.2 is related to the number of ions per unit volume of solution. If 0.1 M $HC_2H_3O_2$ has about the same brightness of 0.001 M HBr, the two solutions have about the same number of ions. Since 0.1 M $HC_2H_3O_2$ has 100 times more solute than 0.001 M HBr, HBr must be dissociated to a much greater extent than $HC_2H_3O_2$. HBr is one of the few molecular acids that is a strong electrolyte. $HC_2H_3O_2$ is a weak electrolyte; if it were a nonelectrolyte, the bulb in Figure 4.2 wouldn't glow.

4.6   Certain pairs of ions form precipitates because their attraction is so strong that they cannot be surrounded and separated by solvent molecules. That is, the attraction between solute particles is greater than the stabilization offered by interaction of individual ions with solvent molecules.

4.8   Use the difference in reactivities with SO_4^{2-} to identify $Pb^{2+}(aq)$ and $Mg^{2+}(aq)$. Test a portion of each solution with $H_2SO_4(aq)$. $Pb^{2+}(aq)$ is an exception to the soluble sulfates rule, so $Pb(NO_3)_2(aq)$ will form a precipitate, while $Mg(NO_3)_2(aq)$ will not.

4.10   Concentration is a ratio of amount of solute to amount of solution or solvent. Thus there are two ways to double the concentration of a solution: double the amount of solute, keeping volume constant or reduce the volume of solution by half, keeping the amount of solute the same.

Electrolytes

4.12   When CH_3OH dissolves, neutral CH_3OH molecules are dispersed throughout the solution. These electrically neutral particles do not carry charge and the solution is nonconducting. When CH_3COOH dissolves, mostly neutral molecules are dispersed throughout the solution. A few of the dissolved molecules ionize to form $H^+(aq)$ and $CH_3COO^-(aq)$. These few ions carry some charge and the solution is weakly conducting.

4.14   Ions are hydrated when they are surrounded by H_2O molecules in aqueous solution.

4.16   (a) $MgI_2(aq) \rightarrow Mg^{2+}(aq) + 2I^-(aq)$

      (b) $Al(NO_3)_3(aq) \rightarrow Al^{3+}(aq) + 3NO_3^-(aq)$

      (c) $HClO_4(aq) \rightarrow H^+(aq) + ClO_4^-(aq)$

      (d) $NaCH_3COO(aq) \rightarrow Na^+(aq) + CH_3COO^-(aq)$

4.18   (a)   acetone (nonelectrolyte): $CH_3COCH_3(aq)$ molecules only; hypochlorous acid (weak electrolyte): $HClO(aq)$ molecules, $H^+(aq)$, ClO^- (aq); ammonium chloride (strong electrolyte): $NH_4^+(aq)$, $Cl^-(aq)$

      (b) NH_4Cl, 0.2 mol solute particles; HClO, between 0.1 and 0.2 mol particles; CH_3OCH_3, 0.1 mol of solute particles

Precipitation Reactions and Net Ionic Equations

4.20   According to Table 4.1:

      (a)   **$Ni(OH)_2$**: insoluble

      (b)   **$PbBr_2$**: insoluble;

      (c)   **$Ba(NO_3)_2$**: soluble

      (d)   **$AlPO_4$**: insoluble

      (e)   **$AgCH_3COO$**: soluble

4.22   In each reaction, the precipitate is in bold type.

      (a) $Ni(NO_3)_2(aq) + 2NaOH(aq) \rightarrow$ **$Ni(OH)_2(s)$** $+ 2NaNO_3(aq)$

      (b)   No precipitate, and, therefore, no reaction. There is no chemical change to any of the reactant ions.

      (c) $Na_2S(aq) + CuCH_3COO(aq) \rightarrow$ **$CuS(s)$** $+ 2NaCH_3COO(aq)$

4.24   Spectator ions are those that do not change during reaction.

      (a) $2Cr^{3+}(aq) + 3CO_3^{2-}(aq) \rightarrow Cr_2(CO_3)_3(s)$; spectators: NH_4^+, SO_4^{2-}

      (b) $Ba^{2+}(aq) + SO_4^{2-}(aq) \rightarrow BaSO_4(s)$; spectators: K^+, NO_3^-

      (c) $Fe^{2+}(aq) + 2OH^-(aq) \rightarrow Fe(OH)_2(s)$; spectators: K^+, NO_3^-

4.26 Br^- and NO_3^- can be ruled out because the Ba^{2+} salts are soluble. (Actually all NO_3^- salts are soluble.) CO_3^{2-} forms insoluble salts with the three cations given; it must be the anion in question.

4.28   (a) $Pb(CH_3COO)_2(aq) + Na_2S(aq) \rightarrow PbS(s) + 2NaCH_3COO(aq)$

           net ionic: $Pb^{2+}(aq) + S^{2-}(aq) \rightarrow PbS$

           $Pb(CH_3COO)_2(aq) + CaCl_2(aq) \rightarrow (PbCl_2)s + Ca(CH_3COO)_2(aq)$

           net ionic: $Pb^{2+}(aq) + 2Cl^-(aq) \rightarrow PbCl_2(s)$

           $Na_2S(aq) + CaCl_2(aq) \rightarrow CaS(aq) + 2NaCl(aq)$

           net ionic: no reaction

      (b)   Spectator ions: Na^+, Ca^{2+}, CH_3COO^-

Acid-Base Reactions

4.30 $NH_3(aq)$ is a weak base, while KOH and $Ca(OH)_2$ are strong bases. $NH_3(aq)$ is only slightly ionized, so even 0.6 M NH_3 is less basic than 0.150 M KOH. $Ca(OH)_2$ has twice as many OH^- per moles as KOH, so 0.100 M $Ca(OH)_2$ is more basic than 0.150 M KOH. The most basic solution is 0.100 M $Ca(OH)_2$.

4.32   (a) NH_3 produces OH^- in aqueous solution by reacting with H_2O (hydrolysis): $NH_3(aq) + H_2O(l) \rightleftharpoons NH_4^+(aq) + OH^-(aq)$. The OH^- causes the solution to be basic.

        (b)   The term "weak" refers to the tendency of HF to dissociate into H^+ and F^- in aqueous solution, not its reactivity toward other compounds.

        (c) H_2SO_4 is a **diprotic** acid; it has two ionizable hydrogens. The first hydrogen completely ionizes to form H^+ and HSO_4^-, but HSO_4^- only **partially** ionizes into H^+ and SO_4^{2-} (HSO_4^- is a weak electrolyte). Thus, an aqueous solution of H_2SO_4 contains a mixture of H^+, HSO_4^- and SO_4^{2-}, with the concentration of HSO_4^- greater than the concentration of SO_4^{2-}.

4.34   All soluble ionic hydroxides from Table 4.1 are listed as strong bases in Table 4.2. Insoluble hydroxides like $Cd(OH)_2$ are not listed as strong bases. "Insoluble" means that less than 1% of the base molecules exist as separated ions and are dissolved. Thus, insoluble hydroxide salts produce too few $OH^-(aq)$ to be considered strong bases.

4.36   Since the solution does conduct some electricity, but less than an equimolar NaCl solution (a strong electrolyte), the unknown solute must be a weak electrolyte. The weak electrolytes in the list of choices are NH_3 and H_3PO_3; since the solution is acidic, the unknown must be **H_3PO_3**.

4.38   (a) $HClO_4$: strong   (b) HNO_3: strong   (c) NH_4Cl: strong

        (d) CH_3OCH_3: non   (e) $CoSO_4$: strong   (f) $C_{12}H_{22}O_{11}$: non

4.40   (a) $HC_2H_3O_2(aq) + KOH(aq) \rightarrow KC_2H_3O_2(aq) + H_2O(l)$

               $HC_2H_3O_2(aq) + OH^-(aq) \rightarrow C_2H_3O_2^-(aq) H_2O(l)$

        (b) $Cr(OH)_3(s) + 3HNO_3(aq) \rightarrow Cr(NO_3)_3(aq) + 3H_2O(l)$

               $Cr(OH)_3(s) + 3H^+(aq) \rightarrow 3H_2O(l) + Cr^{3+}(aq)$

        (c) $Ca(OH)_2(aq) + 2HClO(aq) \rightarrow Ca(ClO)_2(aq) + 2H_2O(l)$

               $HClO(aq) + OH^-(aq) \rightarrow ClO^-(aq) + H_2O(l)$

4.42   (a) $FeO(s) + 2H^+(aq) \rightarrow H_2O(l) + Fe^{2+}(aq)$

        (b) $NiO(s) + 2H^+(aq) \rightarrow H_2O(l) + Ni^{2+}(aq)$

4.44 $K_2O(aq) + H_2O(l) \rightarrow 2KOH(aq)$, molecular; $O^{2-}(aq) + H_2O(l) \rightarrow 2OH^-(aq)$, net ionic

        base: (H^+ ion acceptor) $O^{2-}(aq)$; acid: (H^+ ion donor) $H_2O(aq)$; spectator: K^+

Oxidation-Reduction Reactions

4.46   Oxidation and reduction can only occur together, not separately. When a metal reacts with oxygen, the metal atoms lose electrons and the oxygen atoms gain electrons. Free electrons do not exist under normal conditions. If electrons are lost by one substance they must be gained by another, and vice versa.

4.48   Elements (metals) from Table 4.5 in region A include Na, Mg, K, and Ca; those from region C are Hg and Au. Let's consider K and Au. Since metals from region A are more readily oxidized than those from region C, K will be oxidized to K^+ and Au^{3+} will be reduced to Au in the redox reaction. (Choose Au^{3+} because it is the Au ion shown in Table 4.5.)

In a balanced redox reaction, the number of electrons lost must equal the number of electrons gained. Since K loses 1 electron in forming K^+, while Au^{3+} gains 3 electrons when forming Au, 3 K atoms must be oxidized for every 1 Au^{3+} that is reduced. This relationship dictates the coefficients in the balanced redox reaction.

$$3K(s) + Au^{3+}(aq) \rightleftharpoons Au(s) + 3K^+(aq)$$

4.50   (a)   +4   (b)   +2   (c)   +3   (d)   –2   (e)   +3   (f)   +6

4.52   (a)   acid-base reaction

           (b)   oxidation-reduction reaction; Fe is reduced, C is oxidized

           (c)   precipitation reaction

           (d)   oxidation-reduction reaction; Zn is oxidized, N is reduced

4.54   (a) $2HCl(aq) + Ni(s) \rightarrow NiCl_2(aq) + H_2(g)$; $Ni(s) + 2H^+(aq) \rightarrow Ni^{2+}(aq) + H_2(g)$

           (b) $H_2SO_4(aq) + Fe(s) \rightarrow FeSO_4(aq) + H_2(g)$; $Fe(s) + 2H^+(aq) \rightarrow Fe^{2+}(aq) + H_2(g)$

             Products with the metal in a higher oxidation state are possible, depending on reaction conditions and acid concentration.

           (c) $2HBr(aq) + Mg(s) \rightarrow MgBr_2(aq) + H_2(g)$; $Mg(s) + 2H^+(aq) \rightarrow Mg^{2+}(aq) + H_2(g)$

           (d) $2CH_3COOH(aq) + Zn(s) \rightarrow ZnCH_3COO(aq) + H_2(g)$;

               $Zn(s) + 2CH_3COOH(aq) \rightarrow Zn^{2+}(aq) + 2CH_3COO^-(aq) + H_2(g)$

4.56   (a) $Mn(s) + NiCl_2(aq) \rightarrow MnCl_2(aq) + Ni(s)$

           (b) $Cu(s) + Cr(C_2H_3O_2)(aq) \rightarrow NR$

           (c) $2Cr(s) + 3NiSO_4(aq) \rightarrow Cr_2(SO_4)_3(aq) + 3Ni(s)$

           (d) $Pt(s) + HBr(aq) \rightarrow NR$

           (e) $H_2(g) + CuCl_2(aq) \rightarrow Cu(s) + 2HCl(aq)$

4.58   (a) $Br_2 + 2NaI \rightarrow 2NaBr + I_2$ indicates that Br_2 is more easily reduced than I_2.

             $Cl_2 + 2NaBr \rightarrow 2NaCl + Br_2$ shows that Cl_2 is more easily reduced than Br_2.

The order for ease of reduction is $Cl_2 > Br_2 > I_2$. Conversely, the order for ease of oxidation is $I^- > Br^- > Cl^-$.

(b)   Since the halogens are nonmetals, they tend to form anions when they react chemically. Nonmetallic character decreases going down a family and so does the tendency to gain electrons during a chemical reaction. Thus, the ease of reduction of the halogen, X_2, decreases going down the family and the ease of oxidation of the halide, X^-, increases going down the family.

(c) $Cl_2 + 2KI \rightarrow 2KCl + I_2$; $Br_2 + LiCl \rightarrow$ no reaction

Solution Composition; Molarity

4.60   (a)   The concentration of the remaining solution is unchanged, assuming the original solution was thoroughly mixed. Molar concentration is a **ratio** of moles solute to liters solution. Although there are fewer moles solute remaining in the flask, there is also less solution volume, so the ratio of moles solute/solution volume remains the same.

        (b)   The concentration of the remaining solution is increased. The moles solute remaining in the flask are unchanged, but the solution volume decreases after evaporation. The ratio of moles solute/solution volume increases.

        (c)   The second solution is five times as concentrated as the first. An equal volume of the more concentrated solution will contain five times as much solute (five times the number of moles and also five times the mass) as the 0.50 M solution. Thus, the mass of solute in the 2.50 M solution is 5×4.5 g = 22.5 g.

Mathematically:

$$\frac{\dfrac{2.50 \text{ mol solute}}{1 \text{ L solution}}}{\dfrac{0.50 \text{ mol solute}}{1 \text{ L solution}}} = \frac{x \text{ grams solute}}{4.5 \text{ g solute}}$$

$$\frac{2.50 \text{ mol solute}}{0.50 \text{ mol solute}} = \frac{x \text{ g solute}}{4.5 \text{ g solute}}; \; 5.0(4.5 \text{ g solute}) = 23 \text{ g solute}$$

The result has 2 sig figs; 22.5 rounds to 23 g solute.

4.62   (a) $M = \dfrac{\text{mol solute}}{\text{L solution}}$; $\dfrac{0.750 \text{ g Na}_2\text{SO}_4}{0.850 \text{ L}} \times \dfrac{1 \text{ mol Na}_2\text{SO}_4}{142.04 \text{ g Na}_2\text{SO}_4} = 6.21 \times 10^{-3} \; M \; \text{Na}_2\text{SO}_4$

        (b) $\text{mol} = M \times L$; $\dfrac{0.0475 \text{ mol KMnO}_4}{1 \text{ L}} \times 0.250 \text{ L} = 1.19 \times 10^{-2} \text{ mol KMnO}_4$

        (c) $L = \dfrac{\text{mol}}{M}$; $\dfrac{0.250 \text{ mol HCl}}{11.6 \text{ mol HCl/L}} = 2.16 \times 10^{-2} \text{ L or } 21.6 \text{ mL}$

4.64   Calculate the mol of Na^+ at the two concentrations; the difference is the mol NaCl required to increase the Na^+ concentration to the desired level.

$$\frac{0.118 \text{ mol}}{L} \times 4.6 \text{ L} = 0.5428 = 0.54 \text{ mol Na}^+$$

$$\frac{0.138\,\text{mol}}{L} \times 4.6\,L = 0.6348 = 0.63\,\text{mol Na}^+$$

$(0.6348 - 0.5428) = 0.092 = 0.09\,\text{mol NaCl}$ (2 decimal places and 1 sig fig)

$$0.092\,\text{mol NaCl} \times \frac{58.5\,\text{g NaCl}}{\text{mol}} = 5.38 = 5\,\text{g NaCl}$$

4.66   *Analyze.* Given: BAC (definition from Exercise 4.65), vol of blood. Find: mass alcohol in bloodstream.

       Plan. Change BAC (g/100 mL) to (g/L), then times vol of blood in L.

       Solve. BAC = 0.10 g/100 mL

$$\frac{0.10\,\text{g alcohol}}{100\,\text{mL blood}} \times \frac{1000\,\text{mL}}{1\,L} \times 5.0\,L\ \text{blood} = 5.0\,\text{g alcohol}$$

4.68 $M = \dfrac{\text{mol}}{L}$; $\text{mol} = \dfrac{g}{MM}$ (MM is the symbol for molar mass in this manual.)

     (a) $\dfrac{0.488\,\text{mol K}_2\text{Cr}_2\text{O}_7}{1\,L} \times 50.0\,\text{mL} \times \dfrac{1\,L}{1000\,\text{mL}} \times \dfrac{294.2\,\text{g K}_2\text{Cr}_2\text{O}_7}{1\,\text{mol K}_2\text{Cr}_2\text{O}_7} = 7.18\,\text{g K}_2\text{Cr}_2\text{O}_7$

     (b) $4.00\,\text{g (NH}_4)_2\text{SO}_4 \times \dfrac{1\,\text{mol (NH}_4)_2\text{SO}_4}{132.2\,\text{g (NH}_4)_2\text{SO}_4} \times \dfrac{1}{400.\,\text{mL}} \times \dfrac{1000\,\text{mL}}{1\,L}$

                                                     $= 0.0756\,M\ (\text{NH}_4)_2\text{SO}_4$

     (c) $1.75\,\text{g CuSO}_4 \times \dfrac{1\,\text{mol CuSO}_4}{159.6\,\text{g CuSO}_4} \times \dfrac{1\,L}{0.0250\,\text{mol CuSO}_4} \times \dfrac{1000\,\text{mL}}{1\,L} = 439\,\text{mL solution}$

4.70   **(a)** $0.1\,M\ \text{CaCl}_2 = 0.2\,M\ \text{Cl}^-$; $0.15\,M\ \text{KCl} = 0.15\,M\ \text{Cl}^-$

           $0.1\,M\ \text{CaCl}_2$ has the higher Cl^- concentration.

     (b) $0.1\,M$ KCl has a higher Cl^- concentration than $0.080\,M$ LiCl. Total volume does not affect concentration.

     (c) $0.050\,M\ \text{HCl} = 0.050\,M\ \text{Cl}^-$; $0.020\,M\ \text{CdCl}_2 = 0.040\,M\ \text{Cl}^-$

4.72   **(a)**   *Plan.* These two solutions have common ions. Find the ion concentration resulting from each solution, then add.

           Solve. total volume = 42.0 mL + 37.6 mL = 79.6 mL

$$\frac{0.170\,M\ \text{NaOH} \times 42.0\,\text{mL}}{79.6\,\text{mL}} = 0.08970 = 0.0897\,M\ \text{NaOH};$$

           $0.0897\,M\ \text{Na}^+$, $0.0897\,M\ \text{OH}^-$

$$\frac{0.400\,M\ \text{NaOH} \times 37.6\,\text{mL}}{79.6\,\text{mL}} = 0.18894 = 0.189\,M\ \text{NaOH};$$

$0.189\ M\ Na^+,\ 0.189\ M\ OH^-$

$M\ Na^+ = 0.08970\ M + 0.18894\ M = 0.27864 = 0.2786\ M\ Na^+$

$M\ OH^- = M\ Na^+ = 0.2786\ M\ OH^-$

(b)   *Plan.* No common ions; just dilution.

      Solve. 44.0 mL + 25.0 mL = 69.0 mL

$$\frac{0.100\ M\ Na_2SO_4 \times 44.0\ mL}{69.0\ mL} = 0.06377 = 0.0638\ M\ Na_2SO_4$$

$2 \times (0.06377\ M) = 0.1275 = 0.128\ M\ Na^+;\ 0.0638\ M\ SO_4^{2-}$

$$\frac{0.150\ M\ KCl \times 25.0\ mL}{69.0\ mL} = 0.054348 = 0.0543\ M\ KCl$$

$0.0543\ M\ K^+,\ 0.0543\ M\ Cl^-$

(c)   *Plan.* Calculate concentration of K^+ and Cl^- due to the added solid. Then sum to get total concentration of Cl^-.

      Solve. $\dfrac{3.60\ g\ KCl}{75.0\ mL\ so\ln} \times \dfrac{1\ mol\ KCl}{74.55\ g\ KCl} \times \dfrac{1000\ mL}{1\ L} = 0.6439 = 0.644\ M\ KCl$

$0.250\ M\ CaCl_2;\ 2(0.250\ M) = 0.500\ M\ Cl^-$

total $Cl^- = 0.644\ M + 0.500\ M = 1.144\ M\ Cl^-,\ 0.644\ M\ K^+,\ 0.250\ M\ Ca^{2+}$

4.74   (a) $V_1 = M_2V_2/M_1;\ \dfrac{0.500\ M\ HNO_3 \times 0.450\ mL}{10.0\ M\ HNO_3} = 0.02250\ L = 22.5\ mL\ conc.\ HNO_3$

       (b) $M_2 = M_1V_1/V_2;\ \dfrac{10.0\ M\ HNO_3 \times 25.0\ mL}{500\ mL} = 0.500\ M\ HNO_3$

4.76   (a)   The amount of $AgNO_3$ needed is:

          $0.150\ M \times 0.1750\ L = 0.02625 = 0.263\ mol\ AgNO_3$

          $0.02625\ mol\ AgNO_3 \times \dfrac{169.88\ g\ AgNO_3}{1\ mol\ AgNO_3} = 4.4594 = 4.46\ g\ AgNO_3$

          Add this amount of solid to a 175 mL volumetric container, dissolve in a small amount of water, bring the total volume to exactly 175 mL, and agitate well.

       (b)   Dilute the 3.6 M HNO_3 to prepare 100 mL of 0.50 M HNO_3. To determine the volume of 3.6 M HNO_3 needed, calculate the moles HNO_3 present in 100 mL of 0.50 M HNO_3 and then the volume of 6.0 M solution that contains this number of moles.

          $0.100\ L \times 0.50\ M = 0.050\ mol\ HNO_3$ needed;

$$L = \frac{mol}{M}; \quad L \, 3.6 \, M \, HNO_3 = \frac{0.050 \, mol \, needed}{3.6 \, M} = 0.01389 \, L = 14 \, mL$$

Thoroughly clean, rinse, and fill a buret with the 3.6 M HNO_3, taking precautions appropriate for working with a relatively concentrated acid. Dispense 14 mL of the 3.6 M acid into a 100 mL volumetric flask, add water to the mark, and mix thoroughly.

4.78 $50.000 \, mL \, glycerol \times \dfrac{1.2656 \, g \, glycerol}{1 \, mL \, glycerol} = 63.280 \, g \, glycerol$

$63.280 \, g \, C_3H_8O_3 \times \dfrac{1 \, mol \, C_3H_8O_3}{92.094 \, g \, C_3H_8O_3} = 0.687124 = 0.68712 \, mol \, C_3H_8O_3$

$M = \dfrac{0.687124 \, mol \, C_3H_8O_3}{0.25000 \, L \, solution} = 2.7485 \, M \, C_3H_8O_3$

Solution Stoichiometry; Titrations

4.80   *Plan.* $M \times L = mol \, Cd(NO_3)_2$; balanced equation $\rightarrow$ mol ratio $\rightarrow$ mol NaOH $\rightarrow$ g NaOH

Solve. $\dfrac{0.500 \, mol \, Cd(NO_3)_2}{1 \, L} \times 0.0350 \, L = 0.0175 \, mol \, Cd(NO_3)_2$

$Cd(NO_3)_2(aq) + 2NaOH(aq) \rightarrow Cd(OH)_2(s) + 2NaNO_3(aq)$

$0.0175 \, mol \, Cd(NO_3)_2 \times \dfrac{2 \, mol \, NaOH}{1 \, mol \, Cd(NO_3)_2} \times \dfrac{40.00 \, g \, NaOH}{1 \, mol \, NaOH} = 1.40 \, g \, NaOH$

4.82   (a) $2HCl(aq) + Ba(OH)_2(aq) \rightarrow BaCl_2(aq) + 2H_2O(l)$

$\dfrac{0.101 \, mol \, Ba(OH)_2}{1 \, L \, Ba(OH)_2} \times 0.0500 \, L \, Ba(OH)_2 \times \dfrac{2 \, mol \, HCl}{1 \, mol \, Ba(OH)_2}$

$\times \dfrac{1 \, L \, HCl}{0.120 \, mol \, HCl} = 0.0842 \, L \, or \, 84.2 \, mL \, HCl \, soln$

(b) $H_2SO_4(aq) + 2NaOH(aq) \rightarrow Na_2SO_4(aq) + 2H_2O(l)$

$0.200 \, g \, NaOH \times \dfrac{1 \, mol \, NaOH}{40.00 \, g \, NaOH} \times \dfrac{1 \, mol \, H_2SO_4}{2 \, mol \, NaOH} \times \dfrac{1 \, L \, H_2SO_4}{0.125 \, mol \, H_2SO_4}$

$= 0.0200 \, L \, or \, 20.0 \, mL \, H_2SO_4 \, soln$

(c) $BaCl_2(aq) + Na_2SO_4(aq) \rightarrow BaSO_4(s) + 2NaCl(aq)$

$752 \, mg = 0.752 \, g \, Na_2SO_4 \times \dfrac{1 \, mol \, Na_2SO_4}{142.1 \, g \, Na_2SO_4} \times \dfrac{1 \, mol \, BaCl_2}{1 \, mol \, Na_2SO_4} \times \dfrac{1}{0.0558 \, L}$

$= 0.0948 \, M \, BaCl_2$

(d) $2HCl(aq) + Ca(OH)_2(aq) \rightarrow CaCl_2(aq) + 2H_2O(l)$

$0.0427 \, L \, HCl \times \dfrac{0.208 \, mol \, HCl}{1 \, L \, HCl} \times \dfrac{1 \, mol \, Ca(OH)_2}{2 \, mol \, HCl} \times \dfrac{74.10 \, g \, Ca(OH)_2}{1 \, mol \, Ca(OH)_2} = 0.329 \, g \, Ca(OH)_2$

4.84   See Exercise 4.81(a) for a more detailed approach.

$$\frac{0.115 \, mol \, NaOH}{1 \, L} \times 0.0425 \, L \times \frac{1 \, mol \, CH_3COOH}{1 \, mol \, NaOH} \times \frac{60.05 \, g \, CH_3COOH}{1 \, mol \, CH_3COOH}$$

$$= 0.29349 = 0.293 \, g \, CH_3COOH \, in \, 3.45 \, mL$$

$$1.00 \, qt \, vinegar \times \frac{1 \, L}{1.057 \, qt} \times \frac{1000 \, mL}{1 \, L} \times \frac{0.29349 \, g \, CH_3COOH}{3.45 \, mL \, vinegar} = 80.5 \, g \, CH_3COOH/qt$$

4.86   The balanced equation for the titration is:

$$Sr(NO_3)_2(aq) + Na_2CrO_4(aq) \rightarrow SrCrO_4(s) + 2NaNO_3(aq)$$

Beginning with a 0.100 L sample, we can do the following conversions:

$$volume \, soln \rightarrow g \, Sr(NO_3)_2 \rightarrow mol \, Sr(NO_3)_2 \rightarrow mol \, Na_2CrO_4 \rightarrow vol \, Na_2CrO_4 \, soln$$

$$0.100 \, L \, soln \times \frac{6.82 \, g \, Sr(NO_3)_2}{0.500 \, L \, soln} \times \frac{1 \, mol \, Sr(NO_3)_2}{211.6 \, g \, Sr(NO_3)_2} \times \frac{1 \, mol \, Na_2CrO_4}{1 \, mol \, Sr(NO_3)_2}$$

$$\times \frac{1 \, L \, soln}{0.0245 \, mol \, Na_2CrO_4} = 0.263 \, L \, Na_2CrO_4 \, soln$$

4.88   (a) $HNO_3(aq) + NaOH(s) \rightarrow NaNO_3(aq) + H_2O(l)$

(b)   Determine the limiting reactant, then the identity and concentration of ions remaining in solution. Assume that the $H_2O(l)$ produced by the reaction does **not** increase the total solution volume.

$$12.0 \, g \, NaOH \times \frac{1 \, mol \, NaOH}{40.00 \, g \, NaOH} = 0.300 \, mol \, NaOH$$

$0.200 \, M \, HNO_3 \times 0.0750 \, L \, HNO_3 = 0.0150 \, mol \, HNO_3.$

The mol ratio is 1:1, so HNO_3 is the limiting reactant. No excess H^+ remains in solution. The remaining ions are OH^- (excess reactant), Na^+, and NO_3^- (spectators).

OH^-:   0.300 mol OH^- initial – 0.0150 mol OH^- react = 0.285 mol OH^- remain

0.285 mol OH^-/0.0750 L soln = 3.80 M OH^-(aq)

Na^+:   0.300 mol Na^+/0.0750 L soln = 4.00 M Na^+(aq)

NO_3^-:   0.0150 mol NO_3^-/0.0750 L = 0.200 M NO_3^-(aq)

(c)   The resulting solution is **basic** because of the large excess of OH^-(aq).

Additional Exercises

4.91   If we know the identity of a solute and need to measure its concentration in solution, titration is a good way to do this if three conditions are met. The solute must be a reactant in a chemical reaction of known stoichiometry, the second reactant must be available as a standard solution of well-known concentration, and the equivalence point of the titration must be detectable, either visually or instrumentally. If these conditions are met, a known quantity of solution can be precisely delivered by pipette or buret to a titration vessel. The unknown concentration is then determined by its stoichiometric relationship to the quantity of standard solution required to reach the equivalence point of the titration. Multiple titrations can be performed to ensure precision of the measurement. In summary, titration works well for measuring the unknown concentration of a solute because a well-known quantity of the solute can be measured volumetrically and titrations are repeatable.

4.93   The two precipitates formed are due to $AgCl(s)$ and $SrSO_4(s)$. Since no precipitate forms on addition of hydroxide ion to the remaining solution, the other two possibilities, Ni^{2+} and Mn^{2+}, are absent.

4.95   (a) $Al(OH)_3(s) + 3H^+(aq) \rightarrow Al^{3+}(aq) + 3H_2O(l)$

(b) $Mg(OH)_2(s) + 2H^+(aq) \rightarrow Mg^{2+}(aq) + 2H_2O(l)$

(c) $MgCO_3(s) + 2H^+(aq) \rightarrow Mg^{2+}(aq) + H_2O(l) + CO_2(g)$

(d) $NaAl(CO_3)(OH)_2(s) + 4H^+(aq) \rightarrow Na^+(aq) + Al^{3+}(aq) + 3H_2O(l) + CO_2(g)$

(e) $CaCO_3(s) + 2H^+(aq) \rightarrow Ca^{2+}(aq) + H_2O(l) + CO_2(g)$

[In (c), (d) and (e), one could also write the equation for formation of bicarbonate, e.g., $MgCO_3(s) + H^+(aq) \rightarrow Mg^{2+} + HCO_3^-(aq)$.]

4.96   (a) $2H^+(aq) + SO_3^{2-}(aq) \rightarrow H_2SO_3(aq)$; sulfurous acid

(b) $H_2SO_3(aq) \rightarrow H_2O(l) + SO_2(g)$; sulfur dioxide

(c)   The boiling point of $SO_2(g)$ is –10°C. It is a gas at room temperature (23°C) and pressure (1 atm).

(d)   (i) $Na_2SO_3(aq) + 2HCl(aq) \rightarrow 2NaCl(aq) + H_2O(l) + SO_2(g)$

$SO_3^{2-}(aq) + 2H^+(aq) \rightarrow H_2O(l) + SO_2(g)$

(ii) $Ag_2SO_3(s) + 2HCl(aq) \rightarrow 2AgCl(s) + H_2O(l) + SO_2(g)$

$Ag_2SO_3(s) + 2H^+(aq) + 2Cl^-(aq) \rightarrow 2AgCl(s) + H_2O(l) + SO_2(g)$

(iii) $KHSO_3(s) + HCl(aq) \rightarrow KCl(aq) + H_2O(l) + SO_2(g)$

$KHSO_3(s) + H^+(aq) \rightarrow K^+(aq) + H_2O(l) + SO_2(g)$

(iv) $ZnSO_3(aq) + 2HCl(aq) \rightarrow ZnCl_2(aq) + H_2O(l) + SO_2(g)$

$SO_3^{2-}(aq) + 2H^+(aq) \rightarrow H_2O(l) + SO_2(g)$

4.98   A metal on Table 4.5 is able to displace the metal cations below it from their compounds. That is, zinc will reduce the cations below it to their metals.

(a) $Zn(s) + Na^+(aq) \rightarrow$ no reaction

(b) $Zn(s) + Pb^{2+}(aq) \rightarrow Zn^{2+}(aq) + Pb(s)$

(c) $Zn(s) + Mg^{2+}(aq) \rightarrow$ no reaction

(d) $Zn(s) + Fe^{2+}(aq) \rightarrow Zn^{2+}(aq) + Fe(s)$

(e) $Zn(s) + Cu^{2+}(aq) \rightarrow Zn^{2+}(aq) + Cu(s)$

(f) $Zn(s) + Al^{3+}(aq) \rightarrow$ no reaction

4.99   (a) $A : La_2O_3$ Metals often react with the oxygen in air to produce metal oxides.

             $B : La(OH)_3$ When metals react with water (HOH) to form H_2, OH^- remains.

             $C : LaCl_3$ Most chlorides are soluble.

             $D : La_2(SO_4)_3$ Sulfuric acid provides $SO_4{}^{2-}$ ions.

     (b) $4La(s) + 3O_2(g) \rightarrow 2La_2O_3(s)$

           $2La(s) + 6HOH(l) \rightarrow 2La(OH)_3(s) + 3H_2(g)$

           (There are no spectator ions in either of these reactions.)

           molecular: $La_2O_3(s) + 6HCl(aq) \rightarrow 2LaCl_3(aq) + 3H_2O(l)$

           net ionic: $La_2O_3(s) + 6H^+(aq) \rightarrow 2La^{3+}(aq) + 3H_2O(l)$

           molecular: $La(OH)_3(s) + 3HCl(aq) \rightarrow LaCl_3(aq) + 3H_2O(l)$

           net ionic: $La(OH)_3(s) + 3H^+(aq) \rightarrow La^{3+}(aq) + 3H_2O(l)$

           molecular: $2LaCl_3(aq) + 3H_2SO_4(aq) \rightarrow La_2(SO_4)_3(s) + 6HCl(aq)$

           net ionic: $2La^{3+}(aq) + 3SO_4{}^{2-}(aq) \rightarrow La_2(SO_4)_3(s)$

     (c)   La metal is oxidized by water to produce $H_2(g)$, so La is definitely above H on the activity series. In fact, since an acid is not required to oxidize La, it is probably one of the more active metals.

4.102 Na^+ must replace the total positive (+) charge due to Ca^{2+} and Mg^{2+}. Think of this as moles of charge rather than moles of particles.

$$\frac{0.020 \text{ mol Ca}^{2+}}{1 \text{ L water}} \times 1.5 \times 10^3 \text{ L} \times \frac{2 \text{ mol + change}}{1 \text{ mol Ca}^{2+}} = 60 \text{ mol of + charge}$$

$$\frac{0.0040 \text{ mol Mg}^{2+}}{1 \text{ L water}} \times 1.5 \times 10^3 \text{ L} \times \frac{2 \text{ mol + charge}}{1 \text{ mol Mg}^{2+}} = 12 \text{ mol of + charge}$$

72 moles of + charge must be replaced; 72 mol Na^+ are needed.

4.103 $H_2C_4H_4O_6 + 2OH^-(aq) \rightarrow C_4H_4O_6{}^{2-}(aq) + 2H_2O(l)$

$$0.02465 \text{ L NaOH soln} \times \frac{0.2500 \text{ mol NaOH}}{1 \text{ L}} \times \frac{1 \text{ mol H}_2\text{C}_4\text{H}_4\text{O}_6}{2 \text{ mol NaOH}} \times \frac{1}{0.0500 \text{ L H}_2\text{C}_4\text{H}_4\text{O}_6}$$

$$= 0.06163 \ M \ H_2C_4H_4O_6 \text{ soln}$$

4.105   mol OH^- from NaOH(aq) + mol OH^- from $Zn(OH)_2$(s) = mol H^+ from HBr

        mol H^+ = M HBr × L HBr = 0.500 M HBr × 0.350 L HBr = 0.175 mol H^+

        mol OH^- from NaOH = M NaOH × L NaOH = 0.500 M NaOH × 0.0885 L NaOH

                                         = 0.04425 = 0.0443 mol OH^-

        mol OH^- from $Zn(OH)_2$(s) = 0.175 mol H^+ – 0.04425 mol OH^- from NaOH = 0.13075

                                         = 0.131 mol OH^- from $Zn(OH)_2$

$$0.13075 \text{ mol OH}^- \times \frac{1 \text{ mol Zn(OH)}_2}{2 \text{ mol OH}^-} \times \frac{99.41 \text{ g Zn(OH)}_2}{1 \text{ mol Zn(OH)}_2} = 6.50 \text{ g Zn(OH)}_2$$

Integrative Exercises

4.107 $Ba^{2+}(aq) + SO_4{}^{2-}(aq) \rightarrow BaSO_4(s)$

$$0.2815 \text{ g BaSO}_4 \times \frac{137.3 \text{ g Ba}}{233.4 \text{ g BaSO}_4} = 0.16560 = 0.1656 \text{ g Ba}$$

$$\text{mass \%} = \frac{\text{g Ba}}{\text{g sample}} \times 100 = \frac{0.16560 \text{ g Ba}}{3.455 \text{ g sample}} \times 100 = 4.793 \text{ \% Ba}$$

4.108   *Plan.* Write balanced equation.

$$\text{mass H}_2\text{SO}_4 \text{ soln} \xrightarrow{\text{mass \%}} \text{mass H}_2\text{SO}_4 \rightarrow \text{mol H}_2\text{SO}_4 \rightarrow \text{mol Na}_2\text{CO}_3 \rightarrow \text{mass Na}_2\text{CO}$$

Solve. $H_2SO_4(aq) + Na_2CO_3(s) \rightarrow Na_2SO_4(aq) + H_2O(l) + CO_2(g)$

$$5.0 \times 10^3 \text{ kg conc. H}_2\text{SO}_4 \times \frac{0.950 \text{ kg H}_2\text{SO}_4}{1.00 \text{ kg conc. H}_2\text{SO}_4} = 4.75 \times 10^3 = 4.8 \times 10^3 \text{ kg H}_2\text{SO}_4$$

$$4.75 \times 10^3 \text{ kg H}_2\text{SO}_4 \times \frac{1 \times 10^3 \text{ g}}{1 \text{ kg}} \times \frac{1 \text{ mol H}_2\text{SO}_4}{98.08 \text{ g H}_2\text{SO}_4} \times \frac{1 \text{ mol Na}_2\text{CO}_3}{1 \text{ mol H}_2\text{SO}_4}$$

$$\times \frac{105.99 \text{ g NaHCO}_3}{1 \text{ mol NaHCO}_3} \times \frac{1 \text{ kg}}{1 \times 10^3 \text{ g}} = 5.133 \times 10^3 = 5.1 \times 10^3 \text{ kg Na}_2\text{CO}_3$$

4.110   (a) $Na_2SO_4(aq) + Pb(NO_3)_2(s) \rightarrow PbSO_4(s) + 2NaNO_3(aq)$

(b)   Calculate mol of each reactant and compare.

$$1.50 \text{ g Pb(NO}_3)_2 \times \frac{1 \text{ mol Pb(NO}_3)_2}{331.2 \text{ g Pb(NO}_3)_2} = 0.004529 = 4.53 \times 10^{-3} \text{ mol Pb(NO}_3)_2$$

$0.100 \, M \, Na_2SO_4 \times 0.125 \text{ L} = 0.0125 \text{ mol Na}_2SO_4$

Since the reactants combine in a 1:1 mol ratio, $Pb(NO_3)_2$ is the limiting reactant.

(c) $Pb(NO_3)_2$ is the limiting reactant, so no Pb^{2+} remains in solution. The remaining ions are: $SO_4{}^{2-}$ (excess reactant), Na^+ and $NO_3{}^-$ (spectators).

$SO_4{}^{2-}$:   0.0125 mol $SO_4{}^{2-}$ initial – 0.00453 mol $SO_4{}^{2-}$ reacted

$$= 0.00797 = 0.0080 \text{ mol SO}_4{}^{2-} \text{ remain}$$

0.00797 mol $SO_4{}^{2-}$ / 0.125 L soln = 0.064 M $SO_4{}^{2-}$

Na^+:   Since the total volume of solution is the volume of $Na_2SO_4(aq)$ added, the concentration of Na^+ is unchanged.

$0.100 \, M \, Na_2SO_4 \times (2 \text{ mol Na}^+ / 1 \text{ mol Na}_2SO_4) = 0.200 \, M \, Na^+$

NO_3^-: 4.53×10^{-3} mol $Pb(NO_3)_2 \times 2$ mol $NO_3^- / 1$ mol $Pb(NO_3)_2$

$$= 9.06 \times 10^{-3} \text{ mol } NO_3^-$$

9.06×10^{-3} mol $NO_3^- / 0.125$ L $= 0.0725$ M NO_3^-

4.111   *Plan.* Cl^- is present in NaCl and $MgCl_2$; using mass %, calculate mass NaCl and $MgCl_2$ in mixture, mol Cl^- in each, then molarity of Cl^- in 0.500 L solution.   *Solve.*

$$7.50 \text{ mixture} \times \frac{0.765 \text{ g NaCl}}{1.00 \text{ g mixture}} \times \frac{1 \text{ mol NaCl}}{58.44 \text{ g NaCl}} \times \frac{1 \text{ mol } Cl^-}{1 \text{ mol NaCl}} = 0.09818 = 0.0982 \text{ mol } Cl^-$$

$$7.50 \text{ mixture} \times \frac{0.065 \text{ g } MgCl_2}{1.00 \text{ g mixture}} \times \frac{1 \text{ mol } MgCl_2}{95.21 \text{ g } MgCl_2} \times \frac{2 \text{ mol } Cl^-}{1 \text{ mol } MgCl} = 0.01024 = 0.010 \text{ mol } Cl^-$$

mol $Cl^- = 0.09818 + 0.01024 = 0.10842 = 0.108$ mol Cl^-; $M = \dfrac{0.10842 \text{ mol } Cl^-}{0.5000 \text{ L}} = 0.217$ M Cl^-

4.112   *Plan.* $M = \dfrac{\text{mol } Br^-}{\text{L seawater}}$; mg $Br^- \rightarrow$ g $Br^- \rightarrow$ mol Br^-;

1 kg seawater $\rightarrow$ g $\xrightarrow{\text{density}}$ mL water $\rightarrow$ L seawater

Solve. 65 mg $Br^- \times \dfrac{1 \text{ g } Br^-}{1000 \text{ mg } Br^-} \times \dfrac{1 \text{ mol } Br^-}{79.90 \text{ g } Br^-} = 8.135 \times 10^{-4} = 8.1 \times 10^{-4}$ mol Br^-

1 kg seawater $\times \dfrac{1000 \text{ g}}{1 \text{ kg}} \times \dfrac{1 \text{ mL water}}{1.025 \text{ g water}} \times \dfrac{1 \text{ L}}{1000 \text{ mL}} = 0.9756$ L

M $Br^- = \dfrac{8.135 \times 10^{-4} \text{ mol } Br^-}{0.9756 \text{ L seawater}} = 8.3 \times 10^{-4}$ M Br^-

4.114   (a) AsO_4^{3-}; +5

(b) Ag_3PO_4 is silver phosphate; Ag_3AsO_4 is silver arsenate

(c)   0.0250 L soln $\times \dfrac{0.102 \text{ mol } Ag^+}{1 \text{ L soln}} \times \dfrac{1 \text{ mol } Ag_3AsO_4}{3 \text{ mol } Ag^+} \times \dfrac{1 \text{ mol As}}{1 \text{ mol } Ag_3AsO_4} \times \dfrac{74.92 \text{ g As}}{1 \text{ mol As}}$

$$= 0.06368 = 0.0637 \text{ g As}$$

mass percent $= \dfrac{0.06368 \text{ g As}}{1.22 \text{ g sample}} \times 100 = 5.22\%$ As

4.116   (a)   *Analyze.* Given: 55 gal of 50 ppb AsO_4^{3-}. Find. g Na_3AsO_4.

Plan. Use the definition of ppb to calculate g AsO_4^{3-} in 55 gal of water. Then change AsO_4^{3-} to g Na_3SO_4 using molar masses. Assume the density of H_2O is 1.00 g/mL.

Solve. 1 billion $= 1 \times 10^9$; 1 ppb $= \dfrac{1 \text{ g solute}}{1 \times 10^9 \text{ g solution}}$

$$\dfrac{1 \text{ g solute}}{1 \times 10^9 \text{ g solution}} \times \dfrac{1 \text{ g solution}}{1 \text{ mL solution}} \times \dfrac{1 \times 10^3 \text{ mL}}{1 \text{ L solution}} = \dfrac{\text{g } AsO_4^{3-}}{1 \times 10^6 \text{ L } H_2O}$$

$$50 \text{ ppb AsO}_4^{3-} = 50 \text{ g AsO}_4^{3-} / 1 \times 10^6 \text{ L H}_2\text{O}$$

$$\frac{50 \text{ g AsO}_4^{3-}}{1 \times 10^6 \text{ L H}_2\text{O}} \times \frac{3.7854 \text{ L}}{1 \text{ gal}} \times 55 \text{ gal} \times \frac{207.89 \text{ g Na}_3\text{AsO}_4}{138.92 \text{ g AsO}_4^{3-}} = 0.015578$$

$$= 0.016 \text{ g Na}_3\text{AsO}_4$$

(b)   Parts per billion, ppb, is a mass ratio. If 90% of the arsenic, As, in the form of arsenate, AsO_4^{3-}, is retained in the bucket, then 90% of the mass of As (or AsO_4^{3-}) is in the bucket and 10% of the As (or AsO_4^{3-}) passes thru. Assuming 1×10^6 L of drinking water, 10% of the 500 g AsO_4^{3-} in the water is 50 g AsO_4^{3-}. Thus, only one pass through the bucket is required to reduce the AsO_4^{3-} concentration in drinking water from 500 ppb to 50 ppb, the acceptable standard.

4.117   (a)   mol HCl initial – mol NH$_3$ from air = mol HCl remaining

$$= \text{mol NaOH required for titration}$$

mol NaOH = 0.0588 M × 0.0131 L = 7.703×10^{-4} = 7.70×10^{-4} mol NaOH

$$= 7.70 \times 10^{-4} \text{ mol HCl remain}$$

mol HCl initial – mol HCl remaining = mol NH$_3$ from air

$(0.0105 \text{ M HCl} \times 0.100 \text{ L}) - 7.703 \times 10^{-4}$ mol HCl = mol NH$_3$

10.5×10^{-4} mol HCl $- 7.703 \times 10^{-4}$ mol HCl $= 2.80 \times 10^{-4} = 2.8 \times 10^{-4}$ mol NH$_3$

$$2.8 \times 10^{-4} \text{ mol NH}_3 \times \frac{17.03 \text{ g NH}_3}{1 \text{ mol NH}_3} = 4.77 \times 10^{-3} = 4.8 \times 10^{-3} \text{ g NH}_3$$

(b)   ppm is defined as molecules of NH$_3$/1×10^6 molecules in air.

Calculate molecules NH$_3$ from mol NH$_3$.

$$2.80 \times 10^{-4} \text{ mol NH}_3 \times \frac{0.022 \times 20^{23} \text{ molecules}}{1 \text{ mol}} = 1.686 \times 10^{20}$$

$$= 1.7 \times 10^{20} \text{ NH}_3 \text{ molecules}$$

Calculate total volume of air processed, then g air using density, then molecules air using molar mass.

$$\frac{10.0 \text{ L}}{1 \text{ min}} \times 10.0 \text{ min} \times \frac{1.20 \text{ g air}}{1 \text{ L air}} \times \frac{1 \text{ mol air}}{29.0 \text{ g air}} \times \frac{6.022 \times 10^{23} \text{ molecules}}{1 \text{ mol}}$$

$$= 2.492 \times 10^{24} = 2.5 \times 10^{24} \text{ air molecules}$$

$$\text{ppm NH}_3 = \frac{1.686 \times 10^{20} \text{ NH}_3 \text{ molecules}}{2.492 \times 10^{24} \text{ air molecules}} \times 1 \times 10^6 = 68 \text{ ppm NH}_3$$

(c)   68 ppm > 50 ppm. The manufacturer is **not** in compliance.

5 Thermochemistry

Visualizing Concepts

5.2 (a) The internal energy, E, of the products is greater than that of the reactants, so the diagram represents an increase in the internal energy of the system.

(b) ΔE for this process is positive, +.

(c) If no work is associated with the process, it is endothermic.

5.3 (a) For an endothermic process, the sign of q is positive; the system gains heat. This is true only for system (iii).

(b) In order for ΔE to be less than 0, there is a net transfer of heat or work from the system to the surroundings. The magnitude of the quantity leaving the system is greater than the magnitude of the quantity entering the system. In system (i), the magnitude of the heat leaving the system is less than the magnitude of the work done on the system. In system (iii), the magnitude of the work done by the system is less than the magnitude of the heat entering the system. None of the systems has $\Delta E < 0$.

(c) In order for ΔE to be greater than 0, there is a net transfer of work or heat to the system from the surroundings. In system (i), the magnitude of the work done on the system is greater than the magnitude of the heat leaving the system. In system (ii), work is done on the system with no change in heat. In system (iii) the magnitude of the heat gained by the system is greater than the magnitude of the work done on the surroundings. $\Delta E > 0$ for all three systems.

5.5 (a) $w = -P\Delta V$. Since ΔV for the process is (–), the sign of w is (+).

(b) $\Delta E = q + w$. At constant pressure, $\Delta H = q$. If the reaction is endothermic, the signs of ΔH and q are (+). From (a), the sign of w is (+), so the sign of ΔE is (+). The internal energy of the system increases during the change. (This situation is described by the diagram (ii) in Exercise 5.3.)

5.7 Cooling 1 kg H_2O releases more heat than cooling 1 kg Al . Equal masses of H_2O and Al are cooled by the same number of °C. Under these circumstances, the amount of heat released on cooling is proportional to the specific heat capacities of the substances. Specific heat capacity is expressed as J/g-K or energy per mass and temperature change. Since mass and temperature change are equal for the two substances, the one with the larger specific heat capacity loses the most heat. From Table 5.2, the specific heat capacity of $H_2O(l)$ is 4.18 J/g-K and of Al(s) is 0.90 J/g-K, so 1 kg H_2O releases more heat than 1 kg Al.

5.8 (a) $N_2(g) + O_2(g) \rightarrow 2NO(g)$. Since $\Delta V = 0$, $w = 0$.

(b) $\Delta H = 90.37$ kJ for production of 1 mol of $NO(g)$. The definition of a formation reaction is one where elements combine to form one mole of a single product. The enthalpy change for such a reaction is the enthalpy of formation.

5.10 No. The standard enthalpy of formation of a compound is the change in enthalpy for the reaction that forms one mole of the compound from elements in their standard states. The equation

$$C(graphite) + 4H(g) + O(g) \rightarrow CH_3OH(l)$$

shows elemental carbon (graphite) in its standard state, but elemental hydrogen and oxygen exist as diatomic gases $H_2(g)$ and $O_2(g)$ at standard conditions. ΔH for this equation does not equal ΔH_f^o for $CH_3OH(l)$.

The Nature of Energy

5.12 (a) The kinetic energy of the ball **decreases** as it moves higher. As the ball moves higher and opposes gravity, kinetic energy is changed into potential energy.

(b) The potential energy of the ball **increases** as it moves higher.

(c) The heavier ball would go **half as high** as the tennis ball. At the apex of the trajectory, all initial kinetic energy has been changed into potential energy. The magnitude of the change in potential energy is $m\ g\ \Delta h$, which is equal to the energy initially imparted to the ball. If the same amount of energy is imparted to a ball with twice the mass, m doubles so Δh is half as large.

5.14 (a) *Plan.* Convert lb → kg, mi/hr → m/s.

Solve. $850\,lb \times \dfrac{1\,kg}{2.205\,lb} = 385.49 = 385\,kg$

$\dfrac{66\,mi}{1\,hr} \times \dfrac{1.6093\,km}{1\,mi} \times \dfrac{1000\,m}{1\,km} \times \dfrac{1\,hr}{60\,min} \times \dfrac{1\,min}{60\,sec} = 29.504 = 30\,m/s$

$E_k = 1/2\,mv^2 = 1/2 \times 385.49\,kg \times (29.504)^2\,m^2/s^2 = 1.7 \times 10^5\,J$

(b) E_k is proportional to v^2, so if speed decreases by a factor of 2, kinetic energy decreases by a factor of 4.

(c) Brakes stop a moving vehicle, so the kinetic energy of the motorcycle is primarily transferred to friction between brakes and wheels, and somewhat to deformation of the tire and friction between the tire and road.

5.16 (a) *Analyze.* Given: 1 kwh; 1 watt = 1 J/s; 1 watt • s = 1 J.

Find: conversion factor for joules and kwh.

Plan. kwh → wh → ws → J

Solve. $1\,kwh \times \dfrac{1000\,w}{1\,kw} \times \dfrac{60\,min}{h} \times \dfrac{60\,s}{min} \times \dfrac{1\,J}{1\,w\text{-}s} = 3.6 \times 10^6\,J$

$1\,kwh = 3.6 \times 10^6\,J$

(b)   *Analyze.* Given: 100 watt bulb. Find: heat in kcal radiated by bulb or person in 24 hr.

Plan. 1 watt = 1 J/s; 1 kcal = 4.184×10^3 J; watt → J/s → J → kcal.   *Solve.*

$$100 \text{ watt} = \frac{100 \text{ J}}{1 \text{ s}} \times \frac{60 \text{ sec}}{\text{min}} \times \frac{60 \text{ min}}{\text{hr}} \times 24 \text{ hr} \times \frac{1 \text{ kcal}}{4.184 \times 10^3 \text{ J}} = 2065 = 2.1 \times 10^3 \text{ kcal}$$

24 hr has 2 sig figs, but 100 watt is ambiguous. The answer to 1 sig fig would be 2×10^3 kcal.

Check. $(1 \times 10^2 \times 6 \times 10^1 \times 6/10^3) \approx 6^3 \times 10 \approx 2000$ kcal

5.18   (a)   The system is *open*, because it exchanges both mass and energy with the surroundings. Mass exchange occurs when solution flows into and out of the apparatus. The apparatus is not insulated, so energy exchange also occurs. Closed systems exchange energy but not mass, while isolated systems exchange neither.

          (b)   If the system is defined as shown, it can be closed by blocking the flow in and out, but leaving the flask full of solution.

5.20   (a)   Heat is the energy transferred from a hotter object to a colder object.

          (b)   Heat is transferred from one object (system) to another until the two objects (systems) are at the same temperature.

5.22   (a)   Electrostatic attraction; no work is done because the particles are held stationary.

          (b)   Magnetic attraction; work is done because the nail is moved a distance.

The First Law of Thermodynamics

5.24   (a) $\Delta E = q + w$

          (b)   The quantities q and w are negative when the system loses heat to the surroundings (it cools), or does work on the surroundings.

5.26   In each case, evaluate q and w in the expression $\Delta E = q + w$. For an exothermic process, q is negative; for an endothermic process, q is positive.

          (a)   q is positive and w is negative. ΔE = 850 J – 382 J = 468 J. The process is endothermic.

          (b)   q is negative and w is essentially zero. ΔE = –3140 J. The process is exothermic.

          (c)   q is negative and w is zero. ΔE = –6.47 kJ. The process is exothermic.

5.28 $E_{el} = \dfrac{\kappa Q_1 Q_2}{r^2}$ For two oppositely charged particles, the sign of E_{el} is negative; the closer the particles, the greater the magnitude of E_{el}.

          (a)   The potential energy becomes less negative as the particles are separated (r increases).

(b) ΔE for the process is positive; the internal energy of the system increases as the oppositely charged particles are separated.

(c) Work is done on the system to separate the particles so w is positive. We have no direct knowledge of the change in q, except that it cannot be large and negative, because overall $\Delta E = q + w$ is positive.

5.30 (a) Independent. Potential energy is a state function.

(b) Dependent. Some of the energy released could be employed in performing work, as is done in the body when sugar is metabolized; heat is not a state function.

(c) Dependent. The work accomplished depends on whether the gasoline is used in an engine, burned in an open flame, or in some other manner. Work is not a state function.

Enthalpy

5.32 (a) When a process occurs under constant external pressure, the enthalpy change (ΔH) equals the amount of heat transferred. $\Delta H = q_p$.

(b) $\Delta H = q_p$. If the system absorbs heat, q and ΔH are positive and the enthalpy of the system increases.

5.34 At constant volume ($\Delta V = 0$), $\Delta E = q_v$. According to the definition of enthalpy, $H = E + PV$, so $\Delta H = \Delta E + \Delta(PV)$. For an ideal gas at constant temperature and volume, $\Delta PV = V\Delta P = RT\Delta n$. For this reaction, there are 2 mol of gaseous product and 3 mol of gaseous reactants, so $\Delta n = -1$. Thus $V\Delta P$ or $\Delta(PV)$ is negative. Since $\Delta H = \Delta E + \Delta(PV)$, the negative $\Delta(PV)$ term means that ΔH will be smaller or more negative than ΔE.

5.36 The gas is the system. If 378 J of heat is added, $q = +378$ J. Work done by the system decreases the overall energy of the system, so $w = -56$ J.

5.38 (a) $ZnCO_3(s) \rightarrow ZnO(s) + CO_2(g)$

$\Delta H = 71.5$ kJ

(b)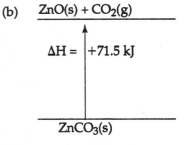

5.40 *Plan.* Consider the sign of an enthalpy change that would convert one of the substances into the other. *Solve.*

(a) $CO_2(s) \rightarrow CO_2(g)$. This change is sublimation, which is endothermic, $+\Delta H$. $CO_2(g)$ has the higher enthalpy.

(b) $H_2 \rightarrow 2H$. Breaking the H–H bond requires energy, so the process is endothermic, $+\Delta H$. Two moles of H atoms have higher enthalpy.

(c) $H_2O(g) \rightarrow H_2(g) + 1/2\ O_2(g)$. Decomposing H_2O into its elements requires energy and is endothermic, $+\Delta H$. One mole of $H_2(g)$ and 0.5 mol $O_2(g)$ at 25°C have the higher enthalpy.

(d) $N_2(g)$ at 100° → $N_2(g)$ at 300°. An increase in the temperature of the sample requires that heat is added to the system, +q and +ΔH. $N_2(g)$ at 300° has the higher enthalpy.

5.42   (a)   The reaction is endothermic, so heat is absorbed by the system during the course of reaction.

(b) $45.0\,g\,CH_3OH \times \dfrac{1\,mol\,CH_3OH}{32.04\,g\,CH_3OH} \times \dfrac{90.7\,kJ}{1\,mol\,CH_3OH} = 127\,kJ$ heat transferred (absorbed)

(c) $25.8\,kJ \times \dfrac{2\,mol\,H_2}{90.7\,kJ} \times \dfrac{2.016\,g\,H_2}{1\,mol\,H_2} = 1.15\,g\,H_2$ produced

The sign of ΔH is reversed for the reverse reaction: $\Delta H = -90.7\,kJ$

(d) $50.9\,g\,CO \times \dfrac{1\,mol\,CO}{28.01\,g\,CO} \times \dfrac{-90.7\,kJ}{1\,mol\,CO} = -165\,kJ$ heat transferred (released)

5.44   (a) $0.632\,mol\,O_2 \times \dfrac{-89.4\,kJ}{3\,mol\,O_2} = -18.83 = -18.8\,kJ$

(b) $8.57\,g\,KCl \times \dfrac{1\,mol\,KCl}{74.55\,g\,KCl} \times \dfrac{-89.4\,kJ}{2\,mol\,KCl} = -5.1386 = -5.14\,kJ$

(c)   Since the sign of ΔH is reversed for the reverse reaction, it seems reasonable that other characteristics would be reversed, as well. If the forward reaction proceeds spontaneously, the reverse reaction is probably not spontaneous. Also, we know from experience that KCl(s) does not spontaneously react with atmospheric $O_2(g)$, even at elevated temperature.

5.46   (a) $3C_2H_2(g) \rightarrow C_6H_6(l)$ $\Delta H = -630\,kJ$

(b) $C_6H_6(l) \rightarrow 3C_2H_2(g)$ $\Delta H = 630\,kJ$
ΔH for the formation of 3 mol of acetylene is 630 kJ. ΔH for the formation of 1 mol of C_2H_2 is then 630 kJ/3 = 210 kJ.

(c)   The exothermic reverse reaction is more likely to be thermodynamically favored.

(d)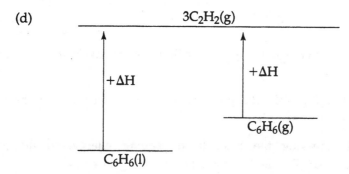

If the reactant is in the higher enthalpy gas phase, the overall ΔH for the reaction has a smaller positive value.

Calorimetry

The specific heat of water to four significant figures, **4.184 J/g - K,** will be used in many of the following exercises; temperature units of K and °C will be used interchangeably.

5.48   *Analyze.* Both objects are heated to 100°C. The two hot objects are placed in the same amount of cold water at the same temperature. Object A raises the water temperature more than object B. *Plan.* Apply the definition of heat capacity to heating the water and heating the objects to determine which object has the greater heat capacity.   *Solve.*

    (a)   Both beakers of water contain the same mass of water, so they both have the same heat capacity. Object A raises the temperature of its water more than object B, so more heat was transferred from object A than from object B. Since both objects were heated to the same temperature initially, object A must have absorbed more heat to reach the 100° temperature. The greater the heat capacity of an object, the greater the heat required to produce a given rise in temperature. Thus, object A has the greater heat capacity.

    (b)   Since no information about the masses of the objects is given, we cannot compare or determine the specific heats of the objects.

5.50   (a)   In Table 5.2, Hg(l) has the smallest specific heat, so it will require the smallest amount of energy to heat 50.0 g of the substance 10 k.

    (b) $50.0 \text{ g Hg(l)} \times 10 \text{ K} \times \dfrac{0.14 \text{ J}}{\text{g - K}} = 70 \text{ J}$

5.52 $62.0 \text{ g ethylene glycol} \times \dfrac{2.42 \text{ J}}{\text{g - K}} \times (40.5°\text{C} - 13.1°\text{C}) = 4.11 \times 10^3 \text{ J}$

5.54   (a)   Following the logic in Solution 5.53, the dissolving process is endothermic, ΔH is positive. The total mass of the solution is (60.0 g H_2O + 3.88 g NH_4NO_3) = 63.88 = 63.9 g. The temperature change of the solution is 23.0 – 18.4 = 4.6°C. The heat lost by the surroundings is

$$63.88 \text{ g solution} \times \dfrac{4.184 \text{ J}}{1 \text{ g - °C}} \times 4.6°\text{C} \times \dfrac{1 \text{ kJ}}{1000 \text{ J}} = 1.229 = 1.2 \text{ kJ}$$

Thus, 1.2 kJ is absorbed when 3.88 g NH_4NO_3(s) dissolves.

$$\dfrac{+1.229 \text{ kJ}}{3.88 \text{ NH}_4\text{NO}_3} \times \dfrac{80.05 \text{ g NH}_4\text{NO}_3}{1 \text{ mol NH}_4\text{NO}_3} = +25.36 = +25 \text{ kJ/mol NH}_4\text{NO}_3$$

    (b)   This process is endothermic, because the temperature of the surroundings decreases, indicating that heat is absorbed by the system.

5.56   (a) $C_6H_5OH(s) + 7O_2(g) \rightarrow 6CO_2(g) + 3H_2O(l)$

    (b) $q_{bomb} = -q_{rxn}; \Delta T = 26.37°\text{C} - 21.36°\text{C} = 5.01°\text{C}$

$$q_{bomb} = \dfrac{11.66 \text{ kJ}}{1°\text{C}} \times 5.01°\text{C} = 58.417 = 58.4 \text{ kJ}$$

At constant volume, $q_v = \Delta E$. ΔE and ΔH are very similar.

$$\Delta H_{rxn} \approx \Delta E_{rxn} = q_{rxn} = -q_{bomb} = \frac{-58.417 \, kJ}{1.800 \, g \, C_6H_5OH} = -32.454 = -32.5 \, kJ/g \, C_6H_5OH$$

$$\Delta H_{rxn} = \frac{-32.454 \, kJ}{1 \, g \, C_6H_5OH} \times \frac{94.11 \, g \, C_6H_5OH}{1 \, mol \, C_6H_5OH} = \frac{-3.054 \times 10^3 \, kJ}{mol \, C_6H_5OH}$$

$$= -3.05 \times 10^3 \, kJ/mol \, C_6H_5OH$$

5.58   (a) $C = 1.640 \, g \, C_6H_5COOH \times \dfrac{26.38 \, kJ}{1 \, g \, C_6H_5COOH} \times \dfrac{1}{4.95°C} = 8.740 = 8.74 \, kJ/°C$

      (b) $\dfrac{8.740 \, kJ}{°C} \times 4.68°C \times \dfrac{1}{1.320 \, g \, sample} = 30.99 = 31.0 \, kJ/g \, sample$

      (c)   If water is lost from the calorimeter, there is less water to heat, so the same amount of heat (kJ) from a reaction would cause a larger increase in the calorimeter temperature. The calorimeter constant, kJ/°C, would decrease, because °C is in the denominator of the expression.

Hess's Law

5.60   (a)   *Analyze/Plan.* Arrange the reactions so that in the overall sum, B, appears in both reactants and products and can be canceled. This is a general technique for using Hess's Law.   *Solve.*

           $\begin{array}{ll} A \rightarrow B & \Delta H = +30 \, kJ \\ \underline{B \rightarrow C} & \underline{\Delta H = +60 \, kJ} \\ A \rightarrow C & \Delta H = +90 \, kJ \end{array}$

      (b)

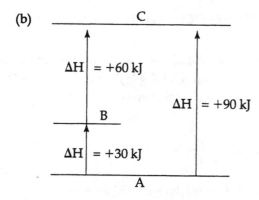

        Check. The process of A forming C can be described as A forming B and B forming C.

5.62 $\begin{array}{ll} 3H_2(g) + 3/2 \, O_2(g) \rightarrow 3H_2O(g) & \Delta H = 3/2(-483.6 \, kJ) \\ \underline{O_3(g) \rightarrow 3/2 \, O_2(g)} & \underline{\Delta H = 1/2(-284.6 \, kJ)} \\ 3H_2(g) + O_3(g) \rightarrow 3H_2O(g) & \Delta H = -867.7 \, kJ \end{array}$

5.64 $\begin{array}{ll} N_2O(g) \rightarrow N_2(g) + 1/2 \, O_2(g) & \Delta H = 1/2 \, (-163.2 \, kJ) \\ NO_2(g) \rightarrow NO(g) + 1/2 \, O_2(g) & \Delta H = 1/2(113.1 \, kJ) \\ \underline{N_2(g) + O_2(g) \rightarrow 2NO(g)} & \underline{\Delta H = 180.7 \, kJ} \\ N_2O(g) + NO_2(g) \rightarrow 3NO(g) & \Delta H = 155.7 \, kJ \end{array}$

Enthalpies of Formation

5.66   (a)   Tables of ΔH_f° are useful because, according to Hess's law, the standard enthalpy of any reaction can be calculated from the standard enthalpies of formation for the reactants and products.

$$\Delta H_{rxn}^{\circ} = \Sigma \Delta H_f^{\circ} \text{ (products)} - \Sigma \Delta H_f^{\circ} \text{ (reactants)}$$

       (b)   The standard enthalpy of formation for any element in its standard state is zero. Elements in their standard states are the reference point for the enthalpy of formation scale.

       (c) $6C(s) + 6H_2(g) + 3O_2(g) \rightarrow C_6H_{12}O_6(s)$

5.68   (a) $1/2\, H_2(g) + 1/2\, Br_2(l) \rightarrow HBr(g)$ $\Delta H_f^{\circ} = -36.23 \text{ kJ}$

       (b) $Ag(s) + 1/2\, N_2(g) + 3/2\, O_2(g) \rightarrow AgNO_3(s)$ $\Delta H_f^{\circ} = -124.4 \text{ kJ}$

       (c) $2Fe(s) + 3/2\, O_2(g) \rightarrow Fe_2O_3(s)$ $\Delta H_f^{\circ} = -822.16 \text{ kJ}$

       (d) $2C(s) + 2H_2(g) + O_2(g) \rightarrow CH_3COOH(l)$ $\Delta H_f^{\circ} = -487.0 \text{ kJ}$

5.70   Use heats of formation to calculate ΔH° for the combustion of butane.

$$C_4H_{10}(l) + 13/2\, O_2(g) \rightarrow 4CO_2(g) + 5H_2O(l)$$

$$\Delta H_{rxn}^{\circ} = 4\Delta H_f^{\circ}\, CO_2(g) + 5\Delta H_f^{\circ}\, H_2O(l) - \Delta H_f^{\circ}\, C_4H_{10}(l) - 13/2\, \Delta H_f^{\circ}\, O_2(g)$$

$$\Delta H_{rxn}^{\circ} = 4(-393.5 \text{ kJ}) + 5(-285.83 \text{ kJ}) - (-147.6 \text{ kJ}) - 13/2(0) = -2855.6 = -2856 \text{ kJ/mol } C_4H_{10}$$

$$5.00 \text{ g } C_4H_{10} \times \frac{1 \text{ mol } C_4H_{10}}{58.123 \text{ g } C_4H_{10}} \times \frac{-2855.6 \text{ kJ}}{1 \text{ mol } C_4H_{10}} = -246 \text{ kJ}$$

5.72   (a) $\Delta H_{rxn}^{\circ} = 2\Delta H_f^{\circ}\, Br_2(l) + 2\Delta H_f^{\circ}\, H_2O(l) - 4\Delta H_f^{\circ}\, HBr(g) - \Delta H_f^{\circ}\, O_2(g)$

           $= 2(0) + 2(-285.83 \text{ kJ}) - 4(-36.23 \text{ kJ}) - 0 = -426.74 \text{ kJ}$

       (b) $\Delta H_{rxn}^{\circ} = \Delta H_f^{\circ}\, Na_2SO_4(s) + \Delta H_f^{\circ}\, H_2O(g) - 2\Delta H_f^{\circ}\, NaOH(s) - \Delta H_f^{\circ}\, SO_3(g)$

           $= -1387.1 \text{ kJ} + (-241.82 \text{ kJ}) - 2(-425.6 \text{ kJ}) - (-395.2 \text{ kJ}) = -382.5 \text{ kJ}$

       (c) $\Delta H_{rxn}^{\circ} = \Delta H_f^{\circ}\, CCl_4(l) + 4\Delta H_f^{\circ}\, HCl(g) - \Delta H_f^{\circ}\, CH_4(g) - 4\Delta H_f^{\circ}\, Cl_2(g)$

           $= -139.3 \text{ kJ} + 4(-92.30 \text{ kJ}) - (-74.8 \text{ kJ}) - 4(0) = -433.7 \text{ kJ}$

       (d) $\Delta H_{rxn}^{\circ} = 2\Delta H_f^{\circ}\, FeCl_3(s) + 3\Delta H_f^{\circ}\, H_2O(g) - \Delta H_f^{\circ}\, Fe_2O_3(g) - 6\Delta H_f^{\circ}\, HCl(g)$

           $= 2(-400 \text{ kJ}) + 3(-241.82 \text{ kJ}) - (-822.16 \text{ kJ}) - 6(-92.30 \text{ kJ}) = -149.5 = -150 \text{ kJ}$

5.74 $\Delta H_{rxn}^{\circ} = \Delta H_f^{\circ}\, Ca(OH)_2(s) + \Delta H_f^{\circ}\, C_2H_2(g) - 2\Delta H_f^{\circ}\, H_2O(l) - \Delta H_f^{\circ}\, CaC_2(s)$

     $-127.2 \text{ kJ} = -986.2 \text{ kJ} + 226.7 \text{ kJ} - 2(-285.83 \text{ kJ}) - \Delta H_f^{\circ}\, CaC_2(s)$

     ΔH_f° for $CaC_2(s) = -60.6 \text{ kJ}$

5.76   (a) $10C(s) + 4H_2(g) \rightarrow C_{10}H_8(s)$ formation

           $C_{10}H_8(s) + 12O_2(g) \rightarrow 10CO_2(g) + 4H_2O(l)$ combustion, $\Delta H^{\circ} = -5154 \text{ kJ}$

       (b) $\Delta H_{rxn}^{\circ} = 10\Delta H_f^{\circ}\, CO_2(g) + 4\Delta H_f^{\circ}\, H_2O(l) - \Delta H_f^{\circ}\, C_{10}H_8(s) - 12\Delta H_f^{\circ}\, O_2(g)$

$$-5154 = 10(-393.5 \text{ kJ}) + 4(-285.83 \text{ kJ}) - \Delta H_f^\circ \text{ } C_{10}H_8(s) - 12(0)$$

$$\Delta H_f^\circ \text{ } C_{10}H_8(s) = 10(-393.5 \text{ kJ}) + 4(-285.83 \text{ kJ}) + 5154 \text{ kJ} = 76 \text{ kJ}$$

Check. The result has 0 decimal places because the heat of combustion has 0 decimal places.

5.78   (a) $CH_3OH(l) + 3/2 \text{ } O_2(g) \rightarrow CO_2(g) + 2H_2O(g)$

        (b) $\Delta H_{rxn}^\circ = \Delta H_f^\circ \text{ } CO_2(g) + 2\Delta H_f^\circ \text{ } H_2O(g) - \Delta H_f^\circ \text{ } CH_3OH(l) - 3/2 \text{ } \Delta H_f^\circ \text{ } O_2(g)$

               $= -393.5 \text{ kJ} + 2(-241.82 \text{ kJ}) - (-238.6 \text{ kJ}) - 3/2(0) = -638.54 = -638.5 \text{ kJ}$

        (c) $\dfrac{-638.54 \text{ kJ}}{\text{mol } CH_3OH} \times \dfrac{1 \text{ mol } CH_3OH}{32.04 \text{ g}} \times \dfrac{0.791 \text{ g}}{\text{mL}} \times \dfrac{1000 \text{ mL}}{\text{L}}$

                                            $= 1.58 \times 10^4 \text{ kJ/L produced}$

        (d) $\dfrac{1 \text{ mol } CO_2}{-638.54 \text{ kJ}} \times \dfrac{44.0095 \text{ g } CO_2}{\text{mol}} = 0.06892 \text{ g } CO_2/\text{kJ emitted}$

Foods and Fuels

5.80   (a)   Fats are appropriate for fuel storage because they are insoluble in water (and body fluids) and have a high fuel value.

        (b)   For convenience, assume 100 g of chips.

$$12 \text{ g protein} \times \dfrac{17 \text{ kJ}}{1 \text{ g protein}} \times \dfrac{1 \text{ Cal}}{4.184 \text{ kJ}} = 48.76 = 49 \text{ Cal}$$

$$14 \text{ g fat} \times \dfrac{38 \text{ kJ}}{1 \text{ g fat}} \times \dfrac{1 \text{ Cal}}{4.184 \text{ kJ}} = 127.15 = 130 \text{ Cal}$$

$$74 \text{ g carbohydrates} \times \dfrac{17 \text{ kJ}}{1 \text{ g carbohydrates}} \times \dfrac{1 \text{ Cal}}{4.184 \text{ kJ}} = 300.67 = 301 \text{ Cal}$$

total Cal = (48.76 + 127.15 + 300.67) = 476.58 = 480 Cal

$$\% \text{ Cal from fat} = \dfrac{127.15 \text{ Cal fat}}{476.58 \text{ total Cal}} \times 100 = 26.68 = 27\%$$

(Since the conversion from kJ to Cal was common to all three components, we would have determined the same percentage by using kJ.)

        (c) $25 \text{ g fat} \times \dfrac{38 \text{ kJ}}{\text{g fat}} = x \text{ g protein} \times \dfrac{17 \text{ kJ}}{\text{g protein}}; \quad x = 56 \text{ g protein}$

5.82   Calculate the fuel value in a pound of M&M® candies.

$$96 \text{ fat} \times \dfrac{38 \text{ kJ}}{1 \text{ g fat}} = 3648 \text{ kJ} = 3.6 \times 10^3 \text{ kJ}$$

$$320 \text{ g carbohydrate} \times \dfrac{17 \text{ kJ}}{1 \text{ g carbohydrate}} = 5440 \text{ kJ} = 5.4 \times 10^3 \text{ kJ}$$

$$21 \text{ g protein} \times \dfrac{17 \text{ kJ}}{1 \text{ g protein}} = 357 \text{ kJ} = 3.6 \times 10^2 \text{ kJ}$$

total fuel value = 3648 kJ + 5440 kJ + 357 kJ = 9445 kJ = 9.4×10^3 kJ/lb

$$\frac{9445\,kJ}{lb} \times \frac{1\,lb}{453.6\,g} \times \frac{42\,g}{serving} = 874.5\,kJ = 8.7 \times 10^2\,kJ/serving$$

$$\frac{874.5\,kJ}{serving} \times \frac{1\,kcal}{4.184\,kJ} \times \frac{1\,Cal}{1\,kcal} = 209.0\,Cal = 2.1 \times 10^2\,Cal/serving$$

Check. 210 Cal is the approximate food value of a candy bar, so the result is reasonable.

5.84 $177\,mL \times \dfrac{1.0\,g\,wine}{1\,mL} \times \dfrac{0.106\,g\,ethanol}{1\,g\,wine} \times \dfrac{1\,mol\,ethanol}{46.1\,g\,ethanol} \times \dfrac{1367\,kJ}{1\,mol\,ethanol} \times \dfrac{1\,Cal}{4.184\,kJ}$

$$= 133 = 1.3 \times 10^2\,Cal$$

Check. A "typical" 6 oz. glass of wine has 150–250 Cal, so this is a reasonable result.

Note that alcohol is responsible for most of the food value of wine.

5.86 $\Delta H_{rxn}^{\circ} = \Delta H_f^{\circ}\,CO_2(g) + 2\Delta H_f^{\circ}\,H_2O(g) - \Delta H_f^{\circ}\,CH_4(g) - 2\Delta H_f^{\circ}\,O_2(g)$

$$= -393.5\,kJ + 2(-241.82\,kJ) - (-74.8\,kJ) - 2(0)\,kJ = -802.3\,kJ$$

$\Delta H_{rxn}^{\circ} = \Delta H_f^{\circ}\,CF_4(g) + 4\Delta H_f^{\circ}\,HF(g) - \Delta H_f^{\circ}\,CH_4(g) - 4\Delta H_f^{\circ}\,F_2(g)$

$$= -679.9\,kJ + 4(-268.61\,kJ) - (-74.8\,kJ) - 4(0)\,kJ = -1679.5\,kJ$$

The second reaction is twice as exothermic as the first. The "fuel values" of hydrocarbons in a fluorine atmosphere are approximately twice those in an oxygen atmosphere. Note that the difference in ΔH° values for the two reactions is in the ΔH_f° for the products, since the ΔH_f° for the reactants is identical.

Additional Exercises

5.88   (a) $E_p = mgh = 52.0\,kg \times 9.81\,m/s^2 \times 10.8\,m = 5509.3\,J = 5.51\,kJ$

(b) $E_k = 1/2\,mv^2;\ v = (2E_k/m)^{1/2} = \left(\dfrac{2 \times 5509\,kg \cdot m^2/s^2}{52.0\,kg}\right)^{1/2} = 14.6\,m/s$

(c)   Yes, the diver does work on entering (pushing back) the water in the pool.

5.89   In the process described, one mole of solid CO_2 is converted to one mole of gaseous CO_2. The volume of the gas is much greater than the volume of the solid. Thus the system (that is, the mole of CO_2) must work against atmospheric pressure when it expands. To accomplish this work while maintaining a constant temperature requires the absorption of additional heat beyond that required to increase the internal energy of the CO_2. The remaining energy is turned into work.

5.91   Freezing is an exothermic process (the opposite of melting, which is clearly endothermic). When the system, the soft drink, freezes, it releases energy to the surroundings, the can. Some of this energy does the work of splitting the can.

5.92   (a) $q = 0$, $w > 0$ (work done to system), $\Delta E > 0$

(b)   Since the system (the gas) is losing heat, the sign of q is negative. The changes in state described in cases (a) and (b) are identical and ΔE is the same in both cases. The distribution of energy transferred as either work or heat is different in the two scenarios. In case (b), more work is required to compress the gas because some heat is lost to the surroundings. (The moral of this story is that the more energy lost by the system as heat, the greater the work on the system required to accomplish the desired change.)

5.94   If a function sometimes depends on path, then it is simply not a state function. Enthalpy is a state function, so ΔH for the two pathways leading to the same change of state pictured in Figure 5.9 must be the same. However, q is not the same for the both. Our conclusion must be that $\Delta H \neq q$ for these pathways. The condition for $\Delta H = q_p$ (other than constant pressure) is that the only possible work on or by the system is pressure-volume work. Clearly, the work being done in this scenario is not pressure-volume work, so $\Delta H \neq q$, even though the two changes occur at constant pressure.

5.95   *Plan.* Change mass of the iceberg to moles, then apply the enthalpy change for melting. 1 million = 1×10^6. *Solve.*

$$1.25 \times 10^6 \text{ metric tons ice} \times \frac{1000 \text{ kg}}{\text{metric ton}} \times \frac{1000 \text{ g}}{\text{kg}} \times \frac{1 \text{ mol } H_2O}{18.02 \text{ g } H_2O} \times \frac{6.01 \text{ kJ}}{\text{mol}} = 4.17 \times 10^{11} \text{ kJ}$$

5.97   Find the heat capacity of 1.7×10^3 gal H_2O.

$$C_{H_2O} = 1.7 \times 10^3 \text{ gal } H_2O \times \frac{4 \text{ qt}}{1 \text{ gal}} \times \frac{1 \text{ L}}{1.057 \text{ qt}} \times \frac{1 \times 10^3 \text{ cm}^3}{1 \text{ L}} \times \frac{1 \text{ g}}{1 \text{ cm}^3} \times \frac{4.184 \text{ J}}{1 \text{ g} \cdot {}^\circ\text{C}}$$

$$= 2.692 \times 10^7 \text{ J}/{}^\circ\text{C} = 2.7 \times 10^4 \text{ kJ}/{}^\circ\text{C}; \text{ then,}$$

$$\frac{2.692 \times 10^7 \text{ J}}{1 {}^\circ\text{C}} \times \frac{1 \text{ g} \cdot {}^\circ\text{C}}{0.85 \text{ J}} \times \frac{1 \text{ kg}}{1 \times 10^3 \text{ g}} \times \frac{1 \text{ brick}}{1.8 \text{ kg}} = 1.8 \times 10^4 \text{ or } 18,000 \text{ bricks}$$

Check. $(1.7 \times \sim 16 \times 10^6)/(\sim 1.6 \times 10^3) \approx 17 \times 10^3$ bricks; the units are correct.

5.98   (a) $q_{Cu} = \dfrac{0.385 \text{ J}}{\text{g} \cdot \text{K}} \times 121.0 \text{ g Cu} \times (30.1{}^\circ\text{C} - 100.4{}^\circ\text{C}) = -3274.9 = -3.27 \times 10^3 \text{ J}$

The negative sign indicates the 3.27×10^3 J are lost by the Cu block.

(b) $q_{H_2O} = \dfrac{4.184 \text{ J}}{\text{g} \cdot \text{K}} \times 150.0 \text{ g } H_2O \times (30.1{}^\circ\text{C} - 25.1{}^\circ\text{C}) = 3138 = 3.1 \times 10^3 \text{ J}$

The positive sign indicates that 3.14×10^3 J are gained by the H_2O.

(c)   The difference in the heat lost by the Cu and the heat gained by the water is 3.275 $\times 10^3$ J – 3.138 $\times 10^3$ J = 0.137 $\times 10^3$ J = 1×10^2 J. The temperature change of the calorimeter is 5.0°C. The heat capacity of the calorimeter in J/K is

$$0.137 \times 10^3 \text{ J} \times \frac{1}{5.0{}^\circ\text{C}} = 27.4 = 3 \times 10 \text{ J/K}.$$

Since q_{H_2O} is known to one decimal place, the difference has one decimal place and the result has 1 sig fig.

If the rounded results from (a) and (b) are used,

$$C_{calorimeter} = \frac{0.2 \times 10^3 \text{ J}}{5.0 {}^\circ\text{C}} = 4 \times 10 \text{ J/K}.$$

(d) $q_{H_2O} = 3.275 \times 10^3 \, J = \dfrac{4.184 \, J}{g \cdot K} \times 150.0 \, g \times (\Delta T)$

$\Delta T = 5.22°C; \; T_f = 25.1°C + 5.22°C = 30.3°C$

5.99   (a)   From the mass of benzoic acid that produces a certain temperature change, we can calculate the heat capacity of the calorimeter.

$\dfrac{0.235 \, g \, benzoic \, acid}{1.642°C \, change \, observed} \times \dfrac{26.38 \, kJ}{1 \, g \, benzoic \, acid} = 3.7755 = 3.78 \, kJ/°C$

Now we can use this experimentally determined heat capacity with the data for caffeine.

$\dfrac{1.525°C \, rise}{0.265 \, g \, caffeine} \times \dfrac{3.7755 \, kJ}{1°C} \times \dfrac{194.2 \, g \, caffeine}{1 \, mol \, caffeine} = 4.22 \times 10^3 \, kJ/mol \, caffeine$

(b)   The overall uncertainty is approximately equal to the sum of the uncertainties due to each effect. The uncertainty in the mass measurement is 0.001/0.235 or 0.001/0.265, about 1 part in 235 or 1 part in 265. The uncertainty in the temperature measurements is 0.002/1.642 or 0.002/1.525, about 1 part in 820 or 1 part in 760. Thus the uncertainty in heat of combustion from each measurement is

$\dfrac{4220}{235} = 18 \, kJ; \quad \dfrac{4220}{265} = 16 \, kJ; \quad \dfrac{4220}{820} = 5 \, kJ; \quad \dfrac{4220}{760} = 6 \, kJ$

The sum of these uncertainties is 45 kJ. In fact, the overall uncertainty is less than this because independent errors in measurement do tend to partially cancel.

5.101   (a) $Mg(s) + 2H_2O(l) \rightarrow Mg(OH)_2(s) + H_2(g)$

$\Delta H_{rxn}^° = \Delta H_f^° \, Mg(OH)_2(s) + \Delta H_f^° \, H_2(g) - 2\Delta H_f^° \, H_2O(l) - \Delta H_f^° \, Mg(s)$

$= -924.7 \, kJ + 0 - 2(-285.83 \, kJ) - 0 = -353.04 = -353.0 \, kJ$

(b)   Use the specific heat of water, 4.184 J/g-°C, to calculate the energy required to heat the water. Use the density of water at 25°C to calculate the mass of H_2O to be heated. (The change in density of H_2O going from 15°C to 85°C does not substantially affect the strategy of the exercise.) Then use the 'heat stoichiometry' in (a) to calculate mass of Mg(s) needed.

$25 \, mL \times \dfrac{0.997 \, g \, H_2O}{mL} \times \dfrac{4.184 \, J}{g \cdot °C} \times 70°C \times \dfrac{1 \, kJ}{1000 \, J} = 7.300 \, kJ = 7.3 \, kJ \, required$

$7.300 \, kJ \times \dfrac{1 \, mol \, Mg}{353.04 \, kJ} \times \dfrac{24.305 \, g \, Mg}{1 \, mol \, Mg} = 0.5026 \, g = 0.50 \, g \, Mg \, needed$

5.102   (a)   For comparison, balance the equations so that 1 mole of CH_4 is burned in each.

$CH_4(g) + O_2(g) \rightarrow C(s) + 2H_2O(l)$ $\Delta H° = -496.9 \, kJ$

$CH_4(g) + 3/2 \, O_2(g) \rightarrow CO(g) + 2H_2O(l)$ $\Delta H° = -607.4 \, kJ$

$CH_4(g) + 2O_2(g) \rightarrow CO_2(g) + 2H_2O(l)$ $\Delta H° = -890.4 \, kJ$

(b) $\Delta H^{\circ}_{rxn} = \Delta H^{\circ}_f\, C(s) + 2\Delta H^{\circ}_f\, H_2O(l) - \Delta H^{\circ}_f\, CH_4(g) - \Delta H^{\circ}_f\, O_2(g)$

        $= 0 + 2(-285.83\ kJ) - (-74.8) - 0 = -496.9\ kJ$

    $\Delta H^{\circ}_{rxn} = \Delta H^{\circ}_f\, CO(g) + 2\Delta H^{\circ}_f\, H_2O(l) - \Delta H^{\circ}_f\, CH_4(g) - 3/2\, \Delta H^{\circ}_f\, O_2(g)$

        $= (-110.5\ kJ) + 2(-285.83\ kJ) - (-74.8\ kJ) - 3/2(0) = -607.4\ kJ$

    $\Delta H^{\circ}_{rxn} = \Delta H^{\circ}_f\, CO_2(g) + 2\Delta H^{\circ}_f\, H_2O(l) - \Delta H^{\circ}_f\, CH_4(g) - 2\Delta H^{\circ}_f\, O_2(g)$

        $= -393.5\ kJ + 2(-285.83\ kJ) - (-74.8\ kJ) - 2(0) = -890.4\ kJ$

(c)   Assuming that $O_2(g)$ is present in excess, the reaction that produces $CO_2(g)$ represents the most negative ΔH per mole of CH_4 burned. More of the potential energy of the reactants is released as heat during the reaction to give products of lower potential energy. The reaction that produces $CO_2(g)$ is the most "downhill" in enthalpy.

5.104   For nitroethane:

$$\frac{1368\ kJ}{1\ mol\ C_2H_5NO_2} \times \frac{1\ mol\ C_2H_5NO_2}{75.072\ g\ C_2H_5NO_2} \times \frac{1.052\ g\ C_2H_5NO_2}{1\ cm^3} = 19.17\ kJ/cm^3$$

For ethanol:

$$\frac{1367\ kJ}{1\ mol\ C_2H_5OH} \times \frac{1\ mol\ C_2H_5OH}{46.069\ g\ C_2H_5OH} \times \frac{0.789\ g\ C_2H_5OH}{1\ cm^3} = 23.4\ kJ/cm^3$$

For methylhydrazine:

$$\frac{1305\ kJ}{1\ mol\ CH_6N_2} \times \frac{1\ mol\ CH_6N_2}{46.072\ g\ CH_6N_2} \times \frac{0.874\ g\ CH_6N_2}{1\ cm^3} = 24.8\ kJ/cm^3$$

Thus, **methylhydrazine** would provide the most energy per unit volume, with ethanol a close second.

5.106   The reaction for which we want ΔH is:

       $4NH_3(l) + 3O_2(g) \rightarrow 2N_2(g) + 6H_2O(g)$

Before we can calculate ΔH for this reaction, we must calculate ΔH_f for $NH_3(l)$.

We know that ΔH_f for $NH_3(g)$ is $-46.2\ kJ$, and that for $NH_3(l) \rightarrow NH_3(g)$, $\Delta H = 23.2\ kJ$

Thus, $\Delta H_{vap} = \Delta H_f\, NH_3(g) - \Delta H_f\, NH_3(l)$.

      $23.2\ kJ = -46.2\ kJ - \Delta H_f\, NH_3(l);\ \Delta H_f\, NH_3(l) = -69.4\ kJ/mol$

Then for the overall reaction, the enthalpy change is:

$\Delta H_{rxn} = 6\Delta H_f\, H_2O(g) + 2\Delta H_f\, N_2(g) - 4\Delta H_f\, NH_3(l) - 3\Delta H_f\, O_2$

     $= 6(-241.82\ kJ) + 2(0) - 4(-69.4\ kJ) - 3(0) = -1173.3\ kJ$

$$\frac{-1173.3\ kJ}{4\ mol\ NH_3} \times \frac{1\ mol\ NH_3}{17.0\ g\ NH_3} = \frac{0.81\ g\ NH_3}{1\ cm^3} \times \frac{1000\ cm^3}{1\ L} = \frac{1.4 \times 10^4\ kJ}{L\ NH_3}$$

(This result has two significant figures because the density is expressed to two figures.)

$$2CH_3OH(l) + 3O_2(g) \rightarrow 2CO_2(g) + 4H_2O(g)$$

$$\Delta H = 2(-393.5 \text{ kJ}) + 4(-241.82 \text{ kJ}) - 2(-239 \text{ kJ}) - 3(0) = -1276 \text{ kJ}$$

$$\frac{-1276 \text{ kJ}}{2 \text{ mol CH}_3\text{OH}} \times \frac{1 \text{ mol CH}_3\text{OH}}{32.04 \text{ g CH}_3\text{OH}} \times \frac{0.792 \text{ g CH}_3\text{OH}}{1 \text{ cm}^3} \times \frac{1000 \text{ cm}^3}{1 \text{ L}} = \frac{1.58 \times 10^4 \text{ kJ}}{\text{L CH}_3\text{OH}}$$

In terms of heat obtained per unit volume of fuel, methanol is a slightly better fuel than liquid ammonia.

5.107   **1,3-butadiene**, C_4H_6, MM = 54.092 g/mol

(a) $C_4H_6(g) + 11/2 \, O_2(g) \rightarrow 4CO_2(g) + 3H_2O(l)$

$$\Delta H^\circ_{rxn} = 4\Delta H^\circ_f \, CO_2(g) + 3\Delta H^\circ_f \, H_2O(l) - \Delta H^\circ_f \, C_4H_6(g) - 11/2 \, \Delta H^\circ_f \, O_2(g)$$

$$= 4(-393.5 \text{ kJ}) + 3(-285.83 \text{ kJ}) - 111.9 \text{ kJ} + 11/2 \, (0) = -2543.4 \text{ kJ/mol } C_4H_6$$

(b) $\dfrac{-2543.4 \text{ kJ}}{1 \text{ mol } C_4H_6} \times \dfrac{1 \text{ mol } C_4H_6}{54.092 \text{ g}} = 47.020 \rightarrow 47 \text{ kJ/g}$

(c) $\% H = \dfrac{6(1.008)}{54.092} \times 100 = 11.18\% \, H$

1-butene, C_4H_8, MM = 56.108 g/mol

(a) $C_4H_8(g) + 6O_2(g) \rightarrow 4CO_2(g) + 4H_2O(l)$

$$\Delta H^\circ_{rxn} = 4\Delta H^\circ_f \, CO_2(g) + 4\Delta H^\circ_f \, H_2O(l) - \Delta H^\circ_f \, C_4H_8(g) - 6\Delta H^\circ_f \, O_2(g)$$

$$= 4(-393.5 \text{ kJ}) + 4(-285.83 \text{ kJ}) - 1.2 \text{ kJ} - 6(0) = -2718.5 \text{ kJ/mol } C_4H_8$$

(b) $\dfrac{-2718.5 \text{ kJ}}{1 \text{ mol } C_4H_8} \times \dfrac{1 \text{ mol } C_4H_8}{56.108 \text{ g } C_4H_8} = 48.451 \rightarrow 48 \text{ kJ/g}$

(c) $\% H = \dfrac{8(1.008)}{56.108} \times 100 = 14.37\% \, H$

n-butane, $C_4H_{10}(g)$, MM = 58.124 g/mol

(a) $C_4H_{10}(g) + 13/2 \, O_2(g) \rightarrow 4CO_2(g) + 5H_2O(l)$

$$\Delta H^\circ_{rxn} = 4\Delta H^\circ_f \, CO_2(g) + 5\Delta H^\circ_f \, H_2O(l) - \Delta H^\circ_f \, C_4H_{10}(g) - 13/2 \, \Delta H^\circ_f \, O_2(g)$$

$$= 4(-393.5 \text{ kJ}) + 5(-285.83 \text{ kJ}) - (-124.7 \text{ kJ}) - 13/2(0)$$

$$= -2878.5 \text{ kJ/mol } C_4H_{10}$$

(b) $\dfrac{-2878.5 \text{ kJ}}{1 \text{ mol } C_4H_{10}} \times \dfrac{1 \text{ mol } C_4H_{10}}{58.124 \text{ g } C_4H_{10}} = 49.523 \rightarrow 50 \text{ kJ/g}$

(c) $\% H = \dfrac{10(1.008)}{58.124} \times 100 = 17.34\% \, H$

(d)   It is certainly true that as the mass % H increases, the fuel value (kJ/g) of the hydrocarbon increases, given the same number of C atoms. A graph of the data in parts (b) and (c) (see below) suggests that mass % H and fuel value are directly proportional when the number of C atoms is constant.

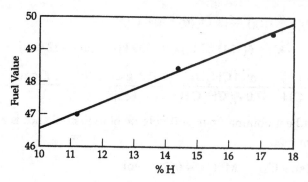

5.108   **(a)** $C_6H_{12}O_6(s) + 6O_2(g) \rightarrow 6CO_2(g) + 6H_2O(l)$

$\Delta H^{\circ}_{rxn} = 6\Delta H^{\circ}_f\, CO_2(g) + 6\Delta H^{\circ}_f\, H_2O(l) - \Delta H^{\circ}_f\, C_6H_{12}O_6(s) - 6\Delta H^{\circ}_f\, O_2(g)$

$= 6(-393.5\text{ kJ}) + 6(-285.83\text{ kJ}) - (-1273\text{ kJ}) - 6(0)$

$= -2803\text{ kJ/mol } C_6H_{12}O_6$

$C_{12}H_{22}O_{11}(s) + 12O_2(g) \rightarrow 12CO_2(g) + 11H_2O(l)$

$\Delta H^{\circ}_{rxn} = 12\Delta H^{\circ}_f\, CO_2(g) + 11\Delta H^{\circ}_f\, H_2O(l) - \Delta H^{\circ}_f\, C_{12}H_{22}O_{11}(s) - 12\Delta H^{\circ}_f\, O_2(g)$

$= 12(-393.5\text{ kJ}) + 11(-285.83\text{ kJ}) - (-2221\text{ kJ}) - 12(0)$

$= -5645\text{ kJ/mol } C_{12}H_{22}O_{11}$

(b) $\dfrac{-2803\text{ kJ}}{1\text{ mol } C_6H_{12}O_6} \times \dfrac{1\text{ mol } C_6H_{12}O_6}{180.2\text{ g } C_6H_{12}O_6} = -\dfrac{15.55\text{ kJ}}{1\text{ g } C_6H_{12}O_6} \rightarrow 16\text{ kJ/g } C_6H_{12}O_6$ (fuel value)

$\dfrac{-5645\text{ kJ}}{1\text{ mol } C_{12}H_{22}O_{11}} \times \dfrac{1\text{ mol } C_{12}H_{22}O_{11}}{342.3\text{ g } C_{12}H_{22}O_{11}} = -\dfrac{16.49\text{ kJ}}{1\text{ g } C_{12}H_{22}O_{11}} \rightarrow 16\text{ kJ/g } C_{12}H_{22}O_{11}$

(fuel value)

(c)   The average fuel value of carbohydrates (Section 5.8) is 17 kJ/g. These two carbohydrates have fuel values (16 kJ/g), slightly lower but in line with this average. (More complex carbohydrates supply more energy and raise the average value.)

5.110   *Plan.* Use dimensional analysis to calculate the amount of solar energy supplied per m² in 1 hr. Use stoichiometry to calculate the amount of plant energy used to produce sucrose per m² in 1 hr. Calculate the ratio of energy for sucrose to total solar energy, per m² per hr.

Solve. 1 W = 1 J/s, 1 kW = 1 kJ/s

$$\frac{1.0\text{ kW}}{m^2} = \frac{1.0\text{ kJ/s}}{m^2} = \frac{1.0\text{ kJ}}{m^2\text{-s}} \times \frac{60\text{ s}}{1\text{ min}} \times \frac{60\text{ min}}{1\text{ hr}} = \frac{3.6 \times 10^3\text{ kJ}}{m^2\text{-hr}}$$

$$\frac{5645\text{ kJ}}{\text{mol sucrose}} \times \frac{1\text{ mol sucrose}}{342.3\text{ g sucrose}} \times \frac{0.20\text{ g sucrose}}{m^2\text{-hr}} = 3.298 = 3.3\text{ kJ/}m^2\text{-hr}$$

for sucrose production

$$\frac{3.298\text{ kJ for sucrose}}{3.6 \times 10^3\text{ kJ total solar}} \times 100 = 0.092\%\text{ sunlight used to produce sucrose}$$

5.111   (a) $6CO_2(g) + 6H_2O(l) \rightarrow C_6H_{12}O_6(s) + 6O_2(g)$, $\Delta H° = 2803$ kJ

This is the reverse of the combustion of glucose (Section 5.8 and Solution 5.108), so $\Delta H° = -(-2803)$ kJ $= +2803$ kJ.

$$\frac{5.5 \times 10^{16} \text{ g CO}_2}{\text{yr}} \times \frac{1 \text{ mol CO}_2}{44.01 \text{ g CO}_2} \times \frac{2803 \text{ kJ}}{6 \text{ mol CO}_2} = 5.838 \times 10^{17} = 5.8 \times 10^{17} \text{ kJ}$$

(b) $1 \text{ W} = 1 \text{ J/s}; 1 \text{ W-s} = 1 \text{ J}$

$$\frac{5.838 \times 10^{17} \text{ kJ}}{\text{yr}} \times \frac{1000 \text{ J}}{\text{kJ}} \times \frac{1 \text{ yr}}{365 \text{ d}} \times \frac{1 \text{ d}}{24 \text{ hr}} \times \frac{1 \text{ hr}}{60 \text{ min}} \times \frac{1 \text{ min}}{60 \text{ s}} \times \frac{1 \text{ W-s}}{\text{J}}$$

$$\times \frac{1 \text{ MW}}{1 \times 10^6 \text{ W}} = 1.851 \times 10^7 \text{ MW} = 1.9 \times 10^7 \text{ MW}$$

$$1.9 \times 10^7 \text{ MW} \times \frac{1 \text{ plant}}{10^3 \text{ MW}} = 1.9 \times 10^4 = 19,000 \text{ nuclear power plants}$$

Integrative Exercises

5.113   The situation in Figure 4.3 is a more complex version of that pictured in Exercise 5.28 and discussed in Solution 5.28. An ionic solid is an orderly arrangement of closely spaced ions, oppositely charged particles. The potential energy of any pair of these ions is described as $E_{el} = \kappa Q_1 Q_2 / r^2$. Separating these oppositely charged particles leads to an increase in the energy of the system, $+ \Delta E$. Work is done to the NaCl by the water molecules. Since both NaCl and water are part of the system, the net amount of work is zero. Since $\Delta E = q + w$, $\Delta E = q$ and both are positive. The dissolving process typically takes place at constant atmospheric pressure, so $\Delta H = q$ and ΔH is also positive.

To verify this conclusion, carry out the dissolution of NaCl in a constant pressure calorimeter. Begin with 1 L of H_2O, record the temperature, add 0.1 mol NaCl, and dissolve completely; record the final temperature. If ΔH is positive, the temperature will decrease.

5.114   (a),(b) $Ag^+(aq) + Li(s) \rightarrow Ag(s) + Li^+(aq)$

$$\Delta H° = \Delta H_f° \text{ Li}^+(aq) - \Delta H_f° \text{ Ag}^+(aq)$$

$$= -278.5 \text{ kJ} - 105.90 \text{ kJ} = -384.4 \text{ kJ}$$

$Fe(s) + 2Na^+(aq) \rightarrow Fe^{2+}(aq) + 2Na(s)$

$$\Delta H° = \Delta H_f° \text{ Fe}^{2+}(aq) - 2\Delta H_f° \text{ Na}^+(aq)$$

$$= -87.86 \text{ kJ} - 2(-240.1 \text{ kJ}) = +392.3 \text{ kJ}$$

$2K(s) + 2H_2O(l) \rightarrow 2KOH(aq) + H_2(g)$

$$\Delta H° = 2\Delta H_f° \text{ KOH}(aq) - 2\Delta H_f° \text{ H}_2O(l)$$

$$= 2(-482.4 \text{ kJ}) - 2(-285.83 \text{ kJ}) = -393.1 \text{ kJ}$$

(c)   Exothermic reactions are more likely to be favored, so we expect the first and third reactions be spontaneous and the second reaction to be nonspontaneous.

(d)   In the activity series of metals, Table 4.5, any metal can be oxidized by the cation of a metal below it on the table.

Ag^+ is below Li, so the first reaction will occur.

Na^+ is above Fe, so the second reaction will not occur.

H^+ (formally in H_2O) is below K, so the third reaction will occur.

These predictions agree with those in part (c).

5.116   (a)   mol Cu $= M \times L = 1.00\ M \times 0.0500\ L = 0.0500$ mol

g $=$ mol $\times$ / $= 0.0500 \times 63.546 = 3.1773 = 3.18$ g Cu

(b)   The precipitate is copper(II) hydroxide, $Cu(OH)_2$.

(c) $CuSO_4(aq) + 2KOH(aq) \rightarrow Cu(OH)_2(s) + K_2SO_4(aq)$, complete

$Cu^{2+}(aq) + 2OH^-(aq) \rightarrow Cu(OH)_2(s)$, net ionic

(d)   The temperature of the calorimeter rises, so the reaction is exothermic and the sign of q is negative.

$$q = -6.2°C \times 100\,g \times \frac{4.184\,J}{1\,g\text{-}°C} = -2.6 \times 10^3\,J = -2.6\,kJ$$

The reaction as carried out involves only 0.050 mol of $CuSO_4$ and the stoichiometrically equivalent amount of KOH. On a molar basis,

$$\Delta H = \frac{-2.6\,kJ}{0.050\,mol} = -52\,kJ \text{ for the reaction as written in part (c)}$$

5.118   (a) $21.83\,g\,CO_2 \times \dfrac{1\,mol\,CO_2}{44.01\,g\,CO_2} \times \dfrac{1\,mol\,C}{1\,mol\,CO_2} \times \dfrac{12.01\,g\,C}{1\,mol\,C} = 5.9572 = 5.957\,g\,C$

$4.47\,g\,H_2O \times \dfrac{1\,mol\,H_2O}{18.02\,g\,H_2O} \times \dfrac{2\,mol\,H}{1\,mol\,H_2O} \times \dfrac{1.008\,g\,H}{mol\,H} = 0.5001 = 0.500\,g\,H$

The sample mass is $(5.9572 + 0.5001) = 6.457$ g

(b) $5.957\,g\,C \times \dfrac{1\,mol\,C}{12.01\,g\,C} = 0.4960\,mol\,C;\ \ 0.4960/0.496 = 1$

$0.500\,g\,H \times \dfrac{1\,mol\,H}{1.008\,g\,H} = 0.496\,mol\,H;\ \ 0.496/0.496 = 1$

The empirical formula of the hydrocarbon is CH.

(c)   Calculate $\Delta H°$ for 6.457 g of the sample.

6.457 g sample $+ O_2(g) \rightarrow 21.83\,g\,CO_2(g) + 4.47\,g\,H_2O(g)$, $\Delta H°_{comb} = -311$ kJ

$\Delta H°_{comb} = \Delta H°\,CO_2(g) + \Delta H°\,H_2O(g) - \Delta H°\,\text{sample} - \Delta H°\,O_2(g)$

$\Delta H°\,\text{sample} = \Delta H°\,CO_2(g) + \Delta H°\,H_2O(g) - \Delta H°_{comb}$

$\Delta H°\,CO_2(g) = 21.83\,g\,CO_2 \times \dfrac{1\,mol\,CO_2}{44.01\,g\,CO_2} \times \dfrac{-393.5\,kJ}{mol\,CO_2} = -195.185 = -195.2\,kJ$

$\Delta H°\,H_2O(g) = 4.47\,g\,H_2O \times \dfrac{1\,mol\,H_2O}{18.02\,g\,H_2O} \times \dfrac{-241.82\,kJ}{mol\,H_2O} = 59.985 = -60.0\,kJ$

ΔH° sample $= -195.185$ kJ $- 59.985$ kJ $- (-311$ kJ$) = 55.83 = 56$ kJ

$$\frac{55.83 \text{ kJ}}{6.457 \text{ g sample}} \times \frac{13.02 \text{ g}}{\text{CH unit}} = 112.6 = 1.1 \times 10^2 \text{ kJ/CH unit}$$

(d)   The hydrocarbons in Appendix C with empirical formula CH are C_2H_2 and C_6H_6.

substance	ΔH_f°/mol	ΔH_f°/CH unit
$C_2H_2(g)$	226.7 kJ	113.4 kJ
$C_6H_6(g)$	82.9 kJ	13.8 kJ
$C_6H_6(l)$	49.0 kJ	8.17 kJ
sample		1.1×10^2 kJ

The calculated value of ΔH_f°/ CH unit for the sample is a good match with acetylene, $C_2H_2(g)$.

5.119   (a) $CH_4(g) \rightarrow C(g) + 4H(g)$ (i) reaction given

$CH_4(g) \rightarrow C(s) + 2H_2(g)$ (ii) reverse of formation

The differences are: the state of C in the products; the chemical form, atoms, or diatomic molecules, of H in the products.

(b)   i. $\Delta H^\circ = \Delta H_f^\circ \, C(g) + 4\Delta H_f^\circ \, H(g) - \Delta H_f^\circ \, CH_4(g)$

$= 718.4$ kJ $+ 4(217.94)$ kJ $- (-74.8)$ kJ $= 1665.0$ kJ

ii. $\Delta H^\circ = \Delta H_f^\circ \, CH_4 = -(-74.8)$ kJ $= 74.8$ kJ

The rather large difference in ΔH° values is due to the enthalpy difference between isolated gaseous C atoms and the orderly, bonded array of C atoms in graphite, C(s), as well as the enthalpy difference between isolated H atoms and H_2 molecules. In other words, it is due to the difference in the enthalpy stored in chemical bonds in C(s) and $H_2(g)$ versus the corresponding isolated atoms.

(c) $CH_4(g) + 4F_2(g) \rightarrow CF_4(g) + 4HF(g)$ $\Delta H^\circ = -1679.5$ kJ

The ΔH° value for this reaction was calculated in Solution 5.86.

$$3.45 \text{ g } CH_4 \times \frac{1 \text{ mol } CH_4}{16.04 \text{ g } CH_4} \times 0.21509 = 0.215 \text{ mol } CH_4$$

$$1.22 \text{ g } F_2 \times \frac{1 \text{ mol } F_2}{38.00 \text{ g } F_2} = 0.03211 = 0.0321 \text{ mol } F_2$$

There are fewer mol F_2 than CH_4, but 4 mol F_2 are required for every 1 mol of CH_4 reacted, so clearly F_2 is the limiting reactant.

$$0.03211 \text{ mol } F_2 \times \frac{-1679.5 \text{ kJ}}{4 \text{ mol } F_2} = -13.48 = -13.5 \text{ kJ heat evolved}$$

6 Electronic Structure of Atoms

Visualizing Concepts

6.1   (a)   Speed is distance traveled per unit time. Measure the distance between the center point and a second reference point, possibly the edge of the container. Using a stop watch, measure the elapsed time between when a wave forms at the center and when it reaches the second reference point. Find the ratio of distance to time.

       (b)   Measure the distance between two wave crests (or troughs or any analogous points on two adjacent waves). Better yet, measure the distance between two crests (or analogous points) that are several waves apart and divide by the number of waves that separate them.

       (c)   Since speed is distance/time, and wavelength is distance, we can calculate frequency by dividing speed by wavelength, $\nu = c/\lambda$.

       (d)   We can measure frequency of the wave by dropping an object such as a cork in the water and counting the number of times per second it moves through a complete cycle of motion.

6.3   (a)   The glowing stove burner is an example of black body radiation, the observational basis for Planck's quantum theory. The wavelengths emitted are related to temperature, with cooler temperatures emitting longer wavelengths and hotter temperatures emitting shorter wavelengths. At the hottest setting, the burner emits orange visible light. At the cooler low setting, the burner emits longer wavelengths out of the visible region, and the burner appears black.

       (b)   If the burner had a super high setting, the emitted wavelengths would be shorter than those of orange light and the glow color would be more blue. (See Figure 6.4 for color variation with wavelength.)

6.4   (a)   Increase. The rainbow has shorter wavelength blue light on the inside and longer wavelength red light on the outside. (See Figure 6.4.)

       (b)   Decrease. Wavelength and frequency are inversely related. Wavelength increases so frequency decreases going from the inside to the outside of the rainbow.

       (c)   The light from the hydrogen discharge tube is not a continuous spectrum, so not all visible wavelengths will be in our "hydrogen discharge rainbow." Starting with the shortest wavelengths, it will be violet followed by blue-violet and blue-green on the inside. Then there will be a gap, and finally a red band. (See the H spectrum in Figure 6.13.)

6.6   (a) $\psi^2(x)$ will be positive or zero at all values of x, and have two maxima with larger magnitudes than the maximum in $\psi(x)$.

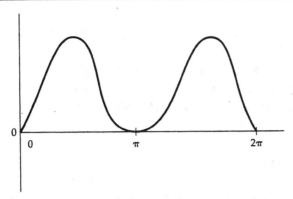

(b)   The greatest probability of finding the electron is at the two maxima in $\psi^2(x)$ at $x = \pi/2$ and $3\pi/2$.

(c)   There is zero probability of finding the electron at $x = \pi$. This value is called a node.

6.7   (a)   1

(b)   p (dumbbell shape, node at the nucleus)

(c)   The lobes in the contour representation would extend farther along the y axis. A larger principle quantum number (4p vs. 3p) implies a greater average distance from the nucleus for electrons occupying the orbital.

The Wave Nature of Light

6.10   (a)   Wavelength (λ) and frequency (ν) are inversely proportional; the proportionality constant is the speed of light (c). $\nu = c/\lambda$.

(b)   Light in the 210–230 nm range is in the ultraviolet region of the spectrum. These wavelengths are slightly shorter than the 400 nm short-wavelength boundary of the visible region.

6.12   (a)   False. Electromagnetic radiation passes through water. The fact that you can see objects through a glass of water should make this clear.

(b)   True.

(c)   False. Infrared light has lower frequencies than visible light.

(d)   False. A foghorn blast is a form of sound waves, which are not accompanied by oscillating electric and magnetic fields.

6.14   Wavelength of (a) gamma rays $<$ (d) yellow (visible) light $<$ (e) red (visible) light $<$ (b) 93.1 MHz FM (radio) waves $<$ (c) 680 kHz or 0.680 MHz AM (radio) waves

6.16   (a) $\nu = c/\lambda$; $\dfrac{2.998 \times 10^8 \text{ m}}{\text{s}} \times \dfrac{1}{10.0 \text{ Å}} \times \dfrac{1 \text{ Å}}{1 \times 10^{-10} \text{ m}} = 3.00 \times 10^{17} \text{ s}^{-1}$

(b) $\lambda = c/\nu$; $\dfrac{2.998 \times 10^8 \text{ m}}{\text{s}} \times \dfrac{1 \text{ s}}{7.6 \times 10^{10}} = 3.94 \times 10^{-3} \text{ m}$

(c)   The 1×10^{-9} m radiation in (a) is X-rays and can be observed by an X-ray detector. Radiation (b) is microwave.

(d) $25.5 \text{ fs} \times \dfrac{1 \times 10^{-15} \text{ s}}{1 \text{ fs}} \times \dfrac{2.998 \times 10^8 \text{ m}}{\text{s}} = 7.64 \times 10^{-6} \text{ m} \ (7.64 \ \mu\text{m})$

6.18   According to Figure 6.4, ultraviolet radiation has both higher frequency and shorter wavelength than infrared radiation. Looking forward to section 6.2, the energy of a photon is directly proportional to frequency (E = hv), so ultraviolet radiation yields more energy from a photovoltaic device.

Quantized Energy and Photons

6.20   Planck's original hypothesis was that energy could only be gained or lost in discreet amounts (quanta) with a certain minimum size. The size of the minimum energy change is related to the frequency of the radiation absorbed or emitted, $\Delta E = hv$, and energy changes occur only in multiples of hv.

Einstein postulated that light itself is quantized, that the minimum energy of a photon (a quantum of light) is directly proportional to its frequency, E = hv. If a photon that strikes a metal surface has less than the threshold energy, no electron is emitted from the surface. If the photon has energy equal to or greater than the threshold energy, an electron is emitted and any excess energy becomes the kinetic energy of the electron.

6.22   (a) $v = c/\lambda = \dfrac{2.998 \times 10^8 \text{ m}}{\text{s}} \times \dfrac{1}{589 \text{ nm}} \times \dfrac{1 \text{ nm}}{1 \times 10^{-9} \text{ m}} = 5.0900 \times 10^{14}$

$= 5.09 \times 10^{14} \text{ s}^{-1}$

(b) $E = hv = 6.626 \times 10^{-34} \text{ J-s} \times 5.0900 \times 10^{14} \text{ s}^{-1} \times \dfrac{6.022 \times 10^{23} \text{ photons}}{\text{mol}}$

$\times \ 0.1 \text{ mol} = 2.03 \times 10^4 \text{ J} = 20.3 \text{ kJ}$

(c) $\Delta E = hv = \dfrac{hc}{\lambda} = \dfrac{6.626 \times 10^{-34} \text{ J-s} \times 2.998 \times 10^8 \text{ m/s}}{589 \text{ nm}} \times \dfrac{1 \text{ nm}}{1 \times 10^{-9} \text{ m}}$

$= 3.37 \times 10^{-19} \text{ J}$

(d)   The 589 nm light emission is characteristic of Na^+. If the pickle is soaked in a different salt long enough to remove all Na^+, the 589 nm light would not be observed. Emission at a different wavelength, characteristic of the new salt, would be observed.

6.24 $E = hv$

$AM : 6.626 \times 10^{-34} \text{ J-s} \times \dfrac{1010 \times 10^3}{1 \text{ s}} = 6.69 \times 10^{-28} \text{ J}$

$FM : 6.626 \times 10^{-34} \text{ J-s} \times \dfrac{98.3 \times 10^6}{1 \text{ s}} = 6.51 \times 10^{-26} \text{ J}$

The FM photon has about 100 times more energy than the AM photon.

6.26 $\dfrac{941 \times 10^3 \text{ J}}{\text{mol N}_2} \times \dfrac{1 \text{ mol}}{6.022 \times 10^{23} \text{ photons}} = 1.563 \times 10^{-18} = 1.56 \times 10^{-18} \text{ J/photon}$

$$\lambda = hc/E = \frac{6.626 \times 10^{-34} \text{ J} \cdot \text{s}}{1.563 \times 10^{-18} \text{ J}} \times \frac{2.998 \times 10^{8} \text{ m}}{1 \text{ s}} = 1.27 \times 10^{-7} \text{ m} = 127 \text{ nm}$$

According to Figure 6.4, this is ultraviolet radiation.

6.28　(a)　The radiation is microwave.

(b)　$E_{photon} = hc/\lambda = \dfrac{6.626 \times 10^{-34} \text{ J} \cdot \text{s}}{3.55 \times 10^{-3} \text{ m}} \times \dfrac{2.998 \times 10^{8} \text{ m}}{1 \text{ s}} = 5.5957 \times 10^{-23}$

$$= 5.60 \times 10^{-23} \text{ J/photon}$$

$$\frac{5.5957 \times 10^{-23} \text{ J}}{1 \text{ photon}} \times \frac{3.2 \times 10^{8} \text{ photons}}{1 \text{ s}} \times \frac{60 \text{ s}}{1 \text{ min}} \times \frac{60 \text{ min}}{1 \text{ hr}} = 6.4463 \times 10^{-11}$$

$$= 6.4 \times 10^{-11} \text{ J/hr}$$

6.30　(a)　$v = E/h = \dfrac{4.41 \times 10^{-19} \text{ J}}{6.626 \times 10^{-34} \text{ J} \cdot \text{s}} = 6.6556 \times 10^{14} = 6.66 \times 10^{14} \text{ s}^{-1}$

(b)　$\lambda = hc/E = \dfrac{6.626 \times 10^{-34} \text{ J} \cdot \text{s}}{4.41 \times 10^{-19} \text{ J}} \times \dfrac{2.998 \times 10^{8} \text{ m}}{\text{s}} = 4.50 \times 10^{-7} \text{ m} = 450 \text{ nm}$

(c)　$E_{439} = hc/\lambda = \dfrac{6.626 \times 10^{-34} \text{ J} \cdot \text{s}}{439 \times 10^{-9} \text{ m}} \times \dfrac{2.998 \times 10^{8} \text{ m}}{\text{s}} = 4.525 \times 10^{-19} = 4.53 \times 10^{-19} \text{ J}$

$$E_K = E_{439} - E_{min} = 4.525 \times 10^{-19} \text{ J} - 4.41 \times 10^{-19} \text{ J} = 0.115 \times 10^{-19} = 1.1 \times 10^{-20} \text{ J}$$

(d)　One electron is emitted per photon. Calculate the number of 439 nm photons in 1.00 µJ. The excess energy in each photon will become the kinetic energy of the electron; it cannot be "pooled" to emit additional electrons.

$$1.00 \text{ µJ} \times \frac{1 \times 10^{-6} \text{ J}}{\text{µJ}} \times \frac{1 \text{ photon}}{4.525 \times 10^{-19} \text{ J}} \times \frac{1 \text{ e}^{-}}{1 \text{ photon}} = 2.21 \times 10^{12} \text{ electrons}$$

Bohr's Model; Matter Waves

6.32　(a)　According to Bohr theory, when hydrogen emits radiant energy, electrons are moving from a higher allowed energy state to a lower one. Since only certain energy states are allowed, only certain energy changes can occur. These allowed energy changes correspond ($\lambda = hc/\Delta E$) to the wavelengths of the lines in the emission spectrum of hydrogen.

(b)　When a hydrogen atom changes from the ground state to an excited state, the single electron moves further away from the nucleus, so the atom "expands".

6.34　(a)　Absorbed.　　(b)　Emitted.　　(c)　Absorbed.

6.36　(a)　$v = E/h = \dfrac{2.044 \times 10^{-18} \text{ J}}{6.626 \times 10^{-34} \text{ J} \cdot \text{s}} = 3.084 \times 10^{15} = 3.08 \times 10^{15} \text{ s}^{-1}$

$$\lambda = c/v = \frac{2.998 \times 10^{8} \text{ m}}{1 \text{ s}} \times \frac{1 \text{ s}}{3.084 \times 10^{15}} = 9.72 \times 10^{-8} \text{ m}$$

Since the sign of ΔE is negative, radiation is emitted.

(b) $\Delta E = -2.18 \times 10^{-18} \, J(1/4 - 1/25) = -4.578 \times 10^{-19} = -4.58 \times 10^{-19} \, J$

$$\nu = \frac{4.578 \times 10^{-19} \, J}{6.626 \times 10^{-34} \, J\text{-}s} = 6.909 \times 10^{14} = 6.91 \times 10^{14} \, s^{-1}; \; \lambda = \frac{2.998 \times 10^8 \, m/s}{6.909 \times 10^{14}/s}$$

$\lambda = 4.34 \times 10^{-7} \, m$. Visible radiation is emitted.

(c) $\Delta E = -2.18 \times 10^{-18} \, J \, (1/36 - 1/9) = 1.817 \times 10^{-19} = 1.82 \times 10^{-19} \, J$

$$\nu = \frac{1.817 \times 10^{-19} \, J}{6.626 \times 10^{-34} \, J\text{-}s} = 2.742 \times 10^{14} = 2.74 \times 10^{14} \, s^{-1}; \; \lambda = \frac{2.998 \times 10^8 \, m/s}{2.742 \times 10^{14}/s}$$

$\lambda = 1.09 \times 10^{-6} \, m$. Radiation is absorbed.

6.38   (a)   Transitions with $n_f = 1$ have larger ΔE values and shorter wavelengths than those with $n_f = 2$. These transitions will lie in the ultraviolet region.

(b) $n_i = 2, n_f = 1$; $\lambda = hc/E = \dfrac{6.626 \times 10^{-34} \, J\text{-}s \times 2.998 \times 10^8 \, m/s}{-2.18 \times 10^{-18} \, J \, (1/1 - 1/4)} = 1.21 \times 10^{-7} \, m$

$n_i = 3, n_f = 1$; $\lambda = hc/E = \dfrac{6.626 \times 10^{-34} \, J\text{-}s \times 2.998 \times 10^8 \, m/s}{-2.18 \times 10^{-18} \, J \, (1/1 - 1/9)} = 1.03 \times 10^{-7} \, m$

$n_i = 4, n_f = 1$; $\lambda = hc/E = \dfrac{6.626 \times 10^{-34} \, J\text{-}s \times 2.998 \times 10^8 \, m/s}{-2.18 \times 10^{-18} \, J \, (1/1 - 1/16)} = 0.972 \times 10^{-7} \, m$

6.40   (a) $2626 \, nm \times \dfrac{1 \times 10^{-9} \, m}{1 \, nm} = 2.626 \times 10^{-6} \, m$;   this line is in the infrared.

(b)   Absorption lines with $n_i = 1$ are in the ultraviolet and with $n_i = 2$ are in the visible. Thus, $n_i \geq 3$, but we do not know the exact value of n_i. Calculate the longest wavelength with $n_i = 3$ ($n_f = 4$). If this is less than 2626 nm, $n_i > 3$.

$$\lambda = hc/E = \frac{6.626 \times 10^{-34} \, J\text{-}s \times 2.998 \times 10^8 \, m/s}{-2.18 \times 10^{-18} \, J \, (1/16 - 1/9)} = 1.875 \times 10^{-6} \, m$$

This wavelength is shorter than 2.626×10^{-6} m, so $n_i > 3$; try $n_i = 4$ and solve for n_f as in Solution 6.39.

$$n_f = \left(\frac{1}{n_i^2} - \frac{hc}{\lambda(2.18 \times 10^{-18} \, J)} \right)^{-1/2} = \left(1/16 - \frac{6.626 \times 10^{-34} \, J\text{-}s \times 2.998 \times 10^8 \, m/s}{2.626 \times 10^{-6} \, m \times 2.18 \times 10^{-18} \, J} \right)^{-1/2} = 6$$

$n_f = 6, n_i = 4$

6.42 $\lambda = h/mv$; change mass to kg and velocity to m/s

mass of muon $= 206.8 \times 9.1094 \times 10^{-28} \, g \times \dfrac{1 \, kg}{1000 \, g} = 1.8838 \times 10^{-28} = 1.88 \times 10^{-28} \, kg$

$$\lambda = \frac{6.626 \times 10^{-34} \, kg\text{-}m^2\text{-}s}{1 \, s^2} \times \frac{1}{1.8838 \times 10^{-28} \, kg} \times \frac{1 \, s}{8.85 \times 10^3 \, m/s} = 3.97 \times 10^{-10} \, m$$

$$= 3.97 \, \text{Å}$$

6.44 $m_e = 9.1094 \times 10^{-31}$ kg (back inside cover of text)

$$\lambda = \frac{6.626 \times 10^{-34} \text{ kg-m}^2\text{-s}}{1 \text{ s}^2} \times \frac{1}{9.1094 \times 10^{-31} \text{ kg}} \times \frac{1 \text{ s}}{9.38 \times 10^6 \text{ m}} = 7.75 \times 10^{-11} \text{ m}$$

$$7.75 \times 10^{-11} \text{ m} \times \frac{1 \text{ Å}}{1 \times 10^{-10} \text{ m}} = 0.775 \text{ Å}$$

Since atomic radii and interatomic distances are on the order of 1–5 Å (Section 2.3), the wavelength of this electron is comparable to the size of atoms.

6.46 $\Delta x \geq = h/4\pi m \Delta v$; use masses in kg, Δv in m/s.

(a) $$\frac{6.626 \times 10^{-34} \text{ J-s}}{4\pi(9.109 \times 10^{-31} \text{ kg})(0.01 \times 10^5 \text{ m/s})} = 6 \times 10^{-8} \text{ m}$$

(b) $$\frac{6.626 \times 10^{-34} \text{ J-s}}{4\pi(1.675 \times 10^{-27} \text{ kg})(0.01 \times 10^5 \text{ m/s})} = 3 \times 10^{-11} \text{ m}$$

(c)   For particles moving with the same uncertainty in velocity, the more massive neutron has a much smaller uncertainty in position than the lighter electron. In our model of the atom, we know where the massive particles in the nucleus are located, but we cannot know the location of the electrons with any certainty, if we know their speed.

Quantum Mechanics and Atomic Orbitals

6.48   (a)   The Bohr model states with 100% certainty that the electron in hydrogen can be found 0.53 Å from the nucleus. The quantum mechanical model, taking the wave nature of the electron and the uncertainty principle into account, is a statistical model that states the probability of finding the electron in certain regions around the nucleus. While 0.53 Å might be the radius with highest probability, that probability would always be less than 100%.

(b)   The equations of classical physics predict the instantaneous position, direction of motion, and speed of a macroscopic particle; they do not take quantum theory or the wave nature of matter into account. For macroscopic particles, these are not significant, but for microscopic particles like electrons, they are crucial. Schrödinger's equation takes these important theories into account to produce a statistical model of electron location given a specific energy.

(c)   The square of the wave function has the physical significance of an amplitude, or probability. The quantity ψ^2 at a given point in space is the probability of locating the electron within a small volume element around that point at any given instant. The total probability, that is, the sum of ψ^2 over all the space around the nucleus, must equal 1.

6.50   (a)   For $n = 3$, there are three l values (2, 1, 0) and nine m_l values ($l = 2$; $m_l = -2, -1, 0, 1, 2$; $l = 1$, $m_l = -1, 0, 1$; $l = 0$, $m_l = 0$).

(b)   For $n = 5$, there are five l values (4, 3, 2, 1, 0) and twenty-five m_l values

($l = 4$, $m_l = -4$ to $+4$; $l = 3$, $m_l = -3$ to $+3$; $l = 2$, $m_l = -2$ to $+2$; $l = 1$, $m_l = -1$ to $+1$; $l = 0$, $= 0$).

In general, for each principal quantum number n there are n l-values and n^2 m_l-values. For each shell, there are n kinds of orbitals and n^2 total orbitals.

6.52   (a)   2, 1, 1; 2, 1, 0; 2, 1 –1   (b) 5, 2, 2; 5, 2, 1; 5, 2, 0; 5, 2, –1; 5, 2, –2

6.54

n	l	m_l	orbital
2	1	–1	2p (example)
1	0	0	1s
3	–3	2	not allowed ($l < n$ and + only)
3	2	–2	3d
2	0	–1	not allowed ($m_l = -l$ to $+l$)
0	0	0	not allowed ($n \neq 0$)
4	2	1	4d
5	3	0	5f

6.56

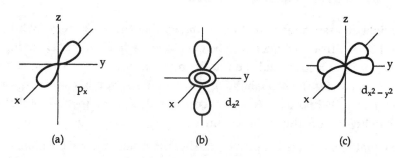

(a)   (b)   (c)

6.58   (a)   In an s orbital, there are $(n - 1)$ nodes.

(b)   The $2p_x$ orbital has one node (the yz plane passing through the nucleus of the atom). The 3s orbital has two nodes.

(c)   Probability density, $\psi^2(r)$, is the probability of finding an electron at a single point, r. The radial probability function, P(r), is the probability of finding an electron at any point that is distance r from the nucleus. Figure 6.19 contains plots of P(r) vs. r for 1s, 2s, and 3s orbitals. The most obvious features of these plots are the radii of maximum probability for the three orbitals, and the number and location of nodes for the three orbitals.

By comparing plots for the three orbitals, we see that as n increases, the number of nodes increases and the radius of maximum probability (orbital size) increases.

(d)   2s = 2p < 3s < 4d < 5s. In the hydrogen atom, orbitals with the same n value are degenerate and energy increases with increasing n value.

Many-Electron Atoms and Electron Configurations

6.60   (a)   The electron with the greater average distance from the nucleus feels a smaller attraction for the nucleus and is higher in energy. Thus the 3p is higher in energy than 3s.

        (b)   Because it has a larger n value, a 3s electron has a greater average distance from the chlorine nucleus than a 2p electron. The 3s electron experiences a smaller attraction for the nucleus and requires less energy to remove from the chlorine atom.

6.62   (a)   The Pauli exclusion principle states that no two electrons can have the same four quantum numbers.

        (b)   An alternate statement of the Pauli exclusion principle is that a single orbital can hold a maximum of two electrons. Thus, the Pauli principle limits the maximum number of electrons in a main shell and its subshells, which determines when a new row of the periodic table begins.

6.64   (a) 4   (b) 14   (c) 2   (d) 2

6.66

Element	(a) C	(b) P	(c) Ne
Electron Configuration	$[He]2s^22p^2$	$[Ne]3s^23p^3$	$[He]2s^22p^6$
Core electrons	2	10	2
Valence electrons	4	5	8
Unpaired electrons	2	3	0

[The concept of "valence electrons" for noble gas elements is problematic, since they are mostly unreactive. We could list the core for neon as [Ne], with no valence or unpaired electrons.]

6.68   (a)   Ga: $[Ar]4s^23d^{10}4p^1$, 1 unpaired electron

        (b)   Ca: $[Ar]4s^2$, 0 unpaired electrons

        (c)   V: $[Ar]4s^23d^3$, 3 unpaired electrons

        (d)   I: $[Kr]5s^24d^{10}5p^5$, 1 unpaired electron

        (e)   Y: $[Kr]5s^24d^1$, 1 unpaired electron

        (f)   Pt: $[Xe]6s^14f^{14}5d^9$, 2 unpaired electrons

        (g)   Lu: $[Xe]6s^24f^{14}5d^1$, 1 unpaired electron

6.70   *Plan.* Write the electron configuration of the neutral transition metal atom, then remove electrons, ns first, then $(n-1)d$, to achieve the cationic charge. *Solve.*

        (a)   Zn: $[Ar]4s^23^{10}$; Zn^{2+} (remove two 4s electrons): $[Ar]3d^{10}$

        (b)   Pt: $[Xe]6s^14f^{14}5d^9$; Pt^{2+} (remove 6s and one 5d electron): $[Xe]4f^{14}5d^8$

        (c)   Cr: $[Ar]4s^13d^5$; Cr^{3+} (remove 4s and two 3d electrons): $[Ar]3d^3$

        (d)   Ti: $[Ar]4s^23d^2$; Ti^{4+} (remove all four valence electrons): $[Ar]$

6.72 (a) 7A (halogens)   (b) 4B   (c) 3A (row 4 and below)

(d) the f-block elements Sm and Pu

6.74 Count the total number of electrons to assign the element.

(a) N: [He]$2s^2 2p^3$ (b) Se: [Ar]$4s^2 3d^{10} 4p^4$ (c) Rh: [Kr]$5s^2 4d^7$

Additional Exercises

6.76 (a) Elements that emit in the visible: Ba (dark blue), Ca (dark blue), K (dark blue), Na (yellow/orange). (The other wavelengths are in the ultraviolet.)

(b) Au: shortest wavelength, highest energy

Na: longest wavelength, lowest energy

(c) $\lambda = c/\nu = \dfrac{2.998 \times 10^8 \text{ m/s}}{6.59 \times 10^{14}/\text{s}} \times \dfrac{1 \text{ nm}}{1 \times 10^{-9} \text{ m}} = 455 \text{ nm}, \quad \text{Ba}$

6.78 (a) $\nu = c/\lambda = \dfrac{2.998 \times 10^8 \text{ m/s}}{320 \text{ nm}} \times \dfrac{1 \text{ nm}}{1 \times 10^{-9} \text{ m}} = 9.37 \times 10^{14} \text{ s}^{-1}$

(b) $E = hc/\lambda = \dfrac{6.626 \times 10^{-34} \text{ J-s} \times 2.998 \times 10^8 \text{ m/s}}{3.20 \times 10^{-7} \text{ m}} \times \dfrac{1 \text{ kJ}}{1000 \text{ J}} \times \dfrac{6.022 \times 10^{23} \text{ photons}}{\text{mole}}$

$= 374 \text{ kJ/mol}$

(c) UV-B photons have shorter wavelength and higher energy.

(d) Yes. The higher energy UV-B photons would be more likely to cause sunburn.

6.79 $E = hc/\lambda \to$ J/photon; total energy = power × time; photons = total energy / J / photon

$E = \dfrac{6.626 \times 10^{-34} \text{ J-s} \times 2.998 \times 10^8 \text{ m/s}}{780 \times 10^{-9} \text{ m}} = 2.5468 \times 10^{-19} = 2.55 \times 10^{-19}$ J/photon

$0.10 \text{ mW} = \dfrac{0.10 \times 10^{-3} \text{ J}}{1 \text{ s}} \times 69 \text{ min} \times \dfrac{60 \text{ s}}{1 \text{ min}} = 0.4140 = 0.41 \text{ J}$

$0.4140 \text{ J} \times \dfrac{1 \text{ photon}}{2.5468 \times 10^{-19} \text{ J}} = 1.626 \times 10^{18} = 1.6 \times 10^{18}$ photons

6.81 $\dfrac{2.6 \times 10^{-12} \text{ C}}{1 \text{ s}} \times \dfrac{1 e^-}{1.602 \times 10^{-19} \text{ C}} \times \dfrac{1 \text{ photon}}{1 e^-} = 1.623 \times 10^7 = 1.6 \times 10^7$ photons/s

$\dfrac{E}{\text{photon}} = hc/\lambda = \dfrac{6.626 \times 10^{-34} \text{ J-s}}{630 \text{ nm}} \times \dfrac{2.998 \times 10^8 \text{ m}}{1 \text{ s}} \times \dfrac{1 \text{ nm}}{1 \times 10^{-9} \text{ m}} \times \dfrac{1.623 \times 10^7 \text{ photon}}{\text{s}}$

$= 5.1 \times 10^{-12} \text{ J/s}$

6.82   (a) $\dfrac{2.00 \times 10^5 \text{ J}}{\text{mol}} \times \dfrac{1 \text{ mol photons}}{6.022 \times 10^{23} \text{ photons}} = 3.321 \times 10^{-19} = 3.32 \times 10^{-19} \text{ J/photon}$

        (b) $\lambda = \dfrac{hc}{E} = \dfrac{6.626 \times 10^{-34} \text{ J-s} \times 2.998 \times 10^8 \text{ m/s}}{3.321 \times 10^{-19} \text{ J}} = 5.98 \times 10^{-7} \text{ m}$

        (c) 5.98×10^{-7} m = 598 nm is well within the visible portion of the electromagnetic spectrum and corresponds to yellow or yellow-orange light. Red light, with wavelengths near or greater than 700 nm, does not have sufficient energy to initiate electron transfer and darken the film.

6.83   (a) $v = c/\lambda;$ $\dfrac{2.998 \times 10^8 \text{ m}}{\text{s}} \times \dfrac{1}{680 \text{ nm}} \times \dfrac{1 \text{ nm}}{1 \times 10^{-9} \text{ m}} = 4.4088 \times 10^{14} = 4.41 \times 10^{14} \text{ s}^{-1}$

        (b)   Calculate J/photon using $E = hc/\lambda$; change to kJ/mol.

        $E_{photon} = \dfrac{6.626 \times 10^{-34} \text{ J-s}}{680 \times 10^{-9} \text{ m}} \times \dfrac{2.998 \times 10^8 \text{ m}}{\text{s}} = 2.9213 \times 10^{-19} = 2.92 \times 10^{-19} \text{ J/photor}$

        $\dfrac{2.9213 \times 10^{-19} \text{ J}}{\text{photon}} \times \dfrac{6.022 \times 10^{23} \text{ photons}}{\text{mol}} \times \dfrac{1 \text{ kJ}}{1000 \text{ J}} = 175.92 = 176 \text{ kJ/mol}$

        (c)   Nothing. The incoming (incident) radiation does not transfer sufficient energy to an electron to overcome the attractive forces holding the electron in the metal.

        (d)   For frequencies greater than v_o, any "extra" energy not needed to remove the electron from the metal becomes the kinetic energy of the ejected electron. The kinetic energy of the electron is directly proportional to this extra energy.

        (e)   Let E_{total} be the total energy of an incident photon, E_{min} be the minimum energy required to eject an electron, and E_k be the "extra" energy that becomes the kinetic energy of the ejected electron.

        $E_{total} = E_{min} + E_k$, $E_k = E_{total} - E_{min} = hv - hv_o$, $E_k = h(v - v_o)$. The slope of the line is the value of h, Planck's constant.

6.85   (a)   Gaseous atoms of various elements in the sun's atmosphere typically have ground state electron configurations. When these atoms are exposed to radiation from the sun, the electrons change from the ground state to one of several allowed excited states. Atoms absorb the wavelengths of light which correspond to these allowed energy changes. All other wavelengths of solar radiation pass through the atmosphere unchanged. Thus, the dark lines are the wavelengths that correspond to allowed energy changes in atoms of the solar atmosphere. The continuous background is all other wavelengths of solar radiation.

        (b)   The scientist should record the absorption spectrum of pure neon or other elements of interest. The black lines should appear at the same wavelengths regardless of the source of neon.

6.86   (a) He^+ is hydrogen-like because it is a one-electron particle. A He atom has two electrons. The Bohr model is based on the interaction of a single electron with the nucleus, but does not accurately account for additional interactions when two or more electrons are present.

(b)   Divide each energy by the smallest value to find the integer relationship.

H: $2.18 \times 10^{-18} / 2.18 \times 10^{-18} = 1$; $Z = 1$

He$^+$: $8.72 \times 10^{-18} / 2.18 \times 10^{-18} = 4$; $Z = 2$

Li^{2+}: $1.96 \times 10^{-17} / 2.18 \times 10^{-18} = 9$; $Z = 3$

The ground-state energies are in the ratio of 1:4:9, which is also the ratio Z^2, the square of the nuclear charge for each particle.

The ground state energy for hydrogen-like particles is:

$E = R_H Z^2$. (By definition, n = 1 for the ground state of a one-electron particle.)

(c)   Z = 6 for C. $E = -2.18 \times 10^{-18}$ J $(6)^2 = -7.85 \times 10^{-17}$ J

6.88   *Plan.* Change keV to J/electron. Calculate v from kinetic energy. $\lambda = h/mv$.   *Solve.*

$$18.6 \text{ keV} \times \frac{1000 \text{ eV}}{\text{keV}} \times \frac{96.485 \text{ kJ}}{1 \text{ eV-mol}} \times \frac{1000 \text{ J}}{1 \text{ kJ}} \times \frac{1 \text{ mol}}{6.022 \times 10^{23} \text{ electrons}}$$

$$= 2.980 \times 10^{-15} = 2.98 \times 10^{-15} \text{ J/electron}$$

$$E_k = mv^2/2; \, v^2 = 2E_k/m; \, v = \sqrt{2E_k/m}$$

$$v = \left(\frac{2 \times 2.980 \times 10^{-15} \text{ kg-m}^2/\text{s}^2}{9.1094 \times 10^{-31} \text{ kg}} \right)^{1/2} = 8.089 \times 10^7 = 8.09 \times 10^7 \text{ m/s}$$

$$\lambda = h/mv = \frac{6.626 \times 10^{-34} \text{ J-s}}{9.1094 \times 10^{-31} \text{ kg} \times 8.089 \times 10^7 \text{ m/s}} \times \frac{1 \text{ kg-m}^2/\text{s}^2}{1 \text{ J}} = 8.99 \times 10^{-12} \text{ m} = 8.99 \text{ pm}$$

6.89   Heisenberg postulated that the dual nature of matter places a limitation on how precisely we can know both the position and momentum of an object. This limitation is significant at the subatomic particle level. The *Star Trek* transporter (presumably) dissembles humans into their protons, neutrons and electrons, moves the particles at high speed (possibly the speed of light) to a new location, and reassembles the particles into the human. Heisenberg's uncertainty principle indicates that if we know the momentum (*mv*) of the moving particles, we can't precisely know their position (*x*). If a few of the subatomic particles don't arrive in exactly the correct location, the human would not be reassembled in their originall form. So, the "Heisenberg compensator" is necessary to make sure that the transported human arrives at the new location intact.

6.91   (a)   Probability density, $[\psi(r)]^2$, is the probability of finding an electron at a single point at distance r from the nucleus. The radial probability function, $4\pi r^2$, is the probability of finding an electron at any point on the sphere defined by radius r. $P(r) = 4\pi r^2 [\psi(r)]^2$ (Figure 6.21).

(b)   The term $4\pi r^2$ explains the differences in plots of the two functions. Plots of the probability density, $[\psi(r)^2]$ for s orbitals shown in Figure 6.23 each have their maximum value at r = 0, with (n – 1) smaller maxima at greater values of r. The plots of radial probability, P(r), for the same s orbitals shown in Figure 6.19 have values of zero at r = 0 and the size of the maxima increases. P(r) is the product of $[\psi(r)]^2$ and $4\pi r^2$. At r = 0, the value of $[\psi(r)]^2$ is finite and large, but the value of

$4\pi r^2$ is zero, so the value of P(r) is zero. As r increases, the values of $[\psi(r)]^2$ vary as shown in Figure 6.23, but the values of $4\pi r^2$ increase continuously, leading to the increasing size of P(r) maxima as r increases.

(c)

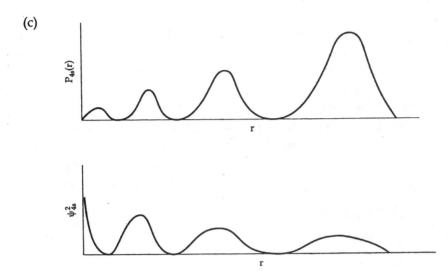

6.92   What the noble gas elements have in common are completed ns and np subshells. Since the Pauli principle limits the number of electrons per orbital to two, this leads to the first three magic numbers, $2(1s^2)$, $10(1s^2 2s^2 2p^6)$, and $18(1s^2 2s^2 2p^6 3s^2 3p^6)$. In the fourth row, (n – 1) d orbitals begin to fill as their energy falls below that of the np orbitals. This leads to the next two magic numbers, $36(1s^2 2s^2 2p^6 3s^2 3p^6 4s^2 3d^{10} 4p^6)$ and $54(1s^2 2s^2 2p^6 3s^2 3p^6 4s^2 3d^{10} 4p^6 5s^2 4d^{10} 5p^6)$. In the sixth row, the energy of the 4f orbitals falls below that of the (n – 1)d and np subshells, and it fills. This explains the final magic number, $86(1s^2 2s^2 2p^6 3s^2 3p^6 4s^2 3d^{10} 4p^6 5s^2 4d^{10} 5p^6 6s^2 4f^{14} 5d^{10} 6p^6)$.

6.93   (a)   The p_z orbital has a nodal plane where z = 0. This is the xy plane.

(b)   The d_{xy} orbital has four lobes and two nodal planes, the two planes where x = 0 and y = 0. These are the yz and xz planes.

(c)   The $d_{x^2-y^2}$ has four lobes and two nodal planes, the planes where $x^2 - y^2 = 0$. These are the planes that bisect the x and y axes and contain the z axis.

6.94   (a)   In the absence of a magnetic field, electrons with opposite m_s values have the same energy. Because electrons with opposite spins will have oppositely oriented magnetic fields, only the interaction of the magnetic fields of the electrons with an external magnetic field will cause the energies of the electrons to be different and observable.

(b)   According to Figure 6.28, the particle with its magnetic field parallel to the external field will have the lower energy. The left electron has its magnetic field oriented parallel to the described magnetic orientation, so it will be lower in energy.

(c)   Microwave photons used to excite unpaired electrons in the ESR experiment have higher energy than radio wave photons used to excite nuclei in NMR.

6.95   (a)   This is the frequency of radiowaves that excite the nuclei from one spin state to the other.

(b) $\Delta E = h\nu = 6.626 \times 10^{-34} \text{ J-s} \times \dfrac{450 \times 10^6}{\text{s}} = 2.98 \times 10^{-25} \text{ J}$

(c)   Since $\Delta E = 0$ in the absence of a magnetic field, it is reasonable to assume that the stronger the external field, the greater ΔE. (In fact, ΔE is directly proportional to field strength). Because ΔE is relatively small [see part (b)], the two spin states are almost equally populated, with a very slight excess in the lower energy state. The stronger the magnetic field, the larger ΔE, the greater number of nuclei in the lower energy spin state. With more nuclei in the lower energy state, more are able to absorb the appropriate radio wave photons and reach the higher energy state. This increases the intensity of the NMR signal, which provides more information and more reliable information than a weak absorption signal.

6.97   (a)   Se: $[\text{Ar}]4s^2 3d^{10}4p^4$

(b)   Rh: $[\text{Kr}]5s^2 4d^7$

(c)   Si: $[\text{Ne}]3s^2 3p^2$

(d)   Hg: $[\text{Xe}]6s^2 4f^{14}5d^{10}$

(e)   Hf: $[\text{Xe}]6s^2 4f^{14}5d^2$

6.98   The core would be the electron configuration of element 118. If no new subshell begins to fill, the condensed electron configuration of element 126 would be similar to those of elements vertically above it on the periodic chart, Pu and Sm. The condensed configuration would be $[118]8s^2 6f^6$. On the other hand, the 5g subshell could begin to fill after 8s, resulting in the condensed configuration $[118]8s^2 5g^6$. Exceptions are also possible (likely).

Integrative Exercises

6.100 $\Delta H^\circ_{rxn} = \Delta H^\circ_f \, O_2(g) + \Delta H^\circ_f \, O(g) - \Delta H^\circ_f \, O_3(g)$

$\Delta H^\circ_{rxn} = 0 + 247.5 \text{ kJ} - 142.3 \text{ kJ} = +105.2 \text{ kJ}$

$\dfrac{105.2 \text{ kJ}}{\text{mol O}_3} \times \dfrac{1 \text{ mol O}_3}{6.022 \times 10^{23} \text{ molecules}} \times \dfrac{1000 \text{ J}}{1 \text{ kJ}} = \dfrac{1.747 \times 10^{-19} \text{ J}}{\text{O}_3 \text{ molecule}}$

$\Delta E = hc/\lambda; \lambda = \dfrac{hc}{\Delta E} = \dfrac{6.626 \times 10^{-34} \text{ J-s} \times 2.998 \times 10^8 \text{ m/s}}{1.747 \times 10^{-19} \text{ J}} = 1.137 \times 10^{-6} \text{ m}$

Radiation with this wavelength is in the infrared portion of the spectrum. (Clearly, processes other than simple photodissociation cause O_3 to absorb ultraviolet radiation.)

6.101   (a)   The electron configuration of Zr is $[\text{Kr}]5s^2 4d^2$ and that of Hf is $[\text{Xe}]6s^2 4f^{14}5d^2$. Although Hf has electrons in f orbitals as the rare earth elements do, the 4f subshell in Hf is filled, and the 5d electrons primarily determine the chemical properties of the element. Thus, Hf should be chemically similar to Zr rather than the rare earth elements.

(b) $ZrCl_4(s) + 4Na(l) \rightarrow Zr(s) + 4NaCl(s)$

This is an oxidation-reduction reaction; Na is oxidized and Zr is reduced.

(c) $2ZrO_2(s) + 4Cl_2(g) + 3C(s) \rightarrow 2ZrCl_4(s) + CO_2(g) + 2CO(g)$

$$55.4\,g\,ZrO_2 \times \frac{1\,mol\,ZrO_2}{123.2\,g\,ZrO_2} \times \frac{2\,mol\,ZrCl_4}{2\,mol\,ZrO_2} \times \frac{233.0\,g\,ZrCl_4}{1\,mol\,ZrCl_4} = 105\,g\,ZrCl_4$$

(d)   In ionic compounds of the type MCl_4 and MO_2, the metal ions have a 4+ charge, indicating that the neutral atoms have lost four electrons. Zr, $[Kr]5s^24d^2$, loses the four electrons beyond its Kr core configuration. Hf, $[Xe]6s^24f^{14}5d^2$, similarly loses its four 6s and 5d electrons, but not electrons from the "complete" 4f subshell.

6.102   (a)   Each oxide ion, O^{2-}, carries a 2- charge. Each metal oxide is a neutral compound, so the metal ion or ions must adopt a total positive charge equal to the total negative charge of the oxide ions in the compound. The table below lists the electron configuration of the neutral metal atom, the positive charge of each metal ion in the oxide, and the corresponding electron configuration of the metal ion.

    i.   K: $[Ar]\,4s^1$ 1+ $[Ar]$

    ii.   Ca: $[Ar]\,4s^2$ 2+ $[Ar]$

    iii.   Sc: $[Ar]\,4s^23d^1$ 3+ $[Ar]$

    iv.   Ti: $[Ar]\,4s^23d^2$ 4+ $[Ar]$

    v.   V: $[Ar]\,4s^23d^3$ 5+ $[Ar]$

    vi.   Cr: $[Ar]\,4s^13d^5$ 6+ $[Ar]$

    Each metal atom loses all (valence) electrons beyond the Ar core configuration. In K_2O, Sc_2O_3 and V_2O_5, where the metal ions have odd charges, two metal ions are required to produce a neutral oxide.

(b)   i.   potassium oxide

    ii.   calcium oxide

    iii.   scandium(III) oxide

    iv.   titanium (IV) oxide

    v.   vanadium (V) oxide

    vi.   chromium (VI) oxide

    (Roman numerals are required to specify the charges on the transition metal ions, because more than one stable ion may exist.)

(c)   Recall that $\Delta H_f^\circ = 0$ for elements in their standard states. In these reactions, M(s) and $H_2(g)$ are elements in their standard states.

    i. $K_2O(s) + H_2(g) \rightarrow 2K(s) + H_2O(g)$

    $\Delta H^\circ = \Delta H_f^\circ\,H_2O(g) + 2\Delta H_f^\circ\,K(s) - \Delta H\,K_2O(s) - \Delta H_f^\circ\,H_2(g)$

    $\Delta H^\circ = -241.82\,kJ + 2(0) - (-363.2\,kJ) - 0 = 121.4\,kJ$

ii. $CaO(s) + H_2(g) \rightarrow Ca(s) + H_2O(g)$

$\Delta H° = \Delta H_f° \, H_2O(g) + \Delta H_f° \, Ca(s) - \Delta H_f° \, CaO(s) - \Delta H_f° \, H_2(g)$

$\Delta H° = -241.82 \, kJ + 0 - (-635.1 \, kJ) - 0 = 393.3 \, kJ$

iii. $TiO_2(s) + 2H_2(g) \rightarrow Ti(s) + 2H_2O(g)$

$\Delta H° = 2\Delta H_f° \, H_2O(g) + \Delta H_f° \, Ti(s) - \Delta H_f° \, TiO_2(s) - 2\Delta H_f° \, H_2(g)$

$= 2(-241.82) + 0 - (-938.7) - 2(0) = 455.1 \, kJ$

iv. $V_2O_5(s) + 5H_2(g) \rightarrow 2V(s) + 5H_2O(g)$

$\Delta H° = 5\Delta H_f° \, H_2O(g) + 2\Delta H_f° \, V(s) - \Delta H_f° \, V_2O_5(s) - 5\Delta H_f° \, H_2(g)$

$= 5(-241.82) + 2(0) - (-1550.6) - 5(0) = 341.5 \, kJ$

(d) $\Delta H_f°$ becomes more negative moving from left to right across this row of the periodic chart. Since Sc lies between Ca and Ti, the median of the two $\Delta H_f°$ values is approximately –785 kJ/mol. However, the trend is clearly not linear. Dividing the $\Delta H_f°$ values by the positive charge on the pertinent metal ion produces the values –363, –318, –235, and –310. The value between Ca^{2+} (–318) and Ti^{4+} (–235) is Sc^{3+} (–277). Multiplying (–277) by 3, a value of approximately –830 kJ results. A reasonable range of values for $\Delta H_f°$ of $Sc_2O_3(s)$ is then –785 to –830 kJ/mol.

6.104   (a) ^{238}U: 92 p, 146 n, 92 e; ^{235}U: 92 p, 143 n, 92 e

In keeping with the definition isotopes, only the number of neutrons is different in the two nuclides. Since the two isotopes have the same number of electrons, they will have the same electron configuration.

(b)   U: $[Rn]7s^2 5f^4$

(c)   From Figure 6.31, the actual electron configuration is $[Rn]7s^2 5f^3 6d^1$. The energies of the 6d and 5f orbitals are very close, and electron configurations of many actinides include 6d electrons.

(d) $^{238}_{92}U \rightarrow ^{234}_{90}Th + ^{4}_{2}He$ ^{234}Th has 90 p, 144 n, 90 e. ^{238}U has lost 2 p, 2 n, 2 e.

These are organized into $^{4}_{2}He$ shown in the nuclear reaction above.

(e)   From Figure 6.31, the electron configuration of Th is $[Rn]7s^2 6d^2$. This is not really surprising because there are so many rare earth electron configurations that are exceptions to the expected orbital filling order. However, Th is the only rare earth that has two d valence electrons. Furthermore, the configuration of Th is different than that of Ce, the element above it on the periodic chart, so the electron configuration is at least interesting.

6.105   In each case, radiant energy from the sun in shown as hν.

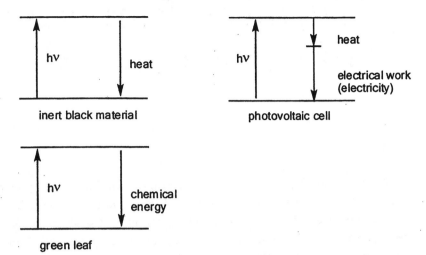

Energy from the sun irradiates the earth without external intervention. In the absence of an appropriate receiver, the energy is dissipated as heat, as the diagram for the inert black material shows. When sunlight hits a material that can convert the energy to a useable form, such as a leaf or a photovoltaic cell, the sun becomes a sustainable energy source.

7 Periodic Properties of the Elements

Visualizing Concepts

7.1 (a) The light bulb itself represents the nucleus of the atom. The brighter the bulb, the more nuclear charge the electron "sees." A frosted glass lampshade between the bulb and our eyes reduces the brightness of the bulb. The shade is analogous to core electrons in the atom shielding outer electrons (our eyes) from the full nuclear charge (the bare light bulb).

(b) Increasing the wattage of the light bulb mimics moving right along a row of the periodic table. The brighter bulb inside the same shade is analogous to having more protons in the nucleus while the core electron configuration doesn't change.

(c) Moving down a family, both the nuclear charge and the core electron configuration changes. To simulate the addition of core electrons farther from the nucleus, we would add larger frosted glass shades as well as increase the wattage of the bulb to show the increase in Z. The effect of the shade should dominate the increase in wattage, so that the brightness of the light decreases moving down a column.

7.3 (a) The bonding atomic radius of A, r_A, is $d_1/2$. The distance d_2 is the sum of the bonding atomic radii of A and X, $r_A + r_X$. Since we know that $r_A = d_1/2$, $d_2 = r_X + d_1/2$, $r_X = d_2 - d_1/2$.

(b) The length of the X-X bond is $2r_X$.

$$2r_X = 2(d_2 - d_1/2) = 2d_2 - d_1.$$

7.4

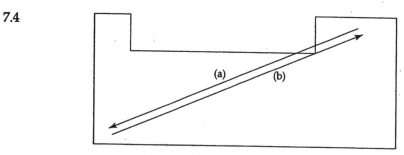

Lines (a) and (b) coincide, but their directions are opposite. Line (a) goes from upper right to lower left, and line (b) from lower left to upper right.

(c) From the diagram, we observe that the trends in bonding atomic radius (size) and ionization energy are opposite each other. As bonding atomic radius increases increases ionization energy decreases, and vice versa.

7.6   (a) $X + 2F_2 \rightarrow XF_4$

(b)   If X is a nonmetal, XF_4 is a molecular compound. If X is a metal, XF_4 is ionic. For an ionic compound with this formula, X would have a charge of 4+, and a much smaller bonding atomic radius than F^-. X in the diagram has about the same bonding radius as F, so it is likely to be a nonmetal.

Periodic Table; Effective Nuclear Charge

7.8   Assuming *eka-* means one place below or under, *eka-manganese* on Table 7.2 is technetium, Tc.

7.10   (a)   The verification of the existence of many new elements by accurately measuring their atomic weights spurred interest in a classification scheme. Mendeleev (and Meyer) noted that certain chemical and physical properties recur periodically when the elements are arranged by increasing atomic weight. The accurate atomic weights provided a common property on which to base a classification scheme of the elements.

(b)   Moseley realized that the characteristic X-ray frequencies emitted by each element were related to a unique integer that he assigned to each element. We now know this integer as the atomic number, the number of protons in the nucleus of an atom. In general, atomic weight increases as atomic number increases, but there are a few exceptions. If elements are arranged by increasing atomic number, a few seeming contradictions in the Mendeleev table (the positions of Ar and K or Te and I) are eliminated.

(c)   The main determining factor of physical and especially chemical properties is electron configuration. For electrically neutral elements, the number of electrons equals the number of protons, which in turn is the atomic number of an element. Atomic weight is related to mass number, protons plus neutrons. The number of neutrons in its nucleus does influence the mass of an atom, but mass is a minor or non-factor in determining properties.

7.12   (a)   Electrostatic attraction for the nucleus lowers the energy of an electron, while electron-electron repulsions increase this energy. The concept of effective nuclear charge allows us to model this increase in the energy of an electron as a smaller net attraction to a nucleus with a smaller positive charge, Z_{eff}.

(b)   In Be (or any element), the 1s electrons are not shielded by any core electrons, so they experience a much greater Z_{eff} than the 2s electrons.

7.14   Follow the method in the preceding question to calculate Z_{eff} values.
(a)   Si: $Z = 14$; $[Ne]3s^23p^2$. 10 electrons in the Ne core. $Z_{eff} = 14 - 10 = 4$
       Cl: $Z = 17$; $[Ne]3s^23p^5$. 10 electrons in the Ne core. $Z_{eff} = 17 - 10 = 7$

(b)   Si: $1s^22s^22p^63s^23p^2$. $S = 0.35(3) + 0.85(8) + 1(2) = 9.85$. $Z_{eff} = 14 - 9.85 = 4.15$
       Cl: $1s^22s^22p^63s^23p^5$. $S = 0.35(6) + 0.85(8) + 1(2) = 10.9$. $Z_{eff} = 17 - 10.9 = 6.10$

(c)   The Slater values of 4.15 (Si) and 6.10 (Cl) are closer to the results of detailed calculations, 4.29 (Si) and 6.12 (Cl).

(d)   The Slater method of approximation more closely approximates the gradual increase in Z_{eff} moving across a row. The 'core 100%-effective' approximation underestimates Z_{eff} for Si but overestimates it for Cl. Slater values are closer to detailed calculations, and a better indication of the change in Z_{eff} moving from Si to Cl.

7.16   Mg < P < K < Ti < Rh. The shielding of electrons in the $n = 3$ shell by 1s, 2s and 2p core electrons in these elements is approximately equal, so the effective nuclear charge increases as Z increases.

Atomic and Ionic Radii

7.18   (a)   Since the quantum mechanical description of the atom does not specify the exact location of electrons, there is no specific distance from the nucleus where the last electron can be found. Rather, the electron density decreases gradually as the distance from the nucleus increases. There is no quantum mechanical "edge" of an atom.

(b)   When nonbonded atoms touch, it is their electron clouds that interact. These interactions are primarily repulsive because of the negative charges of electrons. Thus, the size of the electron clouds determines the nuclear approach distance of nonbonded atoms.

7.20   The distance between Si atoms in solid silicon is two times the bonding atomic radius from Figure 7.7. The Si–Si distance is 2×1.11 Å = 2.22 Å.

7.22   Bi–I = 2.81 Å = $r_{Bi} + r_I$. From Figure 7.7, $r_I = 1.33$ Å.

r_{Bi} = [Bi–I] – r_I = 2.81 Å – 1.33 Å = 1.48 Å.

7.24   (a)   The vertical difference in radius is due to a change in principal quantum number of the outer electrons. The horizontal difference in radius is due to the change in electrostatic attraction between the outer electron and a nucleus with one more or one fewer proton. Adding or subtracting a proton has a much smaller radius effect than moving from one principal quantum level to the next.

(b)   Si < Al < Ge < Ga. This order is predicted by the trends in increasing atomic radius moving to the left in a row and down a column of the periodic chart, assuming that changes moving down a column are larger [see part (a)]. That is, the order above assumes that the change from Si to Ge is larger than the change from Si to Al. This order is confirmed by the values in Figure 7.7.

7.26   (a)   Na < Ca < Ba   (b)   As < Sb < Sn

(c)   Be < Si < Al. This order assumes the increase in radius from the second to the third row is greater than the decrease moving right in the third row. Radii in Figure 7.7 confirm this assumption.

7.28   (a)   As Z stays constant and the number of electrons increases, the electron-electron repulsions increase, the electrons spread apart, and the ions become larger.

$I^- > I > I^+$

(b)   Going down a column, the increasing average distance of the outer electrons from the nucleus causes the size of particles with like charge to increase.

$Ca^{2+} > Mg^{2+} > Be^{2+}$

(c)   Fe: $[Ar]4s^2 3d^6$; Fe^{2+}: $[Ar]3d^6$; Fe^{3+}: $[Ar]3d^5$. The 4s valence electrons in Fe are on average farther from the nucleus than the 3d electrons, so Fe is larger than Fe^{2+}. Since there are five 3d orbitals, in Fe^{2+} at least one orbital must contain a pair of electrons. Removing one electron to form Fe^{3+} significantly reduces repulsion, increasing the nuclear charge experienced by each of the other d electrons and decreasing the size of the ion. $Fe > Fe^{2+} > Fe^{3+}$

7.30   The order of radii is $Ca > Ca^{2+} > Mg^{2+}$, so the largest sphere is Ca, the intermediate one is Ca^{2+}, and the smallest is Mg^{2+}.

7.32   (a) Cl^-: Ar   (b) Sc^{3+}: Ar

(c) Fe^{2+}: $[Ar]3d^6$. Fe^{2+} has 24 electrons. Neutral Cr has 24 electrons, $[Ar]4s^1 3d^5$. Because transition metals fill the *s* subshell first but also lose *s* electrons first when they form ions, many transition metal ions do not have isoelectronic neutral atoms.

(d) Zn^{2+}: $[Ar]3d^{10}$; no isoelectronic neutral atom [same reason as (c)].

(e) Sn^{4+}: $[Kr]4d^{10}$; no isoelectronic neutral atom [same reason as (c)], but Sn^{4+} is isoelectronic with Cd^{2+}.

7.34   (a) K^+ (larger Z) is smaller.

(b) Cl^- and K^+: $[Ne]3s^2 3p^6$. 10 core electrons
Cl^-, $Z = 17$. $Z_{eff} = 17 - 10 = 7$
K^+, $Z = 19$. $Z_{eff} = 19 - 10 = 9$

(c)   Valence electron, $n = 3$; 7 other $n = 3$ electrons; eight $n = 2$ electrons; two $n = 1$ electrons. $S = 0.35(7) + 0.85(8) + 1(2) = 11.25$
Cl^-: $Z_{eff} = 17 - 11.25 = 5.75$. K^+: $Z_{eff} = 19 - 11.25 = 7.75$

(d)   For isoelectronic ions, the electron configurations and therefore shielding values (S) are the same. Only the nuclear charge changes. So, as nuclear charge (Z) increases, effective nuclear charge (Z_{eff}) increases and ionic radius decreases.

7.36   (a) $Se < Se^{2-} < Te^{2-}$ (b) $Co^{3+} < Fe^{3+} < Fe^{2+}$ (c) $Ti^{4+} < Sc^{3+} < Ca$ (d) $Be^{2+} < Na^+ < Ne$

7.38   Make a table of d(measured), d(ionic radii) and d(covalent radii). Use these values to make comparisons for (b) and (c). The estimated distances are just the sum of the various radii from Figure 7.8.

(a)

	d(measured), Å	d(ionic radii), Å	d(covalent radii), Å
Li–F	2.01	2.09	2.05
Na–Cl	2.82	2.83	2.53
K–Br	3.30	3.34	3.10
Rb–I	3.67	3.72	3.44

(b) The agreement between measured distances in specific ionic compounds, and predicted distances based on ionic radii is not perfect. Ionic radii are averages compiled from distances in many ionic compounds containing the ion in question. The sum of these average radii may not give an exact match for the distance in any specific compound, but it will give good distance estimates for many ionic compounds. Also, there is uncertainty in all measured data. Note that all estimates from ionic radii are within 0.08 Å of the measured distances.

(c) Distance estimates from bonding atomic radii are not as accurate as those from ionic radii. This indicates that the bonding in these four compounds is more accurately described as ionic, rather than covalent. The details of these two models will be discussed in Chapter 8.

Ionization Energies; Electron Affinities

7.40 (a) $Sn(g) \rightarrow Sn^+(g) + 1e^-$; $Sn^+(g) \rightarrow Sn^{2+}(g) + 1e^-$

(b) $Ti^{3+}(g) \rightarrow Ti^{4+}(g) + 1e^-$

7.42 (a) The effective nuclear charges of Li and Na are similar, but the outer electron in Li has a smaller n-value and is closer to the nucleus than the outer electron in Na. More energy is needed to overcome the greater attraction of the Li electron for the nucleus.

(b) Sc: [Ar] $4s^2 3d^1$; Ti: [Ar] $4s^2 3d^2$. The fourth ionization of titanium involves removing a 3d valence electron, while the fourth ionization of Sc requires removing a 3p electron from the [Ar] core. The effective nuclear charges experienced by the two 3d electrons in Ti are much more similar than the effective nuclear charges of a 3d valence electron and a 3p core electron in Sc. Thus, the difference between the third and fourth ionization energies of Sc is much larger.

(c) The electron configuration of Li^+ is $1s^2$ or [He] and that of Be^+ is [He]$2s^1$. Be^+ has one more valence electron to lose while Li^+ has the stable noble gas configuration of He. It requires much more energy to remove a 1s core electron close to the nucleus of Li^+ than a 2s valence electron farther from the nucleus of Be^+.

7.44 (a) Moving from F to I in group 7A, first ionization energies decrease and atomic radii increase. The greater the atomic radius, the smaller the electrostatic attraction of an outer electron for the nucleus and the smaller the ionization energy of the element.

(b)   First ionization energies increase slightly going from K to Kr and atomic sizes decrease. As valence electrons are drawn closer to the nucleus (atom size decreases), it requires more energy to completely remove them from the atom (first ionization energy increases). Each trend has a discontinuity at Ga, owing to the increased shielding of the 4p electrons by the filled 3d subshell.

7.46   (a)   Ti. Effective nuclear charge increases moving both right across a row and up a family. The 4s valence electrons in Ti experience the greater Z_{eff} and have greater first ionization energy than 6s electrons of Ba. Recall that transition metals like Ti lose ns electrons first when forming ions.

(b)   Cu. The 4s electrons of Cu are closer to the nucleus and shielded mainly by an [Ar] core, while the 5s electrons of Ag are further from the nucleus and shielded by a [Kr] core. Recall that transition elements lose ns electrons first when forming ions.

(c)   Cl. Effective nuclear charge increases moving both right across a row and up a family. Valence electrons in Cl, which is to the right and above Ge, experience the greater Z_{eff} and have the larger first ionization energy.

(d)   Sb. Z_{eff} and first ionization energy increase moving up a family and right across a row. Even the excess nuclear charge (Z) associated with filling the 4f subshell between Sb and Pb does not totally offset these trends.

7.48   (a) Cr^{3+}: $[Ar]3d^3$

(b) N^{3-}: $[He]2s^22p^6 = [Ne]$, noble-gas configuration

(c) Sc^{3+}: [Ar], noble-gas configuration   (d) Cu^{2+}: $[Ar]3d^9$

(e) Tl^+: $[Xe]6s^24f^{14}5d^{10}$ (f) Au^+: $[Xe]4f^{14}5d^{10}$

7.50   (a) Cu^{2+}, 1 unpaired electron   (b) Tl^+, 0 unpaired electrons

7.52 $Li + 1e^- \rightarrow Li^-$; $Be + 1e^- \rightarrow Be^-$
$[He]2s^1$ $[He]2s^2$ $[He]2s^2$ $[He]2s^22p^1$

Adding an electron to Li completes the 2s subshell. The added electron experiences essentially the same effective nuclear charge as the other valence electron, except for the repulsion of pairing electrons in an orbital. There is an overall stabilization; ΔE is negative.

An extra electron in Be would occupy the higher energy 2p subshell. This electron is shielded from the full nuclear charge by the 2s electrons and does not experience a stabilization in energy; ΔE is positive.

7.54   Ionization energy of F^-: $F^-(g) \rightarrow F(g) + 1e^-$

Electron affinity of F: $F(g) + 1e^- \rightarrow F^-(g)$

The two processes are the reverse of each other. The energies are equal in magnitude but opposite in sign. $I_1 (F^-) = -E (F)$

7.56 $Mg^+(g) + 1e^- \rightarrow Mg(g)$
$[Ne]3s^1$ $\qquad\qquad$ $[Ne]3s^2$

This process is the reverse of the first ionization of Mg. The magnitude of the energy change for this process is the same as the magnitude of the first ionization energy of Mg, 738 kJ/mol.

Properties of Metals and Nonmetals

7.58 $S < Si < Ge < Ca$. S is a nonmetal, Si and Ge are metalloids, and Ca is a metal. We expect that electrical conductivity increases as metallic character increases. Since metallic character increases going down a column and to the left in a row, the order of increasing electrical conductivity is as shown above.

7.60 Metallic character increases moving down a family and to the left in a period. Use these trends to select the element with greater metallic character.

    (a)   Li $\qquad$ (b) Na $\qquad$ (c) Sn $\qquad$ (d) Al

7.62 Follow the logic in Sample Exercise 7.8. Scandium is a metal, so we expect Sc_2O_3 to be ionic. Metal oxides are usually basic and react with acid to form a salt and water. We choose $HNO_3(aq)$ as the acid for our equation.

$Sc_2O_3(s) + 6HNO_3(aq) \rightarrow 2Sc(NO_3)_3(aq) + 3H_2O(l)$.

The net ionic equation is:

$Sc_2O_3(s) + 6H^+(aq) \rightarrow 2Sc^{3+}(aq) + 3H_2O(l)$

7.64 The more nonmetallic the central atom, the more acidic the oxide. In order of increasing acidity: $CaO < Al_2O_3 < SiO_2 < CO_2 < P_2O_5 < SO_3$

7.66 (a) $XCl_4(l) + 2H_2O(l) \rightarrow XO_2(s) + 4HCl(g)$. The second product is $HCl(g)$.

    (b) If X were a metal, both the oxide and the chloride would be high melting solids. If X were a nonmetal, XO_2 would be a nonmetallic, molecular oxide and probably gaseous, like CO_2, NO_2, and SO_2. Neither of these statements describes the properties of XO_2 and XCl_4, so X is probably a metalloid.

    (c) Use the *Handbook of Chemistry* to find formulas and melting points of oxides, and formulas and boiling points of chlorides of selected metalloids.

metalloid	formula of oxide	m.p. of oxide	formula of chloride	b.p. of chloride
boron	B_2O_3	460°C	BCl_3	12°C
silicon	SiO_2	~1700°C	$SiCl_4$	58°C
germanium	GeO GeO_2	710°C ~1100°C	$GeCl_2$ $GeCl_4$	decomposes 84°C
arsenic	As_2O_3 As_2O_5	315°C 315°C	$AsCl_3$	132°C

Boron, arsenic, and, by analogy, antimony, do not fit the description of X, because the formulas of their oxides and chlorides are wrong. Silicon and germanium, in the same family, have oxides and chlorides with appropriate formulas. Both SiO_2 and GeO_2 melt above 1000°C, but the boiling point of $SiCl_4$ is much closer to that of XCl_4. Element X is silicon.

7.68   (a) $K_2O(s) + H_2O(l) \rightarrow 2KOH(aq)$

    (b) $P_2O_3(l) + 3H_2O(l) \rightarrow 2H_3PO_3(aq)$

    (c) $Cr_2O_3(s) + 6HCl(aq) \rightarrow 2CrCl_3(aq) + 3H_2O(l)$

    (d) $SeO_2(s) + 2KOH(aq) \rightarrow K_2SeO_3(aq) + H_2O(l)$

Group Trends in Metals and Nonmetals

7.70   (a)   Rb: $[Kr]5s^1$, r = 2.11 Å   Ag: $[Kr]5s^14d^{10}$, r = 1.53 Å

The electron configurations both have a [Kr] core and a single 5s electron; Ag has a completed 4d subshell as well. The radii are very different because the 5s electron in Ag experiences a much greater effective nuclear charge. Ag has a much larger Z (47 vs. 37), and although the 4d electrons in Ag shield the 5s electron somewhat, the increased shielding does not compensate for the large increase in Z.

    (b)   Ag is much less reactive (less likely to lose an electron) because its 5s electron experiences a much larger effective nuclear charge and is more difficult to remove.

7.72   (a)   Cs is much more reactive than Li toward H_2O because its valence electron is less tightly held (greater n value), and Cs is more easily oxidized.

    (b)   The purple flame indicates that the metal is potassium (see Figure 7.26).

    (c) $\quad K_2O_2(s) \quad + \quad H_2O(l) \rightarrow \quad H_2O_2(aq) \quad + \quad K_2O(aq)$
potassium peroxide   hydrogen peroxide

7.74   (a) $2Cs(s) + 2H_2O(l) \rightarrow 2CsOH(aq) + H_2(g)$

    (b) $Sr(s) + 2H_2O(l) \rightarrow Sr(OH)_2(aq) + H_2(g)$

    (c) $2Na(s) + O_2(g) \rightarrow Na_2O_2(s)$ (See Equation [7.21].)

    (d) $Ca(s) + I_2(s) \rightarrow CaI_2(s)$

7.76   (a)   The reactions of the alkali metals with hydrogen and with a halogen are redox reactions. In both classes of reaction, the alkali metal loses electrons and is oxidized. Both hydrogen and the halogen gain electrons and are reduced. The product is an ionic solid, where either hydride ion, H^-, or a halide ion, X^-, is the anion and the alkali metal is the cation.

    (b) $Ca(s) + F_2(g) \rightarrow CaF_2(s)$ $Ca(s) + H_2(g) \rightarrow CaH_2(s)$

Both products are ionic solids containing Ca^{2+} and the corresponding anion in a 1:2 ratio.

7.78   *Plan.* Predict the physical and chemical properties of At based on the trends in properties in the halogen (7A) family. *Solve.*

(a)   F, at the top of the column, is a gas; I, immediately above At, is a solid; the melting points of the halogens increase going down the column. At is likely to be a solid at room temperature.

(b)   All halogens form ionic compounds with Na; they have the generic formula NaX. The compound formed by At will have the formula NaAt.

7.80   Xe has a lower ionization energy than Ne. The valence electrons in Xe are much farther from the nucleus than those of Ne ($n = 5$ vs $n = 2$) and much less tightly held by the nucleus; they are more "willing" to be shared than those in Ne. Also, Xe has empty 5d orbitals that can help to accommodate the bonding pairs of electrons, while Ne has all its valence orbitals filled.

7.82   (a) $Cl_2(g) + H_2O(l) \rightarrow HCl(aq) + HOCl(aq)$

(b) $Ba(s) + H_2(g) \rightarrow BaH_2(s)$

(c) $2Li(s) + S(s) \rightarrow Li_2S(s)$

(d) $Mg(s) + F_2(g) \rightarrow MgF_2(s)$

Additional Exercises

7.84   (a)   4s

(b)   To a first approximation, s and p valence electrons do not shield each other, so we expect the 4s and 4p electrons in As to experience a similar Z_{eff}. However, since s electrons have a finite probability of being very close to the nucleus (Figure 7.4), they experience less shielding than p electrons with the same n-value. Since $Z_{eff} = Z - S$ and Z is the same for all electrons in As, if S is smaller for 4s than 4p, Z_{eff} will be greater for 4s electrons and they will have a lower energy.

7.86   Close approach by two positively charged nuclei is impossible because of the large electrostatic repulsion between like-charged particles at small distances. The additional space between the nuclei in a molecule like F_2 is occupied by bonding electrons, which are electrostatically stabilized by attraction to both nuclei. The electrons also provide a buffer between the two nuclei.

7.87   (a) $Z_{eff} = Z - S$. According to our simple model, moving from C to N, causes Z to increase by 1 and S to remain the same, so Z_{eff} is greater by 1 for N than for C.

(b)   Using Slater's rules, Z increases by 1 moving from C to N, but S also increases by 0.35, the value for an electron with the same n value as the one of interest. The increase in Z_{eff} from C to N should be $(1 - 0.35) = 0.65$.

(c)   In this case, Slater's rules predict the change in Z_{eff} more accurately than the simple model in (a).

(d) In O, $[He]2s^22p^4$, one of the p orbitals is doubly occupied, which significantly increases electron-electron repulsion. This leads to an overall higher energy for the 2p electrons. In our model, this appears as a larger S and a smaller Z_{eff} for O. The change from N to O is then smaller.

7.89 (a) The estimated distances in the table below are the sum of the radii of the group 5A elements and H from Figure 7.7.

bonded atoms	estimated distance	measured distance
P – H	1.43	1.419
As – H	1.56	1.519
Sb – H	1.75	1.707

In general, the estimated distances are a bit longer than the measured distances. This probably shows a systematic bias in either the estimated radii or in the method of obtaining the measured values.

(b) The principal quantum number of the outer electrons and thus the average distance of these electrons from the nucleus increases from P (n = 3) to As (n = 4) to Sb (n = 5). This causes the systematic increase in M – H distance.

7.90 Ge – H distance = $r_{Ge} + r_H = 1.22 + 0.37 = 1.59Å$

Ge – Cl distance = $r_{Ge} + r_{Cl} = 1.22 + 0.99 = 2.21$ Å

7.92 (a) Hg^{2+}

(b) No. According to Figure 2.24, Hg is not essential for life, even in trace amounts.

(c) Zn^{2+}: $[Ar]3d^{10}$, r = 0.88 Å; Cd^{2+}: $[Kr]4d^{10}$, r = 1.09 Å;
Hg^{2+}: $[Xe]4f^{14}5d^{10}$, r ≈ 1.19 Å.

If there were no 4f electrons in Hg^{2+}, we would expect an ionic radius of around 1.29 Å, an increase of ~0.20 Å due to the increase in principal quantum number of the valence electrons. However, the increase in Z due to filling of the 4f orbitals is not completely offset by shielding. The 5d valence electrons in Hg^{2+} experience a greater than expected Z_{eff} which largely offsets the increase in principal quantum number; ionic radius of Hg^{2+} is smaller than expected. This phenomenon is known as the *lanthanide contraction* and affects the physical properties of elements in the sixth period and beyond. See also Solution 7.91.

(d) Since the ionic radius of Hg^{2+} is similar to that of Cd^{2+}, Hg^{2+} will be physiologically more similar to Cd^{2+}.

(e) By common knowledge, and verified with WebElements.com™, both Hg and Hg^{2+} are extremely toxic to humans.

7.93 (a) $2Sr(s) + O_2(g) \rightarrow 2SrO(s)$

(b) Assume that the corners of the cube are at the centers of the outermost O^{2-} ions, and that the edges pass through the centers of perimeter Sr^{2+} ions. The length of an edge is then $r(O^{2-}) + 2r(Sr^{2+}) + r(O^{2-}) = 2r(O^{2-}) + 2r(Sr^{2+}) = 2(1.32\ \text{Å}) + 2(1.26\ \text{Å}) = 5.16\ \text{Å}$.

(c) Density is the ratio of mass to volume.

$$d = \frac{\text{mass SrO in cube}}{\text{vol cube}} = \frac{\#\,\text{SrO units} \times \text{mass of SrO}}{\text{vol cube}}$$

Calculate the mass of 1 SrO unit in grams and the volume of the cube in cm^3; solve for number of SrO units.

$$\frac{103.62\ \text{g SrO}}{\text{mol}} \times \frac{1\ \text{mol SrO}}{6.022 \times 10^{23}\ \text{SrO units}} = 1.7207 \times 10^{-22} = 1.721 \times 10^{-22}\ \text{g/SrO unit}$$

$$V = (5.16)^3\ \text{Å}^3 \times \frac{(1 \times 10^{-8})^3\ \text{cm}^3}{\text{Å}^3} = 1.3739 \times 10^{-22} = 1.37 \times 10^{-22}\ \text{cm}^3$$

$$d = \frac{\#\ \text{of SrO units} \times 1.7207 \times 10^{-22}\ \text{g/SrO unit}}{1.3739 \times 10^{-22}\ \text{cm}^3} = 5.10\ \text{g/cm}^3$$

$$\#\ \text{of SrO units} = 5.10\ \text{g/cm}^3 \times \frac{1.3739 \times 10^{-22}\ \text{cm}^3}{1.7207 \times 10^{-22}\ \text{g/SrO unit}} = 4.07\ \text{units}$$

Since the number of formula units must be an integer, there are four SrO formula units in the cube. Using average values for ionic radii to estimate the edge length probably leads to the small discrepancy.

7.95 The statement is somewhat true, but more accurate if changed to read: "A negative value for the electron affinity of an atom occurs when the outermost electrons only incompletely shield the added electron from the nucleus." This new statement totally explains the negative electron affinity of Br and the positive value for Kr. For Br^-, the electron is added to the 4p subshell and is incompletely shielded by the "other" 4s and 4p electrons. For Kr^-, the electron is added to the 5s subshell, which is effectively shielded by the spherical Kr core.

7.97 (a) P: [Ne] $3s^2 3p^3$; S: [Ne] $3s^2 3p^4$. In P, each 3p orbital contains a single electron, while in S one 3p orbital contains a pair of electrons. Removing an electron from S eliminates the need for electron pairing and reduces electrostatic repulsion, so the overall energy required to remove the electron is smaller than in P, even though Z is greater.

(b) C: [He] $2s^2 2p^2$; N: [He] $2s^2 2p^3$; O: [He] $2s^2 2p^4$. An electron added to a N atom must be paired in a relatively small 2p orbital, so the additional electron-electron repulsion more than compensates for the increase in Z and the electron affinity is smaller (less exothermic) than that of C. In an O atom, one 2p orbital already contains a pair of electrons, so the additional repulsion from an extra electron is offset by the increase in Z and the electron affinity is greater (more exothermic). Note from Figure 7.14 that the electron affinity of O is only slightly more exothermic than that of C, although the value of Z has increased by 2.

(c) O^+: [He] $2s^2 2p^3$; O^{2+}: [He] $2s^2 2p^2$; F: [He] $2s^2 2p^5$; F^+: [He] $2s^2 2p^4$. Both 'core-only' [Z_{eff} (F) = 7; Z_{eff} (O^+) = 6] and Slater [Z_{eff} (F) = 5.2; Z_{eff} (O^+) = 4.9] predict that F has a greater Z_{eff} than O^+. Variation in Z_{eff} does not offer a satisfactory explanation. The decrease in electron-electron repulsion going from F to F^+ energetically favors ionization and causes it to be less endothermic than the second ionization of O, where there is no significant decrease in repulsion.

(d) Mn^{2+}: [Ar]$3d^5$; Mn^{3+}: [Ar] $3d^4$; Cr^{2+}: [Ar] $3d^4$; Cr^{3+}: [Ar] $3d^3$; Fe^{2+}: [Ar] $3d^6$; Fe^{3+}: [Ar] $3d^5$. The third ionization energy of Mn is expected to be larger than that of Cr because of the larger Z value of Mn. The third ionization energy of Fe is less than that of Mn because going from $3d^6$ to $3d^5$ reduces electron repulsions, making the process less endothermic than predicted by nuclear charge arguments.

7.99   (a)   For both H and the alkali metals, the added electron will complete an *ns* subshell (1s for H and *ns* for the alkali metals) so shielding and repulsion effects will be similar. For the halogens, the electron is added to an *np* subshell, so the energy change is likely to be quite different.

(b)   True. Only He has a smaller estimated "bonding" atomic radius, and no known compounds of He exist. The electron configuration of H is $1s^1$. The single 1s electron experiences no repulsion from other electrons and feels the full unshielded nuclear charge. It is held very close to the nucleus. The outer electrons of all other elements that form compounds are shielded by a spherical inner core of electrons and are less strongly attracted to the nucleus, resulting in larger atomic radii.

(c)   Ionization is the process of removing an electron from an atom. For the alkali metals, the *ns* electron being removed is effectively shielded by the core electrons, so ionization energies are low. For the halogens, a significant increase in nuclear charge occurs as the *np* orbitals fill, and this is not offset by an increase in shielding. The relatively large effective nuclear charge experienced by *np* electrons of the halogens is similar to the unshielded nuclear charge experienced by the H 1s electron. Both H and the halogens have large ionization energies.

7.100   Since Xe reacts with F_2, and O_2 has approximately the same ionization energy as Xe, O_2 will probably react with F_2. Possible products would be O_2F_2, analogous to XeF_2, or OF_2.

$$O_2(g) + F_2(g) \rightarrow O_2F_2(g)$$
$$O_2(g) + 2F_2(g) \rightarrow 2OF_2(g)$$

7.102   Sr: [Kr]$5s^2$, Z = 38. Ca: [Ar]$4s^2$, Z = 20. Sr and Ca are in the same family. They have the same valence electron configuration so we expect their chemical properties to be similar. Both are metals that form cations with +2 charge. From trends, we expect Sr to have a larger covalent radius than Ca, and Sr^{2+} to have a larger ionic radius than Ca^{2+}; Figure 7.8 corroborates this relationship. However, the size difference is not as great as we might expect. The [Kr] core of Sr includes a full 3d subshell, which increases the Z and Z_{eff} for Sr and Sr^{2+} relative to Ca and Ca^{2+}.

Ca and Sr both react with water at room temperature to form Ca^{2+}(aq) and Sr^{2+}(aq). The predominant species in water supplies (very dilute aqueous solutions) and in the form for uptake by plants are Ca^{2+}(aq) and Sr^{2+}(aq). The main factors that determine transport properties are size and charge. Since Ca^{2+} and Sr^{2+} have the same charge and similar size, it is not surprising that they are transported together and assimilated by organisms similarly. Since they have similar properties, they are likely to interact with bio-molecules similarly. So, "normal" (nonradioactive) Sr acts like Ca, which is not only safe, but essential to organisms. This is why "normal" Sr is not very dangerous, but radioactive Sr is lethal. Radioactive Sr replaces Ca and is readily incorporated into organisms.

7.103   Moving one place to the right in a horizontal row of the table, for example, from Li to Be, there is an increase in ionization energy. Moving downward in a given family, for example from Be to Mg, there is usually a decrease in ionization energy. Similarly, atomic size decreases in moving one place to the right and increases in moving downward. Thus, two elements such as Li and Mg that are diagonally related tend to have similar ionization energies and atomic sizes. This in turn gives rise to some similarities in chemical behavior. Note, however, that the valences expected for the elements are not the same. That is, lithium still appears as Li^+, magnesium as Mg^{2+}.

7.104   (a)   *Plan.* Use qualitative physical (bulk) properties to narrow the range of choices, then match melting point and density to identify the specific element.   *Solve.*

Hardness varies widely in metals and nonmetals, so this information is not too useful. The relatively high density, appearance, and ductility indicate that the element is probably less metallic than copper. Focus on the block of nine main group elements centered around Sn. Pb is not a possibility because it was used as a comparison standard. The melting point of the five elements closest to Pb are:

Tl, 303.5°C; In, 156.1°C; Sn, 232°C; Sb, 630.5°C; Bi, 271.3°C

The best match is In. To confirm this identification, the density of In is 7.3 g/cm^3, also a good match to properties of the unknown element.

(b)   In order to write the correct balanced equation, determine the formula of the oxide product from the mass data, assuming the unknown is In.

5.08 g oxide – 4.20 g In = 0.88 g O

4.20 g In/114.82 g/mol = 0.0366 mol In; 0.0366/0.0366 = 1

0.88 g O/16.00 g/mol = 0.0550 mol O; 0.0550/0.0366 = 1.5

Multiplying by 2 produces an integer ratio of 2 In: 3 O and a formula of In_2O_3. The balanced equation is: $4 In(s) + 3O_2(g) \rightarrow 2 In_2O_3(s)$

(c)   According to Figure 7.2, the element In was discovered between 1843–1886. The investigator who first recorded this data in 1822 could have been the first to discover In.

Integrative Exercises

7.105   (a) $\nu = c/\lambda;\ 1\ \text{Hz} = 1\ \text{s}^{-1}$

$$\text{Ne: } \nu = \frac{2.998 \times 10^8\ \text{m/s}}{14.610\ \text{Å}} \times \frac{1\ \text{Å}}{1 \times 10^{-10}\ \text{m}} = 2.052 \times 10^{17}\ \text{s}^{-1} = 2.052 \times 10^{17}\ \text{Hz}$$

$$\text{Ca: } \nu = \frac{2.998 \times 10^8\ \text{m/s}}{3.358 \times 10^{-10}\ \text{m}} = 8.928 \times 10^{17}\ \text{Hz}$$

$$\text{Zn: } \nu = \frac{2.998 \times 10^8\ \text{m/s}}{1.435 \times 10^{-10}\ \text{m}} = 20.89 \times 10^{17}\ \text{Hz}$$

$$\text{Zr: } \nu = \frac{2.998 \times 10^8\ \text{m/s}}{0.786 \times 10^{-10}\ \text{m}} = 38.14 \times 10^{17} = 38.1 \times 10^{17}\ \text{Hz}$$

$$\text{Sn: } \nu = \frac{2.998 \times 10^8\ \text{m/s}}{0.491 \times 10^{-10}\ \text{m}} = 61.06 \times 10^{17} = 61.1 \times 10^{17}\ \text{Hz}$$

(b)

Element	Z	ν	$\nu^{1/2}$
Ne	10	2.052×10^{17}	4.530×10^8
Ca	20	8.928×10^{17}	9.449×10^8
Zn	30	20.89×10^{17}	14.45×10^8
Zr	40	38.14×10^{17}	19.5×10^8
Sn	50	61.06×10^{17}	24.7×10^8

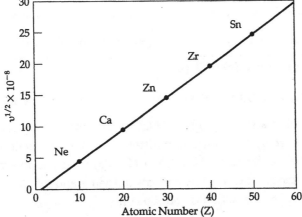

(c)   The plot in part (b) indicates that there is a linear relationship between atomic number and the square root of the frequency of the X-rays emitted by an element. Thus, elements with each integer atomic number should exist. This relationship allowed Moseley to predict the existence of elements that filled "holes" or gaps in the periodic table.

(d)   For Fe, Z = 26. From the graph, $v^{1/2} = 12.5 \times 10^8$, $v = 1.56 \times 10^{18}$ Hz.

$$\lambda = c/v = \frac{2.998 \times 10^8 \text{ m/s}}{1.56 \times 10^{18} \text{ s}^{-1}} \times \frac{1 \text{ Å}}{1 \times 10^{-10} \text{ m}} = 1.92 \text{ Å}$$

(e) $\lambda = 0.980 \text{ Å} = 0.980 \times 10^{-10} \text{ m}$

$$v = c/\lambda = \frac{2.998 \times 10^8 \text{ m/s}}{0.980 \times 10^{-10} \text{ m}} = 30.6 \times 10^{17} \text{ Hz}; \ v^{1/2} = 17.5 \times 10^8$$

From the graph, $v^{1/2} = 17.5 \times 10^8$, Z = 36. The element is krypton, Kr.

7.107   (a) $E = hc/\lambda$; 1 nm = 1×10^{-9} m; 58.4 nm = 58.4×10^{-9} m;

1 eV = 96.485 kJ/mol, 1 eV - mol = 96.485 kJ

$$E = \frac{6.626 \times 10^{-34} \text{ J-s} \times 2.998 \times 10^8 \text{ m/s}}{58.4 \times 10^{-9} \text{ m}} = 3.4015 \times 10^{-18} = 3.40 \times 10^{-18} \text{ J/photon}$$

$$\frac{3.4015 \times 10^{-18} \text{ J}}{\text{photon}} \times \frac{1 \text{ kJ}}{1000 \text{ J}} \times \frac{6.022 \times 10^{23} \text{ photons}}{\text{mol}} \times \frac{1 \text{ eV - mol}}{96.485 \text{ kJ}} = 21.230 = 21.2 \text{ eV}$$

(b) $Hg(g) \rightarrow Hg^+(g) + 1e^-$

(c) $I_1 = E_{58.4} - E_K = 21.23 \text{ eV} - 10.75 \text{ eV} = 10.48 = 10.5 \text{ eV}$

$$10.48 \text{ eV} \times \frac{96.485 \text{ kJ}}{1 \text{ eV - mol}} = 1.01 \times 10^3 \text{ kJ/mol}$$

(d)   From Figure 7.12, iodine (I) appears to have the ionization energy closest to that of Hg, approximately 1000 kJ/mol.

7.108   (a) $Na(g) \rightarrow Na^+(g) + 1e^-$ (ionization energy of Na)

$Cl(g) + 1e^- \rightarrow Cl^-(g)$ (electron affinity of Cl)
$$\overline{\quad Na(g) + Cl(g) \rightarrow Na^+(g) + Cl^-(g) \quad}$$

(b) $\Delta H = I_1 (Na) + E_1(Cl) = +496 \text{ kJ} - 349 \text{ kJ} = +147 \text{ kJ}$, endothermic

(c)   The reaction $2Na(s) + Cl_2(g) \rightarrow 2NaCl(s)$ involves many more steps than the reaction in part (a). One important difference is the production of NaCl(s) versus NaCl(g). The condensation NaCl(g) $\rightarrow$ NaCl(s) is very exothermic and is the step that causes the reaction of the elements in their standard states to be exothermic, while the gas phase reaction is endothermic.

7.110   (a) $r_{Bi} = r_{BiBr_3} - r_{Br} = 2.63 \text{ Å} - 1.14 \text{ Å} = 1.49 \text{ Å}$

(b) $Bi_2O_3(s) + 6HBr(aq) \rightarrow 2BiBr_3(aq) + 3H_2O(l)$

(c) Bi_2O_3 is soluble in acid solutions because it act as a base and undergoes acid-base reactions like the one in part (b). It is insoluble in base because it cannot acts as an acid. Thus, Bi_2O_3 is a basic oxide, the oxide of a metal. Based on the properties of its oxide, Bi is characterized as a metal.

(d)   Bi: $[Xe]6s^2 4f^{14} 5d^{10} 6p^3$. Bi has five outer electrons in the 6p and 6s subshells. If all five electrons participate in bonding, compounds such as BiF_5 are possible. Also, Bi has a large enough atomic radius (1.49 Å) and low-energy orbitals available to accommodate more than four pairs of bonding electrons.

(e)   The high ionization energy and relatively large negative electron affinity of F, coupled with its small atomic radius, make it the most electron withdrawing of the halogens. BiF_5 forms because F has the greatest tendency to attract electrons from Bi. Also, the small atomic radius of F reduces repulsions between neighboring bonded F atoms. The strong electron withdrawing properties of F are also the reason that only F compounds of Xe are known.

7.111   (a) $4KO_2(s) + 2CO_2(g) \rightarrow 2K_2CO_3(s) + 3O_2(g)$

(b)   K, +1; O, –1/2 (O_2^- is superoxide ion); C, +4; O, –2 → K, +1; C, +4; O, –2; O, 0

(c) $18.0 \text{ g } CO_2 \times \dfrac{1 \text{ mol } CO_2}{44.01 \text{ g } CO_2} \times \dfrac{4 \text{ mol } KO_2}{2 \text{ mol } CO_2} \times \dfrac{71.10 \text{ g } KO_2}{1 \text{ mol } KO_2} = 58.2 \text{ g } KO_2$

$18.0 \text{ g } CO_2 \times \dfrac{1 \text{ mol } CO_2}{44.01 \text{ g } CO_2} \times \dfrac{3 \text{ mol } O_2}{2 \text{ mol } CO_2} \times \dfrac{32.00 \text{ g } O_2}{1 \text{ mol } O_2} = 19.6 \text{ g } O_2$

8 Basic Concepts of Chemical Bonding

Visualizing Concepts

8.1 *Analyze/Plan.* Count the number of electrons in the Lewis symbol. This corresponds to the 'A'-group number of the family.   *Solve.*

(a) Group 14 or 4A

(b) Group 2 or 2A

(c) Group 15 or 5A

(These are the appropriate groups in the s and p blocks, where Lewis symbols are most useful.)

8.3 *Analyze/Plan.* Count the valence electrons in the orbital diagram, take ion charge into account, and find the element with this orbital electron count on the periodic chart. Write the complete electron configuration for the ion.   *Solve.*

(a) This ion has seven 3d electrons. Transition metals, or d-block elements, have valence electrons in d-orbitals. Transition metal ions first lose electrons from the 4s orbital, then from 3d if required by the charge. This 2+ ion has lost two electrons from 4s, none from 3d. The transition metal with seven 3d-electrons is cobalt, Co.

(b) The electron configuration of Co is $[Ar]4s^23d^7$. (The configuration of Co^{2+} is $[Ar]3d^7$).

8.4 *Analyze/Plan.* This question is a "reverse" Lewis structure. Count the valence electrons shown in the Lewis structure. For each atom, assume zero formal charge and determine the number of valence electrons an unbound atom has. Name the element.   *Solve.*

A: 1 shared e^- pair = 1 valence electron + 3 unshared pairs = 7 valence electrons, F

E: 2 shared pairs = 2 valence electrons + 2 unshared pairs = 6 valence electrons, O

D: 4 shared pairs = 4 valence electrons, C

Q: 3 shared pairs = 3 valence electrons + 1 unshared pair = 5 valence electrons, N

X: 1 shared pair = 1 valence electron, no unshared pairs, H

Z: same as X, H

Check. Count the valence electrons in the Lewis structure. Does the number correspond to the molecular formula CH_2ONF? 12 e^- pair in the Lewis structure. $CH_2ONF = 4 + 2 + 6 + 5 + 7 = 24 e^-$, 12 e^- pair. The molecular formula we derived matches the Lewis structure.

8.6   *Analyze/Plan.* Given an oxyanion of the type XO_4^{n-}, find the identity of X from elements in the third period. Use the generic Lewis structure to determine the identity of X, and to draw the ion-specific Lewis structures. Use the definition of formal charge, [# of valence electrons – # of nonbonding electrons – (# bonding electrons/2)], to draw Lewis structures where X has a formal charge of zero. *Solve.*

(a)   According to the generic Lewis structure, each anion has 12 nonbonding and 4 bonding electron pairs, for a total of 32 electrons. Of these 32 electrons, the 4 O atoms contribute $(4 \times 6) = 24$, and the overall negative charges contribute 1, 2 or 3. # X electrons = 32 – 24 – n.

For n = 1–, X has $(32 - 24 - 1) = 7$ valence electrons. X is Cl, and the ion is ClO_4^-.

For n = 2–, X has $(32 - 24 - 2) = 6$ valence electrons. X is S, and the ion is SO_4^{2-}.

For n = 3–, X has $(32 - 24 - 3) = 5$ valence electrons. X is P, and the ion is PO_4^{3-}.

Check. The identity of the ions is confirmed in Figure 2.27.

(b)   In the generic Lewis structure, X has 0 nonbonding electrons and $(8/2) = 4$ bonding electrons. Differences in formal charge are due to difference in the number of valence electrons on X.

For PO_4^{3-}, formal charge of P is $(5 - 4) = +1$.

For SO_4^{2-}, formal charge of S is $(6 - 4) = +2$.

For ClO_4^-, formal charge of Cl is $(7 - 4) = +3$.

(c)   In order to reduce the formal charge of X to zero, X must have more bonding electrons. This is accomplished by changing the appropriate number of lone pairs on O to multiple bonds between X and O.

(d)   In part (c) the Lewis structures that cause the formal charge on X to be zero all violate the octet rule. According to Section 8.7, the best single Lewis structure for an anion is the one that obeys the octet rule.

Lewis Symbols

8.8   (a)   Atoms will gain, lose or share electrons to achieve the nearest noble-gas electron configuration. Except for H and He, this corresponds to eight electrons in the valence shell, thus the term octet rule.

(b)   S: $[Ne]3s^23p^4$ A sulfur atom has six valence electrons, so it must gain two electrons to achieve an octet.

(c) $1s^22s^22p^3 = [He]2s^22p^3$ The atom (N) has five valence electrons and must gain three electrons to achieve an octet.

8.10   (a)   Ti: [Ar]$4s^2 3d^2$. Ti has four (4) valence electrons. These valence electrons are available for chemical bonding, while core electons do not participate in chemical bonding.

        (b)   Hf: [Xe]$6s^2 4f^{14} 5d^2$

        (c)   If Hf and Ti both behave as if they have four (4) valence electrons, the 6s and 5d orbitals in Hf behave as valence orbitals and the 4f behaves as a core orbital. This is reasonable because 4f is complete and 4f electrons are, on average, closer to the nucleus than 5d or 6s electrons.

8.12   (a) $\overset{\cdot}{Ca}\cdot$ (b) $\cdot\overset{\cdot\cdot}{\underset{\cdot}{P}}\cdot$ (c) $\left[\overset{\cdot\cdot}{\underset{\cdot\cdot}{:Mg:}}\right]^{2+}$ or Mg^{2+} (d) $\left[\overset{\cdot\cdot}{\underset{\cdot\cdot}{:S:}}\right]^{2-}$ or S^{2-}

Ionic Bonding

8.14 $\overset{\cdot}{Ca}\cdot$ + $\cdot\overset{\cdot\cdot}{\underset{\cdot\cdot}{F}}:$ + $\cdot\overset{\cdot\cdot}{\underset{\cdot\cdot}{F}}:$ ⟶ Ca^{2+} + 2$\left[\overset{\cdot\cdot}{\underset{\cdot\cdot}{:F:}}\right]$

8.16   (a)   BaF$_2$ (b) CsCl   (c) Li$_3$N   (d) Al$_2$O$_3$

8.18   (a)   Zn^{2+}: [Ar]$3d^{10}$

        (b)   Te^{2-}: [Kr]$5s^2 4d^{10} 5p^6$ = [Xe], noble-gas configuration

        (c)   Sc^{3+}: [Ar], noble-gas configuration

        (d)   Rh^{3+}: [Kr]$4d^6$

        (e)   Tl$^+$: [Xe]$6s^2 4f^{14} 5d^{10}$

        (f)   Bi^{3+}:[Xe]$6s^2 4f^{14} 5d^{10}$

8.20   (a)   NaCl, 788 kJ/mol; KF, 808 kJ/mol

        The two factors that affect lattice energies are ionic charge and radius. The ionic charges, 1+ and 1–, are the same in the two compounds. Since lattice energy is inversely proportional to the ion separation (d), we expect the compound with the smaller lattice energy, NaCl, to have the larger ion separation. That is, the K–F distance should be shorter than the Na–Cl distance.

        (b)   Na–Cl, 1.16 Å + 1.67 Å = 2.83 Å

        K–F, 1.52 Å + 1.19 Å = 2.71 Å

        This estimate of the relative ion separations agrees with the estimate from lattice energies. Ionic radii indicate that the K–F distance is shorter than the Na–Cl distance.

8.22   (a)   According to Equation 8.4, electrostatic attraction increases with increasing charges of the ions and decreases with increasing radius of the ions. Thus, lattice energy (i) increases as the charges of the ions increase and (ii) decreases as the sizes of the ions increase.

(b)   KBr < NaF < MgO < ScN. This order is confirmed by the lattice energies given in Table 8.2.   ScN has the highest lattice energy, because its ions have 3+ and 3– charges. Na^+ is smaller than K^+, and F^- is smaller than Br^-. The ion separation is smaller in NaF, so it has the larger lattice energy.

8.24   (a)   The ion charges in CaF_2 and BaF_2 are the same, 2+ for the cations and 1– for the anions. Ba^{2+} is a larger cation than Ca^{2+}, so the ion separation, d, is greater in BaF_2 and the lattice energy is smaller than that of CaF_2.

        (b)   The ions have 1+ and 1– charges in all three compounds. In NaCl the cationic and anionic radii are smaller than in the other two compounds, so it has the largest lattice energy. In RbBr and CsBr, the anion is the same, but the Cs cation is larger, so CsBr has the smaller lattice energy.

        (c)   In BaO, the magnitude of the charges of both ions is 2; in KF, the magnitudes are 1. Charge considerations alone predict that BaO will have the higher lattice energy. The distance effect is less clear; O^{2-} and F^- are isoelectronic, so F^-, with the larger Z, has a slightly smaller radius. Ba^{2+} is two rows lower on the periodic chart than K^+, but it has a greater positive charge, so the radii are probably similar. In any case, the ionic separations in the two compounds are not very different, and the charge effect dominates.

8.26   By analogy to the Born-Haber cycle for NaCl(s), Figure 8.4, the enthalpy of formation for $NaCl_2(s)$ is

$$\Delta H_f^o\, NaCl_2(s) = -\Delta H_{latt} NaCl_2 + \Delta H_f^o\, Na(g) + 2\,\Delta H_f^o\, Cl(g) + I_1(Na) + I_2(Na) + 2E(Cl)$$

        (a) $\Delta H_f^o\, NaCl_2(s) = -\Delta H_{latt} NaCl_2 + 107.7\text{ kJ} + 2(121.7\text{ kJ}) + 496\text{ kJ} + 4562\text{ kJ}$

                                                                                                $+\ 2(-349\text{ kJ})$

        $\Delta H_f^o\, NaCl_2(s) = -\Delta H_{latt} NaCl_2 + 4711\text{ kJ}$

        The collective energy of the "other" steps in the cycle (vaporization and ionization of Na^{2+}, dissociation of Cl_2 and electron affinity of Cl) is +4711 kJ. In order for the sign of $\Delta H_f^o\, NaCl_2$ to be negative, the lattice energy would have to be greater than 4711 kJ.

        (b) $\Delta H_f^o\, NaCl_2(s) = -(2326\text{ kJ}) + 4711\text{ kJ} = 2385\text{ kJ}$

        This value is large and positive.

8.28   (a) $MgCl_2$, 2326 kJ; $SrCl_2$, 2127 kJ. Since the ionic radius of Ca^{2+} is greater than that of Mg^{2+}, but less than that of Sr^{2+}, the ion separation (d) in $CaCl_2$ will be intermediate as well. We expect the lattice energy of $CaCl_2$ to be in the range 2200-2250 kJ.

        (b)   By analogy to Figure 8.4:

        $\Delta H_{latt} = -\Delta H_f^o\, CaCl_2 + \Delta H_f^o\, Ca(g) + 2\Delta H_f^o\, Cl(g) + I_1(Ca) + I_2(Ca) + 2E(Cl)$

        $\quad = -(-795.8\text{ kJ}) + 179.3\text{ kJ} + 2(121.7\text{ kJ}) + 590\text{ kJ} + 1145\text{ kJ} + 2(-349\text{ kJ}) = +2256\text{ kJ}$

        This value is near the range predicted in part (a).

Covalent Bonding, Electronegativity, and Bond Polarity

8.30   K and Ar. K is an active metal with one valence electron. It is most likely to achieve an octet by losing this single electron and to participate in ionic bonding. Ar has a stable octet of valence electrons; it is not likely to form chemical bonds of any type.

8.32

$$:\ddot{F}\cdot \;+\; :\ddot{F}\cdot \;+\; :\ddot{F}\cdot \;+\; \cdot\ddot{P}: \;\longrightarrow\; :\ddot{F}-\overset{\displaystyle :\ddot{F}:}{\underset{\displaystyle :\ddot{F}:}{P}}:$$

8.34   **(a)**   The H atoms must be terminal because H can form only one bond.

               $14\,e^-$, $7\,e^-$ pairs

$$H-\ddot{\underset{..}{O}}-\ddot{\underset{..}{O}}-H$$

        (b)   From Solution 8.33, O_2 has a double bond. The O–O bond in H_2O_2 is a single bond, and thus longer than the O–O bond in O_2.

8.36   **(a)**   The electronegativity of the elements increases going from left to right across a row of the periodic chart.

        (b)   Electronegativity decreases going down a family of the periodic chart.

        (c)   Generally, the trends in electronegativity are the same as those in ionization energy and opposite those in electron affinity. That is, the more positive the ionization energy and the more negative the electron affinity (ignoring a few exceptions), the greater the electronegativity of an element.

8.38   Electronegativity increases going up and to the right in the periodic table.

        (a)   O   **(b)**   Al   **(c)**   Cl   **(d)**   F

8.40   The more different the electronegativity values of the two elements, the more polar the bond.

        (a)   O–F < C–F < Be–F. This order is clear from the periodic trend.

        (b)   S–Br < C–P < O–Cl. Refer to the electronegativity values in Figure 8.6 to confirm the order of bond polarity. The 3 pairs of elements all have the same positional relationship on the periodic chart. The more electronegative element is one row above and one column to the left of the less electronegative element. This leads us to conclude that ΔEN is similar for the 3 bonds, which is confirmed by values in Figure 8.6. The most polar bond, O–Cl, involves the most electronegative element, O. Generally, the largest electronegativity differences tend to be between row 2 and row 3 elements. The 2 bonds in this exercise involving elements in row 2 and row 3 do have slightly greater ΔEN than the S–Br bond, between elements in rows 3 and 4.

        (c)   C–S < N–O < B–F. You might predict that N–O is least polar since the elements are adjacent on the table. However, the big decrease going from the second row to the third means that the electronegativity of S is not only less than that of O, but essentially the same as that of C. C–S is the least polar.

8.42   (a)   The more electronegative element, Br, will have a stronger attraction for the shared electrons and adopt a partial negative charge.

          (b)   Q is the charge at either end of the dipole.

$$Q = \frac{\mu}{r} = \frac{1.21 D}{2.49 \text{ Å}} \times \frac{1 \text{ Å}}{1 \times 10^{-10} \text{ m}} \times \frac{3.34 \times 10^{-30} \text{ C-m}}{1 D} \times \frac{1 e}{1.60 \times 10^{-19} \text{ C}}$$

$$= 0.1014 = 0.101 e$$

The charges on I and Br are 0.101 *e*.

8.44   Generally, compounds formed by a metal and a nonmetal are described as ionic, while compounds formed from two or more nonmetals are covalent. However, substances with metals in a high oxidation states often have properties of molecular compounds.

          (a) $TiCl_4$, metal and nonmetal, Ti(IV) is a relatively high oxidation state, molecular (by contrast with CaF_2, which is definitely ionic), titanium tetrachloride

               CaF_2, metal and nonmetal, ionic, calcium fluoride

          (b) ClF_3, two nonmetals, molecular, chlorine trifluoride

               VF_3, metal and nonmetal, ionic, vanadium(III) fluoride

          (c) $SbCl_5$, metalloid and nonmetal, molecular, antimony pentachloride

               AlF_3, metal and nonmetal, ionic, aluminum fluoride

Lewis Structures; Resonance Structures

8.46   (a)   12 e⁻, 6 e⁻ pairs

          (b)   14 valence e⁻, 7 e⁻ pairs

          (c)   50 valence e⁻, 25 e⁻ pairs

(Choose the Lewis structure that obeys the octet rule, Section 8.7)

          (d)   26 valence e⁻, 13 e⁻ pairs

          (e)   26 valence e⁻, 13 e⁻ pairs

(Choose the Lewis structure that obeys they octet rule, Section 8.7.)

          (f)   10 e⁻, 5 e⁻ pairs

8.48   (a)   26 e⁻, 13 e⁻ pairs

$$:\ddot{\text{F}}-\overset{|}{\text{P}}-\ddot{\text{F}}:$$
$$|$$
$$:\ddot{\text{F}}:$$

The octet rule is satisfied for all atoms in the structure.

(b)   F is more electronegative than P. Assuming F atoms hold all shared electrons, the oxidation number of each F is –1. The oxidation number of P is +3.

(c)   Assuming perfect sharing, the formal charges on all F and P atoms are 0.

(d)   The oxidation number on P is +3; the formal charge is 0. These represent extremes in the possible electron distribution, not the best picture. By virtue of their greater electronegativity, the F atoms carry a partial negative charge, and the P atom a partial positive charge.

8.50   Formal charges are given near the atoms, oxidation numbers are listed below the structures.

(a)   18 e⁻, 9 e⁻ pairs   (b)   24 e⁻, 12 e⁻ pairs

$$:\ddot{\text{O}}-\ddot{\text{S}}=\ddot{\text{O}}$$
$$\;-1\quad +1\quad\;\; 0$$

ox. #: S, +4; O, –2

$$-1:\ddot{\text{O}}-\overset{+2}{\text{S}}=\ddot{\text{O}}\; 0$$
$$|$$
$$:\ddot{\text{O}}:$$
$$-1$$

ox. #: S, +6; O, –2

(c)   26 e⁻, 13 e⁻ pairs

$$\left[-1:\ddot{\text{O}}-\overset{+1}{\ddot{\text{S}}}-\ddot{\text{O}}:-1\right]^{2-}$$
$$|$$
$$:\ddot{\text{O}}:$$
$$-1$$

ox. #: S, +4; O, –2

(d) $SO_2 < SO_3 < SO_3^{2-}$

Double bonds are shorter than single bonds. SO_2 has two resonance structures with alternating single and double bonds, for an approximate average "one-and-a-half" bond. SO_3 has three resonance structures with one double and two single bonds, for an approximately, "one-and-a-third" bond. SO_3^{2-} has all single bonds. The order of increasing bond length is the order of decreasing bond type.

SO_2 (1.5) < SO_3 (1.3) < SO_3^{2-} (1.0).

8.52   (a)   16 e⁻, 8 e⁻ pairs

$$\left[\ddot{\text{O}}=\text{N}=\ddot{\text{O}}\right]^+ \longleftrightarrow \left[:\text{O}\equiv\text{N}-\ddot{\text{O}}:\right]^+ \longleftrightarrow \left[:\ddot{\text{O}}-\text{N}\equiv\text{O}:\right]^+$$

(b)   More than one correct Lewis structure can be drawn, so resonance structures are needed to accurately describe the structure.

114

(c) NO_2^+ has 16 valence electrons. Consider other triatomic molecules involving second-row nonmetallic elements. O_3^{2+} or C_3^{4-} are not "common" (or stable). CO_2 is common and matches the description (as does N_3^-, azide ion).

8.54   The Lewis structures are as follows:

5 e⁻ pairs   9 e⁻ pairs

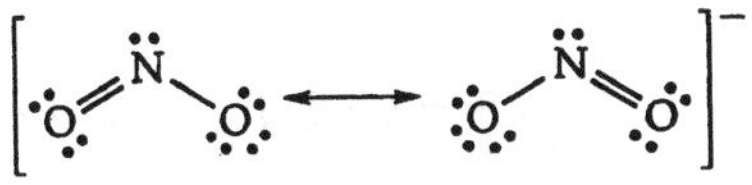

12 e⁻ pairs

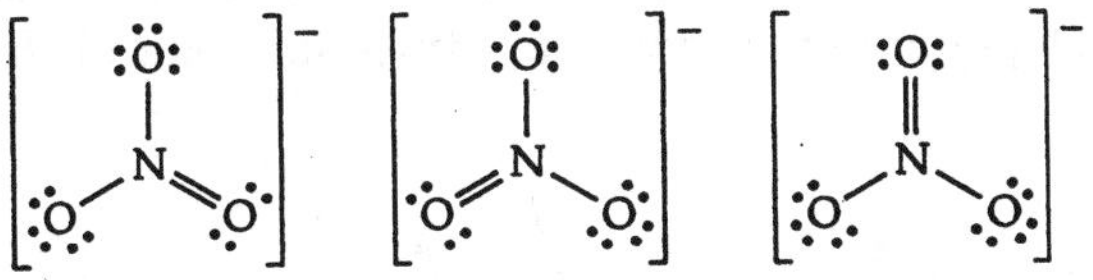

The average number of electron pairs in the N–O bond is 3.0 for NO^+, 1.5 for NO_2^-, and 1.33 for NO_3^-. The more electron pairs shared between two atoms, the shorter the bond. Thus the N–O bond lengths vary in the order $NO^+ < NO_2^- < NO_3^-$.

8.56   (a)

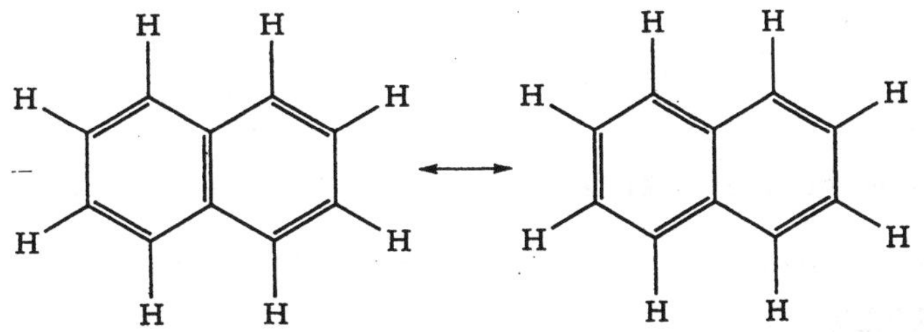

(b)   The resonance model of this molecule has bonds that are neither single nor double, but somewhere in between. This results in bond lengths that are intermediate between C–C single and C=C double bond lengths.

(c)

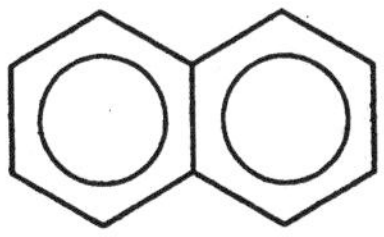

Exceptions to the Octet Rule

8.58   Carbon, in group 14, needs to form four single bonds to achieve an octet, as in CH_4. Nitrogen, in group 15, needs to form three, as in NH_3. If G = group number and n = the number of single bonds, G + n = 18 is a general relationship for the representative non-metals.

Check: O as in H_2O (G = 16) + (n = 2 bonds) = 18

8.60   In the third period, atoms have the space and available orbitals to accommodate extra electrons. Since atomic radius increases going down a family, elements in the third period and beyond are less subject to destabilization from additional electron-electron repulsions. Also, the third shell contains d orbitals that are relatively close in energy to 3s and 3p orbitals (the ones that accommodate the octet) and provide an allowed energy state for the extra electrons.

8.62   (a)   8 e⁻, 4 e⁻ pairs

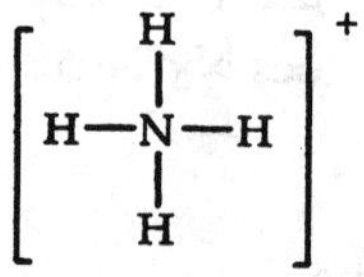

$$\left[\begin{array}{c} H \\ | \\ H-N-H \\ | \\ H \end{array}\right]^{+}$$

(b)   16 e⁻, 8 e⁻ pairs

$$\left[:\ddot{S}-C\equiv N:\right]^{-} \longleftrightarrow \left[\ddot{S}=C=\ddot{N}:\right]^{-} \longleftrightarrow \left[:S\equiv C-\ddot{N}:\right]^{-}$$

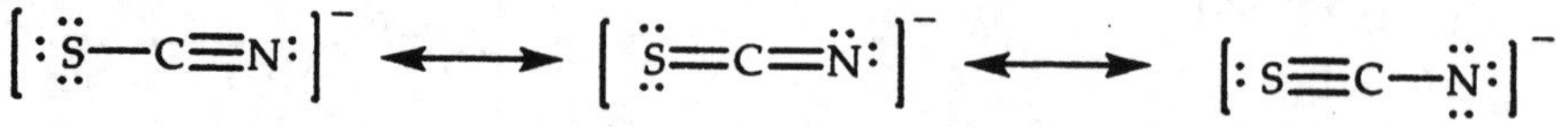

Three resonance structures, all obey the octet rule. The middle structure is probably the largest contributor to the actual structure. (See Sample Exercise 8.9.)

(c)   26 e⁻, 13 e⁻ pairs

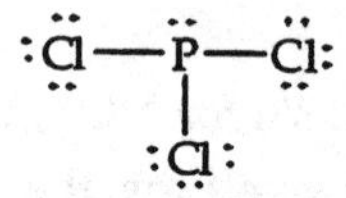

$$:\ddot{C}l-\ddot{P}-\ddot{C}l: \\ | \\ :\ddot{C}l:$$

(d)   34 e⁻, 17 e⁻ pairs

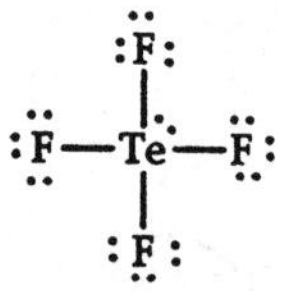

$$:\ddot{F}: \\ | \\ :\ddot{F}-\ddot{Te}-\ddot{F}: \\ | \\ :\ddot{F}:$$

Does not obey the octet rule.

(e)   22 e⁻, 11 e⁻ pair

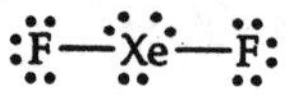

$$:\ddot{F}-\ddot{Xe}-\ddot{F}:$$

Does not obey the octet rule.

8.64   (a)   19 e⁻, 9.5 e⁻ pairs, odd electron molecule

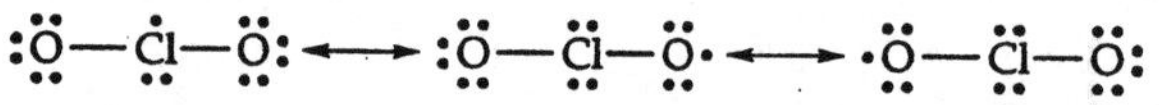

$$:\ddot{O}-\ddot{C}l-\ddot{O}: \longleftrightarrow :\ddot{O}-\ddot{C}l-\dot{O}\cdot \longleftrightarrow \cdot\ddot{O}-\ddot{C}l-\ddot{O}:$$

(b)   None of the structures satisfies the octet rule. In each structure, one atom has only 7 e⁻ around it. If a molecule has an odd number of electrons in the valence shell, no Lewis structure can satisfy the octet rule.

(c) 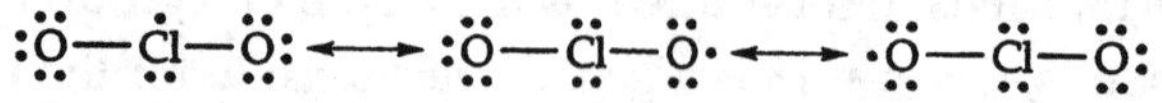 $$:\ddot{O}-\ddot{C}l-\ddot{O}: \longleftrightarrow :\ddot{O}-\ddot{C}l-\dot{O}\cdot \longleftrightarrow \cdot\ddot{O}-\ddot{C}l-\ddot{O}:$$
           −1   +2   −1   −1   +1   0   0   +1   −1

Formal charge arguments predict that the two resonance structures with the odd electron on O are most important. This contradicts electronegativity arguments, which would predict that the less electronegative atom, Cl, would be more likely to have fewer than 8 e⁻ around it.

Bond Enthalpies

8.66   (a) $\Delta H = 3D(C-Br) + D(C-H) + D(Cl-Cl) - 3D(C-Br) - (C-Cl) - D(H-Cl)$

            $= D(C-H) + D(Cl-Cl) - D(C-Cl) - D(H-Cl)$

       $\Delta H = 413 + 242 - 328 - 431 = -104 \text{ kJ}$

   (b) $\Delta H = 4D(C-H) + 2D(C-S) + 2D(S-H) + D(C-C) + 2D(H-Br)$

            $-4D(S-H) - D(C-C) - 2D(C-Br) - 4D(C-H)$

         $= 2D(C-S) + 2D(H-Br) - 2D(S-H) - 2D(C-Br)$

       $\Delta H = 2(259) + 2(366) - 2(339) - 2(276) = 20 \text{ kJ}$

   (c) $\Delta H = 4D(N-H) + D(N-N) + D(Cl-Cl) - 4D(N-H) - 2D(N-Cl)$ (

         $= D(N-N) + D(Cl-Cl) - 2D(N-Cl)$

       $\Delta H = 163 + 242 - 2(200) = 5 \text{ kJ}$

8.68   *Plan.* Draw structural formulas so bonds can be visualized.   *Solve.*

   (a)

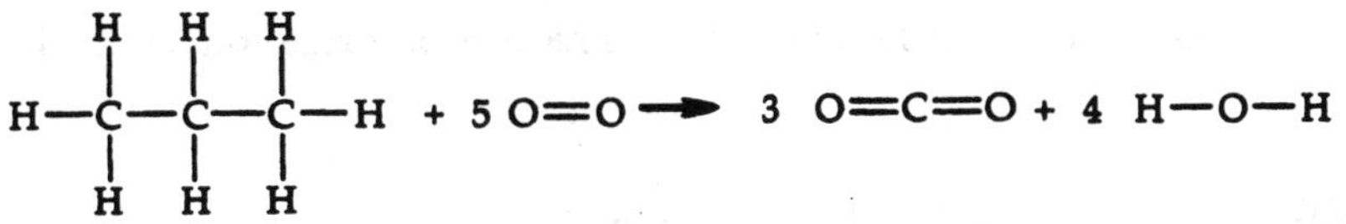

      $\Delta H = 2D(C-C) + 8D(C-H) + 5D(O=O) - 6D(C=O) - 8D(O-H)$

        $= 2(348) + 8(413) + 5(495) - 6(799) - 8(463) = -2023 \text{ kJ}$

   (b)

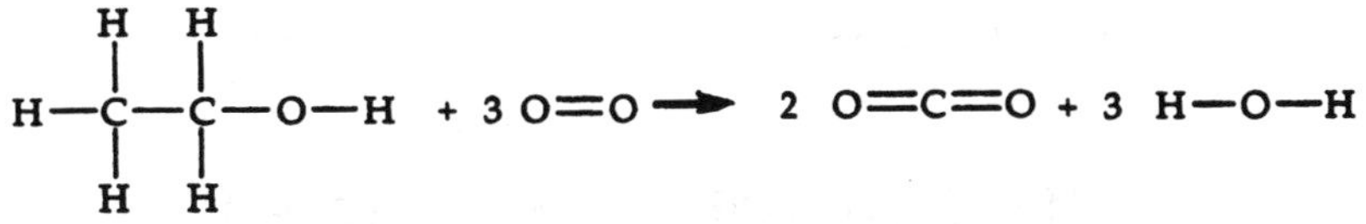

      $\Delta H = D(C-C) + 5D(C-H) + D(C-O) + D(O-H) + 3D(O=O) - 4D(C=O) - 6D(O-H)$

        $= 348 + 5(413) + 358 + 3(495) - 4(799) - 5(463) = -1255 \text{ KJ}$

   (c)   *Plan.* Use bond enthalpies to calculate ΔH for the reaction with $S_8(g)$ as a product. Then,

       $8H_2S(g) \rightarrow 8H_2(g) + S_8(g)$ ΔH

           $\underline{S_8(g) \rightarrow S_8(s)}$ $\underline{-\Delta H_f^\circ \text{ for } S_8(g)}$

       $8H_2S(g) \rightarrow 8H_2(g) + S_8(s)$ $\Delta H_{rxn} = [\Delta H - \Delta H_f^\circ S_8(g)]$

      $\Delta H = 16D(S-H) - 8(H-H) - 8(S-S)$

        $= 16(339) - 8(436) - 8(266) = -192 \text{ kJ}$

      $\Delta H_{rxn} = \Delta H - \Delta H_f^\circ S_8(g) = -192 \text{ kJ} - 102.3 \text{ kJ} = -294.3 = -294 \text{ kJ}$

8.70 (a)

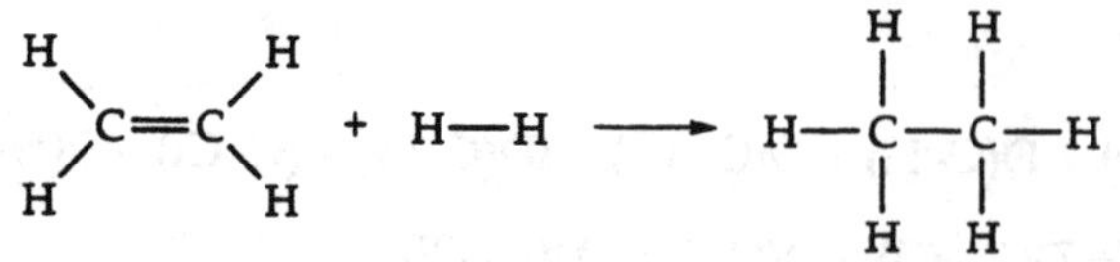

$$H_2C{=}CH_2 + H{-}H \longrightarrow H_3C{-}CH_3$$

$$\Delta H = 4D(C{-}H) + D(C{=}C) + D(H{-}H) - 6D(C{-}H) - D(C{-}C)$$

$$= D(C{=}C) + D(H{-}H) - 2D(C{-}H) - D(C{-}C)$$

$$\Delta H = 614 + 436 - 2(413) - 348 = -124 \text{ kJ}$$

(b) $\Delta H^\circ = \Delta H_f^\circ\ C_2H_6(g) - \Delta H_f^\circ\ C_2H_4(g) - \Delta H_f^\circ\ H_2(g)$

$$= -84.68 - 52.30 - 0 = -136.98 \text{ kJ}$$

The values of ΔH for the reaction differ because the bond enthalpies used in part (a) are average values that can differ from one compound to another. For example, the exact enthalpy of a C-H bond in C_2H_4 is probably not equal to the enthalpy of a C-H bond in C_2H_6. Thus, reaction enthalpies calculated from average bond enthalpies are estimates. On the other hand, standard enthalpies of formation are measured quantities and should lead to accurate reaction enthalpies. The advantage of average bond enthalpies is that they can be used for reactions where no measured enthalpies of formation are available.

8.72 (a) (i) 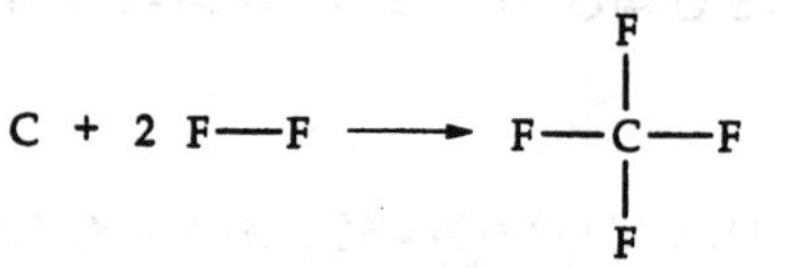 $C + 2\ F{-}F \longrightarrow F{-}CF_2{-}F$ (CF$_4$)

$$\Delta H = 2D(F{-}F) - 4D(C{-}F) = 2(155) - 4(485) = -1630 \text{ kJ}$$

(ii) 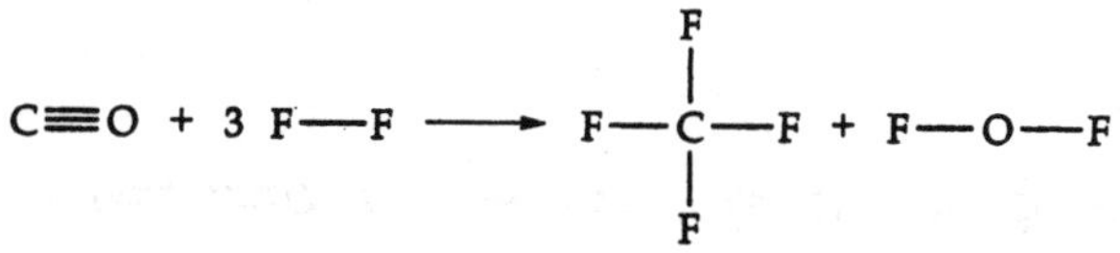 $C{\equiv}O + 3\ F{-}F \longrightarrow F{-}CF_2{-}F + F{-}O{-}F$

$$\Delta H = D(C{\equiv}O) + 3D(F{-}F) - 4D(C{-}F) - 2D(O{-}F)$$

$$= 1072 + 3(155) - 4(485) - 2(190) = -783 \text{ kJ}$$

(iii) 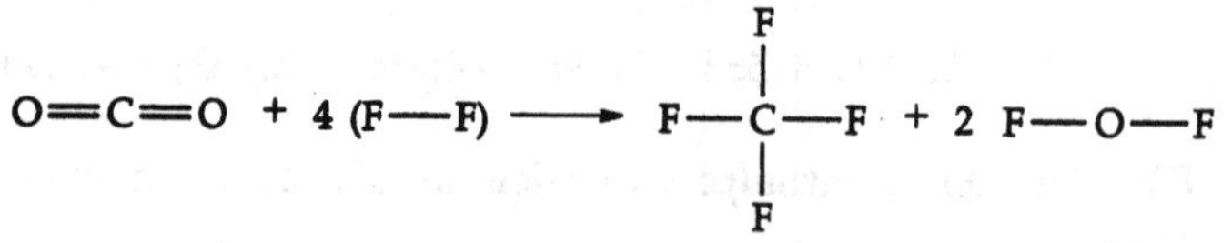 $O{=}C{=}O + 4\ (F{-}F) \longrightarrow F{-}CF_2{-}F + 2\ F{-}O{-}F$

$$\Delta H = 2D(C{=}O) + 4D(F{-}F) - 4D(C{-}F) - 4D(O{-}F)$$

$$= 2(799) + 4(155) - 4(485) - 4(190) = -482 \text{ kJ}$$

Reaction (i) is most exothermic.

(b)   The more oxygen atoms bound to carbon, the less exothermic the reaction in this series.

Additional Exercises

8.74 (a) Lattice energy is proportional to $Q_1 Q_2 / d$. For each of these compounds, $Q_1 Q_2$ is the same. The anion H^- is present in each compound, but the ionic radius of the cation increases going from Be to Ba. Thus, the value of d (the cation-anion separation) increases and the ratio $Q_1 Q_2 / d$ decreases. This is reflected in the decrease in lattice energy going from BeH_2 to BaH_2.

(b) Again, $Q_1 Q_2$ for ZnH_2 is the same as that for the other compounds in the series and the anion is H^-. The lattice energy of ZnH_2, 2870 kJ, is closest to that of MgH_2, 2791 kJ. The ionic radius of Zn^{2+} is similar to that of Mg^{2+}.

8.76 AlN and ScN have the same charges on cations (3+) and anions (3–), so differences in lattice energy are due to differences in ion separation (d). With the same anion in both compounds, any separation difference depends on the difference in ionic radii of Al^{3+} and Sc^{3+}. The Al^{3+} cation is isoelectronic with Ne in the second row, while Sc^{3+} is isoelectronic with Ar in the third row. Size increases going down a family, so the ionic radius of Al^{3+} is smaller than that of Sc^{3+}. Lattice energy is inversely proportional to ion separation, so AlN, with the smaller separation, has the larger lattice energy.

8.77
$$E = \frac{-8.99 \times 10^9 \text{ J-m}}{C^2} \times \frac{4(1.60 \times 10^{-19} \text{ C})^2}{(1.14 + 1.26) \times 10^{-10} \text{ m}} = -3.836 \times 10^{-18} = -3.84 \times 10^{-18} \text{ J}$$

On a molar basis: $(-3.836 \times 10^{-18} \text{ J})(6.022 \times 10^{23}) = -2.310 \times 10^6 \text{ J} = -2310 \text{ kJ}$

Note that the absolute value of this potential energy is less than the lattice energy of CaO, 3414 kJ/mol. The difference represents the added energy of putting all the $Ca^{2+}O^{2-}$ ion pairs together in a three-dimensional array, similar to the one in Figure 8.3.

8.78 $E = Q_1 Q_2 / d$; $\quad k = 8.99 \times 10^9$ J-m/coul^2

(a) Na^+, Br^-: $E = \dfrac{-8.99 \times 10^9 \text{ J-m}}{C^2} \times \dfrac{(1 \times 1.60 \times 10^{-19} \text{ C})^2}{(1.16 + 1.82) \times 10^{-10} \text{ m}} = -7.7230 \times 10^{-19}$

$$= -7.72 \times 10^{-19} \text{ J}$$

The sign of E is negative because one of the interacting ions is an anion; this is an attractive interaction.

On a molar basis: $-7.723 \times 10^{-19} \times 6.022 \times 10^{23} = -4.65 \times 10^5 \text{ J} = -465 \text{ kJ}$

(b) Rb^+, Br^-: $E = \dfrac{-8.99 \times 10^9 \text{ J-m}}{C^2} \times \dfrac{(1 \times 1.60 \times 10^{-19} \text{ C})^2}{(1.66 + 1.82) \times 10^{-10} \text{ m}} = -6.61 \times 10^{-19} \text{ J}$

On a molar basis: $-3.98 \times 10^5 \text{ J} = -398 \text{ kJ}$

(c) Sr^{2+}, S^{2-}: $E = \dfrac{-8.99 \times 10^9 \text{ J-m}}{C^2} \times \dfrac{(2 \times 1.60 \times 10^{-19} \text{ C})^2}{(1.32 + 1.70) \times 10^{-10} \text{ m}} = -3.05 \times 10^{-18} \text{ J}$

On a molar basis: $-1.84 \times 10^6 \text{ J} = -1.84 \times 10^3 \text{ kJ}$

8.80 Molecule (b) H_2S and ion (c) NO_2^- contain polar bonds. The atoms that form the bonds (H–S) and N–O) have different electronegativity values.

8.81 (a) $2NaAlH_4(s) \rightarrow 2NaH(s) + 2Al(s) + 3H_2(g)$

(b)   Hydrogen is the only nonmetal in $NaAlH_4$, so we expect it to be most electronegative. (The position of H on the periodic table is problematic. Its electronegativity does not fit the typical trend for Gp 1A elements.) For the two metals, Na and Al, electronegativity increases moving up and to the right on the periodic table, so Al is more electronegative. The least electronegative element in the compound is Na.

(c)   Covalent bonds hold polyatomic anions together; elements involved in covalent bonding have smaller electronegativity differences than those that are involved in ionic bonds. Possible covalent bonds in $NaAlH_4$ are Na–H and Al–H. Al and H have a smaller electronegativity difference than Na and H and are more likely to form covalent bonds. The anion has an overall 1– charge, so it can be thought of as four hydride ions and one Al^{3+} ion. The formula is AlH_4^-. For the purpose of counting valence electrons, assume neutral atoms.

$8\ e^-$, $4\ e^-$ pairs

$$\left[\begin{array}{c} H \\ | \\ H-Al-H \\ | \\ H \end{array} \right]$$

8.82   (a)   B–O. The most polar bond will be formed by the two elements with the greatest difference in electronegativity. Since electronegativity increases moving right and up on the periodic chart, the possibilities are B–O and Te–O. These two bonds are likely to have similar electronegativitiy differences (3 columns apart vs. 3 rows apart). Values from Figure 8.6 confirm the similarity, and show that B–O is slightly more polar.

(b)   Te–I. Both are in the fifth row of the periodic chart and have the two largest covalent radii among this group of elements.

(c) TeI_2. Te needs to participate in two covalent bonds to satisfy the octet rule, and each I atom needs to participate in one bond, so by forming a TeI_2 molecule, the octet rule can be satisfied for all three atoms.

$$:\ddot{\underset{..}{I}}—\ddot{\underset{..}{Te}}—\ddot{\underset{..}{I}}:$$

(d) B_2O_3. Although this is probably not a purely ionic compound, it can be understood in terms of gaining and losing electrons to achieve a noble-gas configuration. If each B atom were to lose $3\ e^-$ and each O atom were to gain $2\ e^-$, charge balance and the octet rule would be satisfied.

P_2O_3. Each P atom needs to share $3\ e^-$ and each O atom $2\ e^-$ to achieve an octet. Although the correct number of electrons seem to be available, a correct Lewis structure is difficult to imagine. In fact, phosphorus (III) oxide exists as P_4O_6 rather than P_2O_3 (Chapter 22).

8.84   To calculate empirical formulas, assume 100 g of sample.

(a) $\dfrac{47.7\ g\,Cr}{51.9961 g\,/\,mol} = 0.9174\ mol\ Cr$; $0.9174/0.9174 = 1\ Cr$

$$\frac{52.3 \text{ g F}}{18.9984 \text{ g/mol}} = 2.753 \text{ mol F}; \ 2.753/0.9174 = 3 \text{ F}$$

The empirical formula of compound 1 is CrF_3.

(b) $\quad \dfrac{45.7 \text{ g Mo}}{95.94 \text{ g/mol}} = 0.4763 \text{ mol Mo}; \ 0.4763/0.4763 = 1 \text{ Mo}$

$$\frac{54.3 \text{ g F}}{18.9984 \text{ g/mol}} = 2.858 \text{ mol F}; \ 2858/0.4763 = 6 \text{ F}$$

The empirical formula of Compound 2 is MoF_6.

(c) The high-melting green powder is ionic and contains the group 6B metal in the lower oxidation state, Cr(III). The green powder is CrF_3, chromium(III) fluoride.

The colorless liquid is molecular and contains the group 6B metal in the higher oxidation state, Mo(VI). The colorless liquid is MoF_6, molybdenum hexafluoride.

8.86 Use the method detailed in Section 8.5, *A Closer Look*, to estimate partial charges from electronegativity values. From Figure 8.6, the electronegativity of Br is 2.8 and of Cl is 3.0.

Br has $2.8/(3.0 + 2.8) = 0.48$ of the charge of the bonding e^- pair.

Cl has $3.0/(3.0 + 2.8) = 0.52$ of the charge of the bonding e^- pair.

This amounts to $0.52 \times 2e = 1.04e$ on Cl or $0.04e$ more than a neutral Cl atom. This implies a –0.04 charge on Cl and +0.04 charge on Br.

From Figure 7.7, the covalent radius of Br is 1.14 Å and of Cl is 0.99 Å. The Br–Cl separation is 2.13 Å.

$$\mu = Qr = 0.04e \times \frac{1.60 \times 10^{-19} \text{ C}}{e} \times 2.13 \text{ Å} \times \frac{1 \times 10^{-10} \text{ m}}{\text{Å}} \times \frac{1 \text{ D}}{3.34 \times 10^{-30} \text{ C·m}} = 0.41 \text{ D}$$

Clearly, this method is approximate. The estimated dipole moment of 0.41 D is within 28% of the measured value of 0.57 D.

8.87 I_3^- has a Lewis structure with an expanded octet of electrons around the central I.

$$:\!\overset{\cdot\cdot}{\underset{\cdot\cdot}{I}}\!—\!\overset{\cdot\cdot}{\underset{\cdot\cdot}{I}}\!—\!\overset{\cdot\cdot}{\underset{\cdot\cdot}{I}}\!:$$

F cannot accommodate an expanded octet because it is too small and has no available d orbitals in its valence shell.

8.89 (a) $\quad 14e^-$, 7 e^- pairs $32 \ e^-$, 16 e^- pairs

$$\left[:\!\overset{\cdot\cdot}{\underset{\cdot\cdot}{Cl}}\!—\!\overset{\cdot\cdot}{\underset{\cdot\cdot}{O}}\!: \right]^-$$

$$\left[\begin{array}{c} :\!\overset{\cdot\cdot}{O}\!: \\ | \\ :\!\overset{\cdot\cdot}{O}\!—Cl—\overset{\cdot\cdot}{O}\!: \\ | \\ :\!\overset{\cdot\cdot}{O}\!: \end{array} \right]^-$$

FC on Cl = $7 - [6 + 1/2(2)] = 0$

FC on Cl = $7 - [0 + 1/2(8)] = +3$

(b) The oxidation number of Cl is +1 in ClO^- and +7 in ClO_4^-.

(c)   The definition of formal charge assumes that all bonding pairs of electrons are equally shared by the two bonded atoms, that all bonds are purely covalent. The definition of oxidation number assumes that the more electronegative element in the bond gets all of the bonding electrons, that the bonds are purely ionic. These two definitions represent the two extremes of how electron density is distributed between bonded atoms.

In ClO^- and ClO_4^-, Cl is the less electronegative element, so the oxidation numbers have a higher positive value than the formal charges. The true description of the electron density distribution is somewhere between the extremes indicated by formal charge and oxidation number.

(d)   Oxidizing power is the tendency of a substance to be reduced, to gain electrons. Oxidation numbers show the maximum electron deficiency (or excess) of a substance. The higher the oxidation number of the central atom in an oxyanion, the greater its electron deficiency and oxidizing power. Formal charges can also be used to show oxidizing (or reducing) power, but trends are less obvious because the magnitudes are smaller.

8.90   (a)   :N≡N—Ö: ⟷ :N̈—N≡O: ⟷ :N̈=N=Ö:
               0 +1 −1   −2 +1 −1   −1 +1 0

In the leftmost structure, the more electronegative O atom has the negative formal charge, so this structure is likely to be most important.

(b)   In general, the more shared pairs of electrons between two atoms, the shorter the bond, and vice versa. That the N–N bond length in N_2O is slightly longer than the typical N≡N indicates that the middle and right resonance structures where the N atoms share less than three electron pairs are contributors to the true structure. That the N–O bond length is slightly shorter than a typical N=O indicates that the middle structure, where N and O share more than two electron pairs, does contribute to the true structure. This physical data indicates that while formal charge can be used to predict which resonance form will be more important to the observed structure, the influence of minor contributors on the true structure cannot be ignored.

8.92   (a) $\Delta H = 5D(C-H) + D(C-C) + D(C-O) + D(O-H) - 6D(C-H) - 2D(C-O)$

$= D(C-C) + D(O-H) - D(C-H) - D(C-O)$

$= 348 \text{ kJ} + 463 \text{ kJ} - 413 \text{ kJ} - 358 \text{ kJ}$

$\Delta H = +40 \text{ kJ}$; ethanol has the lower enthalpy

(b) $\Delta H = 4D(C-H) + D(C-C) + 2D(C-O) - 4D(C-H) - D(C-C) - D(C=O)$

$= 2D(C-O) - D(C=O)$

$= 2(358 \text{ kJ}) - 799 \text{ kJ}$

$\Delta H = -83 \text{ kJ}$; acetaldehyde has the lower enthalpy

(c) $\Delta H = 8D(C-H) + 4D(C-C) + D(C=C) - 8D(C-H) - 2D(C-C) - 2D(C=C)$

       $= 2D(C-C) - D(C=C)$

       $= 2(348 \text{ kJ}) - 614 \text{ kJ}$

$\Delta H = +82 \text{ kJ}$; cyclopentene has the lower enthalpy

(d) $\Delta H = 3D(C-H) + D(C-N) + D(C \equiv N) - 3D(C-H) - D(C-C) - D(C \equiv N)$

       $= D(C-N) - D(C-C)$

       $= 293 \text{ kJ} - 348 \text{ kJ}$

$\Delta H = -55 \text{ kJ}$; acetonitrile has the lower enthalpy

8.93   (a)

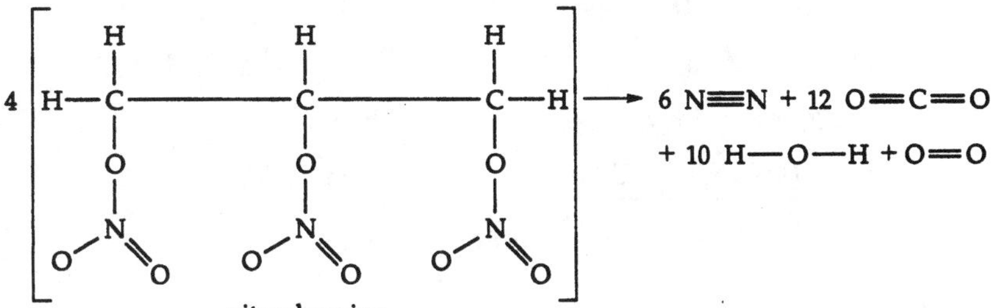

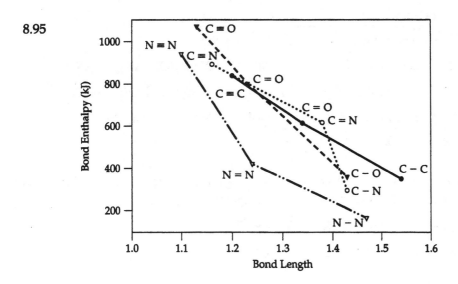

nitroglycerine

$\Delta H = 20D(C-H) + 8D(C-C) + 12D(C-O) + 24D(O-N) + 12D(N=O)$

         $- [6D(N \equiv N) + 24D(C=O) + 20D(H-O) + D(O=O)]$

$\Delta H = 20(413) + 8(348) + 12(358) + 24(201) + 12(607)$

         $- [6(941) + 24(799) + 20(463) + 495]$

    $= -7129 \text{ kJ}$

$$1.00 \text{ g } C_3H_5N_3O_9 \times \frac{1 \text{ mol } C_3H_5N_3O_9}{227.1 \text{ g } C_3H_5N_3O_9} \times \frac{-7129 \text{ kJ}}{4 \text{ mol } C_3H_5N_3O_9} = 7.85 \text{ kJ/g } C_3H_5N_3O_9$$

(b) $4C_7H_5N_3O_6(s) \rightarrow 6N_2(g) + 7CO_2(g) + 10H_2O(g) + 21C(s)$

8.95

When comparing the same pair of bonded atoms (C–N vs. C=N vs. C≡N), the shorter the bond the greater the bond energy, but the two quantities are not necessarily directly proportional. The plot clearly shows that there are no simple length/strength correlations for single bonds alone, double bonds alone, triple bonds alone, or among different pairs of bonded atoms (all C–C bonds vs. all C–N bonds, etc.).

Integrative Exercises

8.98   (a) $Sr(s) \rightarrow Sr(g)$ $\Delta H_f^\circ \; Sr(g) \; [\Delta H_{sub}^\circ \; Sr(s)]$

               $Sr(g) \rightarrow Sr^+(g) + 1\,e^-$ $I_1 \; Sr$

               $Sr^+(g) \rightarrow Sr^{2+}(g) + 1\,e^-$ $I_2 \; Sr$

               $Cl_2(g) \rightarrow 2Cl(g)$ $2\,\Delta H_f^\circ \; Cl(g) \; [D(Cl_2)]$

               $2Cl(g) + 2\,e^- \rightarrow 2Cl^-(g)$ $2E_1 \; Cl$

               $\underline{SrCl_2(s) \rightarrow Sr(s) + Cl_2(g)}$ $\underline{-\Delta H_f^\circ \; SrCl_2}$

               $SrCl_2(s) \rightarrow Sr^{2+}(g) + 2Cl^-(g)$ ΔH_{latt}

     (b) $\Delta H_f^\circ \; SrCl_2(s) = \Delta H_f^\circ \; Sr(g) + I_1(Sr) + I_2(Sr) + 2\Delta H_f^\circ \; Cl(g) + 2E(Cl) - \Delta H_{latt} \; SrCl_2$

           $\Delta H_f^\circ \; SrCl_2(s) = 164.4\;kJ + 549\;kJ + 1064\;kJ + 2(121.7)\;kJ + 2(-349)\;kJ - 2127\;kJ$

                     $= -804\;kJ$

8.99   The pathway to the formation of K_2O can be written:

        $2K(s) \rightarrow 2K(g)$ $2\Delta H_f^\circ \; K(g)$

        $2K(g) \rightarrow 2K^+(g) + 2\,e^-$ $2\,I_1(K)$

        $1/2\,O_2(g) \rightarrow O(g)$ $\Delta H_f^\circ \; O(g)$

        $O(g) + 1\,e^- \rightarrow O^-(g)$ $E_1(O)$

        $O^-(g) + 1\,e^- \rightarrow O^{2-}(g)$ $E_2(O)$

        $\underline{2K^+(g) + O^{2-}(g) \rightarrow K_2O(s)}$ $\underline{-\Delta H_{latt} \; K_2O(s)}$

        $2K(s) + 1/2\,O_2(g) \rightarrow K_2O(s)$ $\Delta H_f^\circ \; K_2O(s)$

        $\Delta H_f^\circ \; K_2O(s) = 2\Delta H_f^\circ \; K(g) + 2\,I_1(K) + \Delta H_f^\circ \; O(g) + E_1(O) + E_2(O) - \Delta H_{latt} \; K_2O(s)$

        $E_2(O) = \Delta H_f^\circ \; K_2O(s) + \Delta H_{latt} \; K_2O(s) - 2\Delta H_f^\circ \; K(g) - 2\,I_t(K) - \Delta H_f^\circ \; O(g) - E_1(O)$

        $E_2(O) = -363.2\;kJ + 2238\;kJ - 2(89.99)\;kJ - 2(419)\;kJ - 247.5\;kJ - (-141)\;kJ$

            $= +750\;kJ$

8.101   (a)   Even though Cl has the greater (more negative) electron affinity, F has a much larger ionization energy, so the electronegativity of F is greater.

          F: $k(IE - EA) = k(1681 - (-328)) = k(2009)$

          Cl: $k(IE - EA) = k(1251 - (-349)) = k(1600)$

(b)   Electronegativiy is the ability of an atom in a molecule to attract electrons to itself. It can be thought of as the ability to hold its own electrons (as measured by ionization energy) and the capacity to attract the electrons of other atoms (as measured by electron affinity). Thus, both properties are relevant to the concept of electronegativity.

(c)   EN = k(IE – EA). For F: 4.0 = k(2009), k = 4.0/2009 = 2.0×10^{-3}

(d)   Cl: EN = 2.0×10^{-3} (1600) = 3.2

      O: EN = 2.0×10^{-3} (1314 – (–141)) = 2.9

These values do not follow the trend on Figure 8.6. The Pauling scale on the figure shows O to be second only to F in electronegativity, more electronegative than Cl. The simple definition EN = k(IE – EA) that employs thermochemical properties of isolated, gas phase atoms does not take into account the complex bonding environment of molecules.

8.102   (a)   Assume 100 g.

$$14.52 \, g \, C \times \frac{1 \, mol}{12.011 \, g \, C} = 1.209 \, mol \, C; \, 1.209/1.209 = 1$$

$$1.83 \, g \, H \times \frac{1 \, mol}{1.008 \, g \, H} = 1.816 \, mol \, H; \, 1.816/1.209 = 1.5$$

$$64.30 \, g \, Cl \times \frac{1 \, mol}{35.453 \, g \, Cl} = 1.814 \, mol \, Cl; \, 1.814/1.209 = 1.5$$

$$19.35 \, g \, O \times \frac{1 \, mol}{15.9994 \, g \, O} = 1.209 \, mol \, O; \, 1.209/1.209 = 1.0$$

Multiplying by 2 to obtain an integer ratio, the empirical formula is $C_2H_3Cl_3O_2$.

(b)   The empirical formula weight is 2(12.0) + 3(1.0) + 3(35.5) + 2(16) = 165.5. The empirical formula is the molecular formula.

(c)   44 e^-, 22 e^- pairs

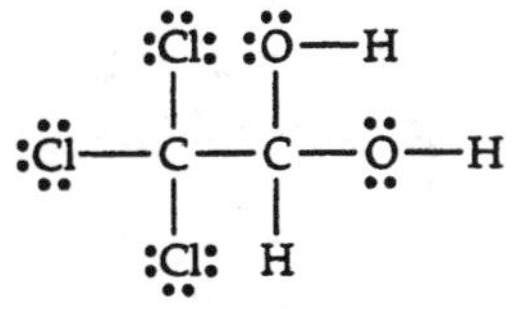

8.104   (a) C_2H_2: 10 e^-, 5 e^- pair N_2: 10 e^-, 5 e^- pair

      H—C≡C—H   :N≡N:

(b) N_2 is an extremely stable, unreactive compound. Under appropriate conditions, it can be either oxidized (Section 22.7) or reduced (Sections 14.7 and 15.2). C_2H_2 is a reactive gas, used in combination with O_2 for welding and as starting material for organic synthesis (Section 25.3).

(c) $2N_2(g) + 5O_2(g) \rightarrow 2N_2O_5(g)$

$2C_2H_2(g) + 5O_2(g) \rightarrow 4CO_2(g) + 2H_2O(g)$

(d) $\Delta H^\circ_{rxn}(N_2) = 2\Delta H^\circ_f \, N_2O_5(g) - 2\Delta H^\circ_f \, N_2(g) - 5\Delta H^\circ_f \, O_2(g)$
$$= 2(11.30) - 2(0) - 5(0) = 22.60 \text{ kJ}$$

$\Delta H^\circ_{ox} = 11.30 \text{ kJ/mol } N_2$

$\Delta H^\circ_{rxn}(C_2H_2) = 4\Delta H^\circ_f \, CO_2(g) + 2\Delta H^\circ_f \, H_2O(g) - 2\Delta H^\circ_f \, C_2H_2(g) - 5\Delta H^\circ_f \, O_2(g)$
$$= 4(-393.5 \text{ kJ}) + 2(-241.82 \text{ kJ}) - 2(226.7 \text{ kJ}) - 5(0)$$
$$= -2511.0 \text{ kJ}$$

$\Delta H^\circ_{ox}(C_2H_2) = -1255.5 \text{ kJ/mol } C_2H_2$

The oxidation of C_2H_2 is highly exothermic, which means that the energy state of the combined products is much lower than that of the reactants. The reaction is "downhill" in an energy sense, and occurs readily. The oxidation of N_2 is mildly endothermic (energy of products higher than reactants) and the reaction does not readily occur. This is in agreement with the general reactivities from part (b).

Referring to bond enthalpies in Table 8.4, when the C–H bonds are taken into account, even more energy is required for bond breaking in the oxidation of C_2H_2 than in the oxidation of N_2. The difference seems to be in the enthalpies of formation of the products. $CO_2(g)$ and $H_2O(g)$ have extremely exothermic ΔH°_f values, which cause the oxidation of C_2H_2 to be energetically favorable. $N_2O_5(g)$ has an endothermic ΔH°_f value, which causes the oxidation of N_2 to be energetically unfavorable.

8.105 (a)   Assume 100 g of compound

$$69.6 \text{g S} \times \frac{1 \text{ mol S}}{32.07 \text{ g}} = 2.17 \text{ mol S}$$

$$30.4 \text{ g N} \times \frac{1 \text{ mol N}}{14.01 \text{ g}} = 2.17 \text{ mol N}$$

S and N are present in a 1:1 mol ratio, so the empirical formula is SN. The empirical formula weight is 46. MM/FW = 184.3/46 = 4 The molecular formula is S_4N_4.

(b)   44 e⁻, 22 e⁻ pairs. Because of its small radius, N is unlikely to have an expanded octet. Begin with alternating S and N atoms in the ring. Try to satisfy the octet rule with single bonds and lone pairs. At least two double bonds somewhere in the ring are required.

These structures carry formal charges on S and N atoms as shown. Other possibilities include:

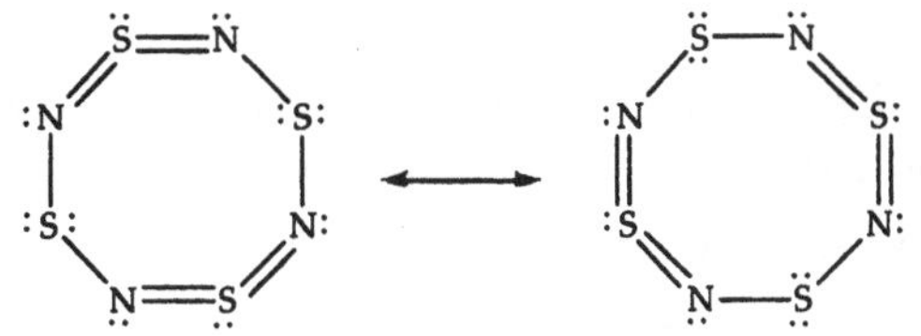

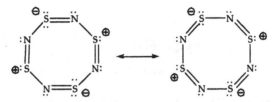

These structures have zero formal charges on all atoms and are likely to contribute to the true structure. Note that the S atoms that are shown with two double bonds are not necessarily linear, because S has an expanded octet. Other resonance structures with four double bonds are.

In either resonance structure, the two 'extra' electron pairs can be placed on any pair of S atoms in ring, leading to a total of 10 resonance structures. The sulfur atoms alternately carry formal charges of +1 and –1. Without further structural information, it is not possible to eliminate any of the above structures. Clearly, the S_4N_4 molecule stretches the limits of the Lewis model of chemical bonding.

(c)   Each resonance structure has 8 total bonds and more than 8 but less than 16 bonding e⁻ pairs, so an "average" bond will be intermediate between a S–N single and double bond. We estimate an average S–N single bond length to be 1.77 Å (sum of bonding atomic radii from Figure 7.7). We do not have a direct value for a S–N double bond length. Comparing double and single bond lengths for C–C (1.34 Å, 1.54 Å), N–N (1.24 Å, 1.47 Å) and O–O (1.21 Å, 1.48 Å) bonds from Table 8.5, we see that, on average, a double bond is approximately 0.23 Å shorter than a single bond. Applying this difference to the S–N single bond length, we estimate the S–N double bond length as 1.54 Å. Finally, the intermediate S–N bond length in S_4N_4 should be between these two values, approximately 1.60–165 Å. (The measured bond length is 1.62 Å.)

(d) $S_4N_4 \rightarrow 4S(g) + 4N(g)$

$\Delta H = 4\Delta H_f^{\circ} S(g) + 4\Delta H_f^{\circ} N(g) - \Delta H_f^{\circ} S_4N_4$

$\Delta H = 4(222.8 \text{ kJ}) + 4(472.7 \text{ kJ}) - 480 \text{ kJ} = 2302 \text{ kJ}$

This energy, 2302 kJ, represents the dissociation of 8 S–N bonds in the molecule; the average dissociation energy of one S–N bond in S_4N_4 is then 2302 kJ/8 bonds = 287.8 kJ.

8.106   (a)   Yes. In the structure shown in the exercise, each P atom needs 1 unshared pair to complete its octet. This is confirmed by noting that only 6 of the 10 valence e⁻ pairs are bonding pairs.

(b)   There are six P–P bonds in P_4.

(c)   20 e⁻, 10 e⁻ pr

$$\ddot{P}\!=\!P\!=\!P\!=\!\ddot{P}$$

In this Lewis structure, the octet rule is satisfied for all atoms. However, it requires P=P, which are uncommon because P has a covalent radius that is too large to accommodate the side-to-side π overlap of parallel p orbitals required for double bond formation.

(d)   From left to right, the formal charges are on the P atoms in the linear structure are –1, +1, +1, –1. In the tetrahedral structure, all formal charges are zero. Clearly the linear structure does not minimize formal charge and is probably less stable than the tetrahedral structure, owing to the difficulty of P=P bond formation (see above).

8.107   (a) $C_6H_6(g) \rightarrow 6H(g) + 6C(g)$

$\Delta H^{\circ} = 6\Delta H_f^{\circ}\ H(g) + 6\Delta H_f^{\circ}\ C(g) - \Delta H_f^{\circ}\ C_6H_6(g)$

$\Delta H^{\circ} = 6(217.94)\ kJ + 6(718.4)\ kJ - 82.9\ kJ = 5535\ kJ$

(b) $C_6H_6(g) \rightarrow 6CH(g)$

(c)

	ΔH°	
$C_6H_6(g) \rightarrow 6H(g) + 6C(g)$		5535 kJ
$6H(g) + 6C(g) \rightarrow 6CH(g)$	$-6D(C\!-\!H)$	$-6(413)$ kJ
$C_6H_6(g) \rightarrow 6CH(g)$		3057 kJ

3057 kJ is the energy required to break the six C–C bonds in $C_6H_6(g)$. The average bond dissociation energy for one carbon-carbon bond in $C_6H_6(g)$ is

$$\frac{3057\ kJ}{6\,C-C\ bonds} = 509.5\ kJ.$$

(d)   The value of 509.5 kJ is between the average value for a C–C single bond (348 kJ) and a C=C double bond (614 kJ). It is somewhat greater than the average of these two values, indicating that the carbon-carbon bond in benzene is a bit stronger than we might expect.

8.108   (a) $Br_2(l) \rightarrow 2Br(g)$ $\Delta H^{\circ} = 2\Delta H_f^{\circ}\ Br(g) = 2(111.8)\ kJ = 223.6\ kJ$

(b) $CCl_4(l) \rightarrow C(g) + 4Cl(g)$

$\Delta H^{\circ} = \Delta H_f^{\circ}\ C(g) + 4\Delta H_f^{\circ}\ Cl(g) - \Delta H_f^{\circ}\ CCl_4(l)$

      $= 718.4\ kJ + 4(121.7)\ kJ - (-139.3)\ kJ = 1344.5$

$$\frac{1344.5\ kJ}{4\,C-Cl\ bonds} = 336.1\ kJ$$

(c)

$$H_2O_2(l) \rightarrow 2H(g) + 2O(g)$$
$$2H(g) + 2O(g) \rightarrow 2OH(g)$$
$$H_2O_2(l) \rightarrow 2OH(g)$$

$$D(O-O)(l) = 2\Delta H_f^{\circ} H(g) + 2\Delta H_f^{\circ} O(g) - \Delta H_f^{\circ} H_2O_2(l) - 2D(O-H)(g)$$

$$= 2(217.94) \text{ kJ} + 2(247.5) \text{ kJ} - (-187.8) \text{ kJ} - 2(463) \text{ kJ}$$

$$= 193 \text{ kJ}$$

(d)   The data are listed below.

bond	D gas kJ/mol	D liquid kJ/mol
Br–Br	193	223.6
C–Cl	328	336.1
O–O	146	192.7

Breaking bonds in the liquid requires more energy than breaking bonds in the gas phase. For simple molecules, bond dissociation from the liquid phase can be thought of in two steps:

molecule (l) → molecule (g)

molecule (g) → atoms (g)

The first step is evaporation or vaporization of the liquid and the second is bond dissociation in the gas phase. Average bond enthalpy in the liquid phase is then the sum of the enthalpy of vaporization for the molecule and the gas phase bond dissociation enthalpies, divided by the number of bonds dissociated. This is greater than the gas phase bond dissociation enthalpy owing to the contribution from the enthalpy of vaporization.

9 Molecular Geometry and Bonding Theories

Visualizing Concepts

9.2 (a) 120°

(b) If the blue balloon expands, the angle between red and green balloons decreases.

(c) Nonbonding (lone) electron pairs exert greater repulsive forces than bonding pairs, resulting in compression of adjacent bond angles.

9.4 (a) 4 e^- domains

(b) The molecule has a non-zero dipole moment, because the C–H and C–F bond dipoles do not cancel each other.

(c) The dipole moment vector bisects the F–C–F and H–C–H angles, with the negative end of the vector toward the F atoms.

9.6 (a) 90° angles are characteristic of hybrids with a d atomic orbital contribution. This pair of orbitals could be sp^3d or sp^3d^2.

(b) Angles of 109.5° are characteristic of sp^3 hybrid orbitals only.

(c) Angles of 120° can be formed by sp^2 hybrids or sp^3d hybrids.

9.8 (a) Recall that π bonds require p atomic orbitals, so the maximum hybridization of a C atom involved in a double bond is sp^2 and in a triple bond is sp. There are 6 C atoms in the molecule. Starting on the left, the hybridizations are: sp^2, sp^2, sp^3, sp, sp, sp^3.

(b) All single bonds are σ bonds. Double and triple bonds each contain 1 σ bond. This molecule has 8 C–H σ bonds and 5 C–C σ bonds, for a total of 13 σ bonds.

(c) Double bonds have 1 π bond and triple bonds have 2 π bonds. This molecule has a total of 3 π bonds.

9.10 (a) The diagram has five electrons in MOs formed by 2p atomic orbitals. C has two 2p electrons, so X must have three 2p electrons. X is N.

(b) The molecule has an unpaired electron, so it is paramagnetic.

(c) Atom X is N, which is more electronegative than C. The atomic orbitals of the more electronegative N are slightly lower in energy than those of C. The lower energy π_{2p} bonding molecular orbitals will have a greater contribution from the lower energy N atomic orbitals. (Higher energy π_{2p}^* MOs will have a greater contribution from higher energy C atomic orbitals.)

130

Molecular Shapes; the VSEPR Model

9.12   (a)   In a symmetrical tetrahedron, the four bond angles are equal to each other, with values of 109.5°. The H–C–H angles in CH_4 and the O–Cl–O angles in ClO_4^- will have values close to 109.5°.

      (b)   'Planar' molecules are flat, so trigonal planar BF_3 is flat. In the trigonal pyramidal NH_3 molecule, the central N atom sits out of the plane of the three H atoms; this molecule is not flat.

9.14   (a)   The number of electron domains in a molecule or ion is the number of bonds (double and triple bonds count as one domain) **plus** the number of nonbonding (lone) electron pairs.

      (b)   A *bonding electron domain* is a region between two bonded atoms that contains one or more pairs of bonding electrons. A *nonbonding electron domain* is localized on a single atom and contains one pair of nonbonding electrons (a lone pair).

9.16   *Analyze/Plan.* See Table 9.1. *Solve.*

      (a)   trigonal planar   (b)   tetrahedral

      (c)   trigonal bipyramidal   (d)   octahedral

9.18   If the electron-domain geometry is trigonal bipyramidal, there are five total electron domains around the central atom. An AB_3 molecule has three bonding domains, so there must be two nonbonding domains on A.

9.20

9.22   bent (b), linear (l), octahedral (oh), seesaw (ss) square pyramidal (sp), square planar (spl), tetrahedral (td), trigonal bipyramidal (tbp), trigonal planar (tr), trigonal pyramidal (tp), T-shaped (T)

	Molecule or ion	Valence electrons	Lewis structure	Electron-domain geometry	Molecular geometry
(a)	PF_3	26		td	tp
(b)	CH_3^+	6	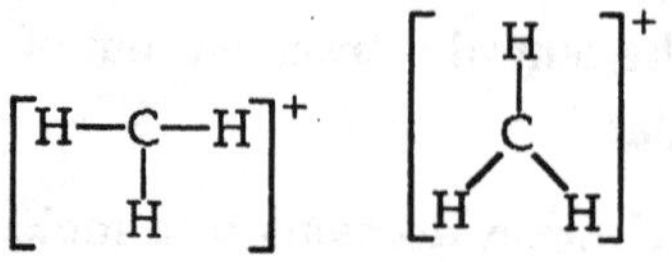	tr	tr
(c)	BrF_3	28	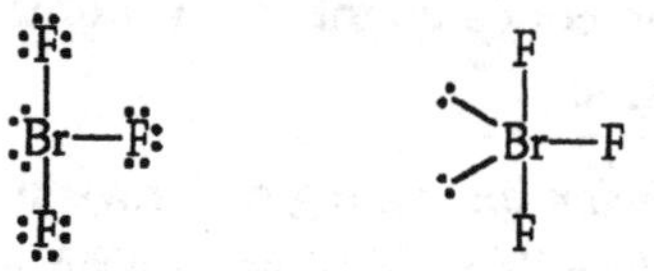	tbp	T
(d)	ClO_4^-	32	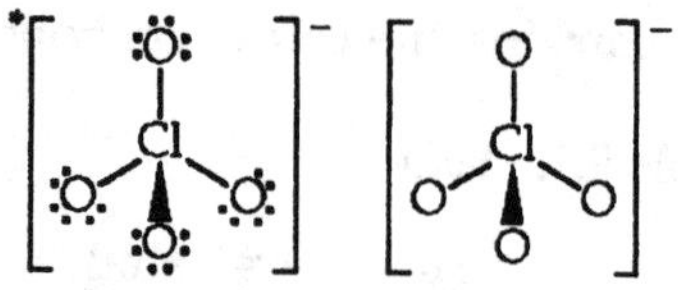	td	td
(e)	XeF_2	22	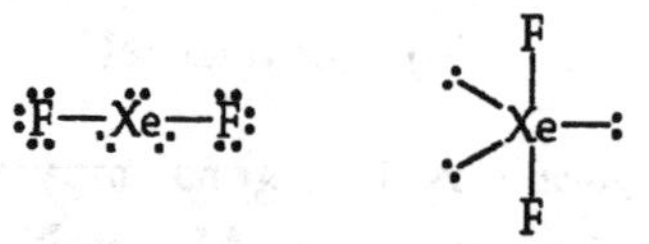	tbp	l
(f)	BrO_2^-	20	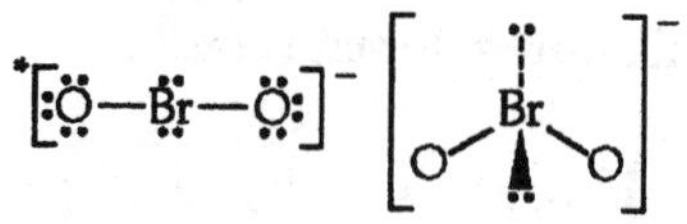	td	b

*More than one resonance structure is possible. All equivalent resonance structures predict the same molecular geometry.

9.24   (a)   Electron-domain geometries: i, octahedral; ii, tedrahedral; iii, trigonal bipyramial

       (b)   nonbonding electron domains: i, 2; ii, 0; iii, 1

       (c)   S or Se. Shape iii has five electron domains, so A must be in or below the third row of the periodic table. This eliminates Be and C. Assuming each F atom has three nonbonding electron domains and forms only single bonds with A, A must have six valence electrons to produce these electron-domain and molecular geometries.

       (d)   Xe. (See Table 9.3) Assuming F behaves typically, A must be in or below the third row and have eight valence electrons. Only Xe fits this description. (Noble gas elements above Xe have not been shown to form molecules of the type AF_4. See Section 7.8.)

9.26   (a)   1 – 109°, 2 – 120°   (b)   3 – 109°, 4 – 120°

       (c)   5 – 109°, 6 – 109°   (d)   7 – 180°, 8 – 109°

9.28 $\left[H—\overset{..}{\underset{..}{N}}—H\right]^-$ $H—\overset{..}{N}—H$ $\left[\begin{array}{c} H \\ | \\ H—N—H \\ | \\ H \end{array}\right]^+$
                                         $\quad\quad\;\; |$
                                         $\quad\quad\; H$

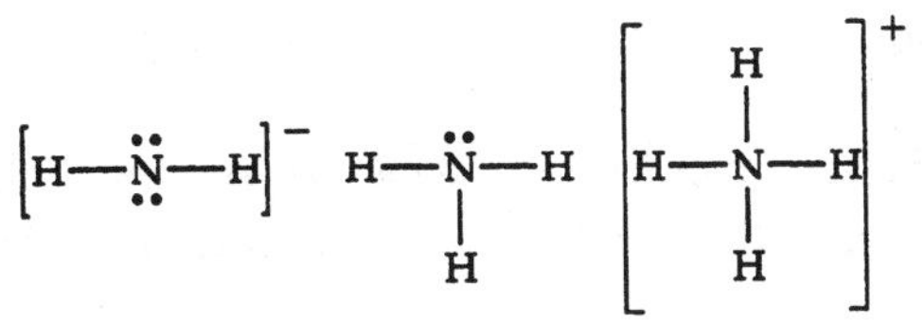

Each species has four electron domains around the N atom, but the number of nonbonding domains decreases from two to zero, going from NH_2^- to NH_4^+. Since nonbonding domains exert greater repulsive forces on adjacent domains, the bond angles expand as the number of nonbonding domains decreases.

9.30   (a) ClO_2^- 20 e$^-$, 10 e$^-$ pr

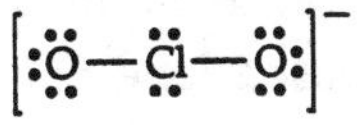

$\left[:\overset{..}{\underset{..}{O}}—\overset{..}{\underset{..}{Cl}}—\overset{..}{\underset{..}{O}}:\right]^-$

4 e$^-$ domains around Cl, tetrahedral e$^-$ domain geometry,

bent molecular geometry bond angle $\lesssim 109.5°$

NO_2^- 18 e$^-$, 9 e$^-$ pr

$\left[\overset{..}{\underset{..}{O}}=\overset{..}{N}—\overset{..}{\underset{..}{O}}:\right]^- \longleftrightarrow \left[:\overset{..}{\underset{..}{O}}—\overset{..}{N}=\overset{..}{\underset{.}{O}}\right]^-$

3 e$^-$ domains about N (both resonance structures), trigonal planar e$^-$ domain geometry bent molecular geometry bond angle $\lesssim 120°$

Both molecular geometries are described as "bent" because both molecules have two nonlinear bonding electron domains. The bond angles (the angle between the two bonding domains) in the two ions are different because the total number of electron domains, and thus the electron domain geometries are different.

   (b) XeF_2 22 e$^-$, 11 e$^-$ pr

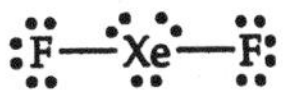

$:\overset{..}{\underset{..}{F}}—\overset{..}{\underset{..}{Xe}}—\overset{..}{\underset{..}{F}}:$

5 e$^-$ domains around Xe, trigonal bipyramidal e$^-$ domain geometry, linear molecular geometry

The question here really is: why do the three nonbonding domains all occupy the equatorial plane of the trigonal bipyramid? In a tbp, there are several different kinds of repulsions, bonding domain-bonding domain (bd-bd), bonding domain-nonbonding domain (bd-nd), and nonbonding domain-nonbonding domain (nd-nd). Each of these can have 90°, 120°, or 180° geometry. Since nonbonding domains occupy more space, 90° nd-nd repulsions are most significant and least desirable. The various electron domains arrange themselves to minimize these 90° nd-nd interactions. The arrangement shown above has no 90° nd-nd repulsions. An arrangement with one or two nonbonding domains in axial positions would lead to at least two 90° nd-nd repulsions, a less stable situation. (To convince yourself, tabulate the number and kinds of repulsions for each possible tbp arrangement of 2bd's and 3nd's.)

Polarity of Polyatomic Molecules

9.32 (a) If PH_3 were planar, the P–H bond dipoles would cancel, and the molecule would be nonpolar. Since PH_3 is polar, the 3 P–H bond dipoles do not cancel, and the molecule can't be planar.

(b) O_3, 18 e$^-$, 9 e$^-$ pr; :Ö=Ö—Ö: ⟷ :Ö—Ö=Ö:

trigonal planar e$^-$ domain geometry
bent molecular geometry

Since all atoms are the same, the individual bond dipoles are zero. However, the central O atom has a lone pair of electrons which cause an unequal electron (and charge) distribution in the molecule. The unopposed lone pair is the source of the dipole moment in O_3.

9.34 (a) For a molecule with polar bonds to be nonpolar, the polar bonds must be (symmetrically) arranged so that the bond dipoles cancel. In most cases, nonbonding e$^-$ domains must be absent from the central atom. Square planar structures may not meet the second condition.

(b) AB_2: linear e$^-$ domain geometry (edg), linear molecular geometry (mg), trigonal bipyramidal edg, linear mg

AB_3: trigonal planar edg, trigonal planar mg

AB_4: tetrahedral edg, tetrahedral mg; octahedral edg, square planar mg

9.36 (a) Nonpolar, in a symmetrical tetrahedral structure (Figure 9.1) the bond dipoles cancel.

(b) Polar, there is an unequal charge distribution due to the nonbonded electron pair on N.

(c) Polar, there is an unequal charge distribution due to the nonbonded electron pair on S.

(d) Nonpolar, the bond dipoles and the nonbonded electron pairs cancel.

(e)   Polar, the C–H and C–Br bond dipoles are not equal and do not cancel.

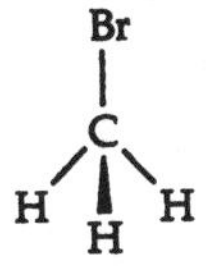

(f)   Nonpolar, in a symmetrical trigonal planar structure, the bond dipoles cancel.

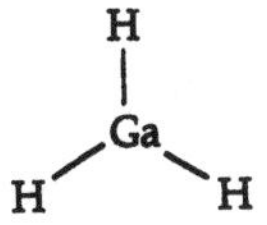

9.38   Each C–Cl bond is polar. The question is whether the vector sum of the C–Cl bond dipoles in each molecule will be nonzero. In the *ortho* and *meta* isomers, the C–Cl vectors are at 60° and 120° angles, respectively, and their resultant dipole moments are nonzero. In the *para* isomer, the C–Cl vectors are opposite, at an angle of 180°, with a resultant dipole moment of zero. The *ortho* and *meta* isomers are polar, the *para* isomer is nonpolar.

Orbital Overlap; Hybrid Orbitals

9.40   (a)

2s   2s

(b)

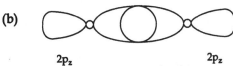

2p$_z$ 2p$_z$

(c)

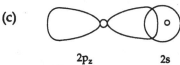

2p$_z$ 2s

9.42   By analogy to the H$_2$ molecule shown in Figure 9.15, as the distance between the atoms decreases, the overlap between their valence orbitals increases. According to Figure 7.7, the bonding atomic radius for the halogens is on the order F < Cl < Br < I. The order of bond lengths in the molecules is I–F < I–Cl < I–Br < I–I. If the extent of orbital overlap increases as the distance between atoms decreases, I–F has the greatest overlap and I$_2$ the least. The order for extent of orbital overlap is I–I < I–Br < I–Cl < I–F.

9.44   In order for atomic orbitals to mix or hybridize, they must have the same principal quantum number. In each principal quantum level, there are a maximum of three *p* orbitals. Any hybrid orbital can have contribution from a maximum of three *p* orbitals. Hybrid orbitals designated sp^4 or sp^5 would require contribution from four or five *p* orbitals, which is not possible.

9.46   (a)   S: $[Ne]3s^2 3p^4$

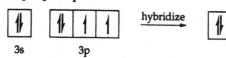

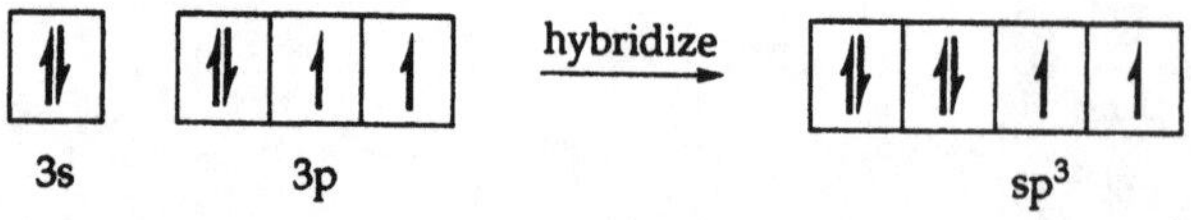

3s   3p   sp³

(b)   The hybrid orbitals are called sp³.

(c)

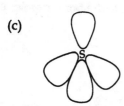

(d)   The hybrid orbitals formed in (a) would not be appropriate for SF_4. There are five electron domains in SF_4, four bonding and one nonbonding, so five hybrid orbitals are required. A set of four sp³ hybrid orbitals could not accommodate all the electron pairs around S.

9.48   (a)   32 e⁻, 16 e⁻ pairs

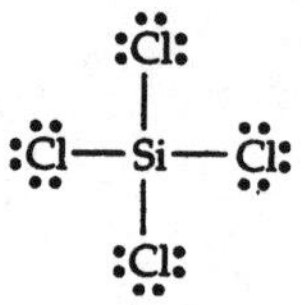

       :Cl̈:
       |
:C̈l—Si—C̈l:
       |
       :C̈l:

4 e⁻ pairs around Si, tetrahedral e⁻ domain geometry, sp³ hybridization

(b)   10 e⁻, 5 e⁻ pairs

H—C≡N:

2 e⁻ domains around C, linear e⁻ domain geometry, sp hybridization

(c)   24 e⁻, 12 e⁻ pairs

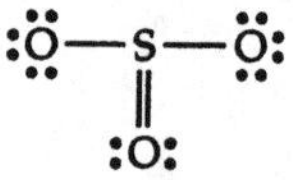

:Ö—S—Ö:
     ‖
    :O:

(other resonance structures are possible)
3 e⁻ domains around S, trigonal planar e⁻ domain geometry, sp² hybridization

(d)   22 e⁻, 11 e⁻ pairs

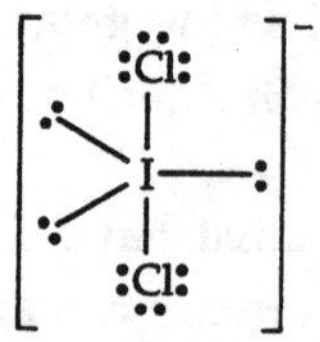

$$\left[\begin{array}{c} :\ddot{C}l: \\ | \\ I—: \\ | \\ :\ddot{C}l: \end{array} \right]^{-}$$

5 e⁻ domains around I, trigonal bipyramidal e⁻ domain geometry, sp³d hybridization (In a trigonal bipyramid, placing nonbonding e⁻ pairs in the equatorial position minimizes repulsion.)

(e)   36 e⁻, 18 e⁻ pairs

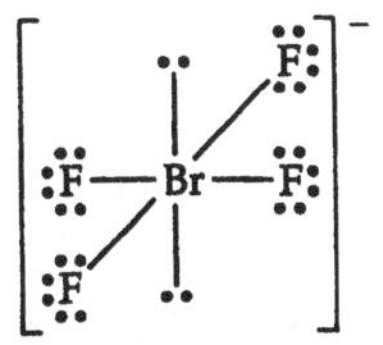

$$\left[\begin{array}{c} \ddot{\text{F}} \\ | \\ :\ddot{\text{F}}\!\!-\!\!\text{Br}\!\!-\!\!\ddot{\text{F}}: \\ | \\ :\ddot{\text{F}} \end{array}\right]^{-}$$

6 e⁻ domains around Br, octahedral e⁻ domain geometry, sp^3d^2 hybridization

Multiple Bonds

9.50   (a)   Two unhybridized p orbitals remain, and the atom can form two pi bonds.

       (b)   It would be much easier to twist or rotate around a single sigma bond. Sigma bonds are formed by end-to-end overlap of orbitals and the bonding electron density is symmetric about the internuclear axis. Rotating (twisting) around a sigma bond can be done without disrupting either the orbital overlap or bonding electron density, without breaking the bond.

            The π part of a double bond is formed by side-to-side overlap of p atomic orbitals perpendicular to the internuclear axis. This π overlap locks the atoms into position and makes twisting difficult. Also, only a small twist (rotation) destroys overlap of the p orbitals and breaks the π bond.

9.52   (a)   H—N̈—N̈—H   :N≡N:
                | |
                H   H

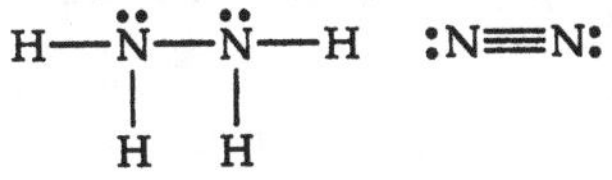

       (b)   The N atoms in N_2H_4 are sp^3 hybridized; there are no unhybridized p orbitals available for π bonding. In N_2, the N atoms are sp hybridized, with two unhybridized p orbitals on each N atom available to form the two π bonds in the N≡N triple bond.

       (c)   The N–N triple bond is N_2 is significantly stronger than the N–N single bond in N_2H_4, because it consists of one σ and two π bonds, rather than a 'plain' sigma bond. Generally, bond strength increases as the extent of orbital overlap increases. The additional overlap from the two π bonds adds to the strength of the N–N bond in N_2.

9.54   (a)   The C bound to O has three electron domains and is sp^2 hybridized; the other three C atoms are sp^3 hybridized.

       (b) $C_4H_8O_2$ has 4(4) + 8(1) + 2(6) = 36 valence electrons.

       (c)   13 pairs or 26 total valence electrons form σ bonds

       (d)   1 pair or 2 total valence electrons form π bonds

       (e)   4 pairs or 8 total valence electrons are nonbonding

9.56   (a)   1, 120°; 2, 120°; 3, 109°

       (b)   1, sp^2; 2, sp^2; 3, sp^3

       (c)   21 σ bonds

9.58   (a)   24 e⁻, 12 e⁻ pairs   (b)

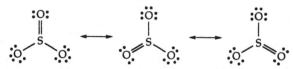

        3 electron domains around S, trigonal planar electron-domain geometry, sp^2 hybrid orbitals

   (c)   The multiple resonance structures indicate delocalized π bonding. All four atoms lie in the trigonal plane of the sp^2 hybrid orbitals. On each atom there is a p atomic orbital perpendicular to this plane in the correct orientation for π overlap. The resulting delocalized π electron cloud is Y-shaped (the shape of the molecule) and has electron density above and below the plane of the molecule.

Molecular Orbitals

9.60   (a)   An MO, since the AOs come from two different atoms.

   (b)   A hybrid orbital, since the AOs are on the same atom.

   (c)   Yes. The Pauli principle, that no two electrons can have the same four quantum numbers, means that an orbital can hold at most two electrons. (Since n, l, and m_1 are the same for a particular orbital and m_s has only two possible values, an orbital can hold at most two electrons). This is true for atomic and molecular orbitals.

9.62   (a)

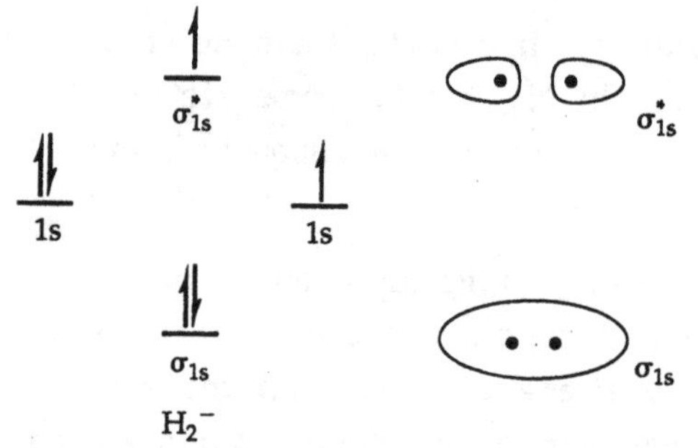

   (b)

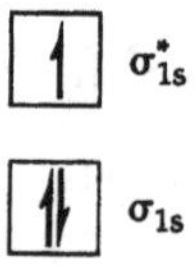

   (c)   Bond order = 1/2 (2-1) = ½

   (d)   If one electron moves from σ_{1s} to σ^*_{1s}, the bond order becomes –1/2. There is a net increase in energy relative to isolated H atoms, so the ion will decompose.

$$H_2^- \xrightarrow{h\nu} H + H^-.$$

9.64   (a)   Zero

(b)   The two π_{2p} molecular orbitals are degenerate; they have the same energy, but they have different spatial orientations 90° apart.

(c)   In the bonding MO the electrons are stabilized by both nuclei. In an antibonding MO, the electrons are directed away from the nuclei, so π_{2p} is lower in energy than π^*_{2p}.

9.66   (a) O_2^{2-} has a bond order of 1.0, while O_2^- has a bond order of 1.5. For the same bonded atoms, the greater the bond order the shorter the bond, so O_2^- has the shorter bond.

(b)   The two possible orbital energy level diagrams are:

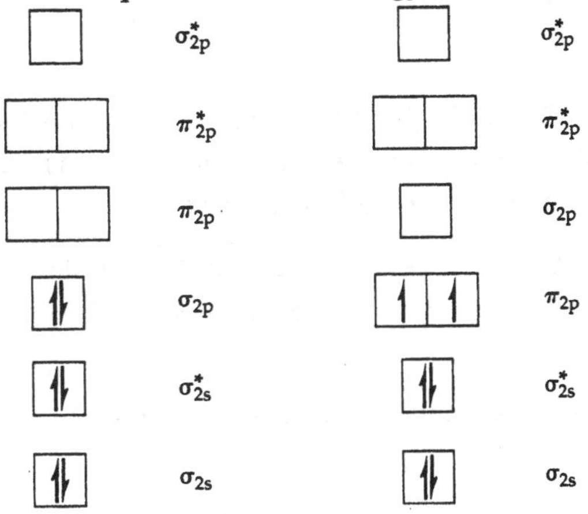

The magnetic properties of a molecule reveal whether it has unpaired electrons. If the σ_{2p} MOs are lower in energy, B_2 has no unpaired electrons. If the π_{2p} MOs are lower in energy than the σ_{2p} MO, there are two unpaired electrons. The magnetic properties of B_2 must indicate that it has unpaired electrons.

(c)   According to Figure 9.46, the two highest-energy electrons of O_2 are in antibonding π^*_{2p} MOs and O_2 has a bond order of 2.0 Removing these two electrons to form O_2^{2+} produces an ion with bond order 3.0. O_2^{2+} has a stronger O–O bond than O_2, because O_2^{2+} has a greater bond order.

9.68   (a)   Substances with unpaired electrons are attracted into a magnetic field. This property is called *paramagnetism*.

(b)   Weigh the substance normally and in a magnetic field, as shown in Figure 9.47. Paramagnetic substances appear to have a larger mass when weighed in a magnetic field.

(c)   See Figures 9.37 and 9.46. O_2^+, one unpaired electron; N_2^{2-}, two unpaired electrons; Li_2^+, one unpaired electron

9.70   Determine the number of "valence" (non-core) electrons in each molecule or ion. Use the homonuclear diatomic MO diagram from Figure 9.43 (shown below) to calculate bond order and magnetic properties of each species. The electronegativity difference between heteroatomics increases the energy difference between the 2s AO on one atom and the 2p AO on the other, rendering the "no interaction" MO diagram in Figure 9.43 appropriate.

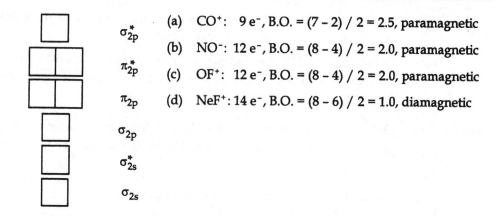

(a) CO^+:   9 e⁻, B.O. = (7 – 2) / 2 = 2.5, paramagnetic

(b) NO^-:   12 e⁻, B.O. = (8 – 4) / 2 = 2.0, paramagnetic

(c) OF^+:   12 e⁻, B.O. = (8 – 4) / 2 = 2.0, paramagnetic

(d) NeF^+: 14 e⁻, B.O. = (8 – 6) / 2 = 1.0, diamagnetic

9.72   (a)   The bond order of NO is [1/2 (8 – 3)] = 2.5. The electron that is lost is in an antibonding molecular orbital, so the bond order in NO^+ is 3.0. The increase in bond order is the driving force for the formation of NO^+.

         (b)   To form NO^-, an electron is added to an antibonding orbital, and the new bond order is [1/2 (8 – 4)] = 2. The order of increasing bond order and bond strength is: $NO^- < NO < NO^+$.

         (c) NO^+ is isoelectronic with N_2, and NO^- is isoelectronic with O_2.

9.74   (a)   I: $5s, 5p_x, 5p_y, 5p_z$; Br: $4s, 4p_x, 4p_y, 4p_z$

         (b)   By analogy to F_2, the BO of IBr will be 1.

         (c)   I and Br have valence atomic orbitals with different principal quantum numbers. This means that the radial extensions (sizes) of the valence atomic orbital that contribute to the MO are different. The n = 5 valence AOs on I are larger than the n = 4 valence AOs on Br.

         (d) σ_{np}^*

         (e)   None

Additional Exercises

9.75   (a)   The physical basis of VSEPR is the electrostatic repulsion of like-charged particles, in this case groups or domains of electrons. That is, owing to electrostatic repulsion, electron domains will arrange themselves to be as far apart as possible.

         (b)   The σ-bond electrons are localized in the region along the internuclear axes. The positions of the atoms and geometry of the molecule are thus closely tied to the locations of these electron pairs. Because the π-bond electrons are distributed above and below the plane that contains the σ bonds, these electron pairs do not, in effect, influence the geometry of the molecule. Thus, all σ- and π-bond electrons localized between two atoms are located in the same electron domain.

9.77   For any triangle, the law of cosines gives the length of side c as $c^2 = a^2 + b^2 - 2ab \cos\theta$.

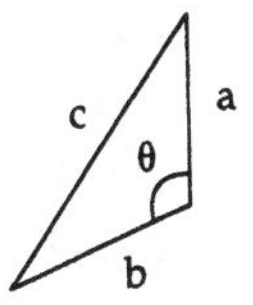

Let the edge length of the cube (uy = vy = vz) = X

The length of the face diagonal (uv) is

$(uv)^2 = (uy)^2 + (vy)^2 - 2(uy)(vy) \cos 90$

$(uv)^2 = X^2 + X^2 - 2(X)(X) \cos 90$

$(uv)^2 = 2X^2; uv = \sqrt{2}X$

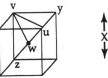

The length of the body diagonal (uz) is

$(uz)^2 = (vz^2) + (uv)^2 - 2(vz)(uv) \cos 90$

$(uz)^2 = X^2 + (\sqrt{2}X)^2 - 2(X)(\sqrt{2}X) \cos 90$

$(uz)^2 = 3X^2; uz = \sqrt{3}X$

For calculating the characteristic tetrahedral angle, the appropriate triangle has vertices u, v, and w. Theta, θ, is the angle formed by sides wu and wv and the hypotenuse is side uv.

wu = wv = uz/2 = $\sqrt{3}/2X$; uv = $\sqrt{2}X$

$(\sqrt{2}X)^2 = (\sqrt{3}/2X)^2 + (\sqrt{3}/2X)^2 - 2(\sqrt{3}/2X)(\sqrt{3}/2) \cos \theta$

$2X^2 = 3/4 X^2 + 3/4 X^2 - 3/2 X^2 \cos \theta$

$2X^2 = 3/2 X^2 - 3/2 X^2 \cos \theta$

$1/2 X^2 = -3/2 X^2 \cos \theta$

$\cos \theta = -(1/2 X^2) / (3/2 X^2) = -1/3 = -0.3333$

$\theta = 109.47°$

9.78   (a)   40 e⁻, 20 e⁻ pairs

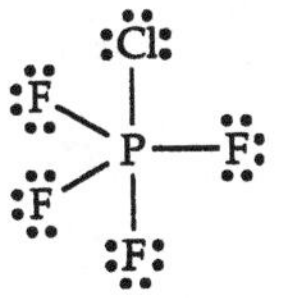

               :Cl:
                 |
       :F |
          >P—F:
       :F |
               :F:

               5 e⁻ domains
               trigonal pyramidal electron domain geometry

   (b)   The greater the electronegativity of the terminal atom, the larger the negative charge centered on the atom, the greater the effective size of the P–X electron domain. A P–F bond will produce a larger electron domain than a P–Cl bond.

   (c)   The molecular geometry (shape) is also trigonal bipyramidal, because all five electron domains are bonding domains. Because we predicted the P–F electron domain to be larger, the maximum number of three P–F bonds will occupy the equatorial plane of the molecule, minimizing the number of 90° P–F to P–F repulsions. This is the same argument that places a "larger" nonbonding domain in the equatorial position of a molecule like SF₄. The P–Cl bond is then axial, as shown in the Lewis structure.

(d)   The molecular geometry is distorted from a perfect trigonal bipyramid because not all electron domains are alike. The 90° P–F to P–F repulsions will be greater than the 90° P–F to P–Cl repulsions, so the F(axial)–P–F angles will be slightly greater than 90°, and the Cl(axial)–P–F angles will be slightly less than 90°. The equatorial F–P–F angles of 120° are distorted little, if at all.

9.80   (a)

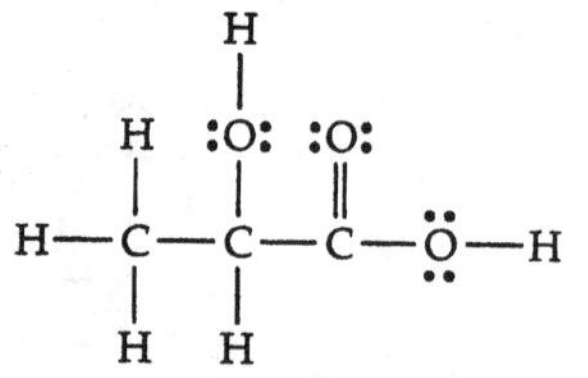

$$
\begin{array}{c}
\overset{\displaystyle H}{\vert} \\
H \quad :\!\ddot{O}: \quad :\!\ddot{O}: \\
\vert \quad\ \vert \quad\ \ \Vert \\
H-\overset{\displaystyle\vert}{\underset{\displaystyle\vert}{C}}-\overset{\displaystyle\vert}{\underset{\displaystyle\vert}{C}}-\overset{\displaystyle}{C}-\ddot{\underset{\displaystyle\cdot\cdot}{O}}-H \\
H \quad H
\end{array}
$$

$3(4) + 3(6) + 6(1) = 36\ e^-,\ 18\ e^-$ pr

(b)   There are 11 σ and 1 π bonds.

(c)   The C=O on the right-hand C atom is shortest. For the same bonded atoms, in this case C and O, the greater the bond order, the shorter the bond.

(d, e)   The right-most C has three e^- domains, so the hybridization is sp^2; bond angles about this C atom are approximately 120°. The middle and left-hand C atoms both have four e^- domains, are sp^3 hybridized, and have bond angles of approximately 109°.

9.82   (a)   The compound on the right has a dipole moment. In the square planar trans structure on the left, all equivalent bond dipoles can be oriented opposite each other, for a net dipole moment of zero.

(b)

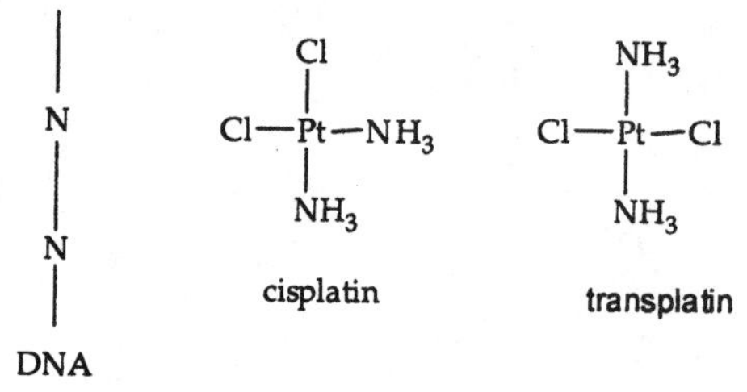

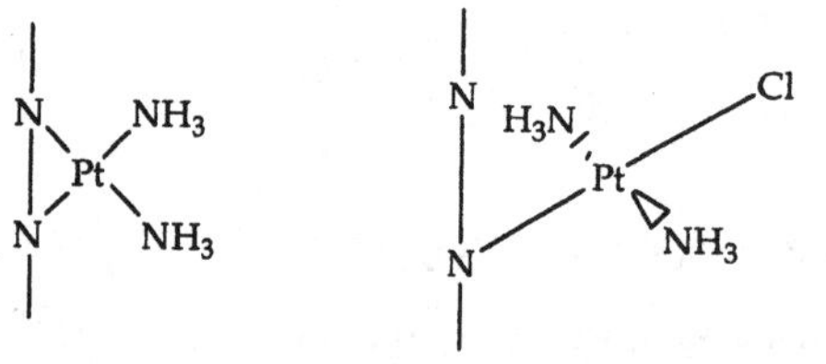

The cis orientation of the Cl atoms in cisplatin means that when they leave, the Pt can bind two adjacent N sites on DNA. This "chelate" orientation (see Chapter 24) tightly binds cisplatin to DNA. Transplatin can bind only one DNA N atom at a time. Thus, to avoid bumping by transplatin NH₃ groups and DNA, the plane of transplatin must rotate away from the DNA backbone. This is a much looser bonding situation than for cisplatin.

9.83

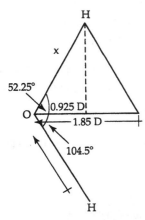

(a)   The bond dipoles in H_2O lie along the O–H bonds with the positive end at H and the negative end at O. The dipole moment vector of the H_2O molecule is the resultant (vector sum) of the two bond dipoles. This vector bisects the H–O–H angle and has a magnitude of 1.85 D with the negative end pointing toward O.

(b)   Since the dipole moment vector bisects the H–O–H bond angle, the angle between one H–O bond and the dipole moment vector is 1/2 the H–O–H bond angle, 52.25°. Dropping a perpendicular line from H to the dipole moment vector creates the right triangle pictured. If x = the magnitude of the O–H bond dipole, x cos (52.25) = 0.925 D. x = 1.51 D.

(c)   The X–H bond dipoles (Table 8.3) and the electronegativity values of X (Figure 8.6) are

	Electronegativity	Bond dipole
F	4.0	1.82
O	3.5	1.51
Cl	3.0	1.08

Since the electronegativity of O is midway between the values for F and Cl, the O–H bond dipole should be approximately midway between the bond dipoles of HF and HCl. The value of the O–H bond dipole calculated in part (b) is consistent with this prediction.

9.84   (a) XeF_6 50 e^-, 25 e^- pairs

(b)   There are seven electron domains around Xe, and the maximum number of e^- domains in Table 9.3 is six.

(c)   Tie seven balloons together and see what arrangement they adopt (seriously! see Figure 9.5). Alternatively, go to the chemical literature where VSEPR was first proposed and see if there is a preferred orientation for seven e^- domains.

(d) Since the hybrid orbitals for five e⁻ domains involve one d orbital and for six pairs, two d orbitals, a reasonable suggestion would be sp^3d^3.

(e) One of the seven e⁻ domains is a nonbonded domain. The question is whether it occupies an axial or equatorial position. The equatorial plane of a pentagonal bipyramid has F–Xe–F angles of 72°. Placing the nonbonded domain in the equatorial plane would create severe repulsions between it and the adjacent bonded domains. Thus, the nonbonded domain will reside in the axial position. The molecular structure is a pentagonal pyramid.

9.86 (a) 16 e⁻, 8 e⁻ pairs

$$\left[\ddot{N}\!=\!N\!=\!\ddot{N}\right]^- \longleftrightarrow \left[:N\!\equiv\!N\!-\!\ddot{N}:\right]^- \longleftrightarrow \left[:\ddot{N}\!-\!N\!\equiv\!N:\right]^-$$

(b) The observed bond length of 1.16 Å is intermediate between the values for N=N, 1.24 Å, and N ≡ N, 1.10 Å. This is consistent with the resonance structures, which indicate contribution from formally double and triple bonds to the true bonding picture in N_3^-.

(c) In each resonance structure, the central N has two electron domains, so it must be sp hybridized. It is difficult to predict the hybridization of terminal atoms in molecules where there are resonance structures because there are a different number of electron domains around the terminal atoms in each structure. Since the "true" electronic arrangement is a combination of all resonance structures, we will assume that the terminal N–N bonds have some triple bond character and that the terminal N atoms are sp hybridized. (There is no experimental measure of hybridization at terminal atoms, since there are no bond angles to observe.)

(d) In each resonance structure, N–N σ bonds are formed by sp hybrids and π bonds are formed by unhybridized p orbitals. Nonbonding e⁻ pairs can reside in sp hybrids or p atomic orbitals.

(e) Recall that electrons in 2s orbitals are on the average closer to the nucleus than electrons in 2p orbitals. Since sp hybrids have greater s orbital character, it is reasonable to expect the radial extension of sp orbitals to be smaller than that of sp^2 or sp^3 orbitals and σ bonds formed by sp orbitals to be slightly shorter than those formed by other hybrid orbitals, assuming the same bonded atoms.

There are no solitary σ bonds in N_3^-. That is, the two σ bonds in N_3^- are each accompanied by at least one π bond between the bonding pair of atoms. Sigma bonds that are part of a double or triple bond must be shorter so that the p orbitals can overlap enough for the π bond to form. Thus, the observation is not applicable to this molecule. (Comparison of C–H bond lengths in C_2H_2, C_2H_4, C_2H_6 and related molecules would confirm or deny the observation.)

9.88 (a) Each C atom is surrounded by three electron domains (two single bonds and one double bond), so bond angles at each C atom will be approximately 120°.

Since there is free rotation around the central C–C single bond, other conformations are possible.

(b)   According to Table 8.5, the average C–C length is 1.54 Å, and the average C=C length is 1.34 Å. While the C=C bonds in butadiene appear "normal," the central C–C is significantly shorter than average. Examination of the bonding in butadiene reveals that each C atom is sp^2 hybridized and the π bonds are formed by the remaining unhybridized 2p orbital on each atom. If the central C–C bond is rotated so that all four C atoms are coplanar, the four 2p orbitals are parallel, and some delocalization of the π electrons occurs.

9.89   (a)   The diagram shows two s atomic orbitals with opposite phases. Because they are spherically symmetric, the interaction of s orbitals can only produce a σ molecular orbital. Because the two orbitals in the diagram have opposite phases, the interaction excludes electron density from the region between the nuclei. The resulting MO has a node between the two nuclei and is labeled σ_{2s}^*. The principal quantum number designation is arbitrary, because it defines only the size of the pertinent AOs and MOs. Shapes and phases of MOs depend only on these same characteristics of the interacting AOs.

(b)   The diagram shows two p atomic orbitals with oppositely phased lobes pointing at each other. End-to-end overlap produces a σ-type MO; opposite phases mean a node between the nuclei and an antibonding MO. The interaction results in a σ_{2p}^* MO.

(c)   The diagram shows parallel p atomic orbitals with like-phased lobes aligned. Side-to-side overlap produces a π-type MO; overlap of like-phased lobes concentrates electron density between the nuclei and a bonding MO. The interaction results in a π_{2p} MO.

9.90   (a) $C_5H_5^-$, 26 e^-, 13 e^- pair

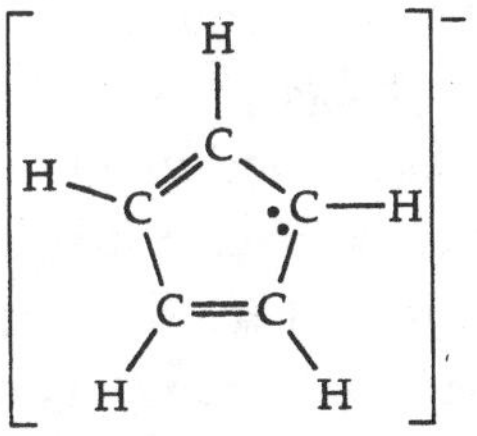

No. According to the single Lewis structure above, the four C atoms involved in double bonds would be sp^2 hybridized, but the C atom with the lone pair would be sp^3 hybridized. Not all C atoms would have the same hybridization.

(b)   Equivalent sp^2 hydridization at all C atoms is consistent with the planar structure of the ion. The VSEPR model applied to the single Lewis structure above does not predict uniform hybridization or planarity of the ion. The VSEPR/Lewis model is consistent with the known structural features of the ion only if the other resonance structures are considered.

(c)   If all C atoms are sp^2 hybridized, as required by the planar structure of the ion, the three hybrid orbitals on each C are used to form the σ framework of the molecule. The unshared pair would then reside in an unhybridized p orbital.

(d)   Yes, there are resonance structures equivalent to the Lewis structure above. It is possible to place the unshared pair on any of the five C atoms, resulting in five equivalent resonance structures (four plus the one above).

(e)   The five resonance structures indicate that there is delocalization of the π electron density in the molecule. The interior circle conveys uniform delocalization over the entire ring, as in benzene.

(f)   In a rigid planar structure with each C atom sp^2 hybridized, the unhybridized p orbitals are aligned parallel, facilitating overlap to form a delocalized π network above and below the plane of the molecule. Since the unshared pair occupies an unhybridized p orbital (part c), it is part of the delocalized π network, along with the four electrons involved in π bonds; the delocalized system contains a total of six electrons.

9.92   Paramagnetic materials appear to weigh more when the mass measurement is made in the presence of a magnetic field. Air contains $O_2(g)$, which is paramagnetic because of its two unpaired electrons in a π_{2p}^* molecular orbital (Figure 9.46). In the presence of a magnetic field, mass measurements made in air would be skewed by the paramagnetism of O_2, and lead to inaccurate results.

9.93   We will refer to azo benzene (on the left) as A and hydrazobenzene (on the right) as H.

(a)   A: sp^2; H: sp^3

(b)   A: Each N and C atom has one unhybridized p orbital. H: Each C atom has one unhybridized p orbital, but the N atoms have no unhybridized p orbitals.

(c)   A: 120°; H: 109°

(d)   Since all C and N atoms in A have unhybridized p orbitals, all can participate in delocalized π bonding. The delocalized π system extends over the entire molecule, including both benzene rings and the azo "bridge." In H, the N atoms have no unhybridized p orbitals, so they cannot participate in delocalized π bonding. Each of the benzene rings in H is delocalized, but the network cannot span the N atoms in the bridge.

(e)   This is consistent with the answer to (d). In order for the unhybridized p orbitals in A to overlap, they must be parallel. This requires a planar σ bond framework where all atoms in the molecule are coplanar.

(f)   For a molecule to be useful in a solar energy conversion device, it must absorb visible light. This requires a HOMO-LUMO energy gap in the visible region. For organic molecules, the size of the gap is related to the number of conjugated π bonds; the more conjugated π bonds, the smaller the gap and the more likely the molecule is to be colored. Azobenzene has seven conjugated π bonds (π network delocalized over the entire molecule) and appears red-orange. Hydrazobenzene has only three conjugated π bonds (π network on benzene rings only) and appears white. Thus, the smaller HOMO-LUMO energy gap in A causes it to be both intensely colored and a more useful molecule for solar energy conversion.

9.94   (a)   H: $1s^1$; F: [He]$2s^2 2p^5$

When molecular orbitals are formed from atomic orbitals, the total number of orbitals is conserved. Since H and F have a total of five valence AOs ($H_{1s} + F_{2s} + 3F_{2p}$), the MO diagram for HF has five MOs.

(b)   H and F have a total of eight valence electrons. Since each MO can hold a maximum of two electrons, four of the five MOs would be occupied.

(c)   No. The MO diagram for NO in Figure 9.49 has eight MOs, and the diagram for HF has only five. The number, type, and energy spacing of the MOs in HF will be different.

(d)

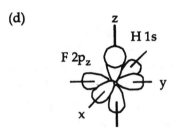

If H and F lie on the z axis, then the $2p_z$ orbital of F will overlap with the 1s orbital of H.

(e)   Since F is more electronegative than H, the valence orbitals on F are at lower energy than those on H.

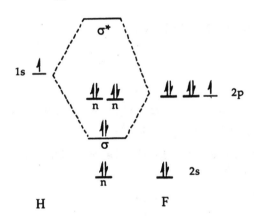

The HF MO diagram has 6 nonbonding, 2 bonding and 0 antibonding electrons. The BO = [2 – 0]/2 = 1. (Nonbonding electrons do not "count" toward bond order.)

(f)   H—$\ddot{\underset{..}{F}}$:

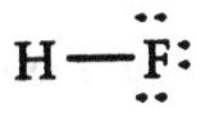

In the Lewis structure for HF, the nonbonding electrons are on the (more electronegative) F atom, as they are in the MO diagram.

9.95   (a)   CO, 10 e⁻, 5 e⁻ pair

:C≡O:

(b)   The bond order for CO, as predicted by the MO diagram in Figure 9.49, is $1/2[8 - 2] = 3.0$. A bond order of 3.0 agrees with the triple bond in the Lewis structure.

(c)   Applying the MO diagram in Figure 9.49 to the CO molecule, the highest energy electrons would occupy the π_{2p} MOs. That is, π_{2p} would be the HOMO, highest occupied molecular orbital. If the true HOMO of CO is a σ-type MO, the order of the π_{2p} and σ_{2p} orbitals must be reversed. Figure 9.45 shows how the interaction of the 2s orbitals on one atom and the 2p orbitals on the other atom can affect the relative energies of the resulting MOs. This 2s–2p interaction in CO is significant enough so that the σ_{2p} MO is higher in energy than the π_{2p} MOs, and the σ_{2p} is the HOMO.

(d)   We expect the atomic orbitals of the more electronegative element to have lower energy than those of the less electronegative element. When atoms of the two elements combine, the lower energy atomic orbitals make a greater contribution to the bonding MOs and the higher energy atomic orbitals make a larger contribution to the antibonding orbitals. Thus, the π_{2p} bonding MOs will have a greater contribution from the more electronegative O atom.

Integrative Exercises

9.96   (a)   Assume 100 g of compound

$$2.1\,g\,H \times \frac{1\,mol\,H}{1.008\,g\,H} = 2.1\,mol\,H; 2.1/2.1 = 1$$

$$29.8\,g\,N \times \frac{1\,mol\,N}{14.01\,g\,N} = 2.13\,mol\,N; 2.13/2.1 \approx 1$$

$$68.1\,g\,O \times \frac{1\,mol\,O}{16.00\,g\,O} = 4.26\,mol\,O; 4.26/2.1 \approx 2$$

The empirical formula is HNO_2; formula weight = 47. Since the approximate molar mass is 50, the molecular formula is HNO_2.

(b)   Assume N is central, since it is unusual for O to be central, and part (d) indicates as much. HNO_2: 18 valence e⁻

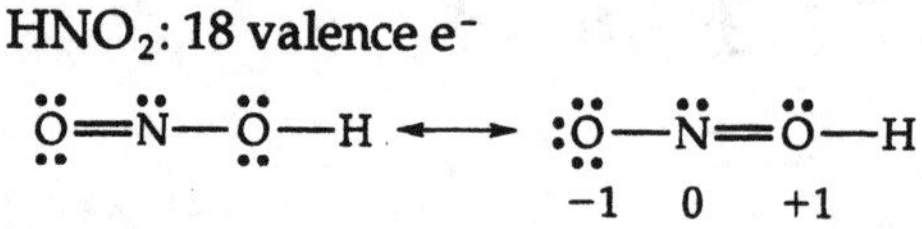

$$\ddot{\underset{\cdot\cdot}{O}}=\ddot{N}-\ddot{\underset{\cdot\cdot}{O}}-H \longleftrightarrow :\ddot{\underset{\cdot\cdot}{O}}-\ddot{N}=\ddot{\underset{\cdot\cdot}{O}}-H$$
$$\qquad\qquad\qquad\qquad\quad -1 \quad\; 0 \quad +1$$

The second resonance form is a minor contributor due to unfavorable formal charges.

(c)   The electron domain geometry around N is trigonal planar with an O–N–O angle of approximately $120°$. If the resonance structure on the right makes a significant contribution to the molecular structure, all four atoms would lie in a plane. If only the left structure contributes, the H could rotate in and out of the molecular plane. The relative contributions of the two resonance structures could be determined by measuring the O–N–O and N–O–H bond angles.

(d)   3 VSEPR e⁻ domains around N, sp^2 hybridization

(e)   3 σ, 1 π for both structures (or for H bound to N).

9.98   (a) PX_3, 26 valence e$^-$, 13$^-$ pairs

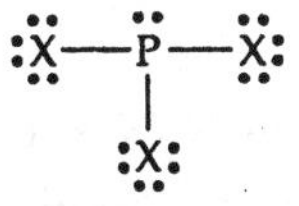

4 electron domains around P, tetrahedral e$^-$ domain geometry,
bond angles ≤ 109°

(b)   As electronegativity increases (I < Br < Cl < F), the X–P–X angles decreases.

(c)   For P–I, ΔEN is (2.5 – 2.1) = 0.4 and the bond dipole is small. For P–F, ΔEN is (4.0 – 2.1) = 1.9 and the bond dipole is large. The greater the ΔEN and bond dipole, the larger the magnitude of negative charge centered on X. The more negative charge centered on X, the greater the repulsion between X and the nonbonding electron pair on P and the smaller the bond angle. (Since electrostatic attractions and repulsions vary as 1/r, the shorter P–F bond may also contribute to this effect.)

(d) $PBrCl_4$, 40 valence electrons, 20 e$^-$ pairs. The molecule will have trigonal bipyramidal electron-domain geometry (similar to PCl_5 in Table 9.3.) Based on the argument in part (c), the P–Br bond will have smaller repulsions with P–Cl bonds than P–Cl bonds have with each other. Therefore, the Br will occupy an axial position in the trigonal bipyramid, so that the more unfavorable P–Cl to P–Cl repulsions can be situated at larger angles in the equatorial plane.

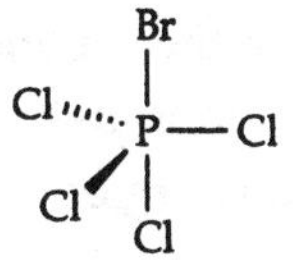

9.100   (a)   C ≡ C   839 kJ/mol   (1 σ, 2 π)

C = C   614 kJ/mol   (1 σ, 1 π)

C – C   348 kJ/mol   (1 σ)

The contribution from 1 π bond would be (614–348) 266 kJ/mol. From a second π bond, (839 – 614), 225 kJ/mol. An average π bond contribution would be (266 + 225)/2 = 246 kJ/mol.

This is $\dfrac{246\,\text{kJ}/\pi\,\text{bond}}{348\,\text{kJ}/\sigma\,\text{bond}} \times 100 = 71\%$ of the average enthalpy of a σ bond.

(b)   N ≡ N   941 kJ/mol

N = N   418 kJ/mol

N – N   163 kJ/mol

first π = (418 – 163) = 255 kJ/mol

second π = (941 – 418) = 523 kJ/mol

average π bond enthalpy = (255 + 523)/2 = 389 kJ/mol

This is $\dfrac{389 \text{ kJ}/\pi \text{ bond}}{163 \text{ kJ}/\sigma \text{ bond}} \times 100 = 240\%$ of the average enthalpy of a σ bond.

N–N σ bonds are weaker than C–C σ bonds, while N–N π bonds are stronger than C–C π bonds. The relative energies of C–C σ and π bonds are similar, while N–N π bonds are much stronger than N–N σ bonds.

(c) N_2H_4, 14 valence e⁻, 7 e⁻ pairs

$$\text{H}\!-\!\overset{\displaystyle ..}{\text{N}}\!-\!\overset{\displaystyle ..}{\text{N}}\!-\!\text{H}$$
$$\quad\ \ |\quad\ |$$
$$\quad\ \ \text{H}\quad \text{H}$$

4 electron domains around N, sp³ hybridization

N_2H_2, 12 valence e⁻, 6 e⁻ pairs

$$\text{H}\!-\!\overset{\displaystyle ..}{\text{N}}\!=\!\overset{\displaystyle ..}{\text{N}}\!-\!\text{H}$$

3 electron domains around N, sp² hybridization

N_2, 10 valence e⁻, 5 e⁻ pairs

:N≡N:

2 electron domains around N, sp hybridization

(d)   In the three types of N–N bonds, each N atom has a nonbonding or lone pair of electrons. The lone pair to bond pair repulsions are minimized going from 109° to 120° to 180° bond angles, making the π bonds stronger relative to the σ bond. In the three types of C–C bonds, no lone-pair to bond-pair repulsions exist, and the σ and π bonds have more similar energies.

9.102   (a)   1 eV = 96.485 kJ/mol

$$H_2: 15.4 \text{ eV} \times \frac{96.485 \text{ kJ/mol}}{1 \text{ eV}} = 1486 = 1.49 \times 10^3 \text{ kJ/mol}$$

$$N_2: 15.6 \text{ eV} \times \frac{96.485 \text{ kJ/mol}}{1 \text{ eV}} = 1505 = 1.51 \times 10^3 \text{ kJ/mol}$$

$$O_2: 12.1 \text{ eV} \times \frac{96.485 \text{ kJ/mol}}{1 \text{ eV}} = 1167 = 1.17 \times 10^3 \text{ kJ/mol}$$

$$F_2: 15.7 \text{ eV} \times \frac{96.485 \text{ kJ/mol}}{1 \text{ eV}} = 1515 = 1.52 \times 10^3 \text{ kJ/mol}$$

(b)

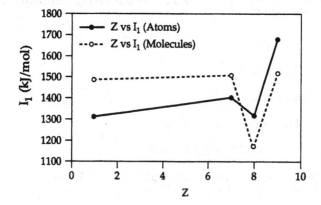

(c)   In general, I_1 for atoms and molecules increases going across a row of the periodic chart. In both cases, there is a discontinuity at oxygen. The details of the trends are different. The deviation at O is larger for the molecules than the atoms, while the increase at F is much greater for the atoms than the molecules.

(d)   According to Figures 9.35 and 9.46, H_2, N_2, and F_2 are diamagnetic and O_2 is paramagnetic. That is, ionization in H_2, N_2, and F_2 has to overcome spin-pairing energy, while ionization of O_2 removes an already unpaired electron. Thus, the ionization energy of O_2 is much less than I_1 for H_2, N_2, and F_2.

Despite differences in bond order, bond length, and the bonding or antibonding nature of the HOMO in H_2, N_2, and F_2, the ionization energies for these molecules are very similar.

9.104   (a)   The molecular and empirical formulas of the four molecules are:

benzene: molecular, C_6H_6; empirical, CH

napthalene: molecular, $C_{10}H_8$; empirical, C_5H_4

anthracene: molecular, $C_{14}H_{10}$; empirical, C_7H_5

tetracene: molecular, $C_{18}H_{12}$, empirical, C_3H_2

(b)   Yes.   Since the compounds all have different empirical formulas, combustion analysis could in principle be used to distinguish them. In practice, the mass % of C in the four compounds is not very different, so the data would have to be precise to at least 3 decimal places and 4 would be better.

(c) $C_{10}H_8(s) + 12O_2(g) \rightarrow 10CO_2(g) + 4H_2O(g)$

(d) $\Delta H_{comb} = 5D(C=C) + 6D(C-C) + 8D(C-H) + 12D(O=O) - 20D(C=O) - 8D(O-H)$

$= 5(614) + 6(348) + 8(413) + 12(495) - 20(799) - 8(463)$

$= -5282 \text{ kJ/mol } C_{10}H_8$

(e)   Yes. For example, the resonance structures of naphthalene are:

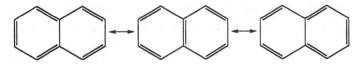

(f)   Colored compounds absorb visible light and appear the color of the visible light that they reflect. Colorless compounds typically absorb shorter wavelength, higher energy light. The energy of light absorbed corresponds to the energy gap between the HOMO and LUMO of the molecule. That tetracene absorbs longer wavelength, lower energy visible light indicates that it has the smallest HOMO-LUMO energy gap of the four molecules. Tetracene also has the most conjugated double bonds of the four molecules. We might conclude that the more conjugated double bonds in an organic molecule, the smaller the HOMO-LUMO energy gap. More information about the absorption spectra of anthracene, naphthalene and benzene is needed to confirm this conclusion.

9.105   (a) – (e)

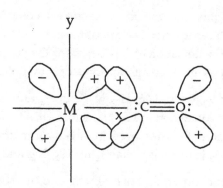

(c)   The two lobes of a p AO have opposite phases. These are shown on the diagram as + and –. An antibonding MO is formed when p AOs with opposite phases interact.

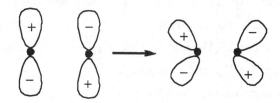

(d)   Note that the d_{xy} AO has lobes that lie between, not on, the x and y axes.

(e)   A π bond forms by overlap of orbitals on M and C. There is electron density above and below, but not along, the M–C axis.

(f)   According to Exercise 9.95, the HOMO of CO is a σ-type MO. So the appropriate MO diagram is shown on the left side of Figure 9.46. A lone CO molecule has 10 valence electrons, the HOMO is σ_{2p} and the bond order is 3.0. The LUMO is π_{2p}^{*}.

When M and CO interact as shown in the π_{2p}^{*} diagram, d–π back bonding causes the π_{2p}^{*} to become partially occupied. Electron density in the π_{2p}^{*} decreases electron density in the bonding molecular orbitals and decreases the BO of the bound CO. The strength of the C–O bond in a metal–CO complex decreases relative to the strength of the C–O bond in an isolated CO molecule.

9.106   (a)   :C̈l—C̈l:

(b)   4 e⁻ domains on each Cl, sp³ hybridization at each Cl

(c)   Since both Cl atoms employ sp³ hybrid orbitals, the Cl–Cl bond is formed by end-to-end, σ overlap of two sp³ hybrid orbitals on different Cl atoms.

(d)   In the AO model, two of the lone pairs occupy mutually perpendicular p orbitals on the same Cl atom. The angle between these two lone pair electron domains is 90°. In the hybrid orbital model, all three lone pairs occupy sp³ hybrid orbitals on the same Cl atom. The angle between these lone pair domains is 109°. If we could measure the "positions" of the lone pairs, we could distinguish between models by the angles between electron domains.

(e)   According to the MO diagram for F_2, and by inference Cl_2, shown in Figure 9.46, the HOMO for Cl_2 is π_{3p}^* and it contains four electrons. If we ionize $Cl_2 \rightarrow Cl_2^+$, the number of antibonding electrons decreases and the BO increases. Cl_2^+ should have a stronger, shorter Cl–Cl bond than Cl_2 has. Conversely, adding an electron to form Cl_2^- adds an electron to the antibonding σ_{3p}^*. This reduces the BO in Cl_2^-, resulting in a weaker, longer Cl–Cl bond.

So, generate Cl_2^+ and Cl_2^- and measure the Cl–Cl distances. If the order of Cl–Cl bond lengths is $Cl_2^+ < Cl_2 < Cl_2^-$, the data supports an MO model.

10 Gases

Visualizing Concepts

10.1   It would be much easier to drink from a straw on Mars. When a straw is placed in a glass of liquid, the liquid level in the straw equals the liquid level in the glass. The atmosphere exerts equal pressure inside and outside the straw. When we drink through a straw, we withdraw air, thereby reducing the pressure on the liquid inside. If only 0.007 atm is exerted on the liquid in the glass, a very small reduction in pressure inside the straw will cause the liquid to rise.

    Another approach is to consider the gravitational force on Mars. Since the pull of gravity causes atmospheric pressure, the gravity on Mars must be much smaller than that on Earth. With a very small Martian gravity holding liquid in a glass, it would be very easy to raise the liquid through a straw.

10.3   At constant temperature and volume, pressure depends on total number of particles (Charles' Law). In order to reduce the pressure by a factor of 2, the number of particles must be reduced by a factor of 2. At the lower pressure, the container would have half as many particles as at the higher pressure.

10.4   (a)   At constant pressure and temperature, the container volume is directly proportional to the number of particles present (Avogadro's Law). As the reaction proceeds, 3 gas molecules are converted to 2 gas molecules, so the container volume decreases. If the reaction goes to completion, the final volume would be 2/3 of the initial volume.

      (b)   At constant volume, pressure is directly proportional to the number of particles (Charles' Law). Since the number of molecules decreases as the reaction proceeds, the pressure also decreases. At completion, the final pressure would be 2/3 the initial pressure.

10.6   (a)   Partial pressure depends on the number of particles of each gas present. Red has the fewest particles, then yellow, then blue. $P_{red} < P_{yellow} < P_{blue}$

      (b) $P_{gas} = \chi_{gas} P_t$. Calculate the mole fraction, χ_{gas} = [mol gas / total moles] or [particles gas / total particles]. This is true because Avogadro's number is a counting number, and mole ratios are also particle ratios.

          χ_{red} = 2 red atoms / 10 total atoms = 0.2; P_{red} = 0.2(0.90 atm) = 0.18 atm

          χ_{yellow} = 3 yellow atoms / 10 total atoms = 0.3; P_{yellow} = 0.3(0.90 atm) = 0.27 atm

          χ_{blue} = 5 blue atoms / 10 total atoms = 0.5; P_{blue} = 0.5(0.90 atm) = 0.45 atm

10.7

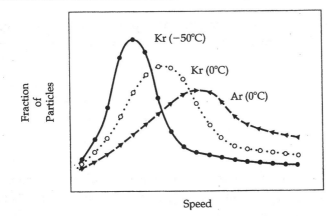

10.9   (a)   Total pressure is directly related to total number of particles (or total mol particles). P(ii) < P(i) = P(iii)

        (b)   Partial pressure of He is directly related to number of He atoms (yellow) or mol He atoms. P_{He}(iii) < P_{He}(ii) < P_{He}(i)

        (c)   Density is total mass of gas per unit volume. We can use the atomic or molar masses of He (4) and N_2(28), as relative masses of the particles.

$$mass(i) = 5(4) + 2(28) = 76$$

$$mass(ii) = 3(4) + 1(28) = 40$$

$$mass(iii) = 2(4) + 5(28) = 148$$

        Since the container volumes are equal, d(ii) < d(i) < d(iii).

        (d)   At the same temperature, all gases have the same "avg" kinetic energy. The average kinetic energies of the particles in the three containers are equal.

10.10 CCl_4, Cl_2 and H_2O would deviate most, while He, N and H_2 would deviate least. At high pressure, gas molecules have relatively little free space in which to move. Both intermolecular attractive forces and the nonzero volume of molecules are important. At low temperature, molecules have less kinetic energy, are less able to overcome attractive forces, and deviations due to intermolecular attractive forces dominate (see Figure 10.24). In Table 10.3, values of *a* show corrections for intermolecular attraction. The gases CCl_4, Cl_2 and H_2O have the largest values of *a*, while He, Ne and H_2 have the smallest. The magnitude of *a* increases as the size and complexity of the molecule increases. CCl_4 and Cl_2 are relatively large gases; H_2O is polar and has hydrogen bonding. He, Ne and H_2 are small, monatomic or nonpolar diatomic. The magnitude of *a* is predictable from molecular structure.

Gas Characteristics; Pressure

10.12   (a)   Because gas molecules are far apart and in constant motion, the gas expands to fill the container. Attractive forces hold liquid molecules together and the volume of the liquid does not change.

        (b) H_2O and CCl_4 molecules are too dissimilar to displace each other and mix in the liquid state. All mixtures of gases are homogeneous. (See Solution 10.11 (c)).

    (c)   Because gas molecules are far apart, the mass present in 1 mL of a gas is very small. The mass of a gas present in 1 L is on the same order of magnitude as the mass of a liquid present in 1 mL.

10.14 $P = m \times a/A$; $1\,Pa = 1\,kg/m\text{-}s^2$; $A = 3.0\,cm \times 4.1\,cm \times 4 = 49.2 = 49\,cm^2$

$$\frac{262\,kg}{49.2\,cm^2} \times \frac{9.81\,m}{s^2} \times \frac{(100)^2\,cm^2}{1\,m^2} = 5.224 \times 10^5 \,\frac{kg}{m\text{-}s^2} = 5.2 \times 10^5\,Pa$$

10.16   Using the relationship derived in Solution 10.15 for two liquids under the influence of gravity, $(d \times h)_{lid} = (d \times h)_{Hg}$. At 752 torr, the height of an Hg barometer is 752 mm.

$$\frac{1.20\,g}{1\,mL} \times h_{lid} = \frac{13.6\,g}{1\,mL} \times 760\,mm;\ h_{lid} = \frac{13.6\,g/mL \times 752\,mm}{1.20\,g/mL} = 8.52 \times 10^3\,mm = 8.52\,m$$

10.18   The mercury would fill the tube completely; there would be no vacuum at the closed end. This is because atmospheric pressure will support a mercury column higher than 70 cm, while our tube is only 50 cm. No mercury flows from the tube into the dish and no vacuum forms at the top of the tube.

10.20   (a) $0.850\,atm \times \dfrac{760\,torr}{1\,atm} = 646\,torr$

        (b) $785\,torr \times \dfrac{101.325\,kPa}{760\,torr} = 105\,kPa$

        (c) $655\,mm\,Hg \times \dfrac{1\,atm}{760\,mm\,Hg} = 0.862\,atm$

        (d) $1.323 \times 10^5\,Pa \times \dfrac{1\,atm}{1.01325 \times 10^5\,Pa} = 1.3057 = 1.306\,atm$

        (e) $2.50\,atm \times \dfrac{1.01325 \times 10^5\,Pa}{1\,atm} \times \dfrac{1\,bar}{1 \times 10^5\,Pa} = 2.53\,bar$

10.22   (a) $\dfrac{1.63105\,Pa}{1\,Titan\,atm} \times \dfrac{1\,Earth\,atm}{101{,}325\,Pa} = \dfrac{1.60972 \times 10^{-5}\,Earth\,atm}{1\,Titan\,atm}$

        (b) $\dfrac{90\,Earth\,atm}{1\,Venus\,atm} \times \dfrac{101.3\,kPa}{1\,Earth\,atm} = \dfrac{9.1 \times 10^3\,kPa}{1\,Venus\,atm}$

10.24   (a)   The atmosphere is exerting 15.4 cm = 154 mm Hg (torr) more pressure than the gas.

$$P_{gas} = P_{atm} - 154\,torr = \left(0.966\,atm \times \frac{760\,torr}{1\,atm}\right) - 154\,torr = 580\,torr$$

        (b)   The gas is exerting 8.7 mm Hg (torr) more pressure than the atmosphere.

$$P_{gas} = P_{atm} + 8.7\,torr = \left(0.99\,atm \times \frac{760\,torr}{1\,atm}\right) + 8.7\,torr = 761.1\,torr = 7.6 \times 10^2\,torr$$

        (Atmospheric pressure of 0.99 atm determines that the result has 2 sig figs.)

The Gas Laws

10.26 *Analyze.* Given: initial P, V, T. Find: final values of P, V, T for certain changes of condition. *Plan.* Select the appropriate gas law relationships from Section 10.3; solve for final conditions, paying attention to units.   *Solve.*

(a) $P_1 V_1 = P_2 V_2$; the proportionality holds true for any pressure or volume units.

$P_1 = 752$ torr, $V_1 = 4.38$ L, $P_2 = 1.88$ atm

$$V_2 = \frac{P_1 V_1}{P_2} = \frac{752 \text{ torr} \times 4.38 \text{ L}}{1.88 \text{ atm}} \times \frac{1 \text{ atm}}{760 \text{ torr}} = 2.31 \text{ L}$$

Check. As pressure increases, volume should decrease; our result agrees with this.

(b) $V_1/T_1 = V_2/T_2$; T must be in Kelvins for the relationship to be true.

$V_1 = 4.38$ L, $T_1 = 21°C = 294$ K, $T_2 = 175°C = 448$ K

$$V_2 = \frac{V_1 T_2}{T_1} = \frac{4.38 \text{ L} \times 448 \text{ K}}{294 \text{ K}} = 6.67 \text{ L}$$

Check. As temperature increases, volume should increase; our result is consistent with this.

10.28 According to Avogadro's hypothesis, the mole ratios in the chemical equation will be volume ratios for the gases if they are at the same temperature and pressure.

$$N_2(g) + 3H_2(g) \rightarrow 2NH_3(g)$$

The volumes of H_2 and N_2 are in a stoichiometric $\dfrac{3.6 \text{ L}}{1.2 \text{ L}}$ or $\dfrac{3 \text{ vol } H_2}{1 \text{ vol } N_2}$ ratio, so either can be used to determine the volume of $NH_3(g)$ produced.

$$1.2 \text{ L } N_2 \times \frac{2 \text{ mol } NH_3}{1 \text{ mol } N_2} = 2.4 \text{ L } NH_3(g) \text{ produced.}$$

The Ideal-Gas Equation

(In *Solutions to Exercises*, the symbol for molar mass is MM.)

10.30 (a) STP stands for standard temperature, 0°C (or 273 K), and standard pressure, 1 atm.

(b) $V = \dfrac{nRT}{P}$; $V = 1 \text{ mol} \times \dfrac{0.08206 \text{ L - atm}}{K \text{ - mol}} \times \dfrac{273 \text{ K}}{1 \text{ atm}}$

$V = 22.4$ L for 1 mole of gas at STP

(c) $25°C + 273 = 298$ K

$V = \dfrac{nRT}{P}$; $V = 1 \text{ mol} \times \dfrac{0.08206 \text{ L - atm}}{K \text{ - mol}} \times \dfrac{298 \text{ K}}{1 \text{ atm}}$

$V = 24.5$ L for 1 mol of gas at 1 atm and 25°C

10.32 $n = g/MM$; $PV = nRT = gRT/MM$; $MM = gRT/PV$.

2-L flask: $MM = 4.8 \text{ RT}/2.0(X) = 2.4 \text{ RT}/X$

3-L flask: $MM = 0.36 \text{ RT}/3.0 (0.1 \text{ X}) = 1.2 \text{ RT}/X$

The molar masses of the two gases are not equal. The gas in the 2-L flask has a molar mass that is twice as large as the gas in the 3-L flask.

10.34   *Analyze/Plan.* Follow the strategy for calculations involving many variables given in Section 10.4. *Solve.*

     (a)   n = 1.50 mol, P = 0.985 atm, T = –6°C = 267 K

$$V = \frac{nRT}{P} = 1.50 \, \text{mol} \times \frac{0.08206 \, \text{L-atm}}{\text{K-mol}} \times \frac{267 \, \text{K}}{0.985 \, \text{atm}} = 33.4 \, \text{L}$$

     (b)   n = 3.33×10^{-3} mol, V = 325 mL = 0.325 L

$$P = 750 \, \text{torr} \times \frac{1 \, \text{atm}}{760 \, \text{torr}} = 0.9868 = 0.987 \, \text{atm}$$

$$T = \frac{PV}{nR} = 0.9868 \, \text{atm} \times \frac{0.325 \, \text{L}}{3.33 \times 10^{-3} \, \text{mol}} \times \frac{1 \, \text{K-mol}}{0.08206 \, \text{L-atm}} = 1174 = 1.17 \times 10^{3} \, \text{K}$$

     (c)   n = 4.67×10^{-2} mol, V = 413 mL = 0.413 L, T = 138°C = 411 K

$$P = \frac{nRT}{V}; = 0.0467 \, \text{mol} \times \frac{0.08206 \, \text{L-atm}}{\text{K-mol}} \times \frac{411 \, \text{K}}{0.413 \, \text{L}} = 3.81 \, \text{atm}$$

     (d)   V = 55.7 L, T = 54°C = 327 K,

$$P = 11.25 \, \text{kPa} \times \frac{1 \, \text{atm}}{101.325 \, \text{kPa}} = 0.11103 = 0.1110 \, \text{atm}$$

$$n = \frac{PV}{RT} = 0.11103 \, \text{atm} \times \frac{\text{K-mol}}{0.08206 \, \text{L-atm}} \times \frac{55.7 \, \text{L}}{327 \, \text{K}} = 0.230 \, \text{mol}$$

10.36   Find the volume of the tube in cm^3; $1 \, cm^3 = 1$ mL.

r = d/2 = 2.5 cm/2 = 1.25 = 1.3 cm; h = 5.5 m = 5.5×10^2 cm

$V = \pi r^2 h = 3.14159 \times (1.25 \, \text{cm})^2 \times (5.5 \times 10^2 \, \text{cm}) = 2.700 \times 10^3 \, \text{cm}^3 = 2.7$ L

$$PV = \frac{g}{MM} RT; \; g = \frac{MM \times PV}{RT}; \; P = 1.78 \, \text{torr} \times \frac{1 \, \text{atm}}{760 \, \text{torr}} = 2.342 \times 10^{-3} = 2.34 \times 10^{-3} \, \text{atm}$$

$$g = \frac{20.18 \, \text{g Ne}}{1 \, \text{mol Ne}} \times \frac{\text{K-mol}}{0.08206 \, \text{L-atm}} \times \frac{2.342 \times 10^{-3} \, \text{atm} \times 2.700 \, \text{L}}{308 \, \text{K}} = 5.049 \times 10^{-3} = 5.0 \times 10^{-3} \, \text{g Ne}$$

10.38 $P_{O_3} = 3.0 \times 10^{-3}$ atm; T = 250 K; V = 1 L (exact)

$$\# \text{ of } O_3 \text{ molecules} = \frac{PV}{RT} \times 6.022 \times 10^{23}$$

$$\# = \frac{3.0 \times 10^{-3} \, \text{atm} \times 1 \, \text{L}}{250 \, \text{K}} \times \frac{\text{K-mol}}{0.08206 \, \text{L-atm}} \times \frac{6.022 \times 10^{23} \, \text{molecules}}{\text{mol}}$$

$$= 8.8 \times 10^{19} \, O_3 \text{ molecules}$$

10.40   (a)   V = 0.250 L, T = 23°C = 296 K, n = 2.30 g C_3H_8 $\times \dfrac{1 \, \text{mol } C_3H_8}{44.1 \, \text{g } C_3H_8} = 0.052154$

$$= 0.0522 \, \text{mol}$$

$$P = \frac{nRT}{V} = 0.052154 \, \text{mol} \times \frac{0.08206 \, \text{L-atm}}{\text{K-mol}} \times \frac{296 \, \text{K}}{0.250 \, \text{L}} = 5.07 \, \text{atm}$$

(b)   STP = 1.00 atm, 273 K

$$V = \frac{nRT}{P} = 0.052154 \, \text{mol} \times \frac{0.08206 \, \text{L-atm}}{\text{K-mol}} \times \frac{273 \, \text{K}}{1.00 \, \text{atm}} = 1.1684 = 1.17 \, \text{L}$$

(c)   °C = 5/9 (°F – 32°); K = °C + 273.15 = 5/9 (130°F – 32°) + 273.15 = 327.59 = 328 K

$$P = \frac{nRT}{V} = 0.052154 \, \text{mol} \times \frac{0.08206 \, \text{L-atm}}{\text{K-mol}} \times \frac{327.59 \, \text{K}}{0.250 \, \text{L}} = 5.608 = 5.61 \, \text{atm}$$

10.42 $V = 65.0 \, \text{L}, T = 23°C = 296 \, \text{K}, P = 16,500 \, \text{kPa} \times \dfrac{1 \, \text{atm}}{101.325} = 162.84 = 163 \, \text{kPa}$

(a) $g = \dfrac{MM \times PV}{RT}; g = \dfrac{32.0 \, \text{g O}_2}{1 \, \text{mol O}_2} \times \dfrac{\text{K-mol}}{0.08206 \, \text{L-atm}} \times \dfrac{162.84 \, \text{atm}}{296 \, \text{K}} \times 65.0 \, \text{L}$

$$= 1.39446 \times 10^4 \, \text{g O}_2 = 13.9 \, \text{kg O}_2$$

(b) $V_2 = \dfrac{P_1 V_1 T_2}{T_1 P_2} = \dfrac{16,500 \, \text{kPa} \times 65.0 \, \text{L} \times 273 \, \text{K}}{296 \, \text{K} \times 101.325 \, \text{kPa}} = 9.76 \times 10^3 \, \text{L}$

(c) $T_2 = \dfrac{P_2 T_1}{P_1} = \dfrac{150.0 \, \text{atm} \times 296 \, \text{K}}{16,500 \, \text{kPa}} \times \dfrac{101.325 \, \text{kPa}}{1 \, \text{atm}} = 272.7 = 273 \, \text{K}$

(d) $P_2 = \dfrac{P_1 V_1 T_2}{V_2 T_1} = \dfrac{16,500 \, \text{kPa} \times 65.0 \, \text{L} \times 297 \, \text{K}}{55.0 \, \text{L} \times 296 \, \text{K}} = 19,566 = 1.96 \times 10^4 \, \text{kPa}$

10.44   mass $= 1800 \times 10^{-9} \, \text{g} = 1.8 \times 10^{-6} \, \text{g}; V = 1 \, \text{m}^3 = 1 \times 10^3 \, \text{L}; T = 273 + 10°\text{C} = 283 \, \text{K}$

(a) $P = \dfrac{gRT}{MM \times V}; P = \dfrac{1.8 \times 10^{-6} \, \text{g Hg} \times 1 \, \text{mol Hg}}{200.6 \, \text{g Hg}} \times \dfrac{0.08206 \, \text{L-atm}}{\text{K-mol}} \times \dfrac{283 \, \text{K}}{1 \times 10^3 \, \text{L}}$

$$= 2.1 \times 10^{-10} \, \text{atm}$$

(b) $\dfrac{1.8 \times 10^{-6} \, \text{g Hg}}{1 \, \text{m}^3} \times \dfrac{1 \, \text{mol Hg}}{200.6 \, \text{g Hg}} \times \dfrac{6.022 \times 10^{23} \, \text{Hg atoms}}{1 \, \text{mol Hg}} = 5.4 \times 10^{15} \, \text{Hg atoms/m}^3$

(c) $1600 \, \text{km}^3 \times \dfrac{1000^3 \, \text{m}^3}{1 \, \text{km}^3} \times \dfrac{1.8 \times 10^{-6} \, \text{g Hg}}{1 \, \text{m}^3} = 2.9 \times 10^6 \, \text{g Hg/day}$

Further Applications of the Ideal-Gas Equation

10.46 $CO_2 < SO_2 < HBr$. For gases at the same conditions, density is directly proportional to molar mass. The order of increasing molar mass is the order of increasing density. CO_2, 44 g/mol $< SO_2$, 64 g/mol $< HBr$, 81 g/mol.

10.48   (b) Xe atoms have a higher mass than N_2 molecules. Because both gases at STP have the same number of molecules per unit volume, the Xe gas must be denser.

10.50   (a) $d = \dfrac{MM \times P}{RT}; MM = 146.1 \, \text{g/mol}, T = 21°\text{C} = 294 \, \text{K}, P = 707 \, \text{torr}$

$$d = \dfrac{146.1 \, \text{g}}{1 \, \text{mol}} \times \dfrac{\text{K-mol}}{0.08206 \, \text{L-atm}} \times \dfrac{707 \, \text{torr}}{294 \, \text{K}} \times \dfrac{1 \, \text{atm}}{760 \, \text{torr}} = 5.63 \, \text{g/L}$$

(b) $MM = \dfrac{dRT}{P} = \dfrac{7.135\,g}{1\,L} \times \dfrac{0.08206\,L\text{-}atm}{K\text{-}mol} \times \dfrac{285\,K}{743\,torr} \times \dfrac{760\,torr}{1\,atm} = 171\,g/mol$

10.52 $MM = \dfrac{gRT}{PV} = \dfrac{0.846\,g}{0.354\,L} \times \dfrac{0.08206\,L\text{-}atm}{K\text{-}atm} \times \dfrac{373\,K}{752\,torr} \times \dfrac{760\,torr}{1\,atm} = 73.9\,g/mol$

10.54 $n_{H_2} = \dfrac{P_{H_2}V}{RT}$; $P = 814\,torr \times \dfrac{1\,atm}{760\,torr} = 1.071 = 1.07\,atm$; $T = 273 + 21°C = 294\,K$

$n_{H_2} = 1.071\,atm \times \dfrac{K\text{-}mol}{0.08206\,L\text{-}atm} \times \dfrac{53.5\,L}{294\,K} = 2.3751 = 2.38\,mol\,H_2$

$2.3751\,mol\,H_2 \times \dfrac{1\,mol\,CaH_2}{2\,mol\,H_2} \times \dfrac{42.10\,g\,CaH_2}{1\,mol\,CaH_2} = 50.0\,g\,CaH_2$

10.56   Follow the logic in Sample Exercise 10.9. The $H_2(g)$ will be used in a balloon, which operates at atmospheric pressure.   Since atmospheric pressure is not explicitly given, assume 1 atm (infinite sig figs).

$n = \dfrac{PV}{RT} = 1 \times \dfrac{3.1150 \times 10^4\,L}{295\,K} \times \dfrac{K\text{-}mol}{0.08206\,L\text{-}atm} = 1.28678 \times 10^3 = 1.29 \times 10^3\,mol\,H_2$

From the balanced equation, 1 mol of Fe produces 1 mol of H_2, so 1.29×10^3 mol Fe are required.

$1.28678 \times 10^3\,mol\,Fe \times \dfrac{55.845\,g\,Fe}{mol\,Fe} \times \dfrac{1\,kg}{1000\,g} = 71.86 = 71.9\,kg\,Fe$

10.58   The gas sample is a mixture of $C_2H_2(g)$ and $H_2O(g)$. Find the partial pressure of C_2H_2, then moles CaC_2 and C_2H_2.

$P_t = 745\,torr = P_{C_2H_2} + P_{H_2O}$. P_{H_2O} at $23°C = 21.07\,torr$

$P_{C_2H_2} = (745\,torr - 21.07\,torr) \times \dfrac{1\,atm}{760\,torr} = 0.95254 = 0.953\,atm$

$0.752\,g\,CaC_2 \times \dfrac{1\,mol\,CaC_2}{64.10\,g} \times \dfrac{1\,mol\,C_2H_2}{1\,mol\,CaC_2} = 0.01173 = 0.0117\,mol\,C_2H_2$

$V = 0.01173\,mol \times \dfrac{0.08206\,L\text{-}atm}{K\text{-}mol} \times \dfrac{296\,K}{0.95254\,atm} = 0.299\,L\,C_2H_2$

Partial Pressures

10.60   (a)   The partial pressure of gas A is **not affected** by the addition of gas C. The partial pressure of A depends only on moles of A, volume of container, and conditions; none of these factors changes when gas C is added.

(b)   The total pressure in the vessel **increases** when gas C is added, because the total number of moles of gas increases.

(c)   The mole fraction of gas B **decreases** when gas C is added. The moles of gas B stay the same, but the total moles increase, so the mole fraction of B (nB/nt) decreases.

10.62   Given mass, V and T of O_2 and He, find the partial pressure of each gas. Sum to find the total pressure in the tank.

$V = 10.0$ L; $T = 19°C$; $19 + 273 = 292$ K

$$n_{O_2} = 51.2 \text{ g O}_2 \times \frac{1 \text{ mol O}_2}{31.999 \text{ g O}_2} = 1.600 = 1.60 \text{ mol O}_2$$

$$n_{He} = 32.6 \text{ g He} \times \frac{1 \text{ mol He}}{4.0026 \text{ g He}} = 8.1447 = 8.14 \text{ mol He}$$

$$P_{O_2} = 1.600 \text{ mol} \times \frac{0.08206 \text{ L-atm}}{K\text{-mol}} \times \frac{292 \text{ K}}{10.0 \text{ L}} = 3.8338 = 3.84 \text{ atm}$$

$$P_{He} = 8.1447 \text{ mol} \times \frac{0.08206 \text{ L-atm}}{K\text{-mol}} \times \frac{292 \text{ K}}{10.0 \text{ L}} = 19.5159 = 19.5 \text{ atm}$$

$$P_t = 3.8338 + 19.5159 = 23.3497 = 23.3 \text{ atm}$$

10.64 $V \text{ C}_4\text{H}_{10}\text{O(l)} \xrightarrow{\text{density}} \text{mass C}_4\text{H}_{10}\text{O} \rightarrow \text{mol C}_4\text{H}_{10}\text{O} \rightarrow P_{C_4H_{10}O}$ at given V, T.

$$P_t = P_{N_2} + P_{O_2} + P_{C_4H_{10}O}; \quad T = 273.15 + 35.0°C = 308.15 = 308.2 \text{ K}$$

(a) $4.00 \text{ mL C}_4\text{H}_{10}\text{O} \times \frac{0.7134 \text{ g C}_4\text{H}_{10}\text{O}}{\text{mL}} \times \frac{1 \text{ mol C}_4\text{H}_{10}\text{O}}{74.12 \text{ g C}_4\text{H}_{10}\text{O}} = 0.0385 \text{ mol C}_4\text{H}_{10}\text{O}$

$$P = \frac{nRT}{V} = 0.03850 \text{ mol} \times \frac{308.15}{5.00 \text{ L}} \times \frac{0.08206 \text{ L-atm}}{K\text{-mol}} = 0.1947 = 0.195 \text{ atm}$$

(b) $P_t = P_{N_2} + P_{O_2} + P_{C_4H_{10}O} = 0.751 \text{ atm} + 0.208 \text{ atm} + 0.195 \text{ atm} = 1.154 \text{ atm}$

10.66 $n_{N_2} = 10.25 \text{ g N}_2 \times \frac{1 \text{ mol}}{28.02 \text{ g}} = 0.3658 \text{ mol}; \quad n_{H_2} = 1.83 \text{ g H}_2 \times \frac{1 \text{ mol}}{2.016 \text{ g}} = 0.9077 = 0.908 \text{ mol}$

$$n_{NH_3} = 7.95 \text{ g NH}_3 \times \frac{1 \text{ mol}}{17.03 \text{ g}} = 0.4668 \text{ mol} = 0.467 \text{ mol}$$

$$n_t = 0.3658 + 0.9077 + 0.4668 = 1.7403 = 1.740 \text{ mol}$$

$$P_{N_2} = \frac{n_{N_2}}{n_t} \times P_t = \frac{0.3658}{1.7403} \times 1.85 \text{ atm} = 0.389 \text{ atm}$$

$$P_{H_2} = \frac{0.9077}{1.7403} \times 1.85 \text{ atm} = 0.965 \text{ atm}; \quad P_{NH_3} = \frac{0.4668}{1.7403} \times 1.85 \text{ atm} = 0.496 \text{ atm}$$

10.68   (a) $n_{O_2} = 5.08 \text{ g O}_2 \times \frac{1 \text{ mol}}{32.00 \text{ g}} = 0.159 \text{ mol}; \quad n_{N_2} = 7.17 \text{ g N}_2 \times \frac{1 \text{ mol}}{28.02 \text{ g}} = 0.256 \text{ mol}$

$$n_{H_2} = 1.32 \text{ g H}_2 \times \frac{1 \text{ mol}}{2.016 \text{ g}} = 0.655 \text{ mol}; \quad n_t = 0.159 + 0.256 + 0.655 = 1.070 \text{ mol}$$

$$\chi_{O_2} = \frac{n_{O_2}}{n_t} = \frac{0.159}{1.07} = 0.149; \quad \chi_{N_2} = \frac{n_{N_2}}{n_t} = \frac{0.256}{1.07} = 0.239$$

$$\chi_{H_2} = \frac{0.655}{1.07} = 0.612$$

(b) $P_{O_2} = n \times \frac{RT}{V}; \quad P_{O_2} = 0.159 \text{ mol} \times \frac{0.08206 \text{ L-atm}}{K\text{-mol}} \times \frac{288 \text{ K}}{12.40 \text{ L}} = 0.303 \text{ atm}$

$$P_{N_2} = 0.256\,\text{mol} \times \frac{0.08206\,\text{L - atm}}{\text{K - mol}} \times \frac{288\,\text{K}}{12.40\,\text{L}} = 0.488\,\text{atm}$$

$$P_{H_2} = 0.655\,\text{mol} \times \frac{0.08206\,\text{L - atm}}{\text{K - mol}} \times \frac{288\,\text{K}}{12.40\,\text{L}} = 1.25\,\text{atm}$$

10.70   Calculate the pressure of the gas in the second vessel directly from mass and conditions using the ideal-gas equation.

(a) $P_{SO_2} = \dfrac{gRT}{MV} = \dfrac{3.00\,\text{g SO}_2}{64.07\,\text{g SO}_2/\text{mol}} \times \dfrac{0.08206\,\text{L - atm}}{\text{K - mol}} \times \dfrac{299\,\text{K}}{10.0\,\text{L}} = 0.11489 = 0.115\,\text{atm}$

(b) $P_{N_2} = \dfrac{gRT}{MV} = \dfrac{2.35\,\text{g N}_2}{28.01\,\text{g N}_2/\text{mol}} \times \dfrac{0.08206\,\text{L - atm}}{\text{K - mol}} \times \dfrac{299\,\text{K}}{10.0\,\text{L}} = 0.20585 = 0.206\,\text{atm}$

(c) $P_t = P_{SO_2} + P_{N_2} = 0.11489\,\text{atm} + 0.20585\,\text{atm} = 0.321\,\text{atm}$

Kinetic-Molecular Theory; Graham's Law

10.72   (a)   False. The average kinetic energy per molecule in a collection of gas molecules is the same for all gases at the same temperature.

(b)   True.

(c)   False. The molecules in a gas sample at a given temperature exhibit a distribution of kinetic energies.

(d)   True.

10.74   Newton's model provides no explanation of the effect of a change in temperature on the pressure of a gas at constant volume or on the volume of a gas at constant pressure. On the other hand, the assumption that the average kinetic energy of gas molecules increases with increasing temperature explains Charles' Law, that an increase in temperature requires an increase in volume to maintain constant pressure.

10.76   (a)   They have the same number of molecules (equal volumes of gases at the same temperature and pressure contain equal numbers of molecules).

(b) N_2 is more dense because it has the larger molar mass. Since the volumes of the samples and the number of molecules are equal, the gas with the larger molar mass will have the greater density.

(c)   The average kinetic energies are equal (statement 5, section 10.7).

(d) CH_4 will effuse faster. The lighter the gas molecules, the faster they will effuse (Graham's Law).

10.78   (a)   *Plan.* The greater the molecular (and molar) mass, the smaller the rms speed of the molecules. Calculate the molar mass of each gas, and place them in decreasing order of mass and increasing order of rms speed. *Solve.*

$CO = 28\,\text{g/mol}$; $SF_6 = 146\,\text{g/mol}$; $H_2S = 34\,\text{g/mol}$; $Cl_2 = 71\,\text{g/mol}$; $HBr = 81\,\text{g/mol}$. In order of increasing speed (and decreasing molar mass):

$SF_6 < HBr < Cl_2 < H_2S < CO$

(b)   *Plan.* Follow the logic of Sample Exercise 10.14. *Solve.*

$$u_{CO} = \sqrt{\frac{3RT}{M}} = \left(\frac{3 \times 8.314 \, kg\text{-}m^2/s^2\text{-}K\text{-}mol \times 300 \, K}{28.0 \times 10^{-3} \, kg/mol}\right)^{1/2} = 5.17 \times 10^2 \, m/s$$

$$u_{Cl_2} = \left(\frac{3 \times 8.314 \, kg\text{-}m^2/s^2\text{-}K\text{-}mol \times 300 \, K}{70.9 \times 10^{-3} \, kg/mol}\right)^{1/2} = 3.25 \times 10^2 \, m/s$$

As expected, the lighter molecule moves at the greater speed.

10.80 $\dfrac{rate^{235}U}{rate^{238}U} = \sqrt{\dfrac{238.05}{235.04}} = \sqrt{1.0128} = 1.0064$

There is a slightly greater rate enhancement for $^{235}U(g)$ atoms than $^{235}UF_6(g)$ molecules (1.0043), because ^{235}U is a greater percentage (100%) of the mass of the diffusing particles than in $^{235}UF_6$ molecules. The masses of the isotopes were taken from *The Handbook of Chemistry and Physics*.

10.82   The time required is proportional to the reciprocal of the effusion rate.

$$\frac{rate\,(X)}{rate\,(O_2)} = \frac{105 \, s}{31 \, s} = \left[\frac{32 \, g \, O_2}{MM_x}\right]^{1/2}; \; MM_x = 32 \, g \, O_2 \times \left[\frac{105}{31}\right]^2 = 370 \, g/mol \, (two \, sig \, figs)$$

Nonideal-Gas Behavior

10.84   Ideal-gas behavior is most likely to occur at high temperature and low pressure, so the atmosphere on Mercury is more likely to obey the ideal-gas law. The higher temperature on Mercury means that the kinetic energies of the molecules will be larger relative to intermolecular attractive forces. Further, the gravitational attractive forces on Mercury are lower because the planet has a much smaller mass. This means that for the same column mass of gas (Figure 10.1), atmospheric pressure on Mercury will be lower.

10.86   The constant a is a measure of the strength of intermolecular attractions among gas molecules; b is a measure of molecular volume. Both increase with increasing molecular mass and structural complexity.

10.88   *Analyze.* Conditions and amount of $CCl_4(g)$ are given. *Plan.* Use ideal-gas equation and van der Waals equation to calculate pressure of gas at these conditions.   *Solve.*

(a) $P = 1.00 \, mol \times \dfrac{0.08206 \, L\text{-}atm}{K\text{-}mol} \times \dfrac{313 \, K}{28.0 \, L} = 0.917 \, atm$

(b) $P = \dfrac{nRT}{V-nb} - \dfrac{an^2}{V^2} = \dfrac{1.00 \times 0.08206 \times 313}{28.0 - (1.00 \times 0.1383)} - \dfrac{20.4(1.00)^2}{(28.0)^2} = 0.896 \, atm$

Check. The van der Waals result indicates that the real pressure will be less than the ideal pressure. That is, intermolecular forces reduce the effective number of particles and the real pressure. This is reasonable for 1 mole of gas at relatively low temperature and pressure.

(c)   According to Table 10.3, CCl_4 has larger a and b values. That is, CCl_4 experiences stronger intermolecular attractions and has a larger molecular volume than Cl_2 does. CCl_4 will deviate more from ideal behavior at these conditions than Cl_2 will.

Additional Exercises

10.90   Only item (b) is satisfactory. Item (c) would not have supported a column of Hg because it is open at both ends. The atmosphere would exert pressure on the top of the column as well as on the reservoir; the column would only be as high as the reservoir and the height would not change with changing pressure. Item (d) is not tall enough to support a nearly 760 mm Hg column. Items (a) and (e) are inappropriate for the same reason: they don't have a uniform cross-sectional area. The height of the Hg column is a direct measure of atmospheric pressure only if the cross-sectional area is constant over the entire tube.

10.91 $P_1 V_1 = P_2 V_2; \; V_2 = P_1 V_1 / P_2$

$$V_2 = \frac{3.0 \, atm \times 1.0 \, mm^3}{695 \, torr} \times \frac{760 \, torr}{1 \, atm} = 3.3 \, mm^3$$

10.93 $P = \dfrac{nRT}{V}; \; n = 1.4 \times 10^{-5} \, mol, \; V = 0.600 \, L, \; T = 23°C = 296 \, K$

$$P = 1.4 \times 10^{-5} \, mol \times \frac{0.08206 \, L\text{-}atm}{K\text{-}mol} \times \frac{296 \, K}{0.600 \, L} = 5.7 \times 10^{-4} \, atm = 0.43 \, mm \, Hg$$

10.94   (a)   Change mass CO_2 to mol CO_2. $P = 1.00 \, atm, \; T = 27°C = 300 \, K$.

$$6 \times 10^6 \, tons \, CO_2 \times \frac{2000 \, lb}{ton} \times \frac{453.6 \, g}{lb} \times \frac{1 \, mol \, CO_2}{44.01 \, g \, CO_2} = 1.237 \times 10^{11} = 1 \times 10^{11} \, mol$$

$$V = \frac{nRT}{P} = 1.237 \times 10^{11} \, mol \times \frac{300 \, K}{1.00 \, atm} \times \frac{0.08206 \, L\text{-}atm}{K\text{-}mol} =$$
$$3.045 \times 10^{12} = 3 \times 10^{12} \, L$$

(b) $1.237 \times 10^{11} \, mol \, CO_2 \times \dfrac{44.01 \, g \, CO_2}{mol \, CO_2} \times \dfrac{1 \, cm^3}{1.2 \, g} \times \dfrac{1 \, L}{1000 \, cm^3} = 4.536 \times 10^9 = 5 \times 10^9 \, L$

(c) $n = 1.237 \times 10^{11} \, mol, \; P = 90 \, atm, \; T = 36°C = 309 \, K$

$$V = \frac{nRT}{P} = 1.237 \times 10^{11} \, mol \times \frac{309 \, K}{90 \, atm} \times \frac{0.08206 \, L\text{-}atm}{K\text{-}mol} = \quad 3.485 \times 10^{10} = 3 \times 10^{10} \, L$$

10.96   Volume of laboratory $= 54 \, m^2 \times 3.1 \, m \times \dfrac{1000 \, L}{1 \, m^3} = 1.674 \times 10^5 = 1.7 \times 10^5 \, L$

Calculate the **total** moles of gas in the laboratory at the conditions given.

$$n_t = \frac{PV}{RT} = 1.00 \, atm \times \frac{K\text{-}mol}{0.08206 \, L\text{-}atm} \times \frac{1.674 \times 10^5 \, L}{297 \, K} = 6.869 \times 10^3 = 6.9 \times 10^3 \, mol \, gas$$

An $Ni(CO)_4$ concentration of 1 part in 10^9 means 1 mol $Ni(CO)_4$ in 1×10^9 total moles of gas.

$$\frac{x \text{ mol Ni(CO)}_4}{6.869 \times 10^3 \text{ mol gas}} = \frac{1}{10^9} = 6.869 \times 10^{-6} \text{ mol Ni(CO)}_4$$

$$6.869 \times 10^{-6} \text{ mol Ni(CO)}_4 \times \frac{170.74 \text{g Ni(CO)}_4}{1 \text{ mol Ni(CO)}_4} = 1.2 \times 10^{-3} \text{ g Ni(CO)}_4$$

10.97 **(a)** mol = g/MM; assume mol Ar = mol X;

$$\frac{\text{g Ar}}{39.948 \text{ g / mol}} = \frac{\text{g X}}{\text{MM X}}; \quad \frac{3.224 \text{ g Ar}}{39.948 \text{ g / mol}} = \frac{8.102 \text{ g X}}{\text{MM X}}$$

$$\text{MM X} = \frac{(8.102 \text{ g X})(39.948 \text{ g / mol})}{3.224 \text{ g Ar}} = 100.39 = 100.4 \text{ g / mol}$$

(b) Assume mol Ar = mol X. For gases, PV = nRT and n = PV/RT. For moles of the two gases to be equal, the implied assumption is that P, V, and T are constant. Since we use the same container for both gas samples, constant V is a good assumption. Constant P and T are not explicitly stated.

We also assume that the gases behave ideally. At ambient conditions, this is a reasonable assumption.

10.99 **(a)** $n = \dfrac{PV}{RT} = 0.980 \text{ atm} \times \dfrac{\text{K - mol}}{0.08206 \text{ L - atm}} \times \dfrac{0.524 \text{ L}}{347 \text{ K}} = 0.018034 = 0.0180 \text{ mol air}$

$$\text{mol O}_2 = 0.018034 \text{ mol air} \times \frac{0.2095 \text{ mol O}_2}{1 \text{ mol air}} = 0.003778 = 0.00378 \text{ mol O}_2$$

(b) $C_8H_{18}(l) + 25/2 \, O_2(g) \rightarrow 8CO_2(g) + 9H_2O(g)$

(The H_2O produced in an automobile engine is in the gaseous state.)

$$0.003778 \text{ mol O}_2 \times \frac{1 \text{ mol C}_8\text{H}_{18}}{12.5 \text{ mol O}_2} \times \frac{114.2 \text{ g C}_8\text{H}_{18}}{1 \text{ mol C}_8\text{H}_{18}} = 0.0345 \text{ g C}_8\text{H}_{18}$$

10.100 **(a)** Pressure percent = mol percent. Change pressure/mol percents to mol fraction. Partial pressure of each gas is mol fraction (χ) times total pressure. $P_x = \chi_x P_t$

$$P_{N_2} = 0.748(0.980 \text{ atm}) = 0.733 \text{ atm}; \quad P_{O_2} = 0.153(0.980 \text{ atm}) = 0.150 \text{ atm}$$

$$P_{CO_2} = 0.037(0.980 \text{ atm}) = 0.03626 = 0.036 \text{ atm}$$

$$P_{H_2O} = 0.062(0.980 \text{ atm}) = 0.06076 = 0.060 \text{ atm}$$

(b) PV = nRT, n = PV/RT; P = 0.036 atm, V = 0.455 L, T = 37°C = 310 K

$$n = 0.03626 \text{ atm} \times \frac{0.455 \text{ L}}{310 \text{ K}} \times \frac{\text{K - mol}}{0.08206 \text{ L - atm}} = 6.486 \times 10^{-4} = 6.5 \times 10^{-4} \text{ mol}$$

(c) $C_6H_{12}O_6 + 6O_2 \rightarrow 6CO_2 + 6H_2O$

$$6.486 \times 10^{-4} \text{ mol CO}_2 \times \frac{1 \text{ mol C}_6\text{H}_{12}\text{O}_6}{6 \text{ mol CO}_2} \times \frac{180.15 \text{ g C}_6\text{H}_{12}\text{O}_6}{1 \text{ mol C}_6\text{H}_{12}\text{O}_6} = 0.01947$$

$$= 0.019 \text{ g C}_6\text{H}_{12}\text{O}_6$$

10.102 $MM_{avg} = \dfrac{dRT}{P} = \dfrac{1.104 \text{ g}}{1 \text{ L}} \times \dfrac{0.08206 \text{ L-atm}}{\text{K-mol}} \times \dfrac{300 \text{ K}}{435 \text{ torr}} \times \dfrac{760 \text{ torr}}{1 \text{ atm}} = 47.48 = 47.5 \text{ g/mol}$

χ = mole fraction O_2; $1 - \chi$ = mole fraction Kr

$47.48 \text{ g} = \chi(32.00) + (1 - \chi)(83.80)$

$36.3 = 51.8 \chi$; $\chi = 0.701$; 70.1% O_2

10.103   **(a)**   The quantity $d/P = MM/RT$ should be a constant at all pressures for an ideal gas. It is not, however, because of nonideal behavior. If we graph d/P vs P, the ratio should approach ideal behavior at low P. At $P = 0$, $d/P = 2.2525$. Using this value in the formula $MM = d/P \times RT$, $MM = 50.46 \text{ g/mol}$.

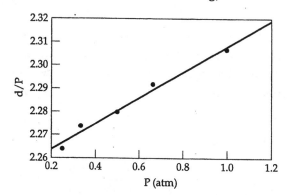

   (b)   The ratio d/P varies with pressure because of the finite volumes of gas molecules and attractive intermolecular forces.

10.105 $u = (3RT/MM)^{1/2}$; $u_2 = 1.100 \, u_1$; $T_1 = -33° = 240 \text{ K}$

$u_1 = (3RT_1/MM)^{1/2}$; $u_1^2 = 3(240)R/MM = 720R/MM$

$u_1 = (720R/MM)^{1/2}$; $u_2 = 1.100u_1 = (1.100)(720R/MM)^{1/2}$

$(1.100)(720R/MM)^{1/2} = (3RT_2/MM)^{1/2}$

$(1.100)^2(720R/MM) = 3RT_2/MM$; $(1.100)^2(720) = 3T_2$

$T_2 = (1.100)(720)/3 = 290.4 = 290 \text{ K} = 17°C$

A 10.0% increase in rms speed (u) requires a 50 K (or 50°C) increase in temperature.

10.106   **(a)**   Assumption 3 states that attractive and repulsive forces between molecules are negligible. All gases in the list are nonpolar. The largest and most structurally complex molecule, SF_6, is most likely to depart from this assumption.

   (b)   The monatomic gas Ne is smallest and least structurally complex, so it will behave most like an ideal gas.

   (c)   Root-mean-square speed is directly related to molecular mass. The lightest gas, CH_4, has the highest rms speed.

   (d)   The heaviest and most structurally complex is SF_6. We guess that this one will occupy the greatest molecular volume relative to total volume. A quantitative measure is the b value in Table 10.3, with units of L/mol. Unfortunately, SF_6 does not appear in Table 10.3.

(e) Average kinetic energy is only related to absolute (K) temperature. At the same temperature, they all have the same average kinetic molecular energy.

(f) Rate of effusion is inversely related to molecular mass. The lighter the molecule, the faster it effuses. Ne and CH_4 have smaller molecular masses and effuse faster than N_2.

10.108 (a) The initial drop in the value of PV/RT is due to attractive forces between molecules. These intermolecular forces cause the molecules to "stick" together and behave as if there are fewer net particles in the sample. At lower pressures, this is the dominant effect. At the same time, the real volume of gas molecules causes the amount of free space in the gas sample to be less than the container volume. Using the container volume to calculate PV/RT gives a value larger than that for an ideal gas (which assumes that the total container volume is free space). At higher pressures, this effect more than compensates for molecular attraction, and PV/RT is greater than 1.

(b) As the temperature of a gas increases, the average kinetic energy of the particles increases. The increased kinetic energy overcomes the attractive forces between molecules and keeps them separate.

10.109 The larger and heavier the particle, in this case a single atom, the more likely it is to deviate from ideal behavior. Other than Rn, Xe is the largest (atomic radius = 1.45 Å), heaviest (molar mass = 131.3 g/mol) and most dense (9.73 g/L) noble gas. Its susceptibility to intermolecular interactions is also demonstrated by its ability to form compounds like XeF_4.

10.111 (a) $120.00 \text{ kg } N_2(g) \times \dfrac{1000 \text{ g}}{1 \text{ kg}} \times \dfrac{1 \text{ mol } N_2}{28.0135 \text{ g N}} = 4283.6 \text{ mol } N_2$

$P = \dfrac{nRT}{V} = 4283.6 \text{ mol} \times \dfrac{0.08206 \text{ L-atm}}{\text{K-mol}} \times \dfrac{553 \text{ K}}{1100.0 \text{ L}} = 176.72 = 177 \text{ atm}$

(b) According to Equation [10.26], $P = \dfrac{nRT}{V - nb} - \dfrac{n^2 a}{V^2}$

$P = \dfrac{(4283.6 \text{ mol})(0.08206 \text{ L-atm/K-mol})(553 \text{ K})}{1100.0 \text{ L} - (4283.6 \text{ mol})(0.0391 \text{ L/mol})} - \dfrac{(4283.6 \text{ mol})^2 (1.39 \text{ L}^2\text{-atm/mol}^2)}{(1100.0 \text{ L})^2}$

$P = \dfrac{194{,}388 \text{ L-atm}}{1100.0 \text{ L} - 167.5 \text{ L}} - 21.1 \text{ atm} = 208.5 \text{ atm} - 21.1 \text{ atm} = 187.4 \text{ atm}$

(c) The pressure corrected for the real volume of the N_2 molecules is 208.5 atm, 31.8 atm higher than the ideal pressure of 176.7 atm. The 21.1 atm correction for intermolecular forces reduces the calculated pressure somewhat, but the "real" pressure is still higher than the ideal pressure. The correction for the real volume of molecules dominates. Even though the value of b is small, the number of moles of N_2 is large enough so that the molecular volume correction is larger than the attractive forces correction.

Integrative Exercises

10.113   *Plan.* Write the balanced equation for the combustion of methanol. Since amounts of both reactants are given, determine the limiting reactant. Use mole ratios to calculate mol H_2O produced, based on the amount of limiting reactant.   *Solve.*

methanol $= CH_3OH(l)$. $2CH_3OH(l) + 3O_2(g) \rightarrow 2CO_2(g) + 4H_2O(g)$

$$25.0\,mL\,CH_3OH \times \frac{0.850\,g\,CH_3OH}{mL} \times \frac{1\,mol\,CH_3OH}{32.04\,g} = 0.6632 = 0.663\,mol\,CH_3OH$$

$$mol\,O_2 = n = \frac{PV}{RT} = 1.00\,atm \times \frac{12.5\,L}{273\,K} \times \frac{K \cdot mol}{0.08206\,L \cdot atm} = 0.5580 = 0.558\,mol\,O_2$$

$$0.558\,mol\,O_2 \times \frac{2\,mol\,CH_3OH}{3\,mol\,O_2} = 0.372\,mol\,CH_3OH$$

0.558 mol O_2 can react with only 0.372 mol CH_3OH, so O_2 is the limiting reactant. Note that a large volume of $O_2(g)$ is required to completely react with a relatively small volume of $CH_3OH(l)$.

$$0.558\,mol\,O_2 \times \frac{4\,mol\,H_2O}{3\,mol\,O_2} = 0.744\,mol\,H_2O$$

10.115   (a)   *Plan.* Use the ideal-gas law to calculate the moles CO_2 that react.

     Solve. P(reacted) = P(initial) – P(final), at constant V, T. Since both CaO and BaO react with CO_2 in a 1:1 mole ratio, mol CaO + mol BaO = mol CO_2. Use molar masses to calculate % CaO in sample.

$$P(reacted) = 730\,torr - 150\,torr = 580\,torr;\ 580\,torr \times \frac{1\,atm}{760\,torr} = 0.76316 = 0.763\,atm$$

$$n = \frac{PV}{RT} = 0.76316\,atm \times \frac{1.0\,L}{298\,K} \times \frac{K \cdot mol}{0.08206\,L \cdot atm} = 0.03121 = 0.0312\,mol\,CO_2$$

  (b)   *Plan.* Use the stoichiometry of the reaction and definition of moles to calculate the mass and Mass % of CaO.

     Solve. $CaO(s) + CO_2(s) \rightarrow CaCO_3(s)$. $BaO(s) + CO_2(g) \rightarrow BaCO_3(s)$

mol CO_2 reacted = mol CaO + mol BaO

Let x = g CaO, 4.00 – x = g BaO

$$0.03121 = \frac{x}{56.08} + \frac{4.00 - x}{153.3}$$

$$0.03121(56.08)(153.3) = 153.3x + 56.08(4.00 - x)$$

$$268.3 = (153.3x - 56.08x) + 224.3$$

$$43.98 = 97.22x,\ x = 0.452 = 0.45\,g\,CaO$$

$$\frac{0.452\,g\,CaO}{4.00\,g\,sample} \times 100 = 11.3 = 11\%\,CaO$$

(By strict sig fig rules, the result has 2 sig figs, because 268 – 224 = 44 has 0 decimal places and 2 sig figs.)

10.116   (a) $5.00 \text{ g HCl} \times \dfrac{1 \text{ mol HCl}}{36.46 \text{ g HCl}} = 0.1371 = 0.137 \text{ mol HCl}$

$5.00 \text{ g NH}_3 \times \dfrac{1 \text{ mol NH}_3}{17.03 \text{ g NH}_3} = 0.2936 = 0.294 \text{ mol NH}_3$

The gases react in a 1:1 mole ratio, HCl is the limiting reactant and is completely consumed. (0.2936 mol – 0.1371 mol) = 0.1565 = 0.157 mol NH_3 remain in the system. $NH_3(g)$ is the only gas remaining after reaction. $V_t = 4.00$ L

(b) $P = \dfrac{nRT}{V} = 0.1565 \text{ mol} \times \dfrac{0.08206 \text{ L-atm}}{\text{K-mol}} \times \dfrac{298 \text{ K}}{4.00 \text{ L}} = 0.957 \text{ atm}$

10.118   (a)   *Analyze/Plan.* $AgF + S_8 \xrightarrow{\Delta} \text{unknown gas}$

The gas probably contains the elements S and F in an unknown mole ratio. (Most compounds containing Ag are ionic and therefore solids.) Calculate the molar mass of the gas from its density at the given conditions. Determine the relative amount of F from the data on the reaction of the gas with water to produce HF. *Solve.*

$MM = \dfrac{dRT}{P} = \dfrac{0.803 \text{ g}}{\text{L}} \times \dfrac{0.08206 \text{ L-atm}}{\text{K-mol}} \times \dfrac{305 \text{ K}}{150 \text{ mm}} \times \dfrac{760 \text{ mm}}{1 \text{ atm}} = 101.83$

$= 102 \text{ g/mol}$

mol F in 480 mL sample: $M \times L = \text{mol}$

0.081 M HF $\times$ 0.080 L = 0.00648 = 0.0065 mol HF = 0.0065 mol F in the sample total
mol gas in 480 mL sample: n = PV/RT

$n = 126 \text{ mm} \times \dfrac{1 \text{ atm}}{760 \text{ mm}} \times \dfrac{0.480 \text{ L}}{301 \text{ K}} \times \dfrac{\text{K-mol}}{0.08206 \text{ L-atm}} = 3.222 \times 10^{-3}$

$= 3.22 \times 10^{-3} \text{ mol}$

mole ratio of S and F:

total g gas = 3.222×10^{-3} mol gas $\times$ 101.83 g/mol; = 0.32808 = 0.328 g gas

g F = 6.48×10^{-3} mol F $\times$ 18.998 g/mol F = 0.12311 = 0.123 g F

g S = 0.32808 – 0.12311 = 0.20497 = 0.205 g S

mol S = 0.205 g S/32.07 g/mol = 0.0639 mol S

0.00639 mol S/0.00648 mol F = 1:1 mole ratio of S:F

The empirical formula is SF; empirical FW = 32.07 + 19.00 = 51.07;

since MM = 102, the empirical formula is S_2F_2

Check. The empirical and molecular formula weights are in an integer ratio, so the result is reasonable.

(b)   26 valence e⁻, 13 e⁻ pairs

(c)   According to VSEPR the electron domain geometry about S in each of the molecules will be tetrahedral, with bond angles of 109° or less. The left molecule will have a structure similar to hydrogen peroxide, H_2O_2; the 4 atoms are not necessarily coplanar, and in fact we expect a dihedral angle of approximately 110°. Since the right molecule has a single central atom, we can describe the molecular geometry as trigonal pyramidal.

From the given bond distances, we expect the single-bond covalent radii to be S = 1.02 Å, F = 0.72 Å. The simple conclusion is that the S–S distances will be ~2.04 Å and the S–F distances ~1.74 Å. In fact, the S–S distance in the left compound is 1.89 Å and in the right it is 1.86 Å. Clearly each of these bonds has some double bond character, as indicated by one of the resonance structures for the right molecule. The actual S–F distances are 1.63 Å (left) and 1.60 Å (right), also shorter than the predicted S–F single bond distance. One possible conclusion is that each of the bonds has some double bond character, that some of the "nonbonding" electron density is incorporated into a delocalized π-bonding network in the molecules.

10.119   (a)   19 e⁻, 9.5 e⁻ pairs

$:\ddot{O}—\dot{\underset{..}{C}l}—\ddot{O}:$

Resonance structures can be drawn with the odd electron on O, but electronegativity considerations predict that it will be on Cl for most of the time.

(b) ClO_2 is very reactive because it is an odd-electron molecule. Adding an electron (reduction) both pairs the odd electron and completes the octet of Cl. Thus, ClO_2 has a strong tendency to gain an electron and be reduced.

(c) ClO_2^-, 20 e⁻, 10 e⁻ pairs

$\left[:\ddot{O}—\ddot{\underset{..}{C}l}—\ddot{O}:\right]^-$

(d)   4 e⁻ domains around Cl, O–Cl–O bond angle ~109°

(e)   Calculate mol Cl_2 from ideal-gas equation; determine limiting reactant; mass ClO_2 via mol ratios.

$$\text{mol } Cl_2 = \frac{PV}{RT} = 1.50 \text{ atm} \times \frac{2.00 \text{ L}}{294 \text{ K}} \times \frac{\text{K-mol}}{0.08206 \text{ L-atm}} = 0.1243 = 0.124 \text{ mol } Cl_2$$

$$10.0 \text{ g NaClO}_2 \times \frac{1 \text{mol NaClO}_2}{90.44 \text{ g}} = 0.1106 = 0.111 \text{ mol NaClO}_2$$

2 mol $NaClO_2$ are required for 1 mol Cl_2, so $NaClO_2$ is the limiting reactant. For every 2 mol $NaClO_2$ reacted, 2 mol ClO_2 are produced, so mol ClO_2 = mol $NaClO_2$.

$$0.1106 \text{ mol } ClO_2 \times \frac{67.45 \text{ g } ClO_2}{\text{mol}} = 7.46 \text{ g } ClO_2$$

10.121   After reaction, the flask contains $IF_5(g)$ and whichever reactant is in excess. Determine the limiting reactant, which regulates the moles of IF_5 produced and moles of excess reactant.

$$I_2(s) + 5F_2(g) \rightarrow 2\,IF_5(g)$$

$$10.0\,g\,I_2 \times \frac{1\,mol\,I_2}{253.8\,g\,I_2} \times \frac{5\,mol\,F_2}{1\,mol\,I_2} = 0.1970 = 0.197\,mol\,F_2$$

$$10.0\,g\,F_2 \times \frac{1\,mol\,F_2}{38.00\,g\,F_2} = 0.2632 = 0.263\,mol\,F_2 \text{ available}$$

I_2 is the limiting reactant; F_2 is in excess.

0.263 mol F_2 available – 0.197 mol F_2 reacted = 0.066 mol F_2 remain.

$$10.0\,g\,I_2 \times \frac{1\,mol\,I_2}{253.8\,g\,I_2} \times \frac{2\,mol\,IF_5}{1\,mol\,I_2} = 0.0788\,mol\,IF_5 \text{ produced}$$

(a) $$P_{IF_5} = \frac{nRT}{V} = 0.0788\,mol \times \frac{0.08206\,L\text{-}atm}{K\text{-}mol} \times \frac{398\,K}{5.00\,L} = 0.515\,atm$$

(b) $$\chi_{IF_5} = \frac{mol\,IF_5}{mol\,IF_5 + mol\,F_2} = \frac{0.0788}{0.0788 + 0.066} = 0.544$$

10.122   (a) $$MgCO_3(s) + 2HCl(aq) \rightarrow MgCl_2(aq) + H_2O(l) + CO_2(g)$$

$$CaCO_3(s) + 2HCl(aq) \rightarrow CaCl_2(aq) + H_2O(l) + CO_2(g)$$

(b) $$n = \frac{PV}{RT} = 743\,torr \times \frac{1\,atm}{760\,torr} \times \frac{K\text{-}mol}{0.08206\,L\text{-}atm} \times \frac{1.72\,L}{301\,K}$$

$$= 0.06808 = 0.0681\,mol\ CO_2$$

(c)   x = g $MgCO_3$, y = g $CaCO_3$, x + y = 6.53 g

mol $MgCO_3$ + mol $CaCO_3$ = mol CO_2 total

$$\frac{x}{84.32} + \frac{y}{100.09} = 0.06808;\ y = 6.53 - x$$

$$\frac{x}{84.32} + \frac{6.53 - x}{100.09} = 0.06808$$

$$100.09x - 84.32x + 84.32(6.53) = 0.06808\,(84.32)(100.09)$$

$$15.77x + 550.610 = 574.549;\ x = 1.52\ g\ MgCO_3$$

$$\text{mass \% } MgCO_3 = \frac{1.52\,g\,MgCO_3}{6.53\,g\,\text{sample}} \times 100 = 23.3\%$$

[By strict sig fig rules, the answer has 2 sig figs: 15.77x + 551 (3 digits from 6.53) = 575; 575 – 551 = 24 (no decimal places, 2 sig figs) leads to 1.5 g $MgCO_3$.]

11 Intermolecular Forces, Liquids, and Solids

Visualizing Concepts

11.2 **(a)(a)** Hydrogen bonding; H–F interactions qualify for this narrowly defined interaction.

(a)(b) London dispersion forces, the only intermolecular forces between nonpolar F_2 molecules.

(a)(c) Ion-dipole forces between Na^+ cation and the negative end of a polar covalent water molecule.

(a)(d) Dipole-dipole forces between oppositely charged portions of two polar covalent SO_2 molecules.

(b) Ion-dipole forces in (a)(c) and hydrogen bonding in (a)(a) are stronger than the other two.

11.3 The viscosity of glycerol will be greater than that of 1-propanol. Viscosity is the resistance of a substance to flow. The stronger the intermolecular forces in a liquid, the greater its viscosity. Hydrogen bonding is the predominant force for both molecules. Glycerol has three times as many O–H groups and many more H-bonding interactions than 1-propanol, so it experiences stronger intermolecular forces and greater viscosity. (Both molecules have the same carbon-chain length, so dispersion forces are similar.)

11.5 The stronger the intermolecular forces, the greater the average kinetic energy required to escape these forces, and the higher the boiling point. $CH_3CH_2CH_2OH$ has hydrogen bonding, by virtue of its –OH group, so it has the higher boiling point. Dispersion forces are similar because molar masses are the same for both molecules.

11.6 **(a)** 360 K, the normal boiling point; 260 K, normal freezing point. The left-most line is the freezing/melting curve, the right-most line is the condensation/boiling curve. The normal boiling and freezing points are the temperatures of boiling and freezing at 1 atm pressure.

(b) The material is solid in the green zone, liquid in the blue zone, and gas in the tan zone. (i) gas (ii) solid (iii) liquid

(c) The triple point, where all three phases are in equilibrium, is the point where the three lines on the phase diagram meet. For this substance, the triple point is approximately 185 K at 0.45 atm.

Molecular Comparisons of Gases, Liquids, and Solids

11.10   (a)   In solids, particles are in essentially fixed positions relative to each other, so the average energy of attraction is stronger than average kinetic energy. In liquids, particles are close together but moving relative to each other. The average attractive energy and average kinetic energy are approximately balanced. In gases, particles are far apart and in constant, random motion. Average kinetic energy is much greater than average energy of attraction.

        (b)   As the temperature of a substance is increased, the average kinetic energy of the particles increases. In a collection of particles (molecules), the state is determined by the strength of interparticle forces relative to the average kinetic energy of the particles. As the average kinetic energy increases, more particles are able to overcome intermolecular attractive forces and move to a less ordered state, from solid to liquid to gas.

        (c)   If a gas is placed under very high pressure, the particles undergo many collisions with the container and with each other. The large number of particle-particle collisions increases the likelihood that intermolecular attractions will cause the molecules to coalesce (liquefy).

11.12   (a)   The average distance between molecules is greater in the liquid state. Density is the ratio of the mass of a substance to the volume it occupies. For the same substance in different states, mass will be the same. The smaller the density, the greater the volume occupied, and the greater the distance between molecules. The liquid at 130° has the lower density (1.08 g/cm^3), so the average distance between molecules is greater.

        (b)   As the temperature of a substance increases, the average kinetic energy and speed of the molecules increases. At the melting point the molecules, on average, have enough kinetic energy to break away from the very orderly array that was present in the solid. As the translational motion of the molecules increases, the occupied volume increases and the density decreases. Thus, the solid density, 1.266 g/cm^3 at 15°C, is greater than the liquid density, 1.08 g/cm^3 at 130°C.

Intermolecular Forces

11.14   Intermolecular forces are based on charge attraction and repulsion. Because substances must be electrically neutral overall, there are opposite charges (full or partial) in every substance. While repulsions occur, net forces are attractive because attractions lower the overall energy of the sample, and matter tends to exist in the lowest possible energy state.

11.16   (a) CH_3OH experiences hydrogen bonding, but CH_3SH does not.

        (b)   Both gases are influenced by London dispersion forces. The heavier the gas particles, the stronger the London dispersion forces. The heavier Xe is a liquid at the specified conditions, while the lighter Ar is a gas.

        (c)   Both gases are influenced by London dispersion forces. The larger, diatomic Cl_2 molecules are more polarizable, experience stronger dispersion forces, and have the higher boiling point.

(d)   Acetone and 2-methylpropane are molecules with similar molar masses and London dispersion forces. Acetone also experiences dipole-dipole forces and has the higher boiling point.

11.18   (a)   True. A more polarizable molecule can develop a larger transient dipole, increasing the strength of electrostatic attractions and dispersion forces among molecules.

(b)   False. The noble gases are all monoatomic. Going down the column, the atomic radius and the size of the electron cloud increase. The larger the electron cloud, the more polarizable the atom, the stronger the London dispersion forces and the higher the boiling point.

(c)   False. The smaller the molecule, the more tightly its electron cloud is held. Tightly held electron clouds are not very polarizable and dispersion forces are weak.

(d)   True. It is usually true that as the number of electrons in a molecule increases, the size of the molecule increases. Larger molecules tend to have diffuse electron clouds, which are more polarizable. Thus, the statement that more electrons lead to increased dispersion forces (and greater polarizability) is correct.

11.20   For molecules with similar structures, the strength of dispersion forces increases with molecular size (molecular weight and number of electrons in the molecule).

(a) Br_2

(b) $CH_3CH_2CH_2CH_2CH_2SH$

(c) $CH_3CH_2CH_2Cl$. These two molecules have the same molecular formula and molecular weight (C_3H_7Cl, molecular weight = 78.5 amu), so the shapes of the molecules determine which has the stronger dispersion forces. According to Figure 11.6, the cylindrical (not branched) molecule will have stronger dispersion forces.

11.22   Both molecules experience hydrogen bonding through their –OH groups and dispersion forces between their hydrocarbon portions. The position of the –OH group in isopropyl alcohol shields it somewhat from approach by other molecules and slightly decreases the extent of hydrogen bonding. Also, isopropyl alcohol is less rod-like (it has a shorter chain) than propyl alcohol, so dispersion forces are weaker. Since hydrogen bonding and dispersion forces are weaker in isopropyl alcohol, it has the lower boiling point.

11.24   (a)   HF has the higher boiling point because hydrogen bonding is stronger than dipole-dipole forces.

(b) $CHBr_3$ has the higher boiling point because it has the higher molar mass, which leads to greater polarizability and stronger dispersion forces.

(c)   ICl has the higher boiling point because it is a polar molecule. For molecules with similar structures and molar masses, dipole-dipole forces are stronger than dispersion forces.

11.26   (a) C_6H_{14}, dispersion; C_8H_{18}, dispersion. C_8H_{18} has the higher boiling point due to greater molar mass and similar strength of forces.

(b) C_3H_8, dispersion; CH_3OCH_3, dipole-dipole, and dispersion. CH_3OCH_3 has the higher boiling point due to stronger intermolecular forces and similar molar mass.

(c) HOOH, hydrogen bonding, dipole-dipole, and dispersion; HSSH, dipole-dipole, and dispersion. HOOH has the higher boiling point due to the influence of hydrogen bonding (Figure 11.7).

(d) NH_2NH_2, hydrogen bonding, dipole-dipole, and dispersion; CH_3CH_3, dispersion. NH_2NH_2 has the higher boiling point due to much stronger intermolecular forces.

11.28 (a) In the solid state, NH_3 molecules are arranged so as to form the maximum number of hydrogen bonds. At the melting point, the average kinetic energy of the molecules is large enough so that they are free to move relative to each other. As they move, old hydrogen bonds break and new ones form, but the strict relative order required for maximum hydrogen bonding is no longer present.

(b) In the liquid state, molecules are moving relative to one another while touching, which makes some hydrogen bonding possible. When molecules achieve enough kinetic energy to vaporize, the distance between them increases beyond the point where hydrogen bonds can form.

Viscosity and Surface Tension

11.30 (a) *Cohesive* forces bind molecules to each other.

Adhesive forces bind molecules to surfaces.

(b) The cohesive forces are hydrogen bonding among water molecules and also hydrogen bonding among cellulose molecules in the paper towel. Adhesive forces are any attractive forces between water and cellulose (the paper towel), likely also hydrogen bonding. If adhesive forces between cellulose and water weren't significant, paper towels wouldn't absorb water.

(c) The shape of a meniscus depends on the strength of the cohesive forces within a liquid relative to the adhesive forces between the walls of the tube and the liquid. Adhesive forces between polar water molecules and silicates in glass (Figure 11.16) are even stronger than cohesive hydrogen-bonding forces among water molecules, so the meniscus is U-shaped (concave-upward).

11.32 (a) H—N̈—N̈—H   H—Ö—Ö—H   H—Ö—H
              | |
              H   H

(b) All have bonds (N–H or O–H, respectively) capable of forming hydrogen bonds. Hydrogen bonding is the strongest intermolecular interaction between neutral molecules and leads to very strong cohesive forces in liquids. The stronger the cohesive forces in a liquid, the greater the surface tension.

Phase Changes

11.34 (a) condensation, exothermic

(b) sublimation, endothermic

(c) vaporization (evaporation), endothermic

(d) freezing, exothermic

11.36 (a) Liquid ethyl chloride at room temperature is far above its boiling point. When the liquid contacts the metal surface, heat sufficient to vaporize the liquid is transferred from the metal to the ethyl chloride, and the heat content of the molecules increases. At constant atmospheric pressure, $\Delta H = q$, so the heat content and the enthalpy content of $C_2H_5Cl(g)$ is higher than that of $C_2H_5Cl(l)$. This indicates that the specific heat of the gas is less than that of the liquid, because the heat content of the gas is starts at a higher level.

(b) Liquid C_2H_5Cl is vaporized (boiled), C_2H_5Cl (g) is warmed to the final temperature, and the solid surface is cooled to the final temperature. The enthalpy of vaporization (ΔH_{vap}) of $C_2H_5Cl(l)$, the specific heat of $C_2H_5Cl(g)$, and the specific heat of the solid surface must be considered.

11.38 Energy released when 200 g of H_2O is cooled from 15°C to 0°C:

$$\frac{4.184 \, J}{g \text{-} K} \times 200 \, g \, H_2O \times 15°C = 12.55 \times 10^3 \, J = 13 \, kJ$$

Energy released when 200 g of H_2O is frozen (there is no change in temperature during a change of state):

$$\frac{334 \, J}{g} \times 200 \, g \, H_2O = 6.68 \times 10^4 \, J = 66.8 \, kJ$$

Total energy released = 12.55 kJ + 66.8 kJ = 79.35 = 79.4 kJ

Mass of freon that will absorb 40.9 kJ when vaporized:

$$79.35 \, kJ \times \frac{1 \times 10^3 \, J}{1 \, kJ} \times \frac{1 \, g \, CCl_2F_2}{289 \, J} = 275 \, g \, CCl_2F_2$$

11.40 Consider the process in steps, using the appropriate thermochemical constant.

Heat the liquid from 10.00°C to 47.6°C, $\Delta T = 37.6°C = 37.6$ K, using the specific heat of the liquid.

$$50.0 \, g \, C_2Cl_3F_3 \times \frac{0.91 \, J}{g \text{-} K} \times 37.6 \, K \times \frac{1 \, kJ}{1000 \, J} = 1.711 = 1.7 \ kJ$$

Boil the liquid at 47.6°C (320.6 K), using the enthalpy of vaporization.

$$50.0 \, g \, C_2Cl_3F_3 \times \frac{1 \, mol \, C_2Cl_3F_3}{187.4 \, g \, C_2Cl_3F_3} \times \frac{27.49 \, kJ}{mol} = 7.3346 = 7.33 \ kJ$$

Heat the gas from 47.6°C to 85.00°C, $\Delta T = 37.4°C = 37.4$ K, using the specific heat of the gas.

$$50.0 \text{ g } C_2Cl_3F_3 \times \frac{0.67 \text{ J}}{\text{g-K}} \times 37.4 \text{ K} \times \frac{1 \text{ kJ}}{1000 \text{ J}} = 1.253 = 1.3 \text{ kJ}$$

The total energy required is 1.711 kJ + 7.335 kJ + 1.253 kJ = 10.299 = 10.3 kJ.

11.42   (a) CCl_3F, CCl_2F_2 and $CClF_3$ are polar molecules that experience dipole-dipole and London dispersion forces with like molecules. CF_4 is a nonpolar compound that experiences only dispersion forces.

(b)   According to Solution 11.41(b), the higher the critical temperature, the stronger the intermolecular attractive forces of a substance. Therefore, the strength of intermolecular attraction increases moving from right to left across the series and as molecular weight increases. $CF_4 < CClF_3 < CCl_2F_2 < CCl_3F$.

(c)   The increasing intermolecular attraction with increasing molecular weight indicates that the critical temperature and pressure of CCl_4 will be greater than that of CCl_3F. Looking at the numerical values in the series, an increase of 88 K in critical temperature and 3.1 atm in critical pressure to the corresponding values for CCl_3F seem reasonable.

Physical Property	CCl_3F	CCl_4(predicted)	CCl_4 (CRC)
Critical Temperature (K)	47.1	557	556.6
Critical Pressure (atm)	43.5	46.6	44.6

The predicted values for CCl_4 are in very good agreement with literature values. The key concept is that dispersion, not dipole-dipole, forces dominate the physical properties in the series.

Vapor Pressure and Boiling Point

11.44   (a)   The pressure difference on the manometer is 130 mm Hg and the gas in the vessel is essentially 100% molecules of the substance in the vapor phase. When the vessel is evacuated, virtually all air is removed. As the frozen liquid warms, it establishes a vapor pressure of 130 mm Hg. This is the pressure difference on the manometer.

(b)   The pressure difference is 1 atm. The gas is 130 mm Hg of the molecular vapor and the rest is air. The liquid vaporizes in contact with the atmosphere, so atmospheric pressure is maintained above the liquid, but the equilibrium gas composition reflects the amount of vapor necessary to maintain 130 mm pressure, plus enough air to maintain a total pressure of 1 atm.

(c)   The pressure difference is 890 mm Hg (1 atm + 130 mm Hg) and the gas is a mixture of 130 mm vapor and 1 atm air. The initial air pressure in the flask is 1 atm and no air is allowed to escape. The gas in the flask is not in equilibrium with the atmosphere and the final pressure in the flask does not equal atmospheric pressure. After a most of the liquid vaporizes, the total gas pressure is the result of 130 mm vapor and 1 atm air.

11.46   (a)   False. The heavier (and larger) CBr_4 has stronger dispersion forces, a higher boiling point, lower vapor pressure and is less volatile.

   (b)   True.

   (c)   False.

   (d)   False

11.48   (a)   On a humid day, there are more gaseous water molecules in the air and more are recaptured by the surface of the liquid, making evaporation slower.

   (b)   At high altitude, atmospheric pressure is lower and water boils at a lower temperature. Because the boiling water is cooler, it takes longer to brew tea at high altitude. (Water may actually boil faster at high altitude, because the boiling temperature is lower.)

11.50   (a)

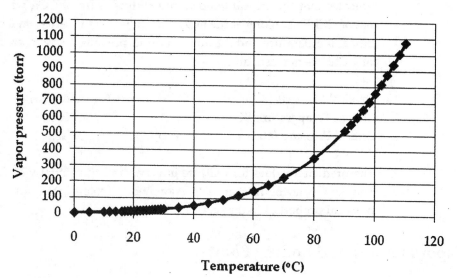

   A plot of vapor pressure vs. temperature data for H_2O from Appendix B is shown above. The vapor pressure of water at body temperature, 37°C, is approximately 50 torr.

   (b)   The data point at 760.0 torr, 100°C is the normal boiling point of H_2O. This is the temperature at which the vapor pressure of H_2O is equal to a pressure of 1 atm or 760 torr.

   (c)   At an external (atmospheric) pressure of 633 torr, the boiling point of H_2O is approximately 96°C.

   (d)   At an external pressure of 774 torr, the boiling point of water is approximately 100.5°C.

   (e)   Follow the logic in Sample Exercise 10.14 to calculate rms speeds at the two temperatures. The rms speed is one way to represent the "average" speed of a large collection of particles.

   $u = (3RT/MM)^{1/2}$. $MM = 18.0 \text{ g/mol} = 18.0 \times 10^{-3} \text{ kg/mol}$

   $R = 8.314 \text{ kg-m}^2/\text{s}^2\text{-mol-K}$. At $T = 96°C = 369$ K,

$$u = \left(\frac{3(8.314 \ kg - m^2 / s^2 - mol - K) \ 369 \ K}{18.0 \times 10^{-3} \ kg / mol} \right)^{1/2} = 715 \ m/s$$

At T = 100.5 °C = 373.6 K,

$$u = \left(\frac{3(8.314 \ kg - m^2 / s^2 - mol - K) \ 373.6 \ K}{18.0 \times 10^{-3} \ kg / mol} \right)^{1/2} = 719.50 = 720 \ m/s$$

The difference in the two rms speeds is less than 1% of the average of the two values. Given the precision of estimating boiling temperatures from the plot, the two rms speeds are essentially equal.

Phase Diagrams

11.52   (a)   The *triple point* on a phase diagram represents the temperature and pressure at which the gas, liquid, and solid phases are in equilibrium.

      (b)   No. A phase diagram represents a closed system, one where no matter can escape and no substance other than the one under consideration is present; air cannot be present in the system. Even if air is excluded, at 1 atm of external pressure, the triple point of water is inaccessible, regardless of temperature [see Sample Exercise 11.6(b)].

11.54   (a)   Solid CO_2 sublimes to form $CO_2(g)$ at a temperature of about –60°C.

      (b)   Solid CO_2 melts to form $CO_2(l)$ at a temperature of about –50°C. The $CO_2(l)$ boils when the temperature reaches approximately –40°C.

11.56   (a)

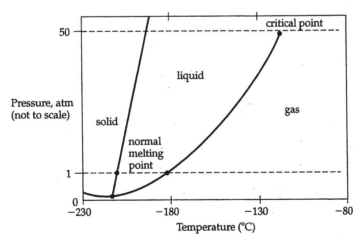

On the diagram above, the triple point is at the dot closest to the x-axis. The normal melting point is at the intersection of the solid-liquid line and the 1-atm dashed line. The normal boiling point is at the intersection of the liquid-gas line and the 1-atm line. The critical point is clearly marked.

      (b) $O_2(s)$ will not float on $O_2(l)$. $O_2(s)$ is denser than $O_2(l)$ because the solid-liquid line on the phase diagram is normal. That is, as pressure increases, the melting temperature increases. [Note that the solid-liquid line for O_2 is nearly vertical, indicating a small difference in the densities of $O_2(s)$ and $O_2(l)$].

(c) $O_2(s)$ will melt when heated at a pressure of 1 atm, since this is a much greater pressure than the pressure at the triple point.

Structures of Solids

11.58 In amorphous silica (SiO_2) the regular structure of quartz is disrupted; the loose, disordered structure, Figure 11.30(b), has many vacant "pockets" throughout. There are fewer SiO_2 groups per volume in the amorphous solid; the packing is less efficient and less dense.

11.60 (a) Ti: 8 corners × 1/8 sphere/corner + [1 center × 1 sphere/center] = 2 Ti atoms

O: 4 faces × 1/2 sphere/face + [2 interior × 1 sphere/interior] = 4 O atoms

Formula: TiO_2

(b) Rutile is an ionic solid; ion-ion forces among Ti^{4+} cations and O^{2-} anions are quite strong, owing to the magnitudes of the charges, and lead to the ordered structure.

(c) From inspection of the unit cell diagram, the Ti at the center of the cell is bound to six (6) O atoms. Each totally interior O atom is bound to three titanium atoms. The coordination number of Ti is 6; the coordination number of O is 3.

11.62 (a) 8 corners × 1/8 atom/corner + 6 faces × ½ atom/face = 4 atoms

(b) Each aluminum atom is in contact with 12 nearest neighbors, 6 in one plane, 3 above that plane, and 3 below. Its coordination number is thus 12.

(c) The length of the face diagonal of a face-centered cubic unit cell is four times the radius of the metal and $\sqrt{2}$ times the unit cell dimension (usually designated a for cubic cells).

$$4 \times 1.43\,\text{Å} = \sqrt{2} \times a;\ a = \frac{4 \times 1.43\,\text{Å}}{\sqrt{2}} = 4.0447 = 4.04\,\text{Å} = 4.04 \times 10^{-8}\,\text{cm}$$

(d) The density of the metal is the mass of the unit cell contents divided by the volume of the unit cell.

$$\text{density} = \frac{4\,\text{Al atoms}}{(4.0447 \times 10^{-8}\,\text{cm})^3} \times \frac{26.98\,\text{g Al}}{6.022 \times 10^{23}\,\text{Al atoms}} = 2.71\,\text{g/cm}^3$$

11.64 Avogadro's number is the number of KCl formula units in 74.55 g of KCl.

$$74.55\,\text{g KCl} \times \frac{1\,\text{cm}^3}{1.984\,\text{g}} \times \frac{(1 \times 10^{10}\,\text{pm})^3}{1\,\text{cm}^3} \times \frac{4\,\text{KCl units}}{628^3\,\text{pm}^3} = 6.07 \times 10^{23}\,\text{KCl formula units}$$

11.66 (a) Na^+, 6   (b) Zn^{2+}, 4   (c) Ca^{2+}, 8

11.68 (a) According to Figure 11.42(b), there are 4 HgS units in a unit cell with the zinc blende structure. [4 complete Hg^{2+} ions, 6(1/2) + 8(1/8) S^{2-} ions]

$$\text{density} = \frac{4\,\text{HgS units}}{(5.852\,\text{Å})^3} \times \frac{232.655\,\text{g}}{6.022 \times 10^{23}\,\text{HgS units}} \times \left(\frac{1\,\text{Å}}{1 \times 10^{-8}\,\text{cm}}\right)^3 = 7.711\,\text{g/cm}^3$$

(b)   We expect Se^{2-} to have a larger ionic radius than S^{2-}, since Se is below S in the chalcogen family and both ions have the same charge. Thus, HgSe will occupy a larger volume and the unit cell edge will be longer.

(c)   For HgSe:

$$density = \frac{4\,HgSe\,units}{(6.085\,Å)^3} \times \frac{279.55\,g\,HgSe}{6.022 \times 10^{23}\,HgSe\,units} \times \left(\frac{1\,Å}{1 \times 10^{-8}\,cm}\right)^3 = 8.241\,g/cm^3$$

Even though HgSe has a larger unit cell volume than HgS, it also has a larger molar mass. The mass of Se is more than twice that of S, while the radius of Se^{2-} is only slightly larger than that of S^{2-} (Figure 7.8). The greater mass of Se accounts for the greater density of HgSe.

Bonding in Solids

11.70   (a)   According to Figure 11.41(a), diamond is a covalent-network solid. Carbon atoms are bound into a three-dimensional network by strong covalent (single) bonds. Silicon, with the same structure, is also a covalent-network solid.

(b)   Si is a metalloid and O is a nonmetal; we expect their bonding to be covalent. Silica, $SiO_2(s)$, will be either molecular or covalent network. By analogy with Si(s), each Si atom will be tetrahedral and participate in four covalent bonds. If the stoichiometry of the solid is SiO_2, a network structure is required for Si to form four single covalent bonds with O. Discreet linear SiO_2 molecules analogous to CO_2 are unlikely, because the covalent radius of Si is too large for effective π-overlap. To confirm this hypothesis, the *Handbook of Chemistry and Physics* lists the melting points of the various forms of $SiO_2(s)$ to be greater than 1600°C. Very high melting points are characteristic of covalent-network solids.

11.72   (a)   ionic   (b)   metallic

(c)   covalent-network   (Based on melting point, it is definitely a network solid. Transition metals in high oxidation states often form bonds with nonmetals that have significant covalent character. It could also be characterized as ionic with same covalent character to the bonds.)

(d)   molecular   (e)   molecular   (f)   molecular

11.74   (a)   metallic

(b)   molecular or metallic (physical properties of metals vary widely)

(c)   covalent-network or ionic   (d)   covalent-network   (e)   ionic

11.76   According to Table 11.7, the solid could be either ionic with low water solubility or network covalent. Due to the extremely high sublimation temperature, it is probably covalent-network.

11.78   (a)   HF, hydrogen bonding versus dipole-dipole for HCl

(b)   C(graphite), covalent-network bonding versus London dispersion forces for CH_4

(c)   KCl, ionic versus dispersion forces for nonpolar Cl_2

(d) MgF_2, higher charge on Mg^{2+} than Li^+

Additional Exercises

11.80   (a)   Correct.

       (b)   The lower boiling liquid must experience less total intermolecular forces.

       (c)   If both liquids are structurally similar nonpolar molecules, the lower boiling liquid has a lower molecular weight than the higher boiling liquid.

       (d)   Correct.

       (e)   At their boiling points, both liquids have vapor pressures of 760 mm Hg.

11.81   (a)   The cis isomer has stronger dipole-dipole forces; the trans isomer is nonpolar. The higher boiling point of the cis isomer supports this conclusion.

       (b)   While boiling points are primarily a measure of strength of intermolecular forces, melting points are influenced by crystal packing efficiency as well as intermolecular forces. Since the nonpolar trans isomer with weaker inter-molecular forces has the higher melting point, it must pack more efficiently.

11.82   (a)   In dibromomethane, CH_2Br_2, the dispersion force contribution will be larger than for CH_2Cl_2, because bromine is more polarizable than the lighter element chlorine. At the same time, the dipole-dipole contribution for CH_2Cl_2 is greater than for CH_2Br_2 because CH_2Cl_2 has a larger dipole moment.

       (b)   Just the opposite comparisons apply to CH_2F_2, which is less polarizable and has a higher dipole moment than CH_2Cl_2.

11.84   The GC base pair, with more hydrogen bonds, is more stable to heating. In order to break up a base pair by heating, sufficient thermal energy must be added to break the existing hydrogen bonds. With 50% more hydrogen bonds, the GC pair is definitely more stable (harder to break apart) than the AT pair.

11.85   The two O–H groups in ethylene glycol are involved in many hydrogen bonding interactions, leading to its high boiling point and viscosity, relative to pentane, which experiences only dispersion forces.

11.86   The more carbon atoms in the hydrocarbon, the longer the chain, the more polarizable the electron cloud, the higher the boiling point. A plot of the number of carbon atoms versus boiling point is shown below. For 8 C atoms, C_8H_{18}, the boiling point is approximately 130°C.

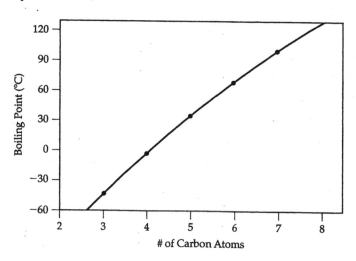

11.87   For a substance above its critical temperature, as pressure increases beyond critical pressure, the solubility of a solute increases. The solubility of the solute is essentially zero below critical pressure. Supercritical CO_2 at very high pressure dissolves caffeine, and the solution leaves the extractor. The pressure reduction value reduces the pressure of CO_2 enough so that the caffeine becomes insoluble. The solid caffeine is deposited in the separator, and the low pressure CO_2 gas is recycled.

11.89   (a)   If the Clausius-Clapeyron equation is obeyed, a graph of ln P vs 1/T(K) should be linear. Here are the data in a form form for graphing.

T(K)	1/T	P(torr)	ln P
280.0	3.571×10^{-3}	32.42	3.479
300.0	3.333×10^{-3}	92.47	4.527
320.0	3.125×10^{-3}	225.1	5.417
330.0	3.030×10^{-3}	334.4	5.812
340.0	2.941×10^{-3}	482.9	6.180

According to the graph, the Clausius-Clapeyron equation is obeyed, to a first approximation.

$$\Delta H_{vap} = -slope \times R; \quad slope = \frac{3.479 - 6.180}{(3.571 - 2.941) \times 10^{-3}} = -\frac{2.701}{0.630 \times 10^{-3}} = -4.29 \times 10^3$$

$$\Delta H_{vap} = -(-4.29 \times 10^3) \times 8.314 \text{ J/K-mol} = 35.7 \text{ kJ/mol}$$

(b)   The normal boiling point is the temperature at which the vapor pressure of the liquid equals atmospheric pressure, 760 torr. From the graph,

ln 760 = 6.63, 1/T for this vapor pressure = 2.828×10^{-3}; T = 353.6 K

11.90   (a)   The Clausius-Clapeyron equation is $\ln P = \frac{-\Delta H_{vap}}{RT} + C.$

For two vapor pressures, P_1 and P_2, measured at corresponding temperatures T_1 and T_2, the relationship is

$$\ln P_1 - \ln P_2 = \left(\frac{-\Delta H_{vap}}{RT_1} + C \right) - \left(\frac{-\Delta H_{vap}}{RT_2} + C \right)$$

$$\ln P_1 - \ln P_2 = \frac{-\Delta H_{vap}}{R} \left(\frac{1}{T_1} - \frac{1}{T_2} \right) + C - C; \quad \ln \frac{P_1}{P_2} = \frac{-\Delta H_{vap}}{R} \left(\frac{1}{T_1} - \frac{1}{T_2} \right)$$

(b) $P_1 = 13.95$ torr, $T_1 = 298$ K; $P_2 = 144.78$ torr, $T_2 = 348$ K

$$\ln \frac{13.95}{144.78} = \frac{-\Delta H_{vap}}{8.314 \text{ J/K-mol}} \left(\frac{1}{298} - \frac{1}{348} \right)$$

$$-2.33974 (8.314 \text{ J/K-mol}) = -\Delta H_{vap} (4.821 \times 10^{-4} /K)$$

$\Delta H_{vap} = 4.035 \times 10^4 = 4.0 \times 10^4$ J/mol = 40 kJ/mol

$[(1/T_1) - (1/T_2)]$ has 2 sig figs and so does the result.

(c)   The normal boiling point of a liquid is the temperature at which the vapor pressure of the liquid is 760 torr.

$P_1 = 144.78$ torr, $T_1 = 348$ K; $P_2 = 760$ torr, $T_2 = $ b.p. of octane

$$\ln\left(\frac{144.78}{760.0}\right) = \frac{-4.035 \times 10^4 \text{ J/mol}}{8.314 \text{ J/K-mol}}\left(\frac{1}{348 \text{ K}} - \frac{1}{T_2}\right)$$

$$\frac{-1.6581}{-4.8533 \times 10^3} = 2.874 \times 10^{-3} - \frac{1}{T_2}; \quad \frac{1}{T_2} = 2.874 \times 10^{-3} - 3.416 \times 10^{-4}$$

$$\frac{1}{T_2} = 2.532 \times 10^{-3} = 2.53 \times 10^{-3}; \quad T_2 = 394 \text{ K} (122°\text{C})$$

This is in good agreement with the literature boiling point of octane, 126°C.

(d) $P_1 = $ vp of octane at 30°C, $T_1 = 303$ K; $P_2 = 144.78$ torr, $T_2 = 348$ K

$$\ln\frac{P_1}{144.78 \text{ torr}} = \frac{-4.035 \times 10^4 \text{ J/mol}}{8.314 \text{ J/K-mol}}\left(\frac{1}{303} - \frac{1}{348}\right)$$

$$\ln\frac{P_1}{144.78 \text{ torr}} = \frac{-4.035 \times 10^4 \text{ J/mol}}{8.314 \text{ J/K-mol}} \times 4.268 \times 10^{-4} = -2.0710 = -2.1$$

$$\frac{P_1}{144.78 \text{ torr}} = e^{-2.0710}; \quad P_1 = 0.12606 \ (144.78) = 18.25 = 2 \times 10^1 \text{ torr}$$

[Strictly speaking, this result has 1 sig fig because (ln = –2.1) has 1 decimal place. In a ln or log, the places left of the decimal show order of magnitude, and places right of the decimal show sig figs in the real number.] The result, ~18 torr at 30°C, is reasonable, given that the vapor pressure of octane at 25°C is 13.95 torr. We expect vapor pressure to increase with temperature.

11.91   Physical data for the two compounds from the *Handbook of Chemistry and Physics*:

	MM	dipole moment	boiling point
CH_2Cl_2	85 g/mol	1.60 D	40.0°C
CH_3I	142 g/mol	1.62 D	42.4°C

(a)   The two substances have very similar molecular structures; each is an unsymmetrical tetrahedron with a single central carbon atom and no hydrogen bonding. Since the structures are very similar, the magnitudes of the dipole-dipole forces should be similar. This is verified by their very similar dipole moments. The heavier compound, CH_3I, will have slightly stronger London dispersion forces. Since the nature and magnitude of the intermolecular forces in the two compounds are nearly the same, it is very difficult to predict which will be more volatile [or which will have the higher boiling point as in part (b)].

(b)   Given the structural similarities discussed in part (a), one would expect the boiling points to be very similar, and they are. Based on its larger molar mass (and dipole-dipole forces being essentially equal) one might predict that CH_3I would have a slightly higher boiling point; this is verified by the known boiling points.

(c)   According to Equation 11.1, $\ln P = \dfrac{-\Delta H_{vap}}{RT} + C$

A plot of $\ln P$ vs. $1/T$ for each compound is linear. Since the order of volatility changes with temperature for the two compounds, the two lines must cross at some temperature; the slopes of the two lines, ΔH_{vap} for the two compounds, and the y-intercepts, C, must be different.

(d) CH_2Cl_2

ln P	T(K)	1/T
2.303	229.9	4.351×10^{-3}
3.689	250.9	3.986×10^{-3}
4.605	266.9	3.747×10^{-3}
5.991	297.3	3.364×10^{-3}

CH_3I

ln P	T(K)	1/T
2.303	227.4	4.398×10^{-3}
3.689	249.0	4.016×10^{-3}
4.605	266.2	3.757×10^{-3}
5.991	298.5	3.350×10^{-3}

For CH_2Cl_2, $-\Delta H_{vap}/R = \text{slope} = \dfrac{(5.991 - 2.303)}{(3.364 \times 10^{-3} - 4.350 \times 10^{-3})} = \dfrac{-3.688}{0.987 \times 10^{-3}}$

$$= -3.74 \times 10^3 = -\Delta H_{vap}/R$$

$\Delta H_{vap} = 8.314 \, (3.74 \times 10^3) = 3.107 \times 10^4 \text{ J/mol} = 31.1 \text{ kJ/mol}$

For CH_3I, $-\Delta H_{vap}/R = \text{slope} = \dfrac{(5.991 - 2.303)}{(3.350 \times 10^{-3} - 4.398 \times 10^{-3})} = \dfrac{-3.688}{1.048 \times 10^{-3}} = -3.519 \times 10^3$

$$= -\Delta H_{vap}/R$$

$\Delta H_{vap} = 8.314 \, (3.519 \times 10^3) = 2.926 \times 10^4 \text{ J/mol} = 29.3 \text{ kJ/mol}$

11.93   In the antifluorite structure, the Li^+ cations occupy the 8 interior positions in the unit cell shown in Figure 11.42(c), while the O^{2-} anions occupy the corners and face-centers.

(a) Li^+, coordination number = 4; O^{2-}, coordination number = 8. Each Li^+ is nearest three O^{2-} anions in face-centers, and one O^{2-} on a corner. Each O^{2-} anion is nearest four Li^+ ions above and four $Li+$ ions below it.

(b)   By analogy to the alkali metal chlorides (NaCl to CsCl), we expect the coordination number of the cation to increase as its ionic radius increases.

(c)   In the A_2O series, the anion remains constant while the cation changes. In order to maintain the 2:1 ratio of cations to anions, all 8 tetrahedral holes (interior of the unit cell) must be occupied by cations. As the cation size increases, the cation becomes too large to sit in the same lattice of O^{2-} anions. As the larger cations expand (push apart) the O^{2-} lattice, the antifluorite structure becomes unstable.

11.94   (a)   The face diagonal of a face-centered cubic unit cell has length $a\sqrt{2}$ and also 4 r, where a is the cubic cell dimension and r is the atomic radius.

$$4\,r = a\sqrt{2}; r = (a\sqrt{2})/4 = (4.078\,\text{Å})(\sqrt{2})/4 = 1.44179 = 1.442\,\text{Å}$$

(b)   Density is the mass of the unit cell contents divided by the unit cell volume (a^3). In a face-centered cubic unit cell, there are 4 Au atoms.

$$\text{density} = \frac{4\,\text{Au atoms}}{(4.078\,\text{Å})^3} \times \frac{196.97\,\text{g}}{6.0221 \times 10^{23}\,\text{Au atoms}} \times \left(\frac{1\,\text{Å}}{1 \times 10^{-8}\,\text{cm}}\right)^3 = 19.29\,\text{g/cm}^3$$

11.96   (a) $n\lambda = 2d\sin\theta$; $n = 1$, $\lambda = 1.54\,\text{Å}$, $\theta = 14.22\,°$; calculate d.

$$d = \frac{n\lambda}{2\sin\theta} = \frac{1 \times 1.54\,\text{Å}}{2\sin(14.22)} = 3.1346 = 3.13\,\text{Å}$$

(b)   Assume the diffracted intensity at 14.22°C is the result of second-order diffraction, $n = 2$.

$$d = \frac{n\lambda}{2\sin\theta} = \frac{2 \times 1.54\,\text{Å}}{2\sin(14.22)} = 6.269 = 6.27\,\text{Å}$$

Note that this is exactly twice the d-spacing calculated assuming $n = 1$.

11.97   (a)   Both diamond (d = 3.5 g/cm³) and graphite (d = 2.3 g/cm³) are covalent-network solids with efficient packing arrangements in the solid state; there is relatively little empty space in their respective crystal lattices. Diamond, with bonded C–C distances of 1.54 Å in all directions, is more dense than graphite, with shorter C–C distances within carbon sheets but longer 3.41 Å separations between sheets (Figure 11.41). Buckminsterfullerene has much more empty space, both inside each C_{60} "ball" and between balls, than either diamond or graphite, so its density will be considerably less than 2.3 g/cm³.

(b)   In a face-centered cubic unit cell, there are 4 complete C_{60} units.

$$\frac{4\,C_{60}\,\text{units}}{(14.2\,\text{Å})^3} \times \frac{720.66\,\text{g}}{6.022 \times 10^{23}\,C_{60}\,\text{units}} \times \left(\frac{1\,\text{Å}}{1 \times 10^{-8}\,\text{cm}}\right)^3 = 1.67\,\text{g/cm}^3$$

(1.67 g/cm³ is the smallest density of the three allotropes, diamond, graphite, and buckminsterfullerene.)

Integrative Exercises

11.99   (a)   In Table 11.4, viscosity increases as the length of the carbon chain increases. Longer molecular chains become increasingly entangled, increasing resistance to flow.

(b) Whereas viscosity depends on molecular chain length in a critical way, surface tension depends on the strengths of intermolecular interactions between molecules. These dispersion forces do not increase as rapidly with increasing chain length and molecular weight as viscosity does.

(c) The –OH group in n-octyl alcohol gives rise to hydrogen bonding among molecules, which increases molecular entanglement and leads to greater viscosity and higher boiling point.

11.100 (a) 24 valence e^-, 12 e^- pairs

$$
\begin{array}{ccc}
H & :O: & H \\
| & \| & | \\
H-C- & C- & C-H \\
| & & | \\
H & & H
\end{array}
$$

The geometry around the central C atom is trigonal planar, and around the two terminal C atoms, tetrahedral.

(b) Polar. The C=O bond is quite polar and the dipoles in the trigonal plane around the central C atom do not cancel.

(c) Dipole-dipole and London-dispersion forces

(d) Since the molecular weights of acetone and 1-propanol are similar, the strength of the London-dispersion forces in the two compounds is also similar. The big difference is that 1-propanol has hydrogen bonding, while acetone does not. These relatively strong attractive forces lead to the higher boiling point for 1-propanol.

11.102 (a) In order for butane to be stored as a liquid at temperatures above its boiling point (–5°C), the pressure in the tank must be greater than atmospheric pressure. In terms of the phase diagram of butane, the pressure must be high enough so that, at tank conditions, the butane is "above" the gas-liquid line and in the liquid region of the diagram.

The pressure of a gas is described by the ideal gas law as P = nRT/V; pressure is directly proportional to moles of gas. The more moles of gas present in the tank the greater the pressure, until sufficient pressure is achieved for the gas to liquify. At the point where liquid and gas are in equilibrium and temperature is constant, liquid will vaporize or condense to maintain the equilibrium vapor pressure. That is, as long as some liquid is present, the gas pressure in the tank will be constant.

(b) If butane gas escapes the tank, butane liquid will vaporize (evaporate) to maintain the equilibrium vapor pressure. Vaporization is an endothermic process, so the butane will absorb heat from the surroundings. The temperature of the tank and the liquid butane will decrease.

(c) $250 \text{ g C}_4\text{H}_{10} \times \dfrac{1 \text{ mol C}_4\text{H}_{10}}{58.12 \text{ g C}_4\text{H}_{10}} \times \dfrac{21.3 \text{ kJ}}{\text{mol}} = 91.6 \text{ kJ}$

$$V = \frac{nRT}{P} = 250\,g \times \frac{1\,mol}{58.12\,g} \times \frac{0.08206\,L\text{-}atm}{mol\text{-}K} \times \frac{308\,K}{755\,torr} \times \frac{760\,torr}{1\,atm} = 109.44 = 109\,L$$

11.103 *Plan.*

(i)   Using thermochemical data from Appendix B, calculate the energy (enthalpy) required to melt and heat the H_2O.

(ii) Using Hess's Law, calculate the enthalpy of combustion, ΔH_{comb}, for C_3H_8.

(iii) Solve the stoichiometry problem.

Solve.

(i)   Heat $H_2O(s)$ from $-20°C$ to $0.0°C$; $5.50 \times 10^3\,g\,H_2O \times \dfrac{2.092\,J}{g\text{-}°C} \times 20°C = 2.301 \times 10^2$

$$= 2.3 \times 10^2\,kJ$$

Melt $H_2O(s)$; $5.50 \times 10^3\,g\,H_2O \times \dfrac{6.008\,kJ}{mol\,H_2O} \times \dfrac{1\,mol\,H_2O}{18.02\,g\,H_2O} = 1834 = 1.83 \times 10^3\,kJ$

Heat $H_2O(l)$ from $0°C$ to $75°C$; $5.50 \times 10^3\,g\,H_2O \times \dfrac{4.184\,J}{g\text{-}°C} \times 75°C = 1726 = 1.7 \times 10^3$

Total energy = 230.1 kJ + 1834 kJ + 1726 kJ = 3790 = 3.8×10^3 kJ

(The result is significant to 100 kJ, limited by 1.7×10^3 kJ)

(ii) $C_3H_8(g) + 5O_2(g) \rightarrow 3CO_2(g) + 4H_2O(l)$

Assume that one product is $H_2O(l)$, since this leads to a more negative ΔH_{comb} and fewer grams of $C_3H_8(g)$ required.

$\Delta H_{comb} = 3\Delta H_f° \, CO_2(g) + 4\Delta H_f° \, H_2O(l) - \Delta H_f° \, C_3H_8(g) - 5\Delta H_f° \, O_2(g)$

$= 3(-393.5\,kJ) + 4\,(-285.83\,kJ) - (-103.85\,kJ) - 5(0) = -2219.97 = -2220\,kJ$

(iii) $3.790 \times 10^3\,kJ\,required \times \dfrac{1\,mol\,C_3H_8}{2219.97\,kJ} \times \dfrac{44.096\,g\,C_3H_8}{1\,mol\,C_3H_8} = 75\,g\,C_3H_8$

(3.8×10^3 kJ required has 2 sig figs and so does the result)

11.104 (a) Low viscosity, low surface tension, and, especially, high thermal conductivity owing to metallic properties.

(b) Metallic bonding between sodium atoms, which persists in the liquid state, is probably the main inhibitor of movement of atoms relative to one another. As temperature increases, thermal motion of the atoms increases and the liquid expands, weakening bonding interactions relative to thermal energies.

11.106 *Plan.* Relative humidity and v.p. of H_2O at given $T \rightarrow P_{H_2O} \rightarrow$ ideal-gas law $\rightarrow$ mol $H_2O(g) \rightarrow H_2O$ molecules. Change $°F \rightarrow °C$, volume of room from $ft^3 \rightarrow L$.

Solve. $°C = 5/9\,(°F - 32)$; $°C = 5/9\,(68\,°F - 32) = 20°C$;

r.h. $= (P_{H_2O}\,in\,air\,/\,v.p.\,of\,H_2O) \times 100$

From Appendix B, v.p. of H_2O at 20°C = 17.54 torr

P_{H_2O} in air = r.h. × v.p. of H_2O/100 = 58 × 17.54 torr/100 = 10.173 = 10 torr

$$V = 12\,\text{ft} \times 10\,\text{ft} \times 8\,\text{ft} \times \frac{12^3\,\text{in}^3}{\text{ft}^3} \times \frac{2.54^3\,\text{cm}^3}{\text{in}^3} \times \frac{1\,\text{L}}{1000\,\text{cm}^3} = 2.718 \times 10^4 = 3 \times 10^4\,\text{L}$$

(The result has 1 sig fig, as does the measurement 8 ft.)

PV = nRT; n = PV/RT

$$n = 10.17\,\text{torr} \times \frac{1\,\text{atm}}{760\,\text{torr}} \times \frac{\text{mol-K}}{0.08206\,\text{L-atm}} \times \frac{2.718 \times 10^4\,\text{L}}{293\,\text{K}} = 15.13 = 2 \times 10^1\,\text{mol}\ H_2O$$

$$15.13\,\text{mol}\ H_2O \times \frac{6.022 \times 10^{23}\,\text{molecules}}{1\,\text{mol}} = 9.110 \times 10^{24} = 9 \times 10^{24}\ H_2O\ \text{molecules}$$

11.107   Data are taken from the 74th edition of the *Handbook of Chemistry and Physics.* T_m = melting point, T_b = boiling point

(a)   W: T_m = 3410°C, T_b = 5660 °C; WF_6: T_m = 2.5°C, T_b = 17.5°C

W is a metal, with strong metallic bonding, and very high T_m and T_b. WF_6 is an octahedral, nonpolar molecule. Even though it has high molar mass, the spherical shape of the molecule prevents extensive molecular contacts. The resulting London dispersion forces are very weak, which leads to the low T_m and T_b.

(b) SO_2: T_m = –72.7°C, T_b = –10°C; SF_4: T_m = –124°C, T_b = –40°C (sublimes)

Both SO_2 and SF_4 are polar covalent molecules with a nonbonding electron pair on the central S atom. The electron-domain geometry in SO_2 is trigonal planar and the molecule shape is bent. The electron-domain geometry in SF_4 is trigonal bipyramidal and the molecular shape is see-saw. Both are gases at ambient temperature and pressure. SF_4 has higher molar mass but lower melting and boiling points than SO_2. This indicates that dipole-dipole forces are more influential on the properties of these molecules and that SF_4 has a smaller dipole moment than SO_2.

(c) SiO_2: T_m = 1723°C, T_b = 2230°C, MM = 60 g/mol

$SiCl_4$: T_m = –70°C, T_b = 57.57°C, MM = 170 g/mol

SiO_2 is a covalent-network substance, with high T_m and T_b. Covalent bonds hold SiO_2 units in a rigid lattice, and high energy is required to break these bonds and melt or boil the substance. $SiCl_4$ is a tetrahedral, nonpolar molecule. Weak dispersion forces between the approximately spherical molecules result in predictably low T_m and T_b.

13 Properties of Solutions

Visualizing Concepts

13.2   Lattice energy is the main component of ΔH_1, the enthalpy required to separate solute particles. If ΔH_1 is too large, the dissolving process is prohibitively endothermic, and the substance is not very soluble.

13.3   (a) < (b) < (c). In Section 13.1, *entropy* is qualitatively defined as randomness or dispersal in space. Container (a) contains only one kind of particle and particles are close together, so (a) has the least entropy. In container (b), the particles occupy approximately the same volume as container (a). However, (b) contains two kinds of particles, homogeneously mixed, so the degree of dispersal and randomness is greater than in (a). Container (c) contains two kinds of homogeneously mixed particles and they occupy a larger volume than in (b), so (c) has the greatest entropy.

13.4   The pink solid is hydrated $CoCl_2$, $CoCl_2 \cdot xH_2O$, where x is a specific integer. The waters of hydration are either associated with Co^{2+}, Cl^-, or sit in specific sites in the crystal lattice. When heated in an oven, the water molecules incorporated into the crystal lattice gradually gain kinetic energy and vaporize. The blue solid is anhydrous $CoCl_2$, absent the waters of hydration and with a different solid-state structure than the pink hydrate.

13.6   Solubility increases in the order Ar, 1.50×10^{-3} M < Kr, 2.79×10^{-3} M < Xe, 5×10^{-5} M, the order of increasing polarizability. As the molar mass of the ideal gas increases, atomic size increases and the electron cloud is less tightly held by the nucleus, causing the cloud to be more polarizable. The greater the polarizability, the stronger the dispersion forces between the gas atoms and water, the more likely the gas atom is to stay dissolved rather than escape the solution, the greater the solubility of the gas.

13.7   Vitamin B_6 is likely to be largely water soluble. The three –OH groups and the —N̈— can enter into many hydrogen bonding interactions with water. The relatively small molecular size indicates that dispersion forces will not play a large role in intermolecular interactions and the hydrogen bonding will dominate. Vitamin E is likely to be largely fat soluble. The long, rod-like hydrocarbon chain will lead to strong dispersion forces among vitamin E and mostly nonpolar fats. Although vitamin E has one –OH and one —Ö— group, the long hydrocarbon chain prevents water from surrounding and separating the vitamin E molecules, reducing its water-solubility.

13.8   According to Figure 13.18, the solubility of CO at 25°C and 1 atm pressure is approximately 0.96 mM. By Henry's Law, $S_g = k\, P_g$. At the same temperature and pressure, k will be the same, so $S_1/P_1 = S_2/P_2$.

$$\frac{0.96\,\text{m}M}{1\,\text{atm}} = \frac{2.5\,\text{m}M}{x\,\text{atm}}; x = \frac{2.5\,\text{m}M \times 1\,\text{atm}}{0.96\,\text{atm}} = 2.6\,\text{atm}$$

13.10   (a)   The blue line represents the solution. According to Raoult's law, the presence of a nonvolatile solute lowers the vapor pressure of a volatile solvent. At any given temperature, the blue line has a lower vapor pressure and represents the solution.

        (b)   The boiling point of a liquid is the temperature at which the vapor pressure of the liquid is equal to atmospheric pressure. Assuming atmospheric pressure of 1.0 atm, the boiling point of the solvent (red line) is approximately 64°C. The boiling point of the solution is approximately 70°C.

13.11   Ideally, 0.50 L. If the volume outside the balloon is very large compared to 0.25 L, solvent will flow across the semipermeable membrane until the molarities of the inner and outer solutions are equal, 0.10 M. This requires an "inner" solution volume twice as large as the initial volume, or 0.50 L. (In reality, osmosis across the balloon membrane is not perfect. The solution concentration inside the balloon will be slightly greater than 0.10 M and the volume of the balloon will be slightly less than 0.50 L.)

13.12   A detergent for solubilizing large hydrophobic proteins (or any other large nonpolar solute, such as greasy dirt) needs a hydrophobic part to interact with the solute, and a hydrophilic part to interact with water. In n-octyl glycoside, the eight-carbon n-octyl chain has strong dispersion interactions with the hydrophobic (nonpolar) protein. The –OH groups on the glycoside (sugar) ring form strong hydrogen bonds with water. This causes the glycoside to dissolve, dragging the hydrophobic protein along with it.

The Solution Process

13.14   (a)   For the same solute, NaCl, in different solvents, solute-solute interactions (ΔH_1) are the same. Because water experiences hydrogen bonding while benzene has only dispersion forces, solvent-solvent interactions (ΔH_2) are greater for water. On the other hand, solute-solvent interactions (ΔH_3) are much weaker between ionic NaCl and nonpolar benzene than between ionic NaCl and polar water. It is the large difference in ΔH_3 that causes NaCl to be soluble in water but not in benzene.

        (b)   Ion-dipole forces between cations and water molecules and relatively small lattice energies (ion-ion forces between cations and anions) lead to strongly hydrated cations.

13.16   From weakest to strongest solvent-solute interactions:

(b), dispersion forces < (c), hydrogen bonding < (a), ion-dipole

13.18   Separation of solvent molecules, ΔH_2, will be smallest in this case, because hydrogen bonding is the weakest of the intermolecular forces involved. ΔH_1 involves breaking ionic bonds, and ΔH_3 involves formation of ion-dipole interactions, both stronger forces than hydrogen bonding.

13.20   KBr is quite soluble in water because of the sizeable increase in disorder of the system (ordered KBr lattice → freely moving hydrated ions) associated with the dissolving process. An increase in disorder or randomness in a process tends to make that process spontaneous.

Saturated Solutions; Factors Affecting Solubility

13.22   (a) $\dfrac{1.22 \text{ mol } MnSO_4 \cdot H_2O}{1 \text{ L soln}} \times \dfrac{169.0 \text{ g } MnSO_4 \cdot H_2O}{1 \text{ mol}} \times 0.100 \text{ L}$

$$= 20.6 \text{ g } MnSO_4 \cdot H_2O/100 \text{ mL}$$

The 1.22 M solution is unsaturated.

(b)   Add a known mass, say 5.0 g, of $MnSO_4 \cdot H_2O$, to the unknown solution. If the solid dissolves, the solution is unsaturated. If there is undissolved $MnSO_4 \cdot H_2O$, filter the solution and weigh the solid. If there is less than 5.0 g of solid, some of the added $MnSO_4 \cdot H_2O$, dissolved and the unknown solution is unsaturated. If there is exactly 5.0 g, no additional solid dissolved and the unknown is saturated. If there is more than 5.0 g, excess solute has precipitated and the solution is supersaturated.

13.24   (a)   at 30°C, $\dfrac{10 \text{ g } KClO_3}{100 \text{ g } H_2O} \times 250 \text{ g } H_2O = 25 \text{ g } KClO_3$

(b) $\dfrac{66 \text{ g } Pb(NO_3)_2}{100 \text{ g } H_2O} \times 250 \text{ g } H_2O = 165 = 1.7 \times 10^2 \text{ g } Pb(NO_3)_2$

(c) $\dfrac{3 \text{ g } Ce_2(SO_4)_3}{100 \text{ g } H_2O} \times 250 \text{ g } H_2O = 7.5 = 8 \text{ g } Ce_2(SO_4)_3$

13.26   Immiscible means that oil and water do not mix homogeneously; they do not dissolve. Many substances are called "oil," but they are typically nonpolar carbon-based molecules with fairly high molecular weights. As such, there are fairly strong dispersion forces among oil molecules. The properties of water are dominated by its strong hydrogen bonding. The dispersion-dipole interactions between water and oil are likely to be weak. Thus, ΔH_1 and ΔH_2 are large and positive, while ΔH_3 is small and negative. The net ΔH_{soln} is large and positive, and mixing does not occur.

13.28   For small n values, the dominant interactions among acid molecules will be hydrogen-bonding. As n increases, dispersion forces between carbon chains become more important and eventually dominate. Thus, as n increases, water solubility decreases and hexane solubility increases.

13.30   *Analyze/Plan.* Water, H_2O, is a polar solvent that forms hydrogen bonds with other H_2O molecules. The more soluble solute in each case will have intermolecular interactions that are most similar to the hydrogen bonding in H_2O. *Solve.*

(a)   Glucose, $C_6H_{12}O_6$, is more soluble because it is capable of hydrogen bonding (Figure 13.12). Nonpolar C_6H_{12} is capable only of dispersion interactions and does not have strong intermolecular interactions with polar (hydrogen bonding) H_2O.

(b)   Ionic sodium propionate, CH_3CH_2COONa, is more soluble. Sodium propionate is a crystalline solid, while propionic acid is a liquid. The increase in disorder or entropy when an ionic solid dissolves leads to significant water solubility, despite the strong ion-ion forces (large ΔH_1) present in the solute (see Solution 13.20).

(c)   HCl is more soluble because it is a strong electrolyte and completely ionized in water. Ionization leads to ion-dipole solute-solvent interactions, and an increase in disorder. CH_3CH_2Cl is a molecular solute capable of relatively weak dipole-dipole solute-solvent interactions and is much less soluble in water.

13.32   Pressure has an effect on O_2 solubility in water because, at constant temperature and volume, pressure is directly related to the amount of O_2 available to dissolve. The greater the partial pressure of O_2 above water, the more O_2 molecules are available for dissolution, and the more molecules that strike the surface of the liquid.

Pressure does not affect the amount or physical properties of NaCl, or ionic solids in general, so it has little influence on the dissolving of NaCl in water.

13.34 $650 \text{ torr} \times \dfrac{1\,atm}{760\,torr} = 0.855\,atm; P_{O_2} = \chi_{O_2}(P_t) = 0.21(0.855\,atm) = 0.1796 = 0.18\,atm$

$$S_{O_2} = kP_{O_2} = \dfrac{1.38 \times 10^{-3}\,mol}{L\text{-}atm} \times 0.1796\,atm = 2.5 \times 10^{-4}\,M$$

Concentrations of Solutions

13.36   (a) $\text{mass \%} = \dfrac{\text{mass solute}}{\text{total mass solution}} \times 100$

$\text{mass solute} = 0.035\,mol\,I_2 \times \dfrac{253.8\,g\,I_2}{1\,mol\,I_2} = 8.883 = 8.9\,g\,I_2$

$\text{mass \% } I_2 = \dfrac{8.883\,g\,I_2}{8.883\,g\,I_2 + 115\,g\,CCl_4} \times 100 = 7.170 = 7.2\%\,I_2$

(b) $\text{ppm} = \dfrac{\text{mass solute}}{\text{total mass solution}} \times 10^6 = \dfrac{0.0079\,g\,Sr^{2+}}{1 \times 10^3\,g\,H_2O} \times 10^6 = 7.9\,ppm\,Sr^{2+}$

13.38   (a) $\dfrac{25.5\,g\,C_6H_5OH}{94.11\,g/mol} = 0.2710 = 0.271\,mol\,C_6H_5OH$

$\dfrac{425\,g\,CH_3CH_2OH}{46.07\,g/mol} = 9.2251 = 9.23\,mol\,CH_3CH_2OH$

$\chi_{C_6H_5OH} = \dfrac{0.2710}{0.2710 + 9.2251} = 0.02853 = 0.0285$

(b) $\text{mass \%} = \dfrac{25.5\,g\,C_6H_5OH}{25.5\,g\,C_6H_5OH + 425\,g\,CH_3CH_2OH} \times 100 = 5.66\%\,C_6H_5OH$

(c) $m = \dfrac{0.2710\,mol\,C_6H_5OH}{0.425\,kg\,CH_3CH_2OH} = 0.6376 = 0.638\,m\,C_6H_5OH$

13.40   (a) $M = \dfrac{\text{mol solute}}{\text{L soln}}; \dfrac{15.0 \text{ g Al}_2(\text{SO}_4)_3}{0.350 \text{ L soln}} \times \dfrac{1 \text{ mol Al}_2(\text{SO}_4)_3}{342.2 \text{ g Al}_2(\text{SO}_4)_3} = 0.125 \, M \text{ AL}_2(\text{SO}_4)_3$

   (b) $\dfrac{5.25 \text{ g Mn(NO}_3)_2 \bullet 2\text{H}_2\text{O}}{0.175 \text{ L soln}} \times \dfrac{1 \text{ mol Mn(NO}_3)_2 \bullet 2\text{H}_2\text{O}}{215.0 \text{ g Mn(NO}_3)_2 \bullet 2\text{H}_2\text{O}} = 0.140 \, M \text{ Mn(NO}_3)_2$

   (c) $M_c \times L_c = M_d \times L_d; 9.00 \, M \text{ H}_2\text{SO}_4 \times 0.0350 \text{ L} = ?M \text{ H}_2\text{SO}_4 \times 0.500 \text{ L}$
         500 mL of 0.630 M H$_2$SO$_4$

13.42   (a) $16.0 \text{ mol H}_2\text{O} \times \dfrac{18.02 \text{ g H}_2\text{O}}{1 \text{ mol H}_2\text{O}} = 288.3 \text{ g H}_2\text{O} = 0.288 \text{ kg H}_2\text{O}$

         $m = \dfrac{1.25 \text{ mol KCl}}{0.2883 \text{ kg H}_2\text{O}} = 4.3358 = 4.34 \, m \text{ KCl}$

   (b) $m = \dfrac{\text{mol solute}}{\text{kg solute}}; \text{mol S}_8 = m \times \text{kg C}_{10}\text{H}_8 = 0.12 \, m \times 0.1000 \text{ kg C}_{10}\text{H}_8 = 0.012 \text{ mol}$

         $0.012 \text{ mol S}_8 \times \dfrac{256.5 \text{ g S}_8}{1 \text{ mol S}_8} = 3.078 = 3.1 \text{ g S}_8$

13.44   (a) $\text{mass \%} = \dfrac{\text{mass C}_6\text{H}_8\text{O}_6}{\text{total mass solution}} \times 100;$

         $\dfrac{80.5 \text{ g C}_6\text{H}_8\text{O}_6}{80.5 \text{ g C}_6\text{H}_8\text{O}_6 + 210 \text{ g H}_2\text{O}} \times 100 = 27.71 = 27.7\% \text{ C}_6\text{H}_8\text{O}_6$

   (b) $\text{mol C}_6\text{H}_8\text{O}_6 = \dfrac{80.5 \text{ g C}_6\text{H}_8\text{O}_6}{176.1 \text{ g/mol}} = 0.4571 = 0.457 \text{ mol C}_6\text{H}_8\text{O}_6$

         $\text{mol H}_2\text{O} = \dfrac{210 \text{ g H}_2\text{O}}{18.02 \text{ g/mol}} = 11.654 = 11.7 \text{ mol H}_2\text{O}$

         $\chi_{\text{C}_6\text{H}_8\text{O}_6} = \dfrac{0.4571 \text{ mol C}_6\text{H}_8\text{O}_6}{0.4571 \text{ mol C}_6\text{H}_8\text{O}_6 + 11.654 \text{ mol H}_2\text{O}} = 0.0377$

   (c) $m = \dfrac{0.4571 \text{ mol C}_6\text{H}_8\text{O}_6}{0.210 \text{ kg H}_2\text{O}} = 2.18 \, m \text{ C}_6\text{H}_8\text{O}_6$

   (d) $M = \dfrac{\text{mol C}_6\text{H}_8\text{O}_6}{\text{L solution}}; 290.5 \text{ g soln} \times \dfrac{1 \text{ mL}}{1.22 \text{ g}} \times \dfrac{1 \text{ L}}{1000 \text{ mL}} = 0.2381 = 0.238 \text{ L}$

         $M = \dfrac{0.4571 \text{ mol C}_6\text{H}_8\text{O}_6}{0.2381 \text{ L soln}} = 1.92 \, M \text{ C}_6\text{H}_8\text{O}_6$

13.46   Given: 9.08 g C$_4$H$_4$S, 1.065 g/mL; 250.0 mL C$_7$H$_8$, 0.867 g/mL

   (a) $\text{mol C}_4\text{H}_4\text{S} = 9.08 \text{ g C}_4\text{H}_4\text{S} \times \dfrac{1 \text{ mol C}_4\text{H}_4\text{S}}{84.15 \text{ g C}_4\text{H}_4\text{S}} = 0.1079 = 0.108 \text{ mol C}_4\text{H}_4\text{S}$

         $\text{mol C}_7\text{H}_8 = \dfrac{0.867 \text{ g}}{1 \text{ mL}} \times 250.0 \text{ mL} \times \dfrac{1 \text{ mol C}_7\text{H}_8}{92.14 \text{ g C}_7\text{H}_8} = 2.352 = 2.35 \text{ mol}$

$$\chi_{C_4H_4S} = \frac{0.1079 \text{ mol } C_4H_4S}{0.1079 \text{ mol } C_4H_4S + 2.352 \text{ mol } C_7H_8} = 0.04386 = 0.0439$$

(b) $m_{C_4H_4S} = \dfrac{\text{mol } C_4H_4S}{\text{kg } C_7H_8}$; $250.0 \text{ mL} \times \dfrac{0.867 \text{ g}}{1 \text{ mL}} \times \dfrac{1 \text{ kg}}{1000 \text{ g}} = 0.2168 = 0.217 \text{ kg } C_7H_8$

$$m_{C_4H_4S} = \frac{0.1079 \text{ mol } C_4H_4S}{0.2168 \text{ kg } C_7H_8} = 0.498 \ m \ C_4H_4S$$

(c) $9.08 \text{ g } C_4H_4S \times \dfrac{1 \text{ mL}}{1.065 \text{ g}} = 8.526 = 8.53 \text{ mL } C_4H_4S$;

$V_{soln} = 8.53 \text{ mL } C_4H_4S + 250.0 \text{ mL } C_7H_8 = 258.5 \text{ mL}$

$$M_{C_4H_4S} = \frac{0.1079 \text{ mol } C_4H_4S}{0.2585 \text{ L soln}} = 0.417 \ M \ C_4H_4S$$

13.48 (a) $\dfrac{1.50 \text{ mol HNO}_3}{1 \text{ L soln}} \times 0.185 \text{ L} = 0.2775 = 0.278 \text{ mol HNO}_3$

(b) Assume that for dilute aqueous solutions, the mass of the solvent is the mass of solution.

$$\frac{1.25 \text{ mol NaCl}}{1 \text{ kg H}_2O} \times \frac{x \text{ mol}}{50.0 \times 10^{-6} \text{ kg}}; x = 6.25 \times 10^{-5} \text{ mol NaCl}$$

(c) $\dfrac{1.50 \text{ g } C_{12}H_{22}O_{11}}{100 \text{ g soln}} = \dfrac{x \text{ g } C_{12}H_{22}O_{11}}{75.0 \text{ g soln}}; x = 1.125 = 1.13 \text{ g } C_{12}H_{22}O_{11}$

$1.125 \text{ g } C_{12}H_{22}O_{11} \times \dfrac{1 \text{ mol } C_{12}H_{22}O_{11}}{342.3 \text{ g } C_{12}H_{22}O_{11}} = 3.287 \times 10^{-3} = 3.29 \times 10^{-3} \text{ mol } C_{12}H_{22}O_{11}$

13.50 (a) $\dfrac{0.110 \text{ mol } (NH_4)_2SO_4}{1 \text{ L soln}} \times 1.50 \text{ L} \times \dfrac{132.2 \text{ g } (NH_4)_2SO_4}{1 \text{ mol } (NH_4)_2SO_4} = 21.81 = 21.8 \text{ g } (NH_4)_2SO_4$

Weigh 21.8 g $(NH_4)_2SO_4$, dissolve in a small amount of water, continue adding water with thorough mixing up to a total solution volume of 1.50 L.

(b) Determine the mass fraction of Na_2CO_3 in the solution:

$$\frac{0.65 \text{ mol Na}_2CO_3}{1000 \text{ g H}_2O} \times \frac{106.0 \text{ g Na}_2CO_3}{1 \text{ mol Na}_2CO_3} = 68.9 \text{ g} = \frac{69 \text{ g Na}_2CO_3}{1000 \text{ g H}_2O}$$

$$\text{mass fraction} = \frac{68.9 \text{ g Na}_2CO_3}{1000 \text{ g H}_2O + 68.9 \text{ g Na}_2CO_3} = 0.06446 = 0.064$$

In 120 g of solution, there are 0.06446(120) = 7.735 = 7.7 g Na_2CO_3.

Weigh out 7.7 g Na_2CO_3 and dissolve it in 120 − 7.7 = 112.3 g H_2O to make exactly 120 g of solution.

(112.3 g H_2O/0.997 g H_2O/mL @ 25° = 112.6 mL H_2O)

(c) $1.20 \, L \times \dfrac{1000 \, mL}{1 \, L} \times \dfrac{1.16 \, g}{1 \, mL} = 1392 \, g \text{ solution}; \; 0.150(1392 \, g \text{ soln}) = 209 \, g \, Pb(NO_3)_2$

Weigh 209 g $Pb(NO_3)$ and add $(1392 - 209) = 1183 \, g \, H_2O$ to make exactly $(1392 = 1.39 \times 10^3) \, g$ or 1.20 L of solution.

$(1183 \, g \, H_2O/0.997 \, g/mL @ 25°C = 1187 \, mL \, H_2O)$

(d)   Calculate the mol HCl necessary to neutralize 5.5 g $Ba(OH)_2$.

$Ba(OH)_2(s) + 2HCl(aq) \rightarrow BaCl_2(aq) + 2H_2O(l)$

$5.5 \, g \, Ba(OH)_2 + \dfrac{1 \, mol \, Ba(OH)_2}{171 \, g \, Ba(OH)_2} \times \dfrac{2 \, mol \, HCl}{1 \, mol \, Ba(OH)_2} = 0.0643 = 0.064 \, mol \, HCl$

$M = \dfrac{mol}{L}; \; L = \dfrac{mol}{M} = \dfrac{0.0643 \, mol \, HCl}{0.50 \, M \, HCl} = 0.1287 = 0.13 \, L = 130 \, mL$

130 mL of 0.50 M HCl are needed.

$M_c \times L_c = M_d \times L_d; \; 6.0 \, M \times L_c = 0.50 \, M \times 0.1287 \, L; \; L_c = 0.01072 \, L = 11 \, mL$

Using a pipette, measure exactly 11 mL of 6.0 M HCl and dilute with water to a total volume of 130 mL.

13.52   *Analyze/Plan.* Assume 1.00 L of solution. Calculate mass of 1 L of solution using density. Calculate mass of NH_3 using mass %, then mol NH_3 in 1.00 L. *Solve.*

$1.00 \, L \text{ soln} \times \dfrac{1000 \, mL}{1 \, L} \times \dfrac{0.90 \, g \text{ soln}}{1 \, mL \text{ soln}} = 9.0 \times 10^2 \, g \text{ soln/L}$

$\dfrac{900 \, g \text{ soln}}{1.00 \, L \text{ soln}} \times \dfrac{28 \, g \, NH_3}{100 \, g \text{ soln}} \times \dfrac{1 \, mol \, NH_3}{17.03 \, g \, NH_3} = 14.80 = 15 \, mol \, NH_3/L \text{ soln} = 15 \, M \, NH_3$

13.54   (a) $\dfrac{0.0750 \, mol \, C_8H_{10}N_4O_2}{1 \, kg \, CHCl_3} \times \dfrac{194.2 \, g \, C_8H_{10}N_4O_2}{1 \, mol \, C_8H_{10}N_4O_2} = 14.565$

$= 14.6 \, g \, C_8H_{10}N_4O_2/kg \, CHCl_3$

$\dfrac{14.565 \, g \, C_8H_{10}N_4O_2}{14.565 \, g \, C_8H_{10}N_4O_2 + 1000.00 \, g \, CHCl_3} \times 100 = 1.436 = 1.44\% \, C_8H_{10}N_4O_2 \text{ by mass}$

(b) $1000 \, g \, CHCl_3 \times \dfrac{1 \, mol \, CHCl_3}{119.4 \, CHCl_3} = 8.375 = 8.38 \, mol \, CHCl_3$

$\chi_{C_8H_{10}N_4O_2} = \dfrac{0.0750}{0.0750 + 8.375} = 0.00888$

13.56   (a)   For gases at the same temperature and pressure, volume % = mol %. The volume and mol % of CO_2 in this breathing air is 4.0%.

(b) $P_{CO_2} = \chi_{CO_2} \times P_t = 0.040 \, (1 \, atm) = 0.040 \, atm$

$M_{CO_2} = \dfrac{P_{CO_2}}{RT} = \dfrac{0.040 \, atm}{310 \, K} \times \dfrac{K \text{-} mol}{0.08206 \, L \text{-} atm} = 1.6 \times 10^{-3} \, M$

Colligative Properties

13.58   (a)   decrease   (b)   decrease

   (c)   increase   (d)   increase

13.60   (a)   An *ideal solution* is a solution that obeys Raoult's Law.

   (b)   *Analyze/Plan.* Calculate the vapor pressure predicted by Raoult's law and compare it to the experimental vapor pressure. Assume ethylene glycol (eg) is the solute. *Solve.*

$$\chi_{H_2O} = \chi_{eg} = 0.500; \ P_A = \chi_A P_A{}^\circ = 0.500(149) \ \text{mm Hg} = 74.5 \ \text{mm Hg}$$

The experimental vapor pressure (P_A), 67 mm Hg, is less than the value predicted by Raoult's law for an ideal solution. The solution is not ideal.

Check. An ethylene glycol-water solution has extensive hydrogen bonding, which causes deviation from ideal behavior. We expect the experimental vapor pressure to be less than the ideal value and it is.

13.62   (a) H_2O vapor pressure will be determined by the mole fraction of H_2O in the solution. The vapor pressure of pure H_2O at 343 K (70°C) = 233.7 torr.

$$\frac{32.5 \ \text{g} \ C_3H_8O_3}{92.10 \ \text{g/mol}} = 0.3529 = 0.353 \ \text{mol}; \quad \frac{125 \ \text{g} \ H_2O}{18.02 \ \text{g/mol}} = 6.937 = 6.94 \ \text{mol}$$

$$P_{H_2O} = \frac{6.937 \ \text{mol} \ H_2O}{6.937 + 0.353} \times 233.7 \ \text{torr} = 222.4 = 222 \ \text{torr}$$

   (b)   Calculate χ_B by vapor pressure lowering; $\chi_B = \Delta P_A / P_A{}^\circ$ (see Solution 13.59(b)). Given moles solvent, calculate moles solute from the definition of mole fraction.

$$\chi_{C_2H_6O_2} = \frac{10.0 \ \text{torr}}{100 \ \text{torr}} = 0.100$$

$$\frac{1.00 \times 10^3 \ \text{g} \ C_2H_5OH}{46.07 \ \text{g/mol}} = 21.71 = 21.7 \ \text{mol} \ C_2H_5OH; \ \text{let} \ y = \text{mol} \ C_2H_6O_2$$

$$\chi_{C_2H_6O_2} = \frac{y \ \text{mol} \ C_2H_6O_2}{y \ \text{mol} \ C_2H_6O_2 + 21.71 \ \text{mol} \ C_2H_5OH} = 0.100 = \frac{y}{y + 21.71}$$

$$0.100 \ y + 2.171 = y; \ 0.900 \ y = 2.171; \ y = 2.412 = 2.41 \ \text{mol} \ C_2H_6O_2$$

$$2.412 \ \text{mol} \ C_2H_6O_2 \times \frac{62.07 \ \text{g}}{1 \ \text{mol}} = 150 \ \text{g} \ C_2H_6O_2$$

13.64   (a)   Since C_6H_6 and C_7H_8 form an ideal solution, we can use Raoult's Law. Since both components are volatile, both contribute to the total vapor pressure of 35 torr.

$$P_t = P_{C_6H_6} + P_{C_7H_8} ; \ P_{C_6H_6} = \chi_{C_6H_6} P_{C_6H_6}^\circ ; \ P_{C_7H_8} = \chi_{C_7H_8} P_{C_7H_8}^\circ$$

$$\chi_{C_7H_8} = 1 - \chi_{C_6H_6} ; \ P_T = \chi_{C_6H_6} P_{C_6H_6}^\circ + (1 - \chi_{C_6H_6}) P_{C_7H_8}^\circ$$

$$35 \ \text{torr} = \chi_{C_6H_6} (75 \ \text{torr}) + (1 - \chi_{C_6H_6}) 22 \ \text{torr}$$

$$13 \ \text{torr} = 53 \ \text{torr} (\chi_{C_6H_6}); \ \chi_{C_6H_6} = \frac{13 \ \text{torr}}{53 \ \text{torr}} = 0.2453 = 0.25; \ \chi_{C_7H_8} = 0.7547 = 0.75$$

(b) $P_{C_6H_6} = 0.2453(75 \text{ torr}) = 18.4 \text{ torr};$ $P_{C_7H_8} = 0.7547(22 \text{ torr}) = 16.6 \text{ torr}$

In the vapor, $\chi_{C_6H_6} = \dfrac{P_{C_6H_6}}{P_t} = \dfrac{18.4 \text{ torr}}{35 \text{ torr}} = 0.53;$ $\chi_{C_7H_8} = 0.47$

13.66   *Analyze/Plan.* ΔT_b depends on mol dissolved particles. Assume 100 g of each solution, calculate mol solute and mol dissolved particles. Glucose and sucrose are molecular solutes, but $NaNO_3$ dissociates into 2 mol particles per mol solute. *Solve.*

10% by mass means 10 g solute in 100 g solution. If we have 10 g of each solute, the one with the smallest molar mass will have the largest mol solute. The molar masses are: glucose, 180.2 g/mol; sucrose, 342.3 g/mol; $NaNO_3$, 85.0 g/mol. $NaNO_3$ has most mol solute, and twice as many dissolved particles, so it will have the highest boiling point. Sucrose has least mol solute and lowest boiling point. Glucose is intermediate.

In order of increasing boiling point: 10% sucrose < 10% glucose < 10% $NaNO_3$.

13.68   0.030 *m* phenol > 0.040 *m* glycerin = 0.020 *m* KBr. Phenol is very slightly ionized in water, but not enough to match the number of particles in a 0.040 *m* glycerin solution. The KBr solution is 0.040 *m* in particles, so it has the same freezing point as 0.040 *m* glycerin, which is a nonelectrolyte.

13.70 $\Delta T = K(m)$; first calculate the **molality** of the solute particles.

(a)   0.30 *m*

(b) $\dfrac{20.0 \text{ g } C_{10}H_{22}}{0.0455 \text{ kg CHCl}_3} \times \dfrac{1 \text{ mol } C_{10}H_{22}}{142.3 \text{ g } C_{10}H_{22}} = 3.089 = 3.09 \text{ m}$

(c) $m = \dfrac{0.45 \text{ mol eg} + 2(0.15) \text{ mol KBr}}{0.150 \text{ kg H}_2O} = \dfrac{0.75 \text{ mol particles}}{0.150 \text{ kg H}_2O} = 5.0 \, m$

Then, f.p. $= T_f - K_f(m)$; b.p. $= T_b + K_b(m)$; T in °C

	m	T_f	$-K_f(m)$	f.p.	T_b	$+K_b(m)$	b.p.
(a)	0.30	−114.6	−1.99(0.30) = −0.60	−115.2	78.4	1.22(0.30) = 0.37	78.8
(b)	3.09	−63.5	−4.68(3.09) = −14.5	−78.0	61.2	3.63(3.09) = 11.2	72.4
(c)	5.0	0.0	−1.86(5.0) = −9.3	−9.3	100.0	0.51(5.0) = 2.6	102.6

13.72   Use ΔT_b = find *m* of aqueous solution, and then use *m* to calculate ΔT_f and freezing point. $K_b = 0.51$, $K_f = 1.86$.

b.p. = 105.0°C; $\Delta T_b = 105.0°C - 100.0°C = 5.0°C$

$\Delta T_b = K_b(m)$; $m = \dfrac{\Delta T_b}{K_b} = \dfrac{5.0 \, ^\circ C}{0.51} = 9.804 = 9.8 \, m$

$\Delta T_f = 1.86°C/m \times 9.804 \, m = 18.24 = 18°C$;   freezing point = 0.0°C − 18.24 °C = −18°C

13.74 $\Pi = MRT$; T = 20°C + 273 = 293 K

$M \text{ (of ions)} = \dfrac{\text{mol NaCl} \times 2}{\text{L soln}} = \dfrac{3.4 \text{ g NaCl}}{1 \text{ L soln}} \times \dfrac{1 \text{ mol NaCl}}{58.4 \text{ g NaCl}} \times \dfrac{2 \text{ mol ions}}{1 \text{ mol NaCl}} = 0.116 = 0.12 \, M$

$$\Pi = \frac{0.116\,\text{mol}}{\text{L}} \times \frac{0.08206\,\text{L - atm}}{\text{K - mol}} \times 293\,\text{K} = 2.8\,\text{atm}$$

13.76 $\Delta T_f = 5.5 - 4.1 = 1.4;$ $m = \dfrac{\Delta T_f}{K_f} = \dfrac{1.4}{5.12} = 0.273 = 0.27\,m$

$$\text{MM lauryl alcohol} = \frac{\text{g lauryl alcohol}}{m \times \text{kg } C_6H_6} = \frac{5.00\,\text{g lauryl alcohol}}{0.273 \times 0.100\,\text{kg } C_6H_6}$$
$$= 1.8 \times 10^2 \text{ g/mol lauryl alcohol}$$

13.78 $M = n/RT = \dfrac{0/605\,\text{atm}}{298\,\text{K}} \times \dfrac{\text{K - mol}}{0.08206\,\text{L - atm}} = 0.02474 = 0.0247\,M$

$$\text{MM} = \frac{\text{g}}{M \times L} = \frac{2.35\,\text{g}}{0.02474\,M \times 0.250\,L} = 380\,\text{g/mol}$$

13.80   If these were ideal solutions, they would have equal ion concentrations and equal ΔT_f values. Data in Table 13.5 indicates that the van't Hoff factors (i) for both salts are less than the ideal values. For 0.030 m NaCl, i is between 1.87 and 1.94, about 1.92. For 0.020 m K_2SO_4, i is between 2.32 and 2.70, about 2.62. From Equation 13.14,

ΔT_f (measured) = $i \times \Delta T_f$ (calculated for nonelectrolyte)

NaCl: ΔT_f (measured) = $1.92 \times 0.030\,m \times 1.86\,°C/m = 0.11\,°C$

K_2SO_4: ΔT_f (measured) = $2.62 \times 0.020\,m \times 1.86\,°C/m = 0.097\,°C$

0.030 m NaCl would have the larger ΔT_f.

The deviations from ideal behavior are due to ion-pairing in the two electrolyte solutions. K_2SO_4 has more extensive ion-pairing and a larger deviation from ideality because of the higher charge on $SO_4{}^{2-}$ relative to Cl^-.

Colloids

13.82   (a)   Suspensions are classified as solutions or colloids according to the size of the dispersed particles. Solute particles have diameters less than 10 Å. Clearly a protein with a molecular mass of 30,000 amu will be longer than 10 Å. The aqueous suspensions are colloids because of the size of protein molecules.

        (b)   Emulsion. An emulsifying agent is one that aids in the formation of an emulsion. It usually has a polar part and a nonpolar part, to facilitate mixing of immiscible liquids with very different molecular polarities.

13.84   (a)   When the colloid *particle mass* becomes large enough so that gravitational and interparticle attractive forces are greater than the kinetic energies of the particles, settling and aggregation can occur.

        (b)   *Hydrophobic* colloids do not attract a sheath of water molecules around them and thus tend to aggregate from aqueous solution. They can be stabilized as colloids by adsorbing charges on their surfaces. The charged particles interact with solvent water, stabilizing the colloid.

(c)   *Charges on colloid particles* can stabilize them against aggregation. Particles carrying like charges repel one another and are thus prevented from aggregating and settling out.

13.86   (a)   The nonpolar hydrophobic tails of soap particles (the hydrocarbon chain of stearate ions) establish attractive intermolecular dispersion forces with the nonpolar oil molecules, while the charged hydrophilic head of the soap particles interacts with H_2O to keep the oil molecules suspended. (This is the mechanism by which laundry detergents remove greasy dirt from clothes.)

         (b)   Electrolytes from the acid neutralize surface charges of the suspended particles in milk, causing the colloid to coagulate.

Additional Exercises

13.88   In this equilibrium system, molecules move from the surface of the solid into solution, while molecules in solution are deposited on the surface of the solid. As molecules leave the surface of the small particles of powder, the reverse process preferentially deposits other molecules on the surface of a single crystal. Eventually, all molecules that were present in the 50 g of powder are deposited on the surface of a 50 g crystal; this can only happen if the dissolution and deposition processes are ongoing.

13.89   Assume that the density of the solution is 1.00 g/mL.

         (a) $4 \text{ ppm } O_2 = \dfrac{4 \text{ mg } O_2}{1 \text{ kg soln}} = \dfrac{4 \times 10^{-3} \text{ g } O_2}{1 \text{ L soln}} \times \dfrac{1 \text{ mol } O_2}{32.0 \text{ g } O_2} = 1.25 \times 10^{-4} = 1 \times 10^{-4} \text{ } M$

         (b) $S_{O_2} = k P_{O_2}; \; P_{O_2} = S_{O_2}/k = \dfrac{1.25 \times 10^{-4} \text{ mol}}{L} \times \dfrac{L\text{-atm}}{1.71 \times 10^{-3} \text{ mol}} = 0.0731 = 0.07 \text{ atm}$

                 $0.0731 \text{ atm} \times \dfrac{760 \text{ mm Hg}}{1 \text{ atm}} = 55.6 = 60 \text{ mm Hg}$

13.91   0.10% by mass means 0.10 g glucose/100 g blood.

         (a) $\text{ppm glucose} = \dfrac{\text{g glucose}}{\text{g solution}} \times 10^6 = \dfrac{0.10 \text{ g glucose}}{100 \text{ g blood}} \times 10^6 = 1000 \text{ ppm glucose}$

         (b) m = mol glucose/kg solvent. Assume that the mixture of nonglucose components is the 'solvent'.

         mass solvent = 100 g blood – 0.10 g glucose = 99.9 g solvent = 0.0999 kg solvent

         $\text{mol glucose} = 0.10 \text{ g} \times \dfrac{1 \text{ mol}}{180.2 \text{ g } C_6H_{12}O_6} = 5.55 \times 10^{-4} = 5.6 \times 10^{-4} \text{ mol glucose}$

         $m = \dfrac{5.55 \times 10^{-4} \text{ mol glucose}}{0.0999 \text{ kg solvent}} = 5.6 \times 10^{-3} \text{ } m \text{ glucose}$

         In order to calculate molarity, solution volume must be known. The density of blood is needed to relate mass and volume.

13.92   *Analyze.* The definition of ppb is (mass solute/mass solution) × 10^9. *Plan.* Use the definition to get g Pb and g solution. Change g Pb to mol Pb, g solution to L solution, calculate molarity. *Solve.*

(a) $9 \text{ ppb} = \dfrac{9 \text{ g Pb}}{1 \times 10^9 \text{ g soln}} \times 10^9$

For dilute aqueous solutions (drinking water) assume that the density of the solution is the density of H_2O.

$$\dfrac{9 \text{ g Pb}}{1 \times 10^9 \text{ g soln}} \times \dfrac{1.0 \text{ g soln}}{\text{mL soln}} \times \dfrac{1000 \text{ mL}}{1 \text{ L}} \times \dfrac{1 \text{ mol Pb}}{207.2 \text{ g Pb}} = 4.34 \times 10^{-8} \ M = 4 \times 10^{-8} \ M$$

(b)   Change 60 m^3 H_2O to cm^3 (mL) H_2O to g H_2O (or g soln).

$$60 \ m^3 \times \dfrac{100^3 \text{ cm}^3}{m^3} \times \dfrac{1 \text{ g } H_2O}{\text{cm}^3 \ H_2O} = 6.0 \times 10^7 \text{ g } H_2O \text{ or soln}$$

$$\dfrac{9 \text{ g Pb}}{1 \times 10^9 \text{ g soln}} \times 6.0 \times 10^7 \text{ g soln} = 0.540 = 0.5 \text{ g Pb}$$

13.94   Mole fraction ethyl alcohol, $\chi_{C_2H_5OH} = \dfrac{P_{C_2H_5OH}}{P^\circ_{C_2H_5OH}} = \dfrac{8 \text{ torr}}{100 \text{ torr}} = 0.08$

$$\dfrac{620 \times 10^3 \text{ g } C_{24}H_{50}}{338.6 \text{ g/mol}} = 1.83 \times 10^3 \text{ mol } C_{24}H_{50}; \quad \text{let } y = \text{mol } C_2H_5OH$$

$\chi_{C_2H_5OH} = 0.08 = \dfrac{y}{y + 1.83 \times 10^3}; \ 0.92 \, y = 146.4; \ y = 1.6 \times 10^2 \text{ mol } C_2H_5OH$

(Strictly speaking, y should have 1 sig fig because 0.08 has 1 sig fig, but this severely limits the calculation.)

$1.6 \times 10^2 \text{ mol } C_2H_5OH \times \dfrac{46 \text{ g } C_2H_5OH}{1 \text{ mol}} = 7.4 \times 10^3 \text{ g or } 7.4 \text{ kg } C_2H_5OH$

13.95   (a)   The solvent vapor pressure over each solution is determined by the total particle concentrations present in the solutions. When the particle concentrations are equal, the vapor pressures will be equal and equilibrium established. The particle concentration of the nonelectrolyte is just 0.050 *M*, the ion concentration of the NaCl is 2 × 0.035 *M* = 0.070 *M*. Solvent will diffuse from the less concentrated nonelectrolyte solution. The level of the NaCl solution will rise, and the level of the nonelectrolyte solution will fall.

(b)   Let x = volume of solvent transferred

$$\dfrac{0.050 \ M \times 30.0 \text{ mL}}{(30.0 - x) \text{ mL}} = \dfrac{0.070 \ M \times 30.0 \text{ mL}}{(30.0 + x) \text{ mL}}; 1.5(30.0 + x) = 2.1(30.0 - x)$$

$45 + 1.5 \, x = 63 - 2.1 \, x; \ 3.6 \, x = 18; \ x = 5.0 = 5 \text{ mL transferred}$

The volume in the nonelectrolyte beaker is (30.0 − 5.0) = 25.0 mL; in the NaCl beaker (30.0 + 5.0) = 35.0 mL.

13.97   Assume constant temperature of all liquids and vapors.

$P_{solution}$ = vapor pressure above the solution

$P^o_{solvent}$ = vapor pressure above pure solvent

$\chi_{solvent}$ = mol fraction solvent, $\chi_{solute} = 1 - \chi_{solvent}$

$\Delta P_{solvent}$ = vapor pressure reduction = $P^o_{solvent} - P_{solution}$

$P_{solution} = \chi_{solvent} P^o_{solvent}$ (Raoult's Law)

$P_{solution} = (1 - \chi_{solute}) P^o_{solvent}$

$P_{solution} = P^o_{solvent} - \chi_{solute} P^o_{solvent}$

$P_{solution} - P^o_{solvent} = -\chi_{solute} P^o_{solvent}$

$-(P_{solution} - P^o_{solvent}) = -(-\chi_{solute} P^o_{solvent})$

$P^o_{solvent} - P_{solution} = \chi_{solute} P^o_{solvent}$

$\Delta P_{solvent} = \chi_{solute} P^o_{solvent}$

13.98   In order to answer this question, you will need to find the physical properties (density, freezing point) of ethylene glycol in a source like the *CRC*. Calculate the freezing point of a solution that is 30% ethylene glycol, $C_2H_6O_2$, and 70% water. Since a car owner would typically use volume measurements to make this solution, assume this is a volume percent concentration. Volume percent is a volume ratio that is valid for any volume unit.   For convenience, assume 30 mL $C_2H_6O_2$, and 70 mL H_2O. The density of $C_2H_6O_2$ is 1.1088 g/mL. The density of H_2O is 0.997 g/mL at 25°C. Find molality and then ΔT_f for water.

$$30 \text{ mL } C_2H_6O_2 \times \frac{1.1088 \text{ g } C_2H_6O_2}{\text{mL}} = 33.264 = 33 \text{ g } C_2H_6O_2$$

$$\frac{33.264 \text{ g } C_2H_6O_2}{70 \text{ mL } H_2O} \times \frac{1 \text{ mol } C_2H_6O_2}{62.1 \text{ g } C_2H_6O_2} \times \frac{1 \text{ mL } H_2O}{0.997 \text{ g } H_2O} \times \frac{1000 \text{ g}}{\text{kg}} = 7.6752 = 7.7 \text{ m}$$

$\Delta T_f = 1.86°C/m \ (7.6752 \ m) = 14.27°C$

$T_f = 0.0°C - 14.27°C = -14.27 = -14°C$

In this 30% solution, ethylene glycol is the solute (present in lesser amount) and water is the solvent (present in greater amount). It is the freezing point of water, 0.0°C, that is depressed by the nonvolatile solute ethylene glycol. If pure ethylene glycol is used in the radiator, it freezes at its regular (not depressed) freezing point, −11.5°C. The freezing point of the solution, −14°C, is lower than the freezing point of pure ethylene glycol.

13.100 The compound with the larger i value is the stronger electrolyte.

$i = \dfrac{\Delta T_f \text{(measured)}}{\Delta T_f \text{(calculated)}}$ The idealized value is 3 for both salts.

$Hg(NO_3)_2$: $m = \dfrac{10.0\,g\,Hg(NO_3)_2}{1.00\,kg\,H_2O} \times \dfrac{1\,mol\,Hg(NO_3)_2}{324.6\,g\,Hg(NO_3)_2} = 0.0308\,m$

ΔT_f (nonelectrolyte) $= -1.86(0.0308) = -0.0573°C$

$i = \dfrac{-0.162°C}{-0.0573°C} = 2.83$

$HgCl_2$: $m = \dfrac{10.0\,g\,HgCl_2}{1.00\,kg\,H_2O} \times \dfrac{1\,mol\,HgCl_2}{271.5\,g\,HgCl_2} = 0.0368\,m$

ΔT_f (nonelectrolyte) $= -1.86(0.0368) = -0.0685°C$

$i = \dfrac{-0.0685}{-0.0685} = 1.00$

With an i value of 2.83, $Hg(NO_3)_2$ is almost completely dissociated into ions; with an

i value of 1.00, the $HgCl_2$ behaves essentially like a nonelectrolyte. Clearly, $Hg(NO_3)_2$ is

the stronger electrolyte.

13.101 (a) $K_b = \dfrac{\Delta T_b}{m};$ $\Delta T_b = 47.46°C - 46.30°C = 1.16°C$

$m = \dfrac{mol\,solute}{kg\,CS_2} = \dfrac{0.250\,mol}{400.0\,mL\,CS_2} \times \dfrac{1\,mL\,CS_2}{1.261\,g\,CS_2} \times \dfrac{1000\,g}{1\,kg} = 0.4956 = 0.496\,m$

$K_b = \dfrac{1.16°C}{0.4956\,m} = 2.34°C/m$

(b) $m = \dfrac{\Delta T_b}{K_b} = \dfrac{(47.08 - 46.30)°C}{2.34°C/m} = 0.333 = 0.33\,m$

$m = \dfrac{mol\,unknown}{kg\,CS_2};$ $m \times kg\,CS_2 = \dfrac{g\,unknown}{MM\,unknown};$ $MM = \dfrac{g\,unknown}{m \times kg\,CS_2}$

$50.0\,mL\,CS_2 \times \dfrac{1.261\,g\,CS_2}{1\,mL} \times \dfrac{1\,kg}{1000\,g} = 0.06305 = 0.0631\,kg\,CS_2$

$MM = \dfrac{5.39\,g\,unknown}{0.333\,m \times 0.06305\,kg\,CS_2} = 257 = 2.6 \times 10^2\,g/mol$

13.103 $M = \dfrac{\Pi}{RT} = \dfrac{57.1\,torr}{298\,K} \times \dfrac{1\,atm}{760\,torr} \times \dfrac{K \cdot mol}{0.08206\,L \cdot atm} = 3.072 \times 10^{-3} = 3.07 \times 10^{-3}\,M$

$\dfrac{0.036\,g\,solute}{100\,g\,H_2O} \times \dfrac{1000\,g\,H_2O}{1\,kg\,H_2O} = 0.36\,g\,solute/kg\,H_2O$

Assuming molarity and molality are the same in this dilute solution, we can then say
0.36 g solute $= 3.072 \times 10^{-3}$ mol; MM $= 117$ g/mol. Because the salt is completely ionized,
the formula weight of the lithium salt is **twice** this calculated value, or **234 g/mol**. The
organic portion, $C_nH_{2n+1}O_2^-$, has a formula weight of 234–7 = 227 g. Subtracting 32 for
the oxygens, and 1 to make the formula C_nH_{2n}, we have C_nH_{2n}, MM = 194 g/mol. Since
each CH_2 unit has a mass of 14, n $\approx$ 194/14 $\approx$ 14. The formula for our salt is $LiC_{14}H_{29}O_2$.

Integrative Exercises

13.105 $\dfrac{0.015\,g\,N_2}{1\,L\,blood} \times \dfrac{1\,mol\,N_2}{28.01\,g\,N_2} = 5.355 \times 10^{-4} = 5.4 \times 10^{-4}\,mol\,N_2/L\,blood$

At 100 ft, the partial pressure of N_2 in air is 0.78 (4.0 atm) = 3.12 atm. This is just four times the partial pressure of N_2 at 1.0 atm air pressure. According to Henry's law, $S_g = kP_g$, a 4-fold increase in P_g results n a 4-fold increase in S_g, the solubility of the gas. Thus, the solubility of N_2 at 100 ft is $4(5.355 \times 10^{-4}\,M) = 2.142 \times 10^{-3} = 2.1 \times 10^{-3}\,M$. If the diver suddenly surfaces, the amount of N_2/L blood released is the difference in the solubilities at the two depths: $(2.142 \times 10^{-3}\,mol/L - 5.355 \times 10^{-4}\,mol/L) = 1.607 \times 10^{-3} = 1.6 \times 10^{-3}\,mol\,N_2/L\,blood$.

At surface conditions of 1.0 atm external pressure and 37°C = 310 K,

$$V = \frac{nRT}{P} = 1.607 \times 10^{-3}\,mol \times \frac{310\,K}{1.0\,atm} \times \frac{0.08206\,L\text{-}atm}{mol\text{-}K} = 0.041\,L$$

That is, 41 mL of tiny N_2 bubbles are released from each L of blood.

13.106   The stronger the intermolecular forces, the higher the heat (enthalpy) of vaporization.

(a)   None of the substances are capable of hydrogen bonding in the pure liquid, and they have similar molar masses. All intermolecular forces are van der Waals forces, dipole-dipole, and dispersion forces. In decreasing order of strength of forces:

acetone > acetaldehyde > ethylene oxide > cyclopropane

The first three compounds have dipole-dipole and dispersion forces, the last only dispersion forces.

(b)   The order of solubility in hexane should be the reverse of the order above. The least polar substance, propane, will be most soluble in hexane. Ethanol, CH_3CH_2OH, is capable of hydrogen bonding with the three polar compounds. Thus, acetaldehyde, acetone, and ethylene oxide should be more soluble than cyclopropane, but without further information we cannot distinguish among the polar molecules.

13.107   For ionic solids, the exothermic part of the solution process is step (3), surrounding the separated ions by solvent molecules. The released energy comes from the attractive interaction of the solvent with the separated ions. In hydrates, one or more water molecules are already associated with the ions, reducing the total energy released during solvation.

13.109   (a) $Zn(s) + H_2SO_4(aq) \rightarrow ZnSO_4(aq) + H_2(g)$

$2.050\,g\,Zn \times \dfrac{1\,mol\,Zn}{65.39\,g\,Zn} = 0.03135\,mol\,Zn$

$1.00\,M\,H_2SO_4 \times 0.0150\,L = 0.0150\,mol\,H_2SO_4$

Since Zn and H_2SO_4 react in a 1:1 mole ratio, H_2SO_4 is the limiting reactant; 0.0150 mol of $H_2(g)$ are produced.

(b) $P = \dfrac{nRT}{V} = \dfrac{0.0150\,mol}{0.122\,L} \times \dfrac{0.08206\,L\text{-}atm}{mol\text{-}K} \times 298\,K = 3.0066 = 3.01\,atm$

(c) $S_{H_2} = kP_{H_2} = \dfrac{7.8 \times 10^{-4}\,mol}{L\text{-}atm} \times 3.0066\,atm = 0.002345 = 2.3 \times 10^{-3}\,M$

$\dfrac{0.002345\,mol\,H_2}{L\,soln} \times 0.0150\,L = 3.518 \times 10^{-5} = 3.5 \times 10^{-5}\,mol\,dissolved\,H_2$

$\dfrac{3.5 \times 10^{-5}\,mol\,dissolved\,H_2}{0.0150\,mol\,H_2\,produced} \times 100 = 0.23\%\,dissolved\,H_2$

This is approximately 2.3 ppt; for every 10,000 H_2 molecules, 23 are dissolved. It was reasonable to ignore dissolved $H_2(g)$ in part (b).

13.110   (a) $\dfrac{1.3 \times 10^{-3}\,mol\,CH_4}{L\,soln} \times 4.0\,L = 5.2 \times 10^{-3}\,mol\,CH_4$

$V = \dfrac{nRT}{P} = \dfrac{5.2 \times 10^{-3}\,mol \times 273\,K}{1.0\,atm} \times \dfrac{0.08206\,L\text{-}atm}{K\text{-}mol} = 0.12\,L$

(b) All three hydrocarbons are nonpolar; they have zero net dipole moment. In CH_4 and C_2H_6, the C atoms are tetrahedral and all bonds are σ bonds. C_2H_6 has a higher molar mass than CH_4, which leads to stronger dispersion forces and greater water solubility. In C_2H_4, the C atoms are trigonal planar and the π electron cloud is symmetric above and below the plane that contains all the atoms. The π cloud in C_2H_4 is an area of concentrated electron density that experiences attractive forces with the positive ends of H_2O molecules. These forces increase the solubility of C_2H_4 relative to the other hydrocarbons.

(c) The molecules have similar molar masses. NO is most soluble because it is polar. The triple bond in N_2 is shorter than the double bond in O_2. It is more difficult for H_2O molecules to surround the smaller N_2 molecules, so they are less soluble than O_2 molecules.

(d) H_2S and SO_2 are polar molecules capable of hydrogen bonding with water. Hydrogen bonding is the strongest force between neutral molecules and causes the much greater solubility. H_2S is weakly acidic in water. SO_2 reacts with water to form H_2SO_3, a weak acid. The large solubility of SO_2 is a sure sign that a chemical process has occurred.

(e) N_2 and C_2H_4. N_2 is too small to be easily hydrated, so C_2H_4 is more soluble in H_2O.

NO (31) and C_2H_6 (30). The structures of these two molecules are very different, yet they have similar solubilities. NO is slightly polar, but too small to be easily hydrated. The larger C_2H_6 is nonpolar, but more polarizable (stronger dispersion forces).

NO (31) and O_2 (32). The slightly polar NO is more soluble than the slightly larger (longer O=O bond than $N \equiv O$ bond) but nonpolar O_2.

13.112   (a) $\Delta T_f = K_f m = K_f \times \dfrac{\text{mol } C_7H_6O_2}{\text{kg } C_6H_6} = K_f \times \dfrac{g\, C_7H_6O_2}{\text{kg } C_6H_6 \times M\, C_7H_6O_2}$

$MM = \dfrac{K_f \times g\, C_7H_6O_2}{\Delta T_f \times \text{kg } C_6H_6} = \dfrac{5.12 \times 0.55}{0.360 \times 0.032} = 2444.4 = 2.4 \times 10^2 \text{ g/mol}$

(b)   The formula weight of $C_7H_6O_2$ is 122 g/mol. The experimental molar mass is twice this value, indicating that benzoic acid is associated into dimers in benzene solution. This is reasonable, since the carboxyl group, –COOH, is capable of strong hydrogen bonding with itself. Many carboxylic acids exist as dimers in solution.

The structure of benzoic acid dimer in benzene solution is:

13.113 $\chi_{CHCl_3} = \chi_{C_3H_6O} = 0.500$

(a)   For an ideal solution, Raoult's Law is obeyed.

$P_t = P_{CHCl_3} + P_{C_3H_6O}; \quad P_{CHCl_3} = 0.5(300\,\text{torr}) = 150\,\text{torr}$

$P_{C_3H_6O} = 0.5(360\,\text{torr}) = 180\,\text{torr}; \quad P_t = 150\,\text{torr} + 180\,\text{torr} = 330\,\text{torr}$

(b)   The real solution has a lower vapor pressure, 250 torr, than an ideal solution of the same composition, 330 torr. Thus, fewer molecules escape to the vapor phase from the liquid. This means that fewer molecules have sufficient kinetic energy to overcome intermolecular attractions. Clearly, even weak hydrogen bonds such as this one are stronger attractive forces than dipole-dipole or dispersion forces. These hydrogen bonds prevent molecules from escaping to the vapor phase and result in a lower than ideal vapor pressure for the solution. There is essentially no hydrogen bonding in the individual liquids.

(c)   According to Coulomb's law, electrostatic attractive forces lead to an overall lowering of the energy of the system. Thus, when the two liquids mix and hydrogen bonds are formed, the energy of the system is decreased and $\Delta H_{soln} < 0$; the solution process is exothermic.

15 Chemical Equilibrium

Visualizing Concepts

15.2 Yes. The first box is pure reactant A. As the reaction proceeds, some A changes to B. In the fourth and fifth boxes, the relative amounts (concentrations) of A and B are constant. Although the reaction is ongoing the rates of A → B and B → A are equal, and the relative amounts of A and B are constant.

15.3 *Analyze.* Given box diagram and reaction type, determine whether K > 1 for the equilibrium mixture depicted in the box.

Plan. Assign species in the box to reactants and products. Write an equilibrium expression in terms of concentrations. Find the relationship between numbers of molecules and concentration. Calculate K.

Solve. Let red = A, blue = X, red and blue pairs = AX. (The colors of A and X are arbitrary.) There are 3A, 2B, and 8AX in the box.

M = mol/L. Since moles is a counting unit for particles, mol ratios and particle ratios are equivalent. We can use numbers of particles in place of moles in the molarity formula. V = 1 L, so in this case, [A] = number of A particles.

$$K = \frac{[AX]}{[A][X]}; \quad [AX] = 8/V = 8; [A] = 3/V = 3; [X] = 2/V = 2. \quad K = \frac{8}{[3][2]} = \frac{8}{6} = 1.33$$

15.5 *Analyze/Plan.* The reaction with the largest equilibrium constant has the largest ratio of products to reactants. Count product and reactant molecules. Calculate ratios and compare. *Solve.*

$$K = \frac{[C_2H_4X_2]}{[C_2H_4][X_2]}. \quad \text{Use numbers of molecules as an adequate measure of concentration.}$$

(While the volume terms don't cancel, they are the same for all parts. For the purpose of comparison, we can ignore volume.) *Solve.*

(a) 8 $C_2H_4Cl_2$, 2 Cl_2, 2 C_2H_4. $K = \dfrac{8}{(2)(2)} = 2$

(b) 6 $C_2H_4Br_2$, 4 Br_2, 4 C_2H_4. $K = \dfrac{6}{(4)(4)} = 0.375 = 0.4$

(c) 3 $C_2H_4I_2$, 7 I_2, 7 C_2H_4. $K = \dfrac{3}{(7)(7)} = 0.0612 = 0.06$

From the smallest to the largest equilibrium constant, (c) < (b) < (a).

Check. By inspection, there are the fewest product molecules and the most reactant molecules in (c); most product and least reactant in (a).

15.7   For the reaction $A_2(g) + B(g) \rightleftharpoons A(g) + AB(g)$, $\Delta n = 0$ and $K_p = K_c$. We can evaluate the equilibrium expression in terms of concentration. Also since $\Delta n = 0$, the volume terms in the expression cancel and we can use number of particles as a measure of moles and molarity. The mixture contains 2A, 4AB and $2A_2$.

$$K_c = \frac{[A][AB]}{[A_2][B]} = \frac{(2)(4)}{(2)(B)} = 2; B = 2$$

2 B atoms should be added to the diagram.

15.8   *Analyze.* Given the diagram and reaction type, calculate the equilibrium constant K_c.

Plan. Analyze the contents of the cylinder. Express them as concentrations, using number of particles as a measure of moles, and $V = 1$ L. Write the equilibrium expression in terms of concentration and calculate K_c.   *Solve.*

(a)   The mixture contains $2A_2$, 2B, 4AB. $[A_2] = 2$, $[B] = 2$, $[AB] = 4$.

$$K_c = \frac{[AB]^2}{[A_2][B]^2} = \frac{(4)^2}{(2)(2)^2} = 2$$

(b)   A decrease in volume favors the reaction with fewer particles. This reaction has two particles in products and three in reactants, so a decrease in volume favors products. The number of AB (product) molecules will increase.

Note that a change in volume does not change the value of K_c. If V decreases, the number of AB molecules must increase in order to maintain the equilibrium value of K_c.

15.10   (a)   Exothermic. In both reaction mixtures (orange and blue), [AB] decreases as T increases.

(b)   In the reaction, there are fewer moles of gas in products than reactants, so greater pressure favors production of products. At any single temperature, [AB] is greater at P = y than at P = x. Since the concentration of the product, AB, is greater at P = y, P = y is the greater pressure.

Equilibrium; The Equilibrium Constant

15.12   (a) $K_c = \frac{[C][D]}{[A][B]}$; if K_c is large, the numerator of the K_c expression is much greater than the denominator and products will predominate at equilibrium.

(b) $K_c = k_f / k_r$; if K_c is large, k_f is larger than k_r and the forward reaction has the greater rate constant.

15.14   (a) $K_c = \dfrac{[O_2]^3}{[O_3]^2}$ (b) $K_c = \dfrac{1}{[Cl_2]^2}$

(c) $K_c = \dfrac{[C_2H_6]^2[O_2]}{[C_2H_4]^2[H_2O]^2}$ (d) $K_c = \dfrac{[CH_4]}{[H_2]^2}$

(e) $K_c = \dfrac{[Cl_2]^2}{[HCl]^4[O_2]}$

homogeneous: (a), (c); heterogeneous: (b), (d), (e)

15.16   (a)   equilibrium lies to right, favoring products ($K_c \gg 1$)

   (b)   equilibrium lies to left, favoring reactants ($K_c \ll 1$)

15.18 $SO_2(g) + Cl_2(g) \rightleftharpoons SO_2Cl_2(g)$, $K_p = 34.5$. $\Delta n = 1 - 2 = -1$

   $K_p = K_c(RT)^{\Delta n}$; $34.5 = K_c(RT)^{-1} = K_c/RT$;

   $K_c = 34.5\ RT = 34.5(0.08206)(303) = 857.81 = 858$

15.20 $2H_2(g) + S_2(g) \rightleftharpoons 2H_2S(g)$, $K_c = 1.08 \times 10^7$ at 700°C. $\Delta n = 2 - 3 = -1$.

   (a) $K_p = K_c(RT)^{\Delta n} = 700°C + 273 = 973\ K$.

   $K_p = 1.08 \times 10^7\ (RT)^{-1} = \dfrac{1.08 \times 10^7}{(0.08206)(973)} = 1.35 \times 10^5$

   (b)   Both K_p and K_c are much greater than one, so the product, H_2S, is **favored** at equilibrium. The equilibrium mixture contains mostly H_2S.

15.22 $K_p = \dfrac{P_{HCl}^4 \times P_{O_2}}{P_{Cl_2}^2 \times P_{H_2O}^2} = 0.0752$

   (a) $K_p = \dfrac{P_{Cl_2}^2 \times P_{H_2O}^2}{P_{HCl}^4 \times P_{O_2}} = \dfrac{1}{0.0752} = 13.298 = 13.3$

   (b) $K_p = \dfrac{P_{HCl}^2 \times P_{O_2}^{1/2}}{P_{Cl_2} \times P_{H_2O}} = (0.0752)^{1/2} = 0.2742 = 0.274$

   (c) $K_p = K_c(RT)^{\Delta n}$; $\Delta n = 2.5 - 2 = 0.5$; $T = 480°C + 273 = 753\ K$

   $K_p = K_c(RT)^{1/2}$, $K_c = K_p/(RT)^{1/2} = 0.2742/[0.08206 \times 753]^{1/2} = 0.03488 = 0.0349$

15.24 $2NO(g) + Br_2(g) \rightleftharpoons 2NOBr(g)$ $K_1 = 2.0$

          $N_2(g) + O_2(g) \rightleftharpoons 2NO(g)$ $K_2 = \dfrac{1}{2.1 \times 10^{30}}$

   _____

   $2NO(g) + Br_2(g) + N_2(g) + O_2(g) \rightleftharpoons 2NOBr(g) + 2NO(g)$

          $N_2(g) + O_2(g) + Br_2(g) \rightleftharpoons 2NOBr(g)$

   $K_c = K_1 \times K_2 = 2.0 \times \dfrac{1}{2.1 \times 10^{30}} = 9.524 \times 10^{-31} = 9.5 \times 10^{-31}$

15.26   (a) $K_p = 1/P_{SO_2}$

   (b) Na_2O is a pure solid. The molar concentration, the ratio of moles of a substance to volume occupied by the substance, is a constant for pure solids and liquids.

Calculating Equilibrium Constants

15.28 $[CH_3OH] = \dfrac{0.0406 \text{ mol}}{2.00 \text{ L}} = 0.0203 \text{ M}$

$[CO] = \dfrac{0.170 \text{ mol CO}}{2.00 \text{ L}} = 0.0850 \text{ M}; \quad [H_2] = \dfrac{0.302 \text{ mol } H_2}{2.00 \text{ L}} = 0.151 \text{ M}$

$K_c = \dfrac{[CH_3OH]}{[CO][H_2]^2} = \dfrac{0.0203}{(0.0850)(0.151)^2} = 10.4743 = 10.5$

15.30 (a) $K_p = \dfrac{P_{PCl_5}}{P_{PCl_3} \times P_{Cl_2}} = \dfrac{1.30 \text{ atm}}{0.124 \text{ atm} \times 0.157 \text{ atm}} = 66.8$

(b) Since $K_p > 1$, products (the numerator of the K_p expression) are favored over reactants (the denominator of the K_p expression).

15.32 (a) Calculate the concentrations of $H_2(g)$ and $Br_2(g)$ and the equilibrium concentration of $H_2(g)$. $M = \text{mol/L}$.

$[H_2]_{init} = 1.374 \text{ g } H_2 \times \dfrac{1 \text{ mol } H_2}{2.0159 \text{ g } H_2} \times \dfrac{1}{2.00 \text{ L}} = 0.34079 = 0.341 \text{ M}$

$[Br_2] = 70.31 \text{ g } Br_2 \times \dfrac{1 \text{ mol } Br_2}{159.81 \text{ g } Br_2} \times \dfrac{1}{2.00 \text{ L}} = 0.21998 = 0.220 \text{ M}$

$[H_2]_{equil} = 0.566 \text{ g } H_2 \times \dfrac{1 \text{ mol } H_2}{2.0159 \text{ g } H_2} \times \dfrac{1}{2.00 \text{ L}} = 0.14038 = 0.140 \text{ M}$

	$H_2(g)$	+	$Br_2(g)$	$\rightleftharpoons$	$2HBr(g)$
initial	0.34079 M		0.21998 M		0
change	−0.20041 M		−0.20041 M		+2(0.20041) M
equil.	0.14038 M		0.01957 M		0.40082 M

The change in H_2 is (0.34079 − 0.14038 = 0.20041 = 0.200). The changes in $[Br_2]$ and [HBr] are set by stoichiometry, resulting in the equilibrium concentrations shown in the table.

(b) $K_c = \dfrac{[HBr]^2}{[H_2][Br_2]} = \dfrac{(0.40082)^2}{(0.14038)(0.01957)} = \dfrac{(0.401)^2}{(0.140)(0.020)} = 58.48 = 58$

The equilibrium concentration of Br_2 has 3 decimal places and 2 sig figs, so the value of K_c has 2 sig figs.

15.34 (a)

	$N_2O_4(g)$	$\rightleftharpoons$	$2NO_2(g)$
initial	1.500 atm		1.000 atm
change	+0.244 atm		−0.488 atm
equil	1.744 atm		0.512 atm

The change in P_{NO_2} is (1.000 − 0.512) = −0.488 atm, so the change in $P_{N_2O_4}$ is +(0.488/2) = +0.244 atm.

(b) $K_p = \dfrac{P_{NO_2}^2}{P_{N_2O_4}} = \dfrac{(0.512)^2}{(1.744)} = 0.1503 = 0.150$

Applications of Equilibrium Constants

15.36   (a)   If the value of Q_c equals the value of K_c, the system is at equilibrium.

       (b)   In the direction of less products (more reactants), to the left.

       (c) $Q_c = 0$ if the concentration of any product is zero.

15.38   Calculate the reaction quotient in each case, compare with

$$K_p = \frac{P_{NH_3}^2}{P_{N_2} \times P_{H_2}^3} = 4.51 \times 10^{-5}$$

       (a) $Q = \dfrac{(98)^2}{(45)(55)^3} = 1.3 \times 10^{-3}$

Since $Q > K_p$, the reaction will shift toward reactants to achieve equilibrium.

       (b) $Q = \dfrac{(57)^2}{(143)(0)^3} = \infty$

Since $Q > K_p$, reaction must shift shift toward reactants to achieve equilibrium. There must be some N_2 present to achieve equilibrium. In this example, the only source of N_2 is the decomposition of NH_3.

       (c) $Q = \dfrac{(13)^2}{(27)(82)^3} = 1.1 \times 10^{-5}$; Q is only slightly less than K_p, so the reaction will

shift slightly toward products to achieve equilibrium.

15.40 $K_p = \dfrac{P_{SO_3}^2}{P_{SO_2}^2 \times P_{O_2}}$; $P_{SO_3} = \left(K_p \times P_{SO_2}^2 \times P_{O_2} \right)^{1/2} = [(0.345)(0.135)^2(0.455)]^{1/2} = 0.0535$ atm

15.42   (a) $K_c = \dfrac{[I]^2}{[I_2]} = 3.1 \times 10^{-5}$

$$[I] = \frac{2.67 \times 10^{-2} \text{ g I}}{10.0 \text{ L}} \times \frac{1 \text{ mol I}}{126.9 \text{ g I}} = 2.1040 \times 10^{-5} = 2.10 \times 10^{-5} M$$

$$[I_2] = \frac{[I]^2}{K_c} = \frac{(2.104 \times 10^{-5})^2}{3.1 \times 10^{-5}} = 1.428 \times 10^{-5} = 1.43 \times 10^{-5} M$$

$$\frac{1.428 \times 10^{-5} \text{ mol I}_2}{L} \times 10.0 \text{ L} \times \frac{253.8 \text{ g I}_2}{\text{mol I}_2} = M = 0.0362 \text{ g I}_2$$

Check. $K_c = \dfrac{(2.104 \times 10^{-5})^2}{1.428 \times 10^{-5}} = 3.1 \times 10^{-5}$

(b) $PV = nRT; P = \dfrac{gRT}{MM\ V}$

$P_{SO_3} = \dfrac{1.17\ g\ SO_3}{80.06\ g/mol} \times \dfrac{0.08206\ L\text{-}atm}{K\text{-}mol} \times \dfrac{700\ K}{2.00\ L} = 0.4197 = 0.420\ atm$

$P_{O_2} = \dfrac{0.105\ g\ O_2}{32.00\ g/mol} \times \dfrac{0.08206\ L\text{-}atm}{K\text{-}mol} \times \dfrac{700\ K}{2.00\ L} = 0.09424 = 0.0942\ atm$

$K_p = 3.0 \times 10^4 = \dfrac{P_{SO_3}^2}{P_{SO_2}^2 \times P_{O_2}}; P_{SO_2} = \left[P_{SO_3}^2 /(K_p)(P_{O_2}) \right]^{1/2}$

$P_{SO_2} = [(0.4197)^2 /(3.0 \times 10^4)(0.09424)]^{1/2} = 7.894 \times 10^{-3} = 7.9 \times 10^{-3}\ atm$

$g\ SO_2 = \dfrac{MM\ PV}{RT} = \dfrac{64.06\ g\ SO_2}{mol\ SO_2} \times \dfrac{K\text{-}mol}{0.08206\ L\text{-}atm} \times \dfrac{7.894 \times 10^{-3}\ atm \times 2.00\ L}{700\ K}$

$= 0.01761 = 0.018\ g\ SO_2$

Check. $K_p = [(0.4197)^2 /(7.894 \times 10^{-3})^2(0.09424] = 3.0 \times 10^4$

15.44 $[Br_2] = [Cl_2] = 0.30\ mol/1.0\ L = 0.30\ M$

	$Br_2(g)$	+	$Cl_2(g)$	$\rightleftharpoons$	$2BrCl(g)$	$K_c = \dfrac{[BrCl]^2}{[Br_2][Cl_2]} = 7.0$
initial	0.30 M		0.30 M		0	
change	–x		–x		+2x	
equil.	(0.30 – x)		(0.30 – x)		+2x	

$7.0 = \dfrac{(2x)^2}{(0.30 - x)^2}$ (We can solve this exactly by taking the square root of both sides.)

$(7.0)^{1/2} = \dfrac{2x}{0.30 - x}$, $2.646(0.30 - x) = 2x$, $0.7937 = 4.646x$, $x = 0.1709 = 0.17\ M$

$[BrCl] = 2x = 0.3417 = 0.34\ M; [Br_2] = [Cl_2] = 0.30 - x = 0.1291 = 0.13\ M$

Check. $K_c = (0.3417)^2 /(0.1291)^2 = 7.0$

15.46 $K_c = [NH_3][H_2S] = 1.2 \times 10^{-4}$. Because of the stoichiometry, equilibrium concentrations of H_2S and NH_3 will be equal; call this quantity y. Then, $y^2 = 1.2 \times 10^{-4}$, $y = 0.010954 = 0.011\ M$.

15.48   (a)   *Analyze/Plan.* If only $PH_3BCl_3(s)$ is present initially, the equation requires that the equilibrium concentrations of $PH_3(g)$ and $BCl_3(g)$ are equal. Write the K_c expression and solve for $x = [PH_3] = [BCl_3]$.   *Solve.*

$K_c = [PH_3][BCl_3]; 1.87 \times 10^{-3} = x^2; x = 0.043243 = 0.0432\ M\ PH_3$ and BCl_3

(b)   Since the mole ratios are 1:1:1, mol $PH_3BCl_3(s)$ required = mol PH_3 or BCl_3 produced.

$$\frac{0.043243 \, \text{mol PH}_3}{\text{L}} \times 0.500 \, \text{L} = 0.02162 = 0.0216 \, \text{mol PH}_3 = 0.0216 \, \text{mol PH}_3\text{BCl}_3$$

$$0.02162 \, \text{mol PH}_3\text{BCl}_3 \times \frac{151.2 \, \text{g PH}_3\text{BCl}_3}{1 \, \text{mol PH}_3\text{BCl}_3} = 3.269 = 3.27 \, \text{g PH}_3\text{BCl}_3$$

In fact, some $PH_3BCl_3(s)$ must remain for the system to be in equilibrium, so a bit more than 3.27 g PH_3BCl_3 is needed.

15.50 $CaCrO_4(s) \rightleftharpoons Ca^{2+}(aq) + CrO_4{}^{2-}(aq)$ $K_c = [Ca^{2+}][CrO_4{}^{2-}] = 7.1 \times 10^{-4}$

At equilibrium, $[Ca^{2+}] = [CrO_4{}^{2-}] = x$

$K_c = 7.1 \times 10^{-4} = x^2$, $x = 0.0266 = 0.027 \, M \, Ca^{2+}$ and $CrO_4{}^{2-}$

LeChâtelier's Principle

15.52 $4NH_3(g) + 5O_2(g) \rightleftharpoons 4NO(g) + 6 H_2O(g)$

(a)   increase $[NH_3]$, increase yield NO

(b)   increase $[H_2O]$, decrease yield NO

(c)   decrease $[O_2]$, decrease yield NO

(d)   decrease container volume, decrease yield NO (fewer moles gas in reactants)

(e)   add catalyst, no change

(f)   increase temperature, decrease yield NO (reaction is exothermic)

15.54   (a)   The reaction must be endothermic $(+\Delta H)$ if heating increases the fraction of products.

(b)   There must be more moles of gas in the products if increasing the volume of the vessel increases the fraction of products.

15.56   (a) $\Delta H° = \Delta H_f° \, CH_3OH(g) - \Delta H_f° \, CO(g) - 2\Delta H_f° \, H_2(g)$

$= -201.2 \, \text{kJ} - (-110.5 \, \text{kJ}) - 0 \, \text{kJ}$

$= -90.7 \, \text{kJ}$

(b)   The reaction is exothermic; an increase in temperature would decrease the value of K and decrease the yield. A low temperature is needed to maximize yield.

(c)   Increasing total pressure would increase the partial pressure of each gas, shifting the equilibrium toward products. The extent of conversion to CH_3OH increases as the total pressure increases.

Additional Exercises

15.58 $2A(g) \rightleftharpoons B(g)$, $K_c = 1$

$\frac{[B]}{[A]^2} = 1$, $[B] = [A]^2$ and $[A] = [B]^{1/2}$

15.59 $CH_4(g) + H_2O(g) \rightarrow CO(g) + 3H_2(g)$

$$K_p = \frac{P_{CO} \times P_{H_2}^3}{P_{CH_4} \times P_{H_2O}} \, ; P = \frac{g\,RT}{MM\,V} \, ; T = 1000\,K$$

$$P_{CO} = \frac{8.62\,g}{28.01\,g/mol} \times \frac{0.08206\,L\text{-}atm}{mol\text{-}K} \times \frac{1000\,K}{5.00\,L} = 5.0507 = 5.05\,atm$$

$$P_{H_2} = \frac{2.60\,g}{2.016\,g/mol} \times \frac{0.08206\,L\text{-}atm}{mol\text{-}K} \times \frac{1000\,K}{5.00\,L} = 21.1663 = 21.2\,atm$$

$$P_{CH_4} = \frac{43.0\,g}{16.04\,g/mol} \times \frac{0.08206\,L\text{-}atm}{mol\text{-}K} \times \frac{1000\,K}{5.00\,L} = 43.9973 = 44.0\,atm$$

$$P_{H_2O} = \frac{48.4\,g}{18.02\,g/mol} \times \frac{0.08206\,L\text{-}atm}{mol\text{-}K} \times \frac{1000\,K}{5.00\,L} = 44.0811 = 44.1\,atm$$

$$K_p = \frac{(5.0507)(21.1663)^3}{(43.9973)(44.0811)} = 24.6949 = 24.7$$

$$K_p = K_c(RT)^{\Delta n}, \, K_c = K_p/(RT)^{\Delta n} \, ; \, \Delta n = 4 - 2 = 2$$

$$K_c = (24.6949)/[(0.08206)(1000)]^2 = 3.6673 \times 10^{-3} = 3.67 \times 10^{-3}$$

15.61   (a) $H_2(g) + S(s) \rightleftharpoons H_2S(g)$ $K_c = [H_2S]/[H_2]$

(b)   Calculate the molarities of H_2S and H_2.

$$[H_2S] = \frac{0.46\,g}{34.1\,g/mol} \times \frac{1}{1.0\,L} = 0.01349 = 0.013\,M$$

$$[H_2] = \frac{0.40\,g}{2.02\,g/mol} \times \frac{1}{1.0\,L} = 0.1980 = 0.20\,M$$

$$K_c = 0.01349/0.1980 = 0.06812 = 0.068$$

(c)   Since S is a pure solid, its concentration doesn't change during the reaction, so [S] does not appear in the equilibrium expression.

15.62   (a) $K_p = \dfrac{P_{Br_2} \times P_{NO}^2}{P_{NOBr}^2} \, ; P = \dfrac{gRT}{PV} \, ; T = 100°C + 273 = 373$

$$P_{Br_2} = \frac{4.19\,g}{159.8\,g/mol} \times \frac{0.08206\,L\text{-}atm}{K\text{-}mol} \times \frac{373}{5.0\,L} = 0.16051 = 0.161\,atm$$

$$P_{NO} = \frac{3.08\,g}{30.01\,g/mol} \times \frac{0.08206\,L\text{-}atm}{K\text{-}mol} \times \frac{373}{5.0\,L} = 0.62828 = 0.628\,atm$$

$$P_{NOBr} = \frac{3.22\,g\,NOBr}{109.9\,g/mol} \times \frac{0.08206\,L\text{-}atm}{K\text{-}mol} \times \frac{373}{5.0\,L} = 0.17936 = 0.179\,atm$$

$$K_p = \frac{(0.16051)(0.62828)^2}{(0.17936)^2} = 1.9695 = 1.97 \qquad K_p = K_c(RT)^{\Delta n}, \, \Delta n = 3 - 2 = 1$$

$$K_c = K_p/RT = 1.9695/(0.08206)(373) = 0.064345 = 0.0643$$

(b) $P_t = P_{Br_2} + P_{NO} + P_{NOBr} = 0.16051 + 0.62828 + 0.17936 = 0.96815 = 0.968\,atm$

15.64 (a) $K_p = \dfrac{P_{NH_3}^2}{P_{N_2} \times P_{H_2}^3} = 4.34 \times 10^{-3}$; $T = 300°C + 273 = 573\,K$

$$P_{NH_3} = \dfrac{gRT}{MM \times V} = \dfrac{1.05\,g}{17.03\,g/mol} \times \dfrac{0.08206\,L\text{-}atm}{K\text{-}mol} \times \dfrac{573\,K}{1.00\,L} = 2.899 = 2.90\,atm$$

	$N_2(g)$ +	$3H_2(g)$	$\rightleftharpoons$	$2NH_3(g)$
initial	0 atm	0 atm		?
change	x	3x		–2x
equil.	x atm	3x atm		2.899 atm

(Remember, only the change line reflects the stoichiometry of the reaction.)

$$K_p = \dfrac{(2.899)^2}{(x)(3x)^3} = 4.34 \times 10^{-3};\ 27\,x^4 = \dfrac{(2.899)^2}{4.34 \times 10^{-3}};\ x^4 = 71.725$$

$x = 2.910 = 2.91\,atm = P_{N_2}$; $P_{H_2} = 3x = 8.730 = 8.73\,atm$

$$g_{N_2} = \dfrac{MM \times PV}{RT} = \dfrac{28.02\,g\,N_2}{mol\,N_2} \times \dfrac{K\text{-}mol}{0.08206\,L\text{-}atm} \times \dfrac{2.910\,atm \times 1.00\,L}{573\,K} = 1.73\,g\,N_2$$

$$g_{H_2} = \dfrac{2.016\,g\,H_2}{mol\,H_2} \times \dfrac{K\text{-}mol}{0.08206\,L\text{-}atm} \times \dfrac{8.730\,atm \times 1.00\,L}{573\,K} = 0.374\,g\,H_2$$

(b)   The initial $P_{NH_3} = 2.899\,atm + 2(2.910\,atm) = 8.719 = 8.72\,atm$

$$g_{NH_3} = \dfrac{17.03\,g\,NH_3}{mol\,NH_3} \times \dfrac{K\text{-}mol}{0.08206\,L\text{-}atm} \times \dfrac{8.719\,atm \times 1.00\,L}{573\,K} = 3.16\,g\,NH_3$$

(c) $P_t = P_{N_2} + P_{H_2} + P_{NH_3} = 2.910\,atm + 8.730\,atm + 2.899\,atm = 14.54\,atm$

15.65

	2IBr	$\rightleftharpoons$	I_2 +	Br_2
initial	0.025 atm		0	0
change	–2x		x	x
equil.	(0.025 – 2x) atm		x	x

$$K_p = 8.5 \times 10^{-3} = \dfrac{P_{I_2} \times P_{Br_2}}{P_{IBr}^2} = \dfrac{x^2}{(0.025-2x)^2};\ \text{Taking the square root of both sides}$$

$$\dfrac{x}{0.025-2x} = (8.5 \times 10^{-3})^{1/2} = 0.0922;\ x = 0.0922(0.025-2x)$$

$x + 0.184x = 0.002305;\ 1.184x = 0.002305;\ x = 0.001947 = 1.9 \times 10^{-3}$

P_{IBr} at equilibrium = $0.025 - 2(1.947 \times 10^{-3}) = 0.02111 = 0.021\,atm$

15.67 $K_p = P_{NH_3} \times P_{H_2S}$; $P_t = 0.614\,atm$

If the equilibrium amounts of NH_3 and H_2S are due solely to the decomposition of $NH_4HS(s)$, the equilibrium pressures of the two gases are equal, and each is 1/2 of the total pressure.

$$P_{NH_3} = P_{H_2S} = 0.614 \text{ atm}/2 = 0.307 \text{ atm}$$

$$K_p = (0.307)^2 = 0.0943$$

15.68   Initial $P_{SO_3} = \dfrac{gRT}{MM\,V} = \dfrac{0.831\,g}{80.07\,g/mol} \times \dfrac{0.08206\,L\text{-}atm}{K\text{-}mol} \times \dfrac{1100\,K}{1.00\,L} = 0.9368 = 0.937 \text{ atm}$

	$2SO_3$	$\rightleftharpoons$	$2SO_2$	$+$	O_2
initial	0.9368 atm		0		0
change	$-2x$		$+2x$		$+x$
equil.	$0.9368-2x$		$2x$		x
[equil.]	0.2104 atm		0.7264 atm		0.3632 atm

$P_t = (0.9368-2x) + 2x + x;\ 0.9368 + x = 1.300 \text{ atm};\ x = 1.300 - 0.9368 = 0.3632 = 0.363 \text{ atm}$

$$K_p = \dfrac{P_{SO_2}^2 \times P_{O_2}}{P_{SO_3}^2} = \dfrac{(0.7264)^2\,(0.3632)}{(0.2104)^2} = 4.3292 = 4.33$$

$K_p = K_p = K_c(RT)^{\Delta n};\ \Delta n = 3 - 2 = 1;\ K_p = K_c(RT)$

$K_c = K_p/RT = 4.3292/[(0.08206)(1100)] = 0.04796 = 0.0480$

15.70 $K_c = [CO_2] = 0.0108;\ [CO_2] = \dfrac{g\,CO_2}{44.01\,g/mol} \times \dfrac{1}{10.0\,L}$

In each case, calculate $[CO_2]$ and determine the position of the equilibrium.

(a) $[CO_2] = \dfrac{4.25\,g}{44.01\,g/mol} \times \dfrac{1}{10.0\,L} = 9.657 \times 10^{-3} = 9.66 \times 10^{-3}\ M$

       $Q = 9.66 \times 10^{-3} > K_c$. The reaction proceeds to the right to achieve equilibrium and the amount of $CaCO_3(s)$ decreases.

(b) $[CO_2] = \dfrac{5.66\,g\,CO_2}{44.01\,g/mol} \times \dfrac{1}{10.0\,L} = 0.0129\ M$

       $Q = 0.0129 > K_c$. The reaction proceeds to the left to achieve equilibrium and the amount of $CaCO_3(s)$ increases.

(c)   6.48 g CO_2 means $[CO_2] > 0.0129\ M$; $Q > 0.0129 > K_c$, the amount of $CaCO_3$ increases.

15.71

	$CO_2(g)$	$+$	$H_2(g)$	$\rightleftharpoons$	$CO(g)$	$+$	$H_2O(g)$
initial	1.50 mol		1.50 mol		0		0
change	$-x$		$-x$		$+x$		$+x$
equil.	$(1.50-x)$mol		$(1.50-x)$mol		x		x

Since $\Delta n = 0$, the volume terms cancel and we can use moles in place of molarity in the K expression.

$$K_c = 0.802 = \frac{[CO][H_2O]}{[CO_2][H_2O]} = \frac{x^2}{(1.50-x)^2}$$

Take the square root of both sides.

$(0.802)^{1/2} = x/(1.50-x);\ 0.8955(1.50-x) = x$

$1.3433 = 1.8955x,\ x = 0.7087 = 0.709$ mol

$[CO] = [H_2O] = 0.7087$ mol$/0.750$ L $= 0.945\ M$

$[CO_2] = [H_2] = (1.50 - 0.709)mol/0.750$ L $= 1.06\ M$

15.72   (a) $[CO_2] = \dfrac{25.0\ g\ CO_2}{44.01\ g\,/\,mol} \times \dfrac{1}{3.00\ L} = 0.18935 = 0.189\ M$

	C(s)	+	CO$_2$(g)	$\rightleftharpoons$	2CO(g)
initial	excess		0.189		0
change	$-x$		$-x$		$+2x$
equil.			0.189$-x$		$+2x$

$K_c = 1.9 = \dfrac{[CO]^2}{[CO_2]} = \dfrac{(2x)^2}{0.189-x};\quad 4x^2 = 1.9(0.189-x);\ 4x^2 + 1.9x - 0.36 = 0.$

Solve the quadratic for x.

$$x = \frac{-1.9 \pm \sqrt{(1.9)^2 - 4(4)(-0.36)}}{2(4)} = 0.14505 = 0.15\ M$$

$[CO] = 2x = 2(0.14505) = 0.2901 = 0.29\ M$

$\dfrac{0.2901\ mol\ CO}{L} \times 3.00\ L \times \dfrac{28.01\ g\ CO}{mol} = 24.38 = 24\ g\ CO$

(b)   The amount of C(s) consumed is related to x. Change M to mol to g C.

$\dfrac{0.14505\ mol}{L} \times 3.00\ L \times 12.01\ g = 5.226 = 5.2\ g\ C$ consumed

(c)   A smaller vessel at the same temperature increases the total pressure of the mixture. The equilibrium shifts to form fewer total moles of gas, which favors reactants. The yield of CO product will be smaller in a smaller vessel.

(d)   If the reaction is endothermic, K is larger at higher temperature. This is confirmed by the two values for K_c, 0.133 at 298 k and 1.0 at 1000 K.

15.74   (a)

	CCl$_4$(g)	$\rightleftharpoons$	C(s) + 2Cl$_2$(g)
initial	2.00 atm		0 atm
change	$-x$ atm		$+2x$ atm
equil.	(2.00$-x$) atm		2x atm

$$K_p = 0.76 = \frac{P_{Cl_2}^2}{P_{CCl_4}} = \frac{(2x)^2}{(2.00-x)}$$

$1.52 - 0.76x = 4x^2$; $4x^2 + 0.76x - 1.52 = 0$

Using the quadratic formula, $a = 4$, $b = 0.76$, $c = -1.52$

$$x = \frac{-0.76 \pm \sqrt{(0.76)^2 - 4(4)(-1.52)}}{2(4)} = \frac{-0.76 + 4.99}{8} = 0.5287 = 0.53 \text{ atm}$$

Fraction CCl_4 reacted $= \dfrac{x \text{ atm}}{2.00 \text{ atm}} = \dfrac{0.53}{2.00} = 0.264 = 26\%$

(b) $P_{Cl_2} = 2x = 2(0.5287) = 1.06 \text{ atm}$

$P_{CCl_4} = 2.00 - x = 2.00 - 0.5287 = 1.47 \text{ atm}$

15.75   (a) $Q = \dfrac{P_{PCl_5}}{P_{PCl_3} \times P_{Cl_2}} = \dfrac{(0.20)}{(0.50)(0.50)} = 0.80$

0.80 (Q) > 0.0870 (K), the reaction proceeds to the left.

(b)

	$PCl_3(g)$	$+$	$Cl_2(g)$	$\rightleftharpoons$	$PCl_5(g)$
initial	0.50 atm		0.50 atm		0.20 atm
change	$+x$ atm		$+x$ atm		$-x$ atm
equil.	$(0.50 + x)$ atm		$(0.50 + x)$ atm		$(0.20 - x)$ atm

(Since the reaction proceeds to the left, P_{PCl_5} must decrease and P_{PCl_3} and P_{Cl_2} must increase.)

$$K_p = 0.0870 = \frac{(0.20-x)}{(0.50+x)(0.50+x)}; \quad 0.0870 = \frac{(0.20-x)}{(0.250 + 1.00\,x + x^2)}$$

$0.0870(0.250 + 1.00x + x^2) = 0.20 - x$; $-0.17825 + 1.0870x + 0.0870x^2 = 0$

$$x = \frac{-1.0870 \pm \sqrt{(1.0870)^2 - 4(0.0870)(-0.17825)}}{2(0.0870)} = \frac{-1.0870 + 1.1152}{0.174} = 0.162$$

$P_{PCl_3} = (0.50 + 0.162) \text{ atm} = 0.662$ $P_{Cl_2} = (0.50 + 0.162) \text{ atm} = 0.662 \text{ atm}$

$P_{PCl_5} = (0.20 - 0.162) \text{ atm} = 0.038 \text{ atm}$

To two decimal places, the pressures are 0.66, 0.66 and 0.04 atm, respectively. When substituting into the K_p expression, pressures to three decimal places yield a result much closer to 0.0870.

(c)   Increasing the volume of the container favors the process where more moles of gas are produced, so the reverse reaction is favored and the equilibrium shifts to the left; the mole fraction of Cl_2 increases.

(d)   For an exothermic reaction, increasing the temperature decreases the value of K; more reactants and fewer products are present at equilibrium and the mole fraction of Cl_2 increases.

15.77 (a) Since the volume of the vessel = 1.00 L, mol = M. The reaction will proceed to the left to establish equilibrium.

$$A(g) + \quad 2B(g) \quad \rightleftharpoons \quad 2C(g)$$

	A(g) +	2B(g)	2C(g)
initial	0 M	0 M	1.00 M
change	+x M	+2x M	–2x M
equil.	x M	2x M	(1.00 – 2x) M

At equilibrium, [C] = (1.00 – 2x) M, [B] = 2x M.

(b) x must be less than 0.50 M (so that [C], 1.00 –2x, is not less than zero).

(c) $K_c = \dfrac{[C]^2}{[A][B]^2}$; $\dfrac{(1.00-2x)^2}{(x)(2x)^2} = 0.25$

$1.00 - 4x + 4x^2 = 0.25(4x)^3$; $x^3 - 4x^2 + 4x - 1 = 0$

(d)

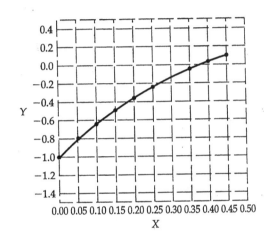

X	Y
0.0	−1.000
0.05	−0.810
0.10	−0.639
0.15	−0.487
0.20	−0.352
0.25	−0.234
0.35	−0.047
0.40	+0.024
0.45	+0.081
~0.383	0.00

(e) From the plot, x ≈ 0.383 M

[A] = x = 0.383 M; [B] = 2x = 0.766 M

[C] = 1.00 – 2x = 0.234 M

Using the K_c expression as a check:

$K_c = 0.25$; $\dfrac{(0.234)^2}{(0.383)(0.766)^2} = 0.24$; the estimated values are reasonable.

15.78 $K_p = \dfrac{P_{O_2} \times P_{CO}^2}{P_{CO_2}^2} \approx 1 \times 10^{-13}$; $P_{O_2} = (0.03)(1\text{ atm}) = 0.03$ atm

$P_{CO} = (0.002)(1\text{ atm}) = 0.002$ atm; $P_{CO_2} = (0.12)(1\text{ atm}) = 0.12$ atm

$Q = \dfrac{(0.03)(0.002)^2}{(0.12)^2} = 8.3 \times 10^{-6} = 8 \times 10^{-6}$

Since Q > K_p, the system will shift to the left to attain equilibrium. Thus a catalyst that promoted the attainment of equilibrium would result in a lower CO content in the exhaust.

15 Chemical Equilibrium

Integrative Exercises

15.81 (a) (i) $K_c = [Na^+]/[Ag^+]$

(ii) $K_c = [Hg^{2+}]^3 / [Al^{3+}]^2$

(iii) $K_c = [Zn^{2+}][H_2] / [H^+]^2$

(b) According to Table 4.5, the activity series of the metals, a metal can be oxidized by any metal cation below it on the table.

(i) Ag^+ is far below Na, so the reaction will proceed to the right and K_c will be large.

(ii) Al^{3+} is above Hg, so the reaction will not proceed to the right and K_c will be small.

(iii) H^+ is below Zn, so the reaction will proceed to the right and K_c will be large.

(c) $K_c < 1$ for this reaction, so Fe^{2+} (and thus Fe) is above Cd on the table. In other words, Cd is below Fe. The value of K_c, 0.06, is small but not extremely small, so Cd will be only a few rows below Fe.

15.82 (a) $AgCl(s) \rightleftharpoons Ag^+(aq) + Cl^-(aq)$

(b) $K_c = [Ag^+][Cl^-]$

(c) Using thermodynamic data from Appendix C, calculate ΔH for the reaction in part (a).

$$\Delta H° = \Delta H_f^° Ag^+(aq) + \Delta H_f^° Cl^-(aq) - \Delta H_f^° AgCl(s)$$

$$\Delta H° = 105.90 \text{ kJ} - 167.2 \text{ kJ} - (-127.0 \text{ kJ}) = 65.7 \text{ kJ}$$

The reaction is endothermic (heat is a reactant), so the solubility of AgCl(s) in $H_2O(l)$ will increase with increasing temperature.

15.84 Consider the energy profile for an exothermic reaction.

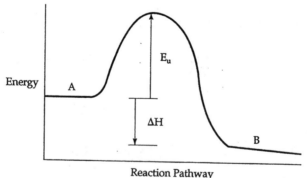

The activation energy in the forward direction, E_{af}, equals E_u, and the activation energy in the reverse reaction, E_{ar}, equals $E_u - \Delta H$. (The same is true for an endothermic reaction because the sign of ΔH is the positive and $E_{ar} < E_{af}$). For the reaction in question,

$$K = \frac{k_f}{k_r} = \frac{A_f e^{-E_{af}/RT}}{A_r e^{-E_{ar}/RT}}$$

Since the ln form of the Arrhenius equation is easier to manipulate, we will consider ln K.

$$\ln K = \ln\left(\frac{k_f}{k_r}\right) = \ln k_f - \ln k_r = \frac{-E_{af}}{RT} + \ln A_f - \left[\frac{-E_{ar}}{RT} + \ln A_r\right]$$

Substituting E_u for E_{af} and $(E_u - \Delta H)$ for E_{ar}

$$\ln K = \frac{-E_u}{RT} + \ln A_f - \left[\frac{-(E_u - \Delta H)}{RT} + \ln A_r\right]; \ \ln K = \frac{-E_u + (E_u - \Delta H)}{RT} + \ln A_f - \ln A_r$$

$$\ln K = \frac{-\Delta H}{RT} + \ln \frac{A_f}{A_r}$$

For the catalyzed reaction, $E_{cat} < E_u$ and $E_{af} = E_{cat}$, $E_{ar} = E_{cat} - \Delta H$. The catalyst does not change the value of ΔH.

$$\ln K_{cat} = \frac{-E_{cat} + (E_{cat} - \Delta H)}{RT} + \ln A_f - \ln A_r$$

$$\ln K_{cat} = \frac{-\Delta H}{RT} + \frac{\ln A_f}{A_r}$$

Thus, assuming A_f and A_r are not changed by the catalyst, $\ln K = \ln K_{cat}$ and $K = K_{cat}$.

15.85 (a) $$P = \frac{gRT}{MM\ V} = \frac{0.300\,g\,H_2S}{34.08\ g/mol\ H_2S} \times \frac{298\,K}{5.00\,L} \times \frac{0.08206\ L\text{-}atm}{mol\text{-}K} = 0.043053$$
$$= 0.0431\ atm$$

(b) $K_p = P_{NH_3} \times P_{H_2S}$. Before solid is added, $Q = P_{NH_3} \times P_{H_2S} = 0 \times 0.0431 = 0$.

Q < K and the reaction will proceed to the right. However, no $NH_4SH(s)$ is present to produce $NH_3(g)$, so the reaction cannot proceed.

(c)

	$NH_4SH(s)$ $\rightleftharpoons$	$NH_3(g)$	+	$H_2S(g)$
initial		0 atm		0.043053 atm
change		+x atm		+x atm
equil.		+x atm		(0.043053+x) atm

Since Q < K initially [part (a)], P_{H_2S} must increase along with P_{NH_3} until equilibrium is established.

$$K_p = P_{NH_3} \times P_{H_2S}; 0.120 = (x)(0.043053 + x); 0 = x^2 + 0.043053\,x - 0.120$$

Solve for x using the quadratic formula.

$$x = \frac{-0.043053 \pm \sqrt{(0.043053)^2 - 4(1)(-0.120)}}{2(1)}; \quad x = 0.3256 = 0.326 \text{ atm}$$

$$P_{NH_3} = 0.326 \text{ atm}; \quad P_{H_2S} = (0.043053 + 0.3256) \text{ atm} = 0.3686 = 0.369 \text{ atm}$$

(d) $\quad \chi_{H_2S} = \dfrac{P_{H_2S}}{P_t} = \dfrac{0.3686 \text{ atm}}{(0.3256 + 0.3686) \text{ atm}} = 0.531$

(e) The minimum amount of $NH_4HS(s)$ required is slightly greater than the number of moles NH_3 present at equilibrium. We can calculate the mol NH_3 present at equilibrium using the ideal-gas equation.

$$n_{NH_3} = \frac{P_{NH_3}V}{RT} = 0.3256 \text{ atm} \times \frac{K \text{-mol}}{0.08206 \text{ L-atm}} \times \frac{5.00 \text{ L}}{298 \text{ K}} = 0.06657$$

$$= 0.0666 \text{ mol } NH_3$$

$$0.06657 \text{ mol } H_2S \times \frac{1 \text{ mol } NH_4SH}{1 \text{ mol } H_2S} \times \frac{51.12 \text{ g } NH_4SH}{1 \text{ mol } NH_4SH} = 3.40 \text{ g } NH_4SH$$

The minimum amount is slightly greater than 3.40 g NH_4HS.

15.87 (a) $\quad H_2O(l) \rightleftharpoons H_2O(g); \quad K_p = P_{H_2O}$

(b) At 30°C, the vapor pressure of $H_2O(l)$ is 31.82 torr. $K_P = P_{H_2O} = 31.82$ torr

$K_p = 31.82 \text{ torr} \times 1 \text{ atm}/760 \text{ torr} = 0.041868 = 0.04187 \text{ atm}$

(c) From part (b), the value of K_p is the vapor pressure of the liquid at that temperature. By definition, vapor pressure = atmospheric pressure = 1 atm at the normal boiling point. $K_p = 1$ atm

15.88 (a)

C-C B.O. = 1   C=C B.O. = 2

(b) $\Delta H = D$ (bond breaking) – D (bond making)

E1: $\quad \Delta H = D(C=Cl) - D(C-Cl) - D(C-C) - 2D(C-Cl)$

$\quad\quad \Delta H = 614 + 242 - 348 - 2(328) = -148 \text{ kJ}$

E2: $\quad \Delta H = D(C-C) + D(C-H) + D(C-Cl) - D(C=C) - D(H-Cl)$

$\quad\quad = 348 + 413 + 328 - 614 - 431 = 44 \text{ kJ}$

(c) E1 is exothermic with $\Delta n = -1$. The yield of $C_2H_4Cl_2(g)$ would decrease with increasing temperature and with increasing container volume.

(d) E2 is endothermic with $\Delta n = 1$. The yield of C_2H_3Cl would increase with increasing temperature and with increasing container volume.

(e) The boiling points of the reactants and products are: C_2H_4, –103.7°C; Cl_2, –34.6°C, $C_2H_4Cl_2$, +83.5°C; C_2H_3Cl, –13.4°C; HCl, –84.9°C.

Because the products of E1 and E2 are optimized by different conditions, carry out the two equilibria in separate reactors. Since E1 is exothermic and $\Delta n = -1$, the reactor on the left should be as small and cold as possible to maximize yield of $C_2H_4Cl_2$. At temperatures below 83.5°C, $C_2H_4Cl_2$ will condense to the liquid and it can be easily transferred to the second (right) reactor.

Since E_2 is endothermic, the reactor on the right should be as large and hot as possible to optimize production of C_2H_3Cl. The outlet stream will be a mixture of $C_2H_3Cl(g)$, $C_2H_4Cl_2(g)$, and $HCl(g)$. This mixture could be run through a heat exchanger to condense and subsequently recycle $C_2H_4Cl_2(l)$. Since HCl has a lower boiling point than C_2H_3Cl, it cannot be removed by condensation. The $C_2H_3Cl(g)$ / $HCl(g)$ mixture could be bubbled through a basic aqueous solution such as $NaHCO_3(aq)$ or $NaOH(aq)$ to remove $HCl(g)$, leaving pure $C_2H_3Cl(g)$.

Other details of reactor design such as the use of catalysts to speed up these reactions, the exact costs and benefits of heat exchange, recycling unreacted components, and separation and recovery of products are issues best resolved by chemical engineers.

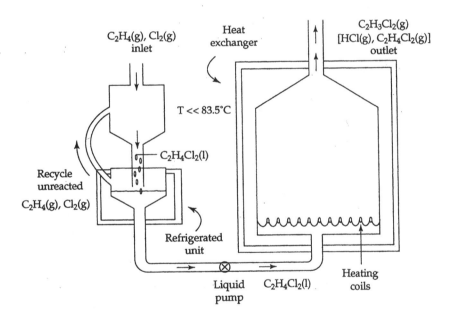

18 Chemistry of the Environment

Visualizing Concepts

18.2   Molecules in the upper atmosphere tend to have multiple bonds because they have sufficiently high bond dissociation enthalpies (Table 8.4) to survive the incoming high energy radiation from the sun. According to Table 8.4, for the same two bonded atoms, multiple bonds have higher bond dissociation enthalpies than single bonds. Molecules with single bonds are likely to undergo photodissociation in the presence of the high energy, short wavelength solar radiation present in the upper atmosphere.

18.4   *Analyze.* Given granite, marble, bronze, and other solid materials, what observations and measurements indicate whether the material is appropriate for an outdoor sculpture? If the material changes (erodes) over time, what chemical processes are responsible?

Plan. An appropriate material resists chemical and physical changes when exposed to environmental conditions. An inappropriate material undergoes chemical reactions with substances in the troposphere, degrading the structural strength of the material and the sculpture.   *Solve.*

(a)   The appearance and mass of the material upon environmental exposure are both indicators of chemical and physical changes. If the appearance and mass of the material are unchanged after a period of time, the material is well-suited for the sculpture because it is inert to chemical and physical changes. Changes in the color or texture of the material's surface indicate that a chemical reaction has occurred, because a different substance with different properties has formed. A decrease in mass indicates that some of the material has been lost, either by chemical reaction or physical change. An increase in mass indicates corrosion. If the mass of the material is unchanged, it is probably inert to chemical and physical environmental changes and suitable for sculpture.

(b)   The two main chemical processes that lead to erosion are reaction with acid rain and corrosion or air oxidation, which is encouraged by acid conditions (see Section 20.8).

Acid rain is primarily H_2SO_3 and/or H_2SO_4, which reacts directly with carbonate minerals such as marble and limestone. Acidic conditions created by acid rain encourage corrosion of metals such as iron, steel, and bronze. Corrosion produces metal oxides which may or may not cling to the surface of the material. If the oxides are washed away, the material will lose mass after corrosion. Physical erosion due to the effects of wind and rain on soft materials such as sandstone also causes mass to decrease.

298

18.6 *Analyze/Plan.* Explain how an ion-exchange column "softens" water. See the Closer Look box on "Water Softening" in Section 18.6.

Solve. The plastic beads in an ion-exchange column contain covalently bound anionic groups such as R–COO⁻ and R–SO₃⁻. These groups have Na⁺ cations associated with them for charge balance. When "hard" water containing Ca^{2+} and other divalent cations passes over the beads, the 2+ cations are attracted to the anionic groups and Na⁺ is displaced. The higher charge on the divalent cations leads to greater electrostatic attractions, which promote the cation exchange. The "soft" water that comes out of the column contains two Na⁺ ions in place of each divalent cation, mostly Ca^{2+} and Mg^{2+}, that remains in the column associated with the plastic beads.

18.8 Some of the missing CO_2 is absorbed by "land plants" (vegetation other than trees) and incorporated into the soil. Soil is the largest land-based carbon reservoir. The amount of carbon-storing capacity of soil is affected by erosion, soil fertility, and other complex factors. For more details, search the internet for "carbon budget."

Earth's Atmosphere

18.10 (a) Boundaries between regions of the atmosphere are at maxima and minima (peaks and valleys) in the atmospheric temperature profile. For example, in the troposphere, temperature decreases with altitude, while in the stratosphere, it increases with altitude. The temperature minimum is the tropopause boundary.

(b) Atmospheric pressure in the troposphere ranges from 1.0 atm to 0.4 atm, while pressure in the stratosphere ranges from 0.4 atm to 0.001 atm. Gas density (g/L) is directly proportional to pressure. The much lower density of the stratosphere means it has the smaller mass, despite having a larger volume than the troposphere.

18.12 $P_{Ar} = \chi_{Ar} \times P_{atm}$; $P_{Ar} = 0.00934 \, (96.5 \text{ kPa}) = 0.901 \text{ kPa}$; $0.901 \text{ kPa} \times \dfrac{760 \text{ torr}}{101.325 \text{ kPa}} = 6.76 \text{ torr}$

$P_{CO_2} = \chi_{CO_2} \times P_{atm}$; $P_{CO_2} = 0.000382 \, (96.5 \text{ kPa}) = 0.0369 \text{ kPa}$; $0.0369 \text{ kPa} \times \dfrac{760 \text{ torr}}{101.325 \text{ kPa}}$
$$= 0.276 \text{ torr}$$

18.14 (a) ppm Ne = mol Ne/1×10^6 mol air; $\chi_{Ne} = 1.818 \times 10^{-5}$ mol Ne/mol air

$$\frac{1.818 \times 10^{-5} \text{ mol Ne}}{1 \text{ mol air}} = \frac{x \text{ mol Ne}}{1 \times 10^6 \text{ mol air}}; x = 18.18 \text{ ppm Ne}$$

(b) $P_{Ne} = \chi_{Ne} \times P_{atm} = 1.818 \times 10^{-5} \times 733 \text{ torr} \times \dfrac{1 \text{ atm}}{760 \text{ torr}} = 1.7534 \times 10^{-5}$

$$= 1.75 \times 10^{-5} \text{ atm}$$

T = 292 K

$$\frac{n_{Ne}}{V} = \frac{P_{Ne}}{RT} = \frac{1.7534 \times 10^{-5} \text{ atm}}{292 \text{ K}} \times \frac{\text{K-mol}}{0.08206 \text{ L-atm}} = 7.3176 \times 10^{-7} = 7.32 \times 10^{-7} \text{ mol/L}$$

$$\frac{7.3176 \times 10^{-7} \text{ mol Ne}}{L} \times \frac{6.022 \times 10^{23} \text{ atoms}}{\text{mol}} = 4.4067 \times 10^{17}$$

$$= 4.41 \times 10^{17} \text{ Ne atoms/L}$$

The Upper Atmosphere; Ozone

18.16 $$\frac{339 \times 10^3 \text{ J}}{1 \text{ mol}} \times \frac{1 \text{ mol}}{6.022 \times 10^{23} \text{ molecules}} = 5.6294 \times 10^{-19} = 5.63 \times 10^{-19} \text{ J/molecule}$$

$$\lambda = \frac{hc}{E} = \frac{(6.626 \times 10^{-34} \text{ J-sec})(3.00 \times 10^8 \text{ m/sec})}{5.6294 \times 10^{-19} \text{ J}} = 3.53 \times 10^{-7} \text{ m} = 353 \text{ nm}$$

$$\frac{293 \times 10^3 \text{ J}}{1 \text{ mol}} \times \frac{1 \text{ mol}}{6.022 \times 10^{23} \text{ molecules}} = 4.8655 \times 10^{-19} = 4.87 \times 10^{-19} \text{ J/molecule}$$

$$\lambda = \frac{(6.626 \times 10^{-34} \text{ J-sec})(3.00 \times 10^8 \text{ m/sec})}{4.8655 \times 10^{-19} \text{ J}} = 4.09 \times 10^{-7} \text{ m} = 409 \text{ nm}$$

Photons of wavelengths longer than 409 nm cannot cause rupture of the C–Cl bond in either CF_3Cl or CCl_4.   Photons with wavelengths between 409 and 353 nm can cause C–Cl bond rupture in CCl_4, but not in CF_3Cl.

18.18   Photodissociation of N_2 is relatively unimportant compared to photodissociation of O_2 for two reasons. The bond dissociation energy of N_2, 941 kJ/mol, is much higher than that of O_2, 495 kJ/mol. Photons with a wavelength short enough to photodissociate N_2 are not as abundant as the ultraviolet photons that lead to photodissociation of O_2. Also, N_2 does not absorb these photons as readily as O_2 so even if a short-wavelength photon is available, it may not be absorbed by an N_2 molecule.

18.20   32 e^-, 16 e^- pr

$$
\begin{array}{ccc}
 & :\!\ddot{F}\!: & \\
 & | & \\
:\!\ddot{C}l\!- & C & -\ddot{C}l\!: \\
 & | & \\
 & :\!\ddot{C}l\!: & \\
\end{array}
$$

CFC–11, $CFCl_3$, contains C–Cl bonds that can be cleaved by UV light in the stratosphere to produce Cl atoms. It is chlorine in atomic form that catalyzes the destruction of stratospheric ozone. CFC–11 is chemically inert and resists decomposition in the troposphere, so that it eventually reaches the stratosphere in molecular form.

18.22   Yes. Assuming $CFBr_3$ reaches the stratosphere intact, it contains C–Br bonds that are even more susceptible to cleavage by UV light than C–Cl bonds. According to Table 8.4, the average C–Br bond dissociation energy is 276 kJ/mol, compared to 328 kJ/mol for C–Cl bonds. Once in atomic form, Br atoms catalyze the destruction of ozone by a mechanism similar to that of Cl atoms.

Chemistry of the Troposphere

18.24 Rainwater is naturally acidic due to the presence of $CO_2(g)$ in the atmosphere. All oxides of nonmetals produce acidic solutions when dissolved in water. Even in the absence of polluting gases such as SO_2, SO_3, NO, and NO_2, CO_2 causes rainwater to be acidic. The important equilibria are:

$$CO_2(g) + H_2O(l) \rightleftharpoons H_2CO_3(aq) \rightleftharpoons H^+(aq) + HCO_3^-(aq).$$

18.26 (a) $Fe(s) + O_2(g) + 4H_3O^+(aq) \rightarrow Fe^{2+}(aq) + 6H_2O(l)$

(b) No. Silver is a "noble" metal. It is relatively resistant to oxidation, and much more resistant than iron. In Table 4.5, The Activity Series of Metals in Aqueous Solution, Ag is much, much lower than Fe and it is below hydrogen, while Fe is above hydrogen. This means that Fe is susceptible to oxidation by acid, while Ag is not.

18.28 (a) Visible (Figure 6.4)

(b) $E_{photon} = hc/\lambda = \dfrac{6.626 \times 10^{-34} \text{ J-s} \times 3.00 \times 10^8 \text{ m/s}}{420 \times 10^{-9} \text{ m}} = 4.733 \times 10^{-19}$

$$= 4.73 \times 10^{-19} \text{ J/photon}$$

$$\dfrac{4.733 \times 10^{-19} \text{ J}}{1 \text{ photon}} \times \dfrac{6.022 \times 10^{23} \text{ photons}}{1 \text{ mol}} \times \dfrac{1 \text{ kJ}}{1000 \text{ J}} = 285 \text{ kJ/mol}$$

(c) $\ddot{O}{=}\overset{\cdot}{N}{-}\ddot{\underset{\cdot\cdot}{O}}{:} + h\nu \longrightarrow \ddot{O}{=}\ddot{N}\cdot + {:}\ddot{\underset{\cdot}{O}}\cdot$

18.30 (a) A *greenhouse gas* absorbs energy in the 10,000–30,000 nm or infrared region. It absorbs wavelengths of radiation emitted by earth and returns it as heat. A non-greenhouse gas is transparent to radiation in this wavelength range.

(b) $Ar(g)$ is monatomic, while $CH_4(g)$ contains 4 C–H bonds. Infrared radiation has insufficient energy to cause electron transitions or bond cleavage; but it has an appropriate amount of energy to cause molecular deformations, bond stretching, and angle bending. Monatomic gases such as Ar cannot "use" infrared radiation and are transparent to it.

The World Ocean

18.32 If the phosphorous is present as phosphate, there is a 1:1 ratio between the molarity of phosphorus and molarity of phosphate. Thus, we can calculate the molarity based on the given mass of P.

$$\dfrac{0.07 \text{ g P}}{1 \times 10^6 \text{ g H}_2\text{O}} \times \dfrac{1 \text{ mol P}}{31 \text{ g P}} \times \dfrac{1 \text{ mol PO}_4^{3-}}{1 \text{ mol P}} \times \dfrac{1 \times 10^3 \text{ g H}_2\text{O}}{1 \text{ L H}_2\text{O}} = 2.26 \times 10^{-6} = 2 \times 10^{-6} M \text{ PO}_4^{3-}$$

18.34 0.05 ppb Au = 0.05 g Au/1×10^9 g seawater

$$\$1{,}000{,}000 \times \dfrac{1 \text{ oz Au}}{\$800} \times \dfrac{1 \text{ lb}}{16 \text{ oz}} \times \dfrac{453.6 \text{ g}}{1 \text{ lb}} = 3.5438 \times 10^4 \text{ g} = 3.54 \times 10^4 \text{ g Au needed}$$

$$3.5438 \times 10^4 \text{ g Au} \times \frac{1 \times 10^9 \text{ g seawater}}{0.05 \text{ g Au}} \times \frac{1 \text{ mL seawater}}{1.03 \text{ g seawater}} \times \frac{1 \text{ L}}{1000 \text{ mL}} = 6.8811 \times 10^{11}$$

$$= 7 \times 10^{11} \text{ L seawater}$$

7×10^{11} L seawater are needed if the process is 100% efficient; since it is only 50% efficient, twice as much seawater is needed.

$6.8811 \times 10^{11} \times 2 = 1.3762 \times 10^{12} = 1 \times 10^{12}$ L seawater

Note that the 1 sig fig in 0.05 ppb Au limits the precision of the calculation.

18.36 Calculate the total ion concentration of sea water by summing the molarities given in Table 18.6. Then use $\Pi = \Delta MRT$ to calculate pressure.

$$M_{total} = 0.55 + 0.47 + 0.028 + 0.054 + 0.010 + 0.010 + 2.3 \times 10^{-3} + 8.3 \times 10^{-4}$$

$$+ 4.3 \times 10^{-4} + 9.1 \times 10^{-5} + 7.0 \times 10^{-5} = 1.1257 = 1.13 \ M$$

$$\Pi = \frac{(1.1257 - 0.02) \text{ mol}}{L} \times \frac{0.08206 \text{ L} \times \text{atm}}{\text{mol-K}} \times 297 \text{ K} = 26.948 = 26.9 \text{ atm}$$

Check. The largest numbers in the molarity sum have 2 decimal places, so M_{total} has 2 decimal places and 3 sig figs. ΔM also has 2 decimal places and 3 sig figs so the calculated pressure has 3 sig figs. Units are correct.

Fresh Water

18.38 (a) Decomposition of organic matter by aerobic bacteria depletes dissolved O_2. A low dissolved oxygen concentration indicates the presence of organic pollutants.

(b) According to Section 13.3, the solubility of $O_2(g)$ (or any gas) in water decreases with increasing temperature.

18.40 $120,000 \text{ persons} \times \dfrac{59 \text{ g } O_2}{1 \text{ person}} \times \dfrac{1 \times 10^6 \text{ g } H_2O}{9 \text{ g } O_2} \times \dfrac{1 \text{ L } H_2O}{1 \times 10^3 \text{ g } H_2O} = 7.9 \times 10^8 = 8 \times 10^8 \text{ L } H_2O$

18.42 (a) Ca^{2+}, Mg^{2+}, Fe^{2+}

(b) Divalent cations (ions with 2+ charges) contribute to water hardness. These ions react with soap to form scum on surfaces or leave undesirable deposits on surfaces, particularly inside pipes, upon heating.

18.44 $Ca(OH)_2$ is added to remove Ca^{2+} as $CaCO_3(s)$, and Na_2CO_3 removes the remaining Ca^{2+}.

$Ca^{+2}(aq) + 2HCO_3^-(aq) + [Ca^{2+}(aq) + 2OH^-(aq)] \rightarrow 2CaCO_3(s) + 2H_2O(l).$

One mole $Ca(OH)_2$ is needed for each 2 moles of $HCO_3^-(aq)$ present.

$$5.0 \times 10^7 \text{ L } H_2O \times \frac{1.7 \times 10^{-3} \text{ mol } HCO_3^-}{1 \text{ L } H_2O} \times \frac{1 \text{ mol } Ca(OH)_2}{2 \text{ mol } HCO_3^-} \times \frac{74 \text{ g } Ca(OH)_2}{1 \text{ mol } Ca(OH)_2}$$

$$= 3.1 \times 10^6 \text{ g } Ca(OH)_2$$

Half of the native HCO_3^- precipitates the added Ca^{2+} so this operation reduces the Ca^{2+} concentration from $5.7 \times 10^{-3} \ M$ to $(5.7 \times 10^{-3} - 8.5 \times 10^{-4}) \ M = 4.85 \times 10^{-3} = 4.9 \times 10^{-3} \ M$. Next we must add sufficient Na_2CO_3 to further reduce $[Ca^{2+}]$ to

$1.1 \times 10^{-3} M$ (20% of the original $[Ca^{2+}]$). We thus need to reduce $[Ca^{2+}]$ by $(4.85 \times 10^{-3} - 1.1 \times 10^{-3}) M = 3.75 \times 10^{-3} = 3.8 \times 10^{-3} M$

$$Ca^{2+}(aq) + CO_3^{-2}(aq) \rightarrow CaCO_3(s).$$

$$5.0 \times 10^7 \text{ L H}_2\text{O} \times \frac{3.75 \times 10^{-3} \text{ mol Ca}^{2+}}{1 \text{ L H}_2\text{O}} \times \frac{1 \text{ mol Na}_2\text{CO}_3}{1 \text{ mol Ca}^{2+}} \times \frac{106 \text{ g Na}_2\text{CO}_3}{1 \text{ mol Na}_2\text{CO}_3}$$
$$= 2.0 \times 10^7 \text{ g Na}_2\text{CO}_3$$

18.46 $Al_2(SO_4)_3$ is a typical coagulant in municipal water purification. It reacts with OH^- in a slightly basic solution to form a gelatinous precipitate that occludes very small particles and bacteria. The precipitate settles slowly and is removed by sand filtration.

Properties of $Al_2(SO_4)_3$ and other useful coagulants are:

- They react with low concentrations of $OH^-(aq)$. That is, K_{sp} of the hydroxide precipitate is very small. The capacity to form a hydroxide precipitates means that no extra salts must be added to form the precipitate. Also, the $[OH^-]$ can be easily adjusted by $Ca(OH)_2$ and other reagents that are part of the purification process.

- The hydroxide precipitate is composed of very small, evenly dispersed particles that do not settle quickly. This is required to remove very small bacteria and viruses from all parts of the liquid, not just the sites of solid formation.

Green Chemistry

18.48   Catalysts increase the rate of a reaction by lowering activation energy, E_a. For an uncatalyzed reaction that requires extreme temperatures and pressures to generate product at a viable rate, finding a suitable catalyst reduces the required temperature and/or pressure, which reduces the amount of energy used to run the process. A catalyst can also increase rate of production, which would reduce the net time and thus energy required to generate a certain amount of product.

18.50
- In either solvent, the reaction is catalyzed, which usually leads to decreased processing temperatures and times, and greater energy efficiency.

- $scCO_2$ is the preferred solvent. It achieves maximum conversion much faster than CH_2Cl_2 solvent. $scCO_2$ reduces processing time, temperature, and energy requirements. It also results in fewer unwanted by-products to be separated and processed. While use of $scCO_2$ increases the amount of a greenhouse gas released to the environment, it eliminates use of CH_2Cl_2, which is implicated in stratospheric ozone depletion. Use of $scCO_2$ rather than CH_2Cl_2 is a good green trade-off.

Additional Exercises

18.52 MM_{avg} at the surface $= 83.8(0.17) + 16.0(0.38) + 32.0(0.45) = 34.73 = 35$ g/mol.

Next, calculate the percentage composition at 200 km. The fractions can be "normalized" by saying that the 0.45 fraction of O_2 is converted into two 0.45 fractions of O atoms, then dividing by the total fractions, $0.17 + 0.38 + 0.45 + 0.45 = 1.45$:

$$MM_{avg} = \frac{83.8(0.17) + 16.0(0.38) + 16.0(0.90)}{1.45} = 23.95 = 24 \text{ g/mol}$$

18.54

$$2[Cl(g) + O_3(g) \rightarrow ClO(g) + O_2(g)] \qquad [18.7]$$
$$2Cl(g) + 2O_3(g) \rightarrow 2ClO(g) + 2O_2(g)$$
$$\underline{2ClO(g) \qquad \rightarrow O_2(g) + 2Cl(g)} \qquad [18.9]$$
$$2Cl(g) + 2O_3(g) + 2ClO(g) \rightarrow 2ClO(g) + 3O_2(g) + 2Cl(g)$$
$$2O_3(g) \xrightarrow{Cl} 3O_2(g) \qquad [18.10]$$

Note that Cl(g) fits the definition of a catalyst in this reaction.

18.55 Chlorofluorocarbons (CFCs), primarily $CFCl_3$ and CF_2Cl_2, are chemically inert and water insoluble. These properties make them valuable as propellants, refrigerants and foaming agents because they are virtually unreactive in the *troposphere* (lower atmosphere) and do not initiate or propagate undesirable reactions. Further, they are water-insoluble and not removed from the atmosphere by rain; they do not end up in the fresh water supply.

These properties render CFCs a long-term problem in the *stratosphere*. Because CFCs are inert and water-insoluble, they are not removed from the troposphere by reaction or dissolution and have very long lifetimes. Virtually the entire mass of released CFCs eventually diffuses into the stratosphere where conditions are right for photo-dissociation and the production of Cl atoms. Cl atoms catalyze the destruction of ozone, O_3.

18.57 In an HFC, C–Cl bonds are replaced by C–F bonds. The bond dissociation enthalpy of a C–F bond is 485 kJ/mol, much more than for a C–Cl bond, 328 kJ/mol (Table 8.4). Although HFCs have long lifetimes in the stratosphere, it is infrequent that light with energy sufficient to dissociate a C–F bond will reach an HFC molecule. F atoms, the bad actors in ozone destruction, are much less likely than Cl atoms to be produced by photodissociation in the stratosphere.

18.58 (a) $\cdot\ddot{\text{O}}$—H

(b) HNO_3 is a major component in acid rain.

(c) While it removes CO, the reaction produces NO_2. The photodissociation of NO_2 to form O atoms is the first step in the formation of tropospheric ozone and photochemical smog.

(d) Again, NO_2 is the initiator of photochemical smog. Also, methoxyl radical, OCH_3, is a reactive species capable of initiating other undesirable reactions.

18.60 Oxygen is present in the atmosphere to the extent of 209,000 parts per million. If CO binds 210 times more effectively than O_2, then the **effective** concentration of CO is 210×125 ppm $= 26,250 = 26,300$ ppm. The fraction of carboxyhemoglobin in the blood leaving the lungs is thus $\frac{26,250}{26,250 + 209,000} = 0.112$. Thus, 11.2 percent of the blood is in the form of carboxyhemoglobin, 88.8 percent as the O_2-bound oxyhemoglobin.

18.62 (a) According to Section 13.3, the solubility of gases in water decreases with increasing temperature. Thus, the solubility of $CO_2(g)$ in the ocean would decrease if the temperature of the ocean increased.

(b) If the solubility of $CO_2(g)$ in the ocean decreased because of global warming, more $CO_2(g)$ would be released into the atmosphere, perpetuating a cycle of increasing temperature and concomitant release of $CO_2(g)$ from the ocean.

18.63 Most of the 390 watts/m^2 radiated from Earth's surface is in the infrared region of the spectrum. Tropospheric gases, particularly $H_2O(g)$ and $CO_2(g)$, absorb much of this radiation and prevent it from escaping into space (Figure 18.12). The energy absorbed by these so-called "greenhouse gases" warms the atmosphere close to Earth's surface and makes the planet livable.

18.65 (a) $NO(g) + h\nu \rightarrow N(g) + O(g)$

(b) $NO(g) + h\nu \rightarrow NO^+(g) + e^-$

(c) $NO(g) + O_3(g) \rightarrow NO_2(g) + O_2(g)$

(d) $3NO_2(g) + H_2O(l) \rightarrow 2HNO_3(aq) + NO(g)$

18.66 (a) CO_3^{2-} is a relatively strong Brønsted-Lowry base and produces OH^- in aqueous solution according to the hydrolysis reaction:

$$CO_3^{2-}(aq) + H_2O(l) \rightleftharpoons HCO_3^-(aq) + OH^-(aq), \quad K_b = 1.8 \times 10^{-4}$$

If $[OH^-(aq)]$ is sufficient for the reaction quotient, Q, to exceed K_{sp} for $Mg(OH)_2$, the solid will precipitate.

(b) $$\frac{125 \text{ mg Mg}^{2+}}{1 \text{ kg soln}} \times \frac{1 \text{ g Mg}^{2+}}{1000 \text{ mg Mg}^{2+}} \times \frac{1.00 \text{ kg soln}}{1.00 \text{ L soln}} \times \frac{1 \text{ mol Mg}^{2+}}{24.305 \text{ g Mg}^{2+}} = 5.143 \times 10^{-3}$$

$$= 5.14 \times 10^{-3} \, M \, Mg^{2+}$$

$$\frac{4.0 \text{ g Na}_2\text{CO}_3}{1.0 \text{ L soln}} \times \frac{1 \text{ mol CO}_3^{2-}}{106.0 \text{ g Na}_2\text{CO}_3} = 0.03774 = 0.038 \, M \, CO_3^{2-}$$

$$K_b = 1.8 \times 10^{-4} = \frac{[HCO_3^-][OH^-]}{[CO_3^{2-}]} \approx \frac{x^2}{0.03774}; \, x = [OH^-] = 2.606 \times 10^{-3}$$

$$= 2.6 \times 10^{-3} \, M$$

(This represents 6.9% hydrolysis, but the result will not be significantly different using the quadratic formula.)

$Q = [Mg^{2+}][OH^-]^2 = (5.143 \times 10^{-3})(2.606 \times 10^{-3})^2 = 3.5 \times 10^{-8}$

K_{sp} for $Mg(OH)_2 = 1.6 \times 10^{-12}$; $Q > K_{sp}$, so $Mg(OH)_2$ will precipitate.

18.68 *Plan.* Calculate the volume of air above Los Angeles and the volume of pure O_3 that would be present at the 84 ppb level. For gases at the same temperature and pressure, volume fractions equal mole fractions. *Solve.*

$$V_{air} = 4000 \text{ mi}^2 \times \frac{(1.6093)^2 \text{ km}^2}{\text{mi}^2} \times \frac{(1000)^2 \text{ m}^2}{1 \text{ km}^2} \times 10 \text{ m} \times \frac{1 \text{ L}}{1 \times 10^{-3} \text{ m}^3} = 1.036 \times 10^{14}$$

$$= 1.0 \times 10^{14} \text{ L air}$$

$$84 \text{ ppb O}_3 = \frac{84 \text{ mol O}_3}{1 \times 10^9 \text{ mol air}} = 8.4 \times 10^{-8} = \chi_{O_3}$$

V (pure O_3) = 8.4 × 10⁻⁸ (1.036 × 10¹⁴ L air) = 8.702 × 10⁶ = 8.7 × 10⁶ L O_3

Values for P and T are required to calculate mol O_3 from volume O_3, using the ideal-gas law. Since these are not specified in the exercise, we will make a reasonable assumption for a sunny April day in Los Angeles. The city is near sea level and temperatures are moderate throughout the year, so P = 1 atm and T = 25°C (78°F) are reasonable values.

PV = nRT, n = PV/RT

$$n = 1.000 \text{ atm} \times \frac{8.702 \times 10^6 \text{ L}}{298 \text{ K}} \times \frac{\text{K-mol}}{0.08206 \text{ L-atm}} = 3.558 \times 10^5 = 3.6 \times 10^5 \text{ mol } O_3$$

Check. Using known conditions to make reasonable estimates and assumptions is a valuable skill for problem solving. Knowing when assumptions are required is an important step in the learning process.

Integrative Exercises

18.70   (a) $8{,}376{,}726 \text{ tons coal} \times \dfrac{83 \text{ ton C}}{100 \text{ ton coal}} \times \dfrac{44.01 \text{ ton } CO_2}{12.01 \text{ ton C}} = 2.5 \times 10^7 \text{ ton } CO_2$

$8{,}376{,}726 \text{ tons coal} \times \dfrac{2.5 \text{ ton S}}{100 \text{ ton coal}} \times \dfrac{64.07 \text{ ton } SO_2}{32.07 \text{ ton S}} = 4.2 \times 10^5 \text{ ton } SO_2$

(b) $CaO(s) + SO_2(g) \rightarrow CaSO_3(s)$

$4.18 \times 10^5 \text{ ton } SO_2 \times \dfrac{55 \text{ ton } SO_2 \text{ removed}}{100 \text{ ton } SO_2 \text{ produced}} \times \dfrac{120.15 \text{ ton } CaSO_3}{64.07 \text{ ton } SO_2}$

$= 4.3 \times 10^5 \text{ ton } CaSO_3$

18.71   *Coarse sand* is removed by coarse sand filtration. *Finely divided particles* and some *bacteria* are removed by precipitation with aluminum hydroxide. Remaining *harmful bacteria* are removed by ozonation. *Trihalomethanes* are removed by either aeration or activated carbon filtration; use of activated carbon might be preferred because it does not involve release of TCMs into the atmosphere. *Dissolved organic substances* are oxidized (and rendered less harmful, but not removed) by both aeration and ozonation. Dissolved *nitrates* and *phosphates* are not removed by any of these processes, but are rendered less harmful by adequate aeration.

18.73   According to Equation [14.12], $\ln([A]_t / [A]_o) = -kt$. $[A]_t = 0.10 [A]_o$

$\ln(0.10 [A]_o / [A]_o) = \ln(0.10) = -(2 \times 10^{-6} \text{ s}^{-1}) \text{ t}$

$t = -\ln(0.10) / 2 \times 10^{-6} \text{ s}^{-1} = 1.151 \times 10^6 \text{ s}$

$1.151 \times 10^6 \text{ s} \times \dfrac{1 \text{ min}}{60 \text{ s}} \times \dfrac{1 \text{ hr}}{60 \text{ min}} \times \dfrac{1 \text{ day}}{24 \text{ hr}} = 13.3 \text{ days } (1 \times 10 \text{ days})$

The value of the rate constant limits the result to 1 sig fig. This implies that there is minimum uncertainty of ± 1 in the tens place of our answer. Realistically, the remediation could take anywhere from 1 to 20 days.

18.74 (i) $ClO(g) + O_3(g) \rightarrow ClO_2(g) + O_2(g)$

$\Delta H_i = \Delta H_f^\circ\, ClO_2(g) + \Delta H_f^\circ\, O_2(g) - \Delta H_f^\circ\, ClO(g) - \Delta H_f^\circ\, O_3(g)$

$\Delta H_i = 102 + 0 - 101 - (142.3) = -141\ kJ$

(ii) $ClO_2(g) + O(g) \rightarrow ClO(g) + O_2(g)$

$\Delta H_{ii} = \Delta H_f^\circ\, ClO(g) + \Delta H_f^\circ\, O_2(g) - \Delta H_f^\circ\, ClO_2(g) - \Delta H_f^\circ\, O(g)$

$\Delta H_{ii} = 101 + 0 - 102 - (247.5) = -249\ kJ$

(overall) $ClO(g) + O_3(g) + ClO_2(g) + O(g) \rightarrow ClO_2(g) + O_2(g) + ClO(g) + O_2(g)$

$$O_3(g) + O(g) \rightarrow 2O_2(g)$$

$\Delta H = \Delta H_i + \Delta H_{ii} = -141\ kJ + (-249)\ kJ = -390\ kJ$

Because the enthalpies of both (i) and (ii) are distinctly exothermic, it is possible that the $ClO - ClO_2$ pair could be a catalyst for the destruction of ozone.

18.76 (a) A rate constant of $M^{-1}s^{-1}$ is indicative of a reaction that is second order overall. For the reaction given, the rate law is probably rate = $k[O][O_3]$. (Although rate = $k[O]^2$ or $k[O_3]^2$ are possibilities, it is difficult to envision a mechanism consistent with either one that would result in two molecules of O_2 being produced.)

(b) Yes. Most atmospheric processes are initiated by collision. One could imagine an activated complex of four O atoms collapsing to form two O_2 molecules. Also, the rate constant is large, which is less likely for a multistep process. The reaction is analogous to the destruction of O_3 by Cl atoms (Equation [18.7]), which is also second order with a large rate constant.

(c) According to the Arrhenius equation, $k = Ae^{-Ea/RT}$. Thus, the larger the value of k, the smaller the activation energy, E_a. The value of the rate constant for this reaction is large, so the activation energy is small.

(d) $\Delta H^\circ = 2\Delta H_f^\circ\, O_2(g) - \Delta H_f^\circ\, O(g) - \Delta H_f^\circ\, O_3(g)$

$\Delta H^\circ = 0 - 247.5\ kJ - 142.3\ kJ = -389.8\ kJ$

The reaction is exothermic, so energy is released; the reaction would raise the temperature of the stratosphere.

18.77 (a) 17 e^-, 8.5 e^- pairs

$\ddot{O}{=}\dot{N}{-}\ddot{\ddot{O}}: \longleftrightarrow :\ddot{\ddot{O}}{-}\dot{N}{=}\ddot{O}$

Owing to its lower electronegativity, N is more likely to be electron deficient and to accommodate the odd electron.

(b) The fact that NO_2 is an electron deficient molecule indicates that it will be highly reactive. Dimerization results in formation of a N—N single bond which completes the octet of both N atoms. NO_2 and N_2O_4 exist in equilibrium in a closed system. The reaction is exothermic, Equation [22.48]. In an urban environment, NO_2 is produced from hot automobile combustion. At these temperatures, equilibrium favors the monomer because the reaction is exothermic.

(c) $2NO_2(g) + 4CO(g) \rightarrow N_2(g) + 4CO_2(g)$

$NO_2(g) + CO(g) \rightarrow NO(g) + CO_2(g)$

NO_2 is an oxidizing agent and CO is a reducing agent, so we expect products to contain N in a more reduced form, NO or N_2, and C in a more oxidized form, CO_2.

(d)   No. Because it is an odd-electron molecule, NO_2 is very reactive. We expect it to undergo chemical reactions or photodissociate before it can migrate to the stratosphere. The expected half-life of an NO_2 molecule is short.

18.79   rate = $k[CF_3CH_2F][OH]$. $k = 1.6 \times 10^8\ M^{-1}\ s^{-1}$ at 4°C.

[CF_3CH_2F] = 6.3×10^8 molecules/cm^3, [OH] = 8.1×10^5 molecules/cm^3

Change molecules/cm^3 to mol/L (*M*) and substitute into the rate law.

$$\frac{6.3 \times 10^8\ \text{molecules}}{cm^3} \times \frac{1\ \text{mol}}{6.022 \times 10^{23}\ \text{molecules}} \times \frac{1000\ cm^3}{1\ L} =$$

$$1.0462 \times 10^{-12} = 1.0 \times 10^{-12}\ M\ CF_3CH_2F$$

$$\frac{8.1 \times 10^5\ \text{molecules}}{cm^3} \times \frac{1\ \text{mol}}{6.022 \times 10^{23}\ \text{molecules}} \times \frac{1000\ cm^3}{1\ L} =$$

$$1.3451 \times 10^{-15} = 1.3 \times 10^{-15}\ M\ OH$$

$$\text{rate} = \frac{1.6 \times 10^8}{M\text{-}s} \times 1.0462 \times 10^{-12}\ M \times 1.3451 \times 10^{-15}\ M = 2.2515 \times 10^{-19} = 2.3 \times 10^{-19}\ M/s$$

18.80   (a)   According to Table 18.1, the mole fraction of CO_2 in air is 0.000375.

$P_{CO_2} = \chi_{CO_2} \times P_{atm} = 0.000375\,(1.00\ \text{atm}) = 3.75 \times 10^{-4}\ \text{atm}$

$C_{CO_2} = kP_{CO_2} = 3.1 \times 10^{-2}\ M/\text{atm} \times 3.75 \times 10^{-4}\ \text{atm} = 1.16 \times 10^{-5} = 1.2 \times 10^{-5}\ M$

(b) H_2CO_3 is a weak acid, so the [H^+] is regulated by the equilibria:

$H_2CO_3(aq) \rightleftharpoons H^+(aq) + HCO_3^-(aq)\ K_{a1} = 4.3 \times 10^{-7}$

$HCO_3^-(aq) \rightleftharpoons H^+(aq) + CO_3^{2-}(aq)\ \ K_{a2} = 5.6 \times 10^{-11}$

Since the value of K_{a2} is small compared to K_{a1}, we will assume that most of the $H^+(aq)$ is produced by the first dissociation.

$K_{a1} = 4.3 \times 10^{-7} = \dfrac{[H^+][HCO_3^-]}{[H_2CO_3]}; [H^+] = [HCO_3^-] = x, [H_2CO_3] = 1.2 \times 10^{-5} - x$

Since K_{a1} and [H_2CO_3] have similar values, we cannot assume x is small compared to 1.2×10^{-5}.

$4.3 \times 10^{-7} = \dfrac{x^2}{(1.2 \times 10^{-5} - x)}; 5.00 \times 10^{-12} - 4.3 \times 10^{-7}\ x = x^2$

$$0 = x^2 + 4.3 \times 10^{-7} x - 5.00 \times 10^{-12}$$

$$x = \frac{-4.3 \times 10^{-7} \pm \sqrt{(4.3 \times 10^{-7})^2 - 4(1)(-5.00 \times 10^{-12})}}{2(1)}$$

$$x = \frac{-4.3 \times 10^{-7} \pm \sqrt{1.85 \times 10^{-13} + 2.00 \times 10^{-11}}}{2} = \frac{-4.3 \times 10^{-7} \pm 4.49 \times 10^{-6}}{2}$$

The negative result is meaningless; $x = 2.03 \times 10^{-6} = 2.0 \times 10^{-6} \, M \, H^+$; pH = 5.69

Since this $[H^+]$ is quite small, the $[H^+]$ from the autoionization of water might be significant. Calculation shows that for $[H^+] = 2.0 \times 10^{-6} \, M$ from H_2CO_3, $[H^+]$ from $H_2O = 5.2 \times 10^{-9} \, M$, which we can ignore.

18.82   (a) $Al(OH)_3(s) \rightleftharpoons Al^{3+}(aq) + 3OH^-(aq)$ $K_{sp} = 1.3 \times 10^{-33} = [Al^{3+}][OH^-]^3$

This is a precipitation conditions problem. At what $[OH^-]$ (we can get pH from $[OH^-]$) will $Q = 1.3 \times 10^{-33}$, the requirement for the onset of precipitation?

$Q = 1.3 \times 10^{-33} = [Al^{3+}][OH^-]^3$. Find the molar concentration of $Al_2(SO_4)_3$ and thus $[Al^{3+}]$.

$$\frac{5.0 \, lb \, Al_2(SO_4)_3}{2000 \, gal \, H_2O} \times \frac{453.6 \, g}{1 \, lb} \times \frac{1 \, mol \, Al_2(SO_4)_3}{342.2 \, g \, Al_2(SO_4)_3} \times \frac{1 \, gal}{4 \, qt} \times \frac{1 \, qt}{0.946 \, L}$$

$$= 8.758 \times 10^{-4} \, M \, Al_2(SO_4)_3 = 1.752 \times 10^{-3} = 1.8 \times 10^{-3} \, M \, Al^{3+}$$

$Q = 1.3 \times 10^{-33} = (1.752 \times 10^{-3})[OH^-]^3$; $[OH^-]^3 = 7.42 \times 10^{-31}$

$[OH^-] = 9.054 \times 10^{-11} = 9.1 \times 10^{-11} \, M$; pOH = 10.04; pH = 14 − 10.04 = 3.96

(b) $CaO(s) + H_2O(l) \rightarrow Ca^{2+}(aq) + 2OH^-(aq)$; $[OH^-] = 9.054 \times 10^{-11}$ mol/L

$$mol \, OH^- = \frac{9.054 \times 10^{-11} \, mol}{1 \, L} \times 2000 \, gal \times \frac{4 \, qt}{1 \, gal} \times \frac{0.946 \, L}{1 \, qt} = 6.852 \times 10^{-7}$$

$$= 6.9 \times 10^{-7} \, mol \, OH^-$$

$$6.852 \times 10^{-7} \, mol \, OH^- \times \frac{1 \, mol \, CaO}{2 \, mol \, OH^-} \times \frac{56.1 \, g \, CaO}{1 \, mol \, CaO} \times \frac{1 \, lb}{453.6 \, g} = 4.2 \times 10^{-8} \, lb \, CaO$$

This is a very small amount of CaO, about 20 μg.

25 The Chemistry of Life: Organic and Biological Chemistry

Visualizing Concepts

25.2   *Analyze/Plan.* Given structural formulas, decide which molecule will undergo addition. Consider which functional groups are present in the molecules, and which are most susceptible to addition.   *Solve.*

Addition reactions are characteristic of alkenes. Molecule (c), an alkene, will readily undergo addition.

Molecule (a) is an aromatic hydrocarbon, which does not typically undergo addition because the delocalized electron cloud is too difficult to disrupt. Molecules (b) and (d) contain carbonyl groups (actually carboxylic acid groups) that do not typically undergo addition, except under special conditions.

25.4   *Analyze.* Given structural formulas, decide which molecules are capable of isomerism, and what type. *Plan.* Analyze each molecule for possible structural, geometric, and optical isomers/enantiomers.   *Solve.*

(a) $C_5H_{11}NO_2$. Structural, geometric and optical. There are many ways to arrange the atoms in molecules with this empirical formula, so there are many structural isomers. There is one point of unsaturation in the given molecule, the C=O group; structural isomers with their point of unsaturation at a C=C group could have geometric isomers as well.   The C atom to which the $-NH_3^+$ group is bound is a chiral center, so there are enantiomers. All amino acids except glycine have two possible enantiomers.

(b) $C_7H_5O_2Cl$. The most obvious isomers for this aromatic compound are ortho, meta, and para geometric isomers. Because the molecule has several points of unsaturation, the number of structural isomers is limited, but there are a few possibilities with two triple bonds. Switching the $-OH$ and $-Cl$ groups also generates a structural isomer.   There are no chiral centers, so no optical isomers.

(c) C_5H_{10}. There are many structural isomers for this empirical formula. The straight-chain alkene shown also has geometric (cis-trans) isomers.

(d) C_3H_8. There are no other structural, geometric, or optical isomers for this molecule.

25.6 *Analyze/Plan.* Follow the logic in Sample Exercise 25.1 to name each compound. Decide which structures are the same compound. *Solve.*

(a) 2,2,4-trimethylpentane

(b) 3-ethyl-2-methylpentane

(c) 2,3,4-trimethylpentane

(d) 2,3,4-trimethylpentane

Structures (c) and (d) are the same molecule.

Introduction to Organic Compounds; Hydrocarbons

25.8

$$N\equiv\underset{7}{C}-\underset{6}{\overset{\overset{\textstyle H}{|}}{\underset{\underset{\textstyle H}{|}}{C}}}-\underset{5}{\overset{\overset{\textstyle H}{|}}{\underset{\underset{\textstyle H}{|}}{C}}}-\underset{4}{\overset{\overset{\textstyle H}{|}}{C}}=\underset{3}{\overset{\textstyle H}{C}}-\underset{2}{\overset{\overset{\textstyle OH}{|}}{\underset{\underset{\textstyle H}{|}}{C}}}-\underset{1}{\overset{\overset{\textstyle O}{||}}{C}}-H$$

(a) C2, C5 and C6 have sp^3 hybridization (4 e$^-$ domains around C)

(b) C7 has sp hybridization (2 e$^-$ domains around C)

(c) C1, C3, and C4 have sp^2 hybridization (3 e$^-$ domains around C)

25.10 From Table 8.4, the bond enthalpies in kJ/mol are: C—H, 413; C—C, 348; C—O, 358; C—Cl, 328. The bond enthalpes indicate that C—H bonds are most difficult to break, and C—Cl bonds least difficult. However, they do not explain the reactivity of C—O bonds, or stability of C—C bonds.

The reactivity of molecules containing C—O and C—Cl bonds is a result of their unequal charge distribution, which attracts reactants that are either electron deficient (electrophilic) or electron rich (nucleophilic).

25.12 All the classifications listed are hydrocarbons; they contain only the elements hydrogen and carbon.

(a) *Alkanes* are hydrocarbons that contain only single bonds.

(b) *Cycloalkanes* contain at least one ring of three or more carbon atoms joined by single bonds. Because it is a type of alkane, all bonds in a cycloalkane are single bonds.

(c) *Alkenes* contain at least one C=C double bond.

(d) *Alkynes* contain at least one C≡C triple bond.

(e) A *saturated hydrocarbon* contains only single bonds. Alkanes and cycloalkanes fit this definition.

(f) An *aromatic hydrocarbon* contains one or more planar, six-membered rings of carbon atoms with delocalized π-bonding throughout the ring.

25.14   cycloalkane, H_2C-CH_2 , C_6H_{12}, saturated

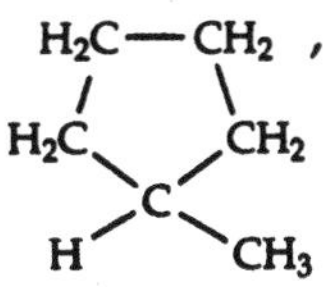

$$H_2C\diagdown\quad\diagup CH_2$$
$$C$$
$$H\diagup\quad\diagdown CH_3$$

cycloalkene, $HC=CH$, C_6H_{10}, unsaturated

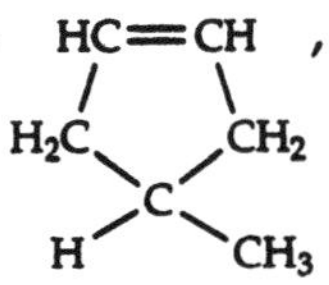

$$H_2C\diagdown\quad\diagup CH_2$$
$$C$$
$$H\diagup\quad\diagdown CH_3$$

alkyne, $CH_3-CH_2-C\equiv C-CH_2-CH_3$, C_6H_{10}, unsaturated

aromatic hydrocarbon, C_6H_6, unsaturated

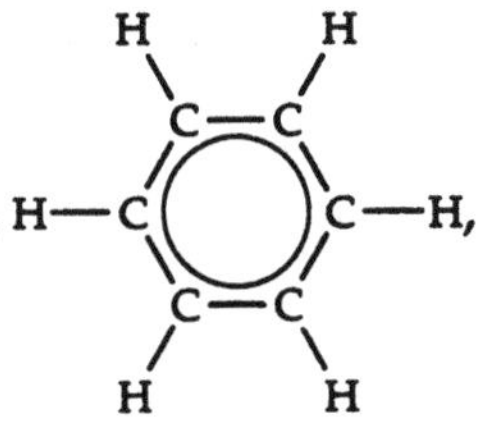

25.16 C_nH_{2n-2}

25.18 $CH_3-CH_2-CH_2-CH=CH_2$
pentene

$CH_3-CH_2-CH=CH-CH_3$ $CH_2=CH-\underset{\underset{CH_3}{|}}{CH}-CH_3$
2-pentene   3-methyl-1-butene

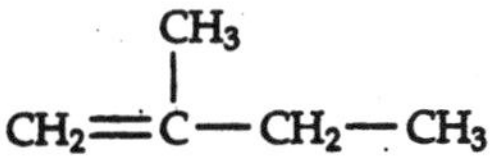

$CH_2=\underset{\underset{CH_3}{|}}{C}-CH_2-CH_3$ $CH_3-\underset{\underset{CH_3}{|}}{C}=CH-CH_3$
2-methyl-1-butene 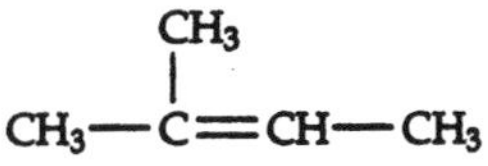   2-methyl-2-butene

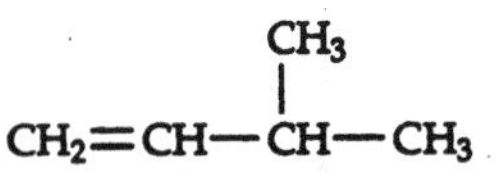

25.20   (a)   109°   (b)   120°   (c)   180°

25.22   (a)   3,3,5-trimethylheptane

(b)   3,4,4-trimethylheptane

(c)

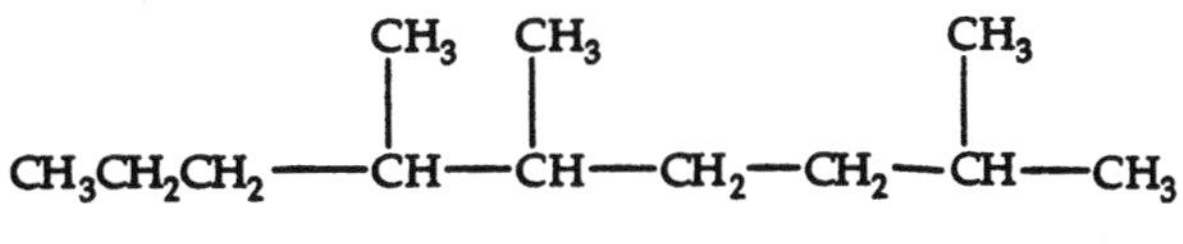

$$CH_3CH_2CH_2-\underset{\underset{CH_3}{|}}{CH}-\underset{\underset{CH_3}{|}}{CH}-CH_2-CH_2-\underset{\underset{CH_3}{|}}{CH}-CH_3$$

(d)

$$CH_3CH_2CH_2CH_2CH_2-\underset{\underset{CH_3}{|}}{CH}-\underset{\underset{CH_3}{|}}{CH}-\underset{\underset{\underset{\underset{\underset{CH_2}{|}}{CH_2}}{|}}{\underset{CH_2}{|}}}{CH}-CH_2-CH_3$$

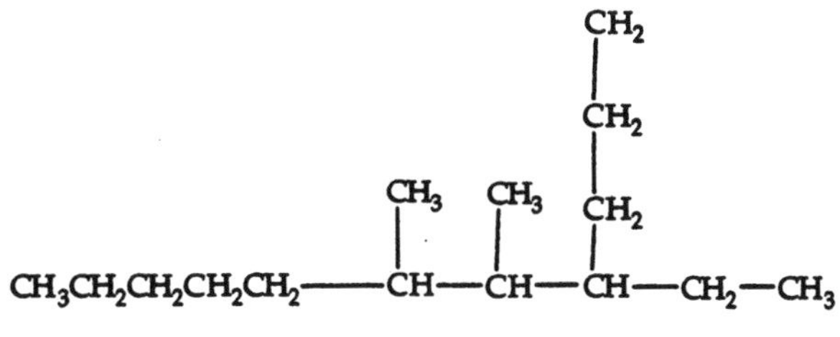

(e)

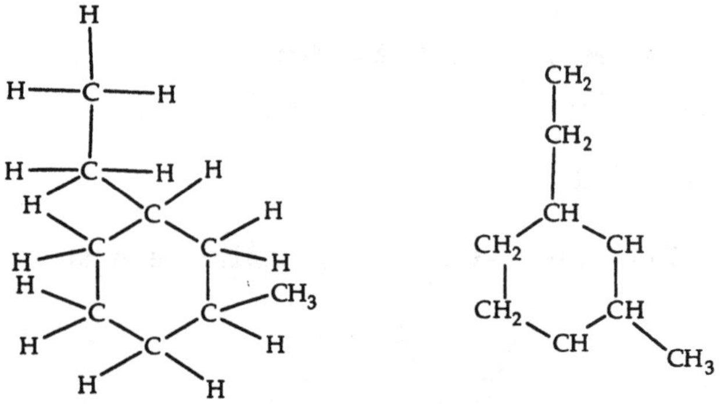

25.24   **(a)**   1,4-dichlorocyclohexane

       (b)   3-chloro-1-propyne

       (c)   *trans*-2-hexene

       (d)   1-chloro-2-methyl-2-phenyl-butane or (1-chloro-2-methyl)-2-butylbenzene

       (e)   *cis*-5-chloro-1,3-pentadiene

25.26   Butene is an alkene, C_4H_8. There are two possible placements for the double bond:

$$CH_2{=}CHCH_2CH_3 \text{ or } CH_3CH{=}CHCH_3$$

             1-butene   2-butene

These two compounds are *structural isomers*. For 2-butene, there are two different, noninterchangeable ways to construct the carbon skeleton (owing to the absence of free rotation around the double bond). These two compounds are *geometric isomers*.

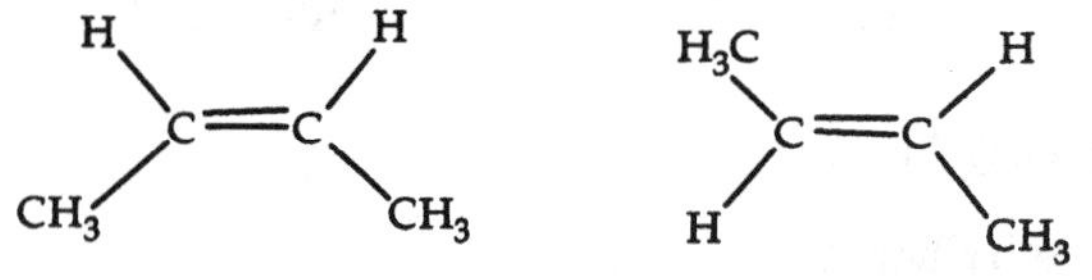

          cis-2-butene   *trans*-2-butene

25.28

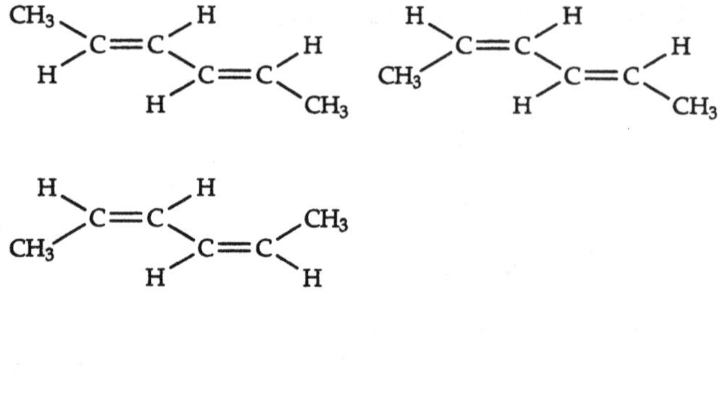

25.30 Octane number can be increased by increasing the fraction of branched-chain alkanes or aromatics, since these have high octane numbers. This can be done by cracking. The octane number also can be increased by adding an anti-knock agent such as tetraethyl lead, $Pb(C_2H_5)_4$ (no longer legal); methyl t-butyl ether (MTBE); or an alcohol, methanol, or ethanol.

Reactions of Hydrocarbons

25.32 (a)

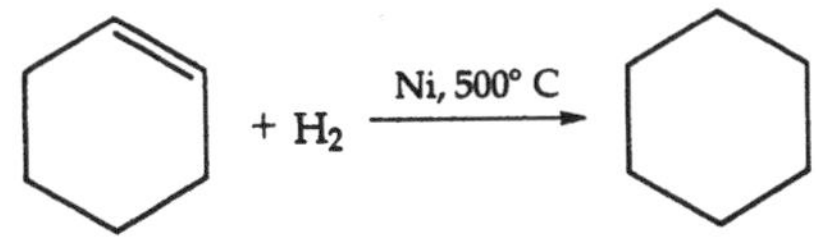

(b)

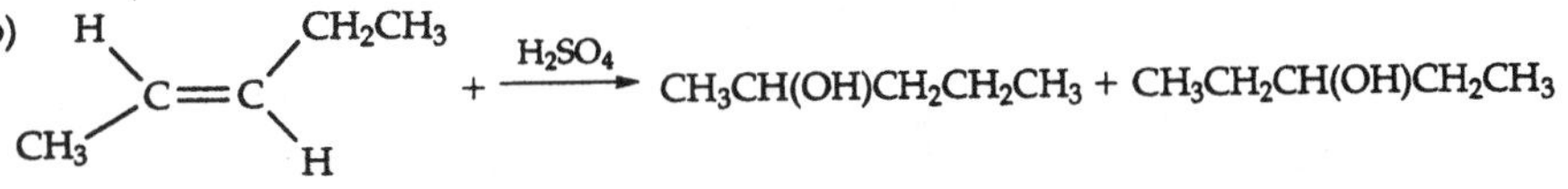

(c)

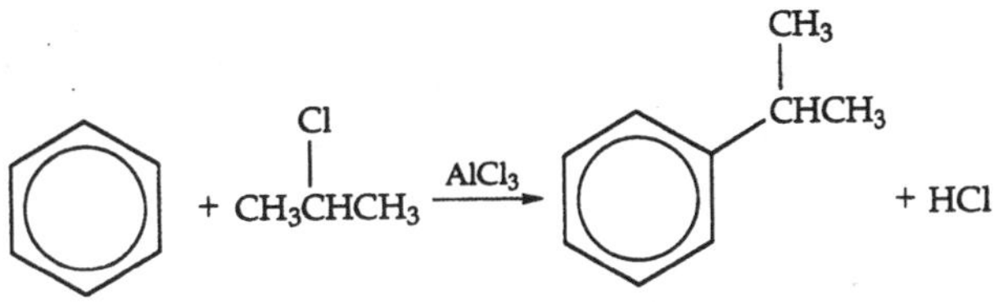

25.34 (a) The reaction of Br_2 with an alkene to form a colorless halogenated alkane is an addition reaction. Aromatic hydrocarbons do not readily undergo addition reactions, because their π-electrons are stabilized by delocalization.

(b) *Plan.* Use a Friedel-Crafts reaction to substitute a $-CH_2CH_3$ onto benzene. Do a second substitution reaction to get *para*-bromoethylbenzene. *Solve.*

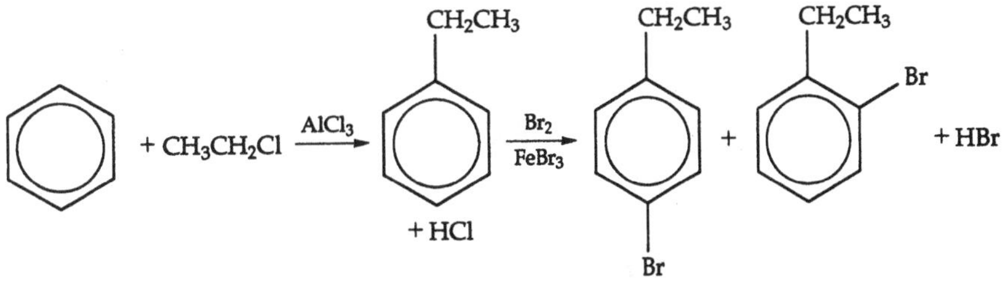

It appears that ortho, meta, and para geometric isomers of bromoethylbenzene would be possible. However, because of electronic effects beyond the scope of this chapter, the ethyl group favors formation of ortho and para isomers, but not the meta. The ortho and para products must be separated by distillation or some other technique.

25.36 The partially positive end of the hydrogen halide, $\overset{\delta^+}{H} - \overset{\delta^-}{X}$, is attached to the π electron cloud of the alkene cyclohexene. The electrons that formed the π bond in cyclohexene form a sigma bond to the H atom of HX, leaving a halide ion, X^-. The intermediate is a carbocation; one of the C atoms formerly involved in the π bond is now bound to a second H atom. The other C atom formerly involved in the π bond carries a full positive charge and forms only three sigma bonds, two to adjacent C atoms and one to H.

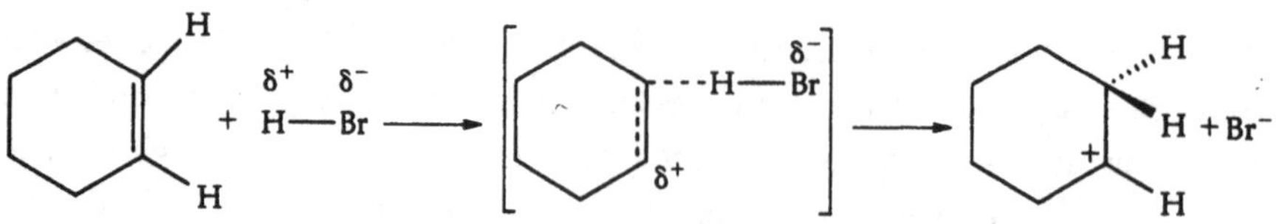

25.38

	ΔH
$C_{10}H_8(l) + 12O_2(g) \rightarrow 10CO_2(g) + 4H_2O(l)$	-5157 kJ
$-[C_{10}H_{18}(l) + 29/2\ O_2(g) \rightarrow 10CO_2(g) + 9H_2O(l)$	$-(-6286)$ kJ
$C_{10}H_8(l) + 5H_2O(l) \rightarrow C_{10}H_{18}(l) + 5/2\ O_2(g)$	$+1129$ kJ
$5/2\ O_2(g) + 5H_2(g) \rightarrow 5H_2O(l)$	$5(-285.8)$ kJ
$C_{10}H_8(l) + 5H_2(g) \rightarrow C_{10}H_{18}(l)$	-300 kJ

Compare this with the heat of hydrogenation of ethylene:

$C_2H_4(g) + H_2(g) \rightarrow C_2H_6(g)$; $\Delta H = -84.7 - (52.3) = -137$ kJ. This value applies to just one double bond. For five double bonds, we would expect about -685 kJ. The fact that hydrogenation of napthalene yields only -300 kJ indicates that the overall energy of the napthalene molecule is lower than expected for five isolated double bonds and that there must be some special stability associated with the aromatic system in this molecule.

Functional Groups and Chirality

25.40 (a) $-\overset{O}{\overset{\|}{C}}-O$, ester

(b) $-Cl$, halocarbon; $-OH$, alcohol (aromatic alcohols are phenols)

(c) $-\overset{O}{\overset{\|}{C}}-NH-$, amide

(d) alkane

(e) $-C{=}C-$, alkene; $-\overset{O}{\overset{\|}{C}}H$, aldehyde

(f) $-\overset{O}{\overset{\|}{C}}-$, ketone

25.42 (a) C_4H_8O, 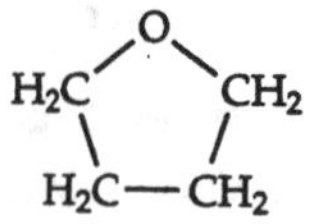

(b) $CH_3CH_2\overset{O}{\overset{\|}{C}}CH_3$, $CH_3CH_2CH_2\overset{O}{\overset{\|}{C}}-H$

$CH_2{=}CH_2CH_2CH_2OH$, $CH_3CH{=}CHCH_2OH$, (cis and trans)
$CH_2{=}CHCH(OH)CH_3$ (enantiomers)

(Structures with the $-OH$ group attached to an alkene carbon atom are not included. These molecules are called "vinyl alcohols" and are not the major form at equilibrium.)

25.44 (a) CH₃CH₂C(=O)—H

(b) CH₃CH₂CH₂CCH₃ (with =O)

(c) CH₃CHCCH₃ (with =O), CH₃ below

(d) CH₃CH₂CHC(=O)—H, CH₃ below

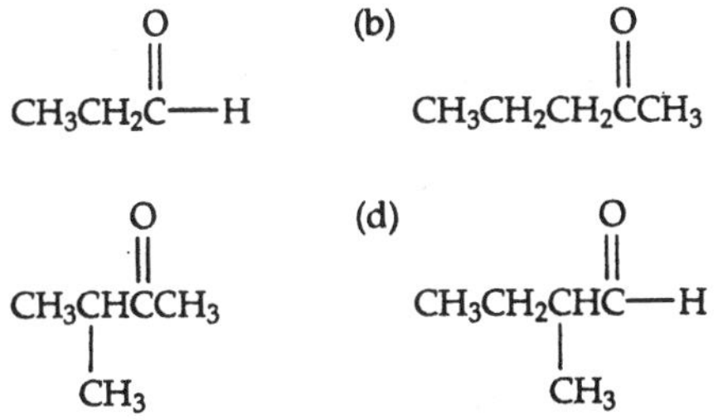

25.46 (a) CH₃CH₂CH₂C(=O)—O—CH₃

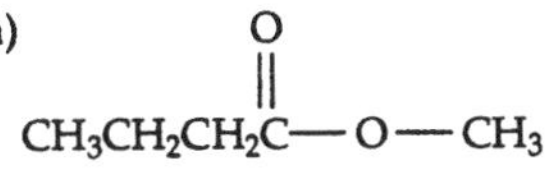

methylbutanoate

(b) (benzene ring)—C(=O)—O—C(CH₃)(H)(CH₃)

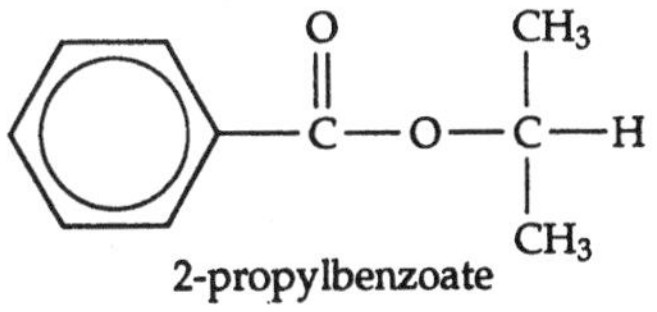

2-propylbenzoate

(c) CH₃CH₂C(=O)—N(CH₃)—CH

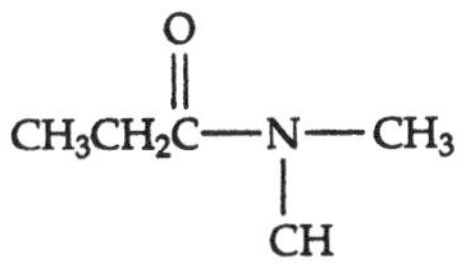

N, N-dimethylpropanamide

25.48 (a) CH₃CH₂CH₂CH₂OH + HOCCH₂CH₃ (with =O) ⟶ CH₃CH₂CH₂CH₂OCCH₂CH₃ (with =O)

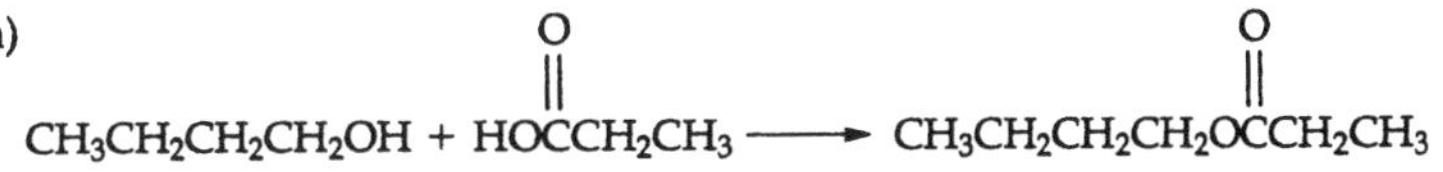

1-butanol   propionic acid   butyl proprionate
(propanoic acid)

(b) CH₃OC(=O)—(benzene ring) + NaOH ⟶ [(benzene ring)—C(=O)(O⁻)]⁻ + Na⁺ + CH₃OH

25.50 2 CH₃COOH(l) ⟶ CH₃COCH₃(l) (with two =O) + H₂O(l)

CH₃C(=O)—[OH + H]—O—C(=O)CH₃ ⟶ CH₃C(=O)—O—C(=O)CH₃ + H₂O

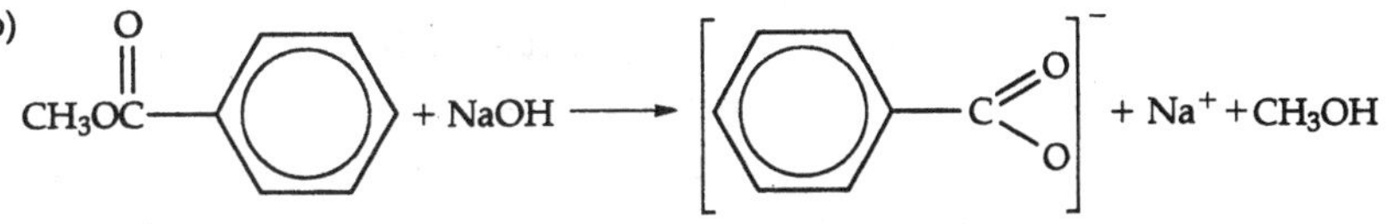

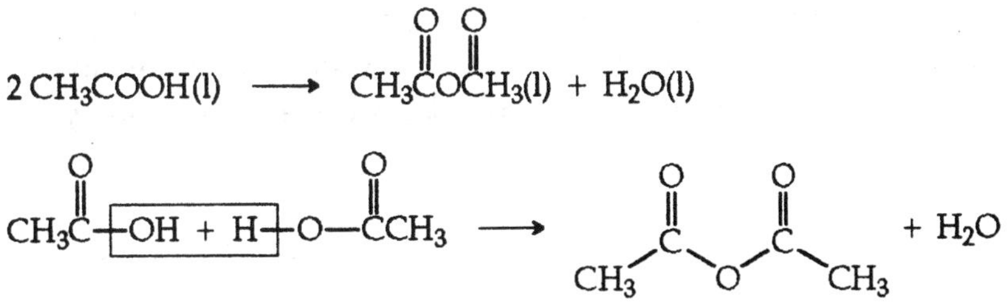

25 Organic and Biological Chemistry

Solutions to Black Exercises

25.52 (a)

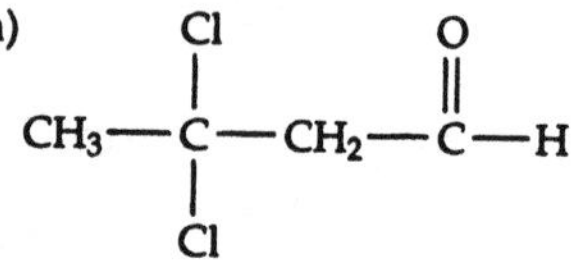

(b)

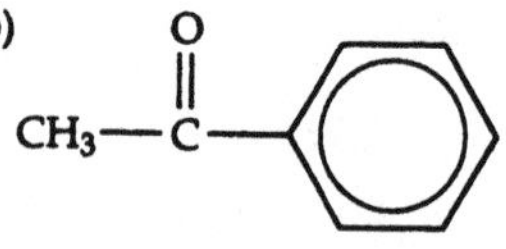

(c)

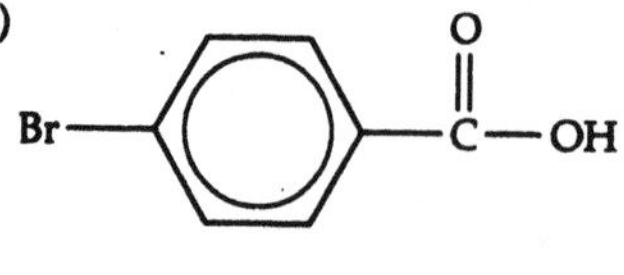

(d)

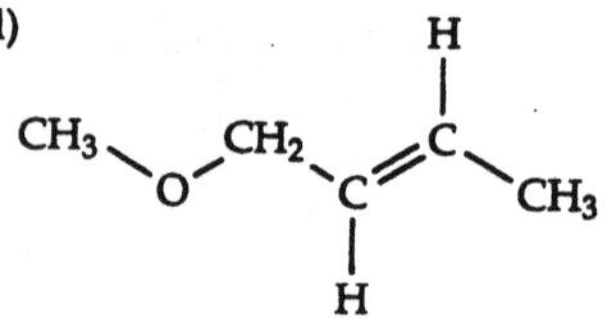

(e)

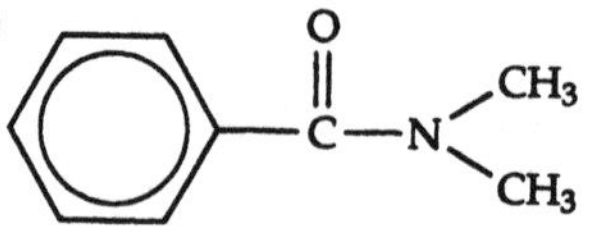

25.54

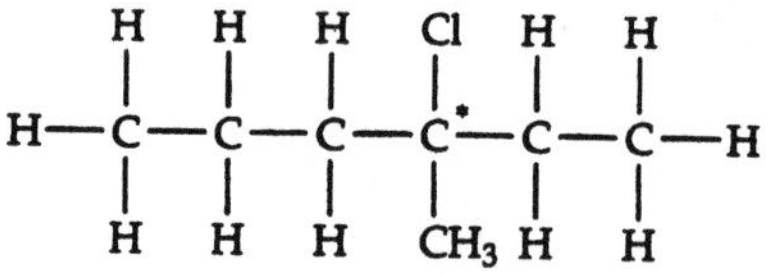

Yes, the molecule has optical isomers. The chiral carbon atom is attached to chloro, methyl, ethyl, and propyl groups. (If the root was a 5-carbon chain, the molecule would not have optical isomers because two of the groups would be ethyl groups.)

Proteins

25.56 The side chains possess three characteristics that may be of importance. They may be bulky (e.g., the phenyl group in phenylalanine) and thus impose restraints on where and how the amino acid can undergo reaction. Secondly, the side chain will be either hydrophobic, containing mostly nonpolar groups such as $(CH_3)_2CH—$ in valine, or hydrophilic, containing a polar group such as —OH in serine. The hydrophobic or hydrophilic nature of the side chain definitely influences solubility and other intermolecular interactions. Finally, the side chain may contain an acidic (e.g., the —COOH group in glutamic acid) or basic (e.g., the $—NH_2$ group in lysine) functional group. These groups will be protonated or deprotonated, depending on the pH of the solution, and determine the variation of properties (including solubility) over a range of pH values. Acidic or basic side chains may also become involved in hydrogen-bonding with other amino acids.

25.58

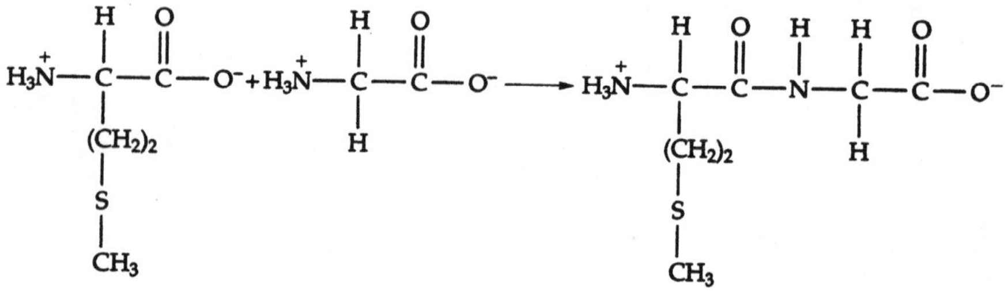

methionine glycine methionylglycine

25.60 (a) Valine, serine, glutamic acid

(b) Six (assuming the tripeptid contains all three amino acids):

Gly-Ser-Glu, GSE; Gly-Glu-Ser, GES; Ser-Gly-Glu, SGE; Ser-Glu-Gly, SEG; Glu-Ser-Gly, ESG; Glu-Gly-Ser, EGS

25.62 The α-helix and β-sheet are examples of regular orientations in protein chains that are termed protein secondary structures. Both patterns are formed by hydrogen bonding. The main difference is that an α-helix is formed by hydrogen bonds between amino acids in the same chain, while a β-sheet is formed by hydrogen bonds between two chains (or a chain with a flexible loop that has bent back on itself to form hydrogen bonds).

An α-helix is a column, with hydrogen bonds between a particular amino acid and a different amino acid several groups away. In Figure 25.26, the pitch of the helix orients hydrogen bonds between every fourth amino acid. A β-sheet has a hydrogen-bonding pattern that zippers together two uncoiled protein strands to form a "pleated" sheet. These two secondary structures are enabled by different amino acid sequences. And, many sequences form neither an α-helix nor a β-sheet.

Carbohydrates and Lipids

25.64 Glucose exists in solution as a cyclic structure in which the aldehyde function on carbon 1 reacts with the OH group of carbon 5 to form what is called a hemiacetal, Figure 25.29. Carbon atom 1 carries an OH group in the hemiacetal form; in α-glucose this OH group is on the opposite side of the ring as the CH_2OH group on carbon atom 5. In the β (beta) form the OH group on carbon 1 is on the same side of the ring as the CH_2OH group on carbon 5.

The condensation product of two glucose units looks like this:

α-linkage   β-linkage

25.66 (a) In the linear form of galactose, the aldehydic carbon is C1. Carbon atoms 2, 3, 4, and 5 are chiral because they each carry four different groups. Carbon 6 is not chiral because it contains two H atoms.

(b)   The structure is best deduced by comparing galactose with glucose, and inverting the configurations at the appropriate carbon atoms. Recall from Solution 25.64 that both the β-form (shown here) and the α-form (OH on carbon 1 on the opposite side of ring as the CH_2OH on carbon 5) are possible.

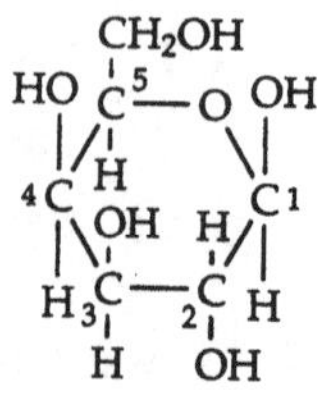

galactose

25.68   The empirical formula of glycogen is $C_6H_{10}O_5$. The six-membered ring form of glucose is the unit that forms the basis of glycogen. The monomeric glucose units are joined by α linkages.

25.70   Consider the fuels ethane, C_2H_6, and ethanol, C_2H_5OH, where one C–H bond has been replaced by C–O–H, a C–O and an O–H bond. Combustion reactions for the two fuels follow.

$C_2H_6 + 7/2 O_2 \rightarrow 2CO_2 + 3H_2O$; $C_2H_5OH + 3O_2 \rightarrow 2CO_2 + 3H_2O$

Both reactions have the same products, so the exothermic (negative) parts of the reaction enthalpies are the same. The difference is in the endothermic (positive) part, the energy required to break bonds of the reactants. According to Table 8.4, the energies required to break bonds in the two sets of reactants follow.

C_2H_6: $6D(C–H) + D(C–C) + 7/2D(O_2) = 6(413) + 348 + 3.5(495) = 4558.5 = 4559$ kJ

C_2H_5OH: $5D(C–H) + D(C–C) + D(C–O) + D(O–H) + 3D(O_2) =$

$5(413) + 348 + 358 + 463 + 3(495) = 4719$ kJ

Since more energy is required to break bonds in the combustion of one mole of ethanol, the reaction is less exothermic overall. Because C_2H_6 has a more exothermic combustion reaction, we say that more energy is "stored" in C_2H_6 than in C_2H_5OH.

Nucleic Acids

25.72

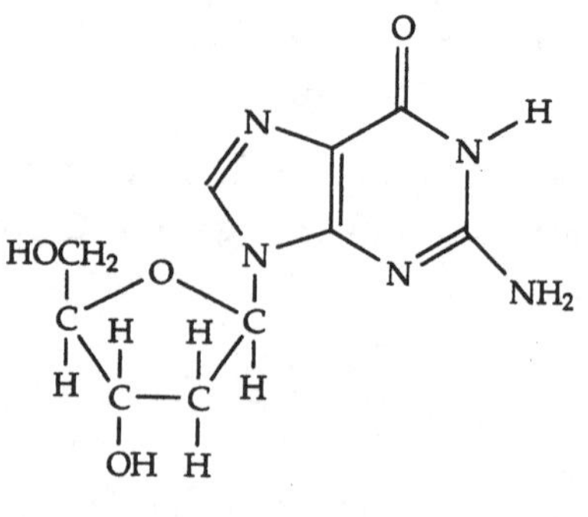

25.74   In the helical structure for DNA, the strands of the polynucleotides are held together by hydrogen-bonding interactions between particular pairs of bases. It happens that adenine and thymine form an especially effective base pair, and that guanine and

cytosine are similarly related. Thus, each adenine has a thymine as its opposite number in the other strand, and each guanine has a cytosine as its opposite number. In the overall analysis of the double strand, total adenine must then equal total thymine, and total guanine equals total cytosine.

25.76　In terms of the "small molecule" components of DNA and RNA, there are two main differences. Both DNA and RNA contain 5-membered ring sugars. In RNA, the sugar is ribose; in DNA the substituent at C2 is –H instead of –OH, and the sugar is deoxyribose. Both include four nitrogen-containing organic bases. Three of these, adenine, guanine and cytosine, occur in both DNA and RNA. The fourth base is thymine in DNA and uracil in RNA; thymine and uracil differ by a single –CH₃ substituent.

In terms of macromolecular structure, DNA is double-stranded and exists as the famous "double helix", while RNA is single-stranded. The seemingly minor structural differences in small-molecule components results in a major difference between the macromolecular structures of DNA and RNA.

Additional Exercises

25.78　*Analyze/Plan.* We are asked the number of structural isomers for two specified carbon chain lengths and a certain number of double bonds. Structural isomers have different connectivity. Since the chain length is specified, we can ignore structural isomers created by branching. We are not asked about geometrical isomers, so we ignore those as well. The resulting question is: How many ways are there to place the specified number of double bonds along the specified C chain? *Solve.*

5 C chain with one double bond: 2 structural isomers

C=C–C–C–C　　C–C=C–C–C

6 C chain with two double bonds: 6 structural isomers

C=C–C=C–C–C　　C=C–C–C=C–C　　C=C–C–C–C=C
C–C=C–C=C–C　　C=C=C–C–C–C　　C–C=C=C–C–C

25.79　Because of the strain in bond angles about the ring, cyclic alkynes with less than eight carbons are not stable. Alkyne carbon atoms preferentially have 180° bond angles; this requires a linear four-carbon group in the ring. Three additional carbons in the ring do not provide enough flexibility to make this possible without gross bond length or angle distortions. It is possible that a ring with eight or more carbons could accommodate an alkyne linkage. The (n–4) carbon atoms in the ring must provide enough flexibility for ring closure without large distortions of C–C bond lengths or angles. [You can test this with models, or by searching online data bases of known compounds.]

25.81　In alkanes, carbon forms only single, sigma bonds. Alkenes contain at least one C–C double bond, consisting of one sigma and one pi bond. Alkynes have a least one C–C triple bond, composed of one sigma and two pi bonds. In both alkenes and alkynes, C atoms are involved in pi overlap. The question is, what feature of Si prevents it from forming double or triple bonds which involve pi overlap.

According to Table 8.5, the average C—C single bond length is 1.54 Å, C=C is 1.34 Å, and C≡C is 1.20 Å. These distances show that pi overlap requires substantially closer approach of the two bonded atoms than sigma overlap alone. The bonding atomic radius of Si is 1.11 Å, while that of C is 0.77 Å (Figure 7.7). The close approach of Si atoms that is required for pi overlap is not possible because of its large bonding atomic radius. Thus, silicon analogs of alkenes and alkynes that involve multiple bonds and pi overlap are virtually unknown. Silicon analogs of alkanes with exclusively sigma overlap are known; the average Si—Si single bond length is 2.22 Å.

25.82   The suffic −ene signifies an alkene, −one a ketone. The molecule has alkene and ketone functional groups.

25.84   Two plausible decomposition reactions are:

(i) $CH_2Cl_2(l) \rightarrow C(s) + H_2(g) + Cl_2(g)$

(ii) $CH_2(NO_2)_2(l) \rightarrow N_2(g) + CO_2(g) + H_2O(g) + 1/2 O_2(g)$

Use bond dissociation energies (Table 8.4) to evaluate approximate ΔH values for each reaction.

(i) $\Delta H = 2D(C{-}H) + 2D(C{-}Cl) - D(H{-}H) - D(Cl{-}Cl)$

         $= 2(413) + 2(328) - 436 - 242 = +804$ kJ

(ii) $\Delta H = 2D(C{-}H) + 2D(C{-}N) + 2D(N{=}O) + 2D(N{-}O) - D(N{\equiv}N) - 2D(C{=}O)$

                                                                $- 2D(O{-}H) - 1/2D(O$

         $= 2(413) + 2(293) + 2(607) + 2(201) - 941 - 2(799) - 2(463) - 1/2(495)$

         $\Delta H = -685$ kJ

Clearly, the decomposition of $CH_2(NO_2)_2$ is thermodynamically favorable, while the decomposition of CH_2Cl_2 is not. In particular, this is because of the stability of N_2 and CO_2 relative to $CH_2(NO_2)_2$. For CH_2Cl_2, no oxygen atoms are available to form stable products such as CO_2 and H_2O.

25.86   (a)

$$\underset{\begin{array}{c}||\\O\end{array}}{CH_3CH_2CH_2COH} \text{ or } \underset{\begin{array}{c}||\\O\end{array}}{(CH_3)_2CHCOH}$$

(c)

(b)
$$\underset{\begin{array}{c}|\\OH\end{array}}{CH_3-}\underset{\begin{array}{c}|\\OH\end{array}}{CH}-CH_2 \text{ or } \underset{\begin{array}{c}|\\OH\end{array}}{CH_2}-CH_2-\underset{\begin{array}{c}|\\OH\end{array}}{CH_2}$$

(d)

414

25.87   The difference between an alcoholic hydrogen and a carboxylic acid hydrogen is two-fold. First, the electronegative carbonyl oxygen in a carboxylic acid withdraws electron density from the O—H bond, rendering the bond more polar and the H more ionizable. Second, the conjugate base of a carboxylic acid, carboxylate anion, exhibits resonance. This stabilizes the conjugate base and encourages ionization of the carboxylic acid. In an alcohol no electronegative atoms are bound to the carbon that holds the —OH group, and the H is tightly bound to the O.

25.88   In order for indole to be planar, the N atom must be sp^2 hybridized. The nonbonded electron pair on N is in a pure p orbital perpendicular to the plane of the molecule. The electrons that form the π bonds in the molecule are also in pure p orbitals perpendicular to the plane of the molecule. Thus, each of these p orbitals is in the correct orientation for π overlap; the delocalized π system extends over the entire molecule and includes the "nonbonded" electron pair on N. The reason that indole is such a weak base (H^+ acceptor) is that the nonbonded electron pair is delocalized and a H^+ ion does not feel the attraction of a full localized electron pair.

25.89   (a)   None

(b)   The carbon bearing the secondary —OH has four different groups attached, and is thus chiral.

(c)   The carbon bearing the —NH_2 group and the carbon bearing the CH_3 group are both chiral.

25.90   In the zwitterion form of a tripeptide present in aqueous solution near pH 7, the terminal carboxyl group is deprotonated and the terminal amino group is protonated, resulting in a net zero charge. The molecule has a net charge only if a side (R) group contains a charged (protonated or deprotonated) group. The tripeptide is positively charged if a side group contains a protonated amine. According to Figure 25.23, the only amino acids with protonated amines in their side groups are arginine (Arg) and lysine (Lys). Of the tripeptides listed, only (a) Gly-Ser-Lys will have a net positive charge at pH 7.

[Note that aspartic acid (Asp) has a deprotonated carboxyl in its side group, so (c) Phe-Tyr-Asp will have a net negative charge at pH 7.]

25.92   Starch, glycogen, and cellulose are all biopolymers built by linking glucose monomers. Starch and glycogen have alpha (α) glucose linkages, where the bridging O atom is on the opposite side of the ring as the CH_2OH group. The smallest repeating unit in starch and glycogen is a single glucose unit. Starch and glycogen can have branched structures, while cellulose is always linear.

Cellulose has beta (β) glucose linkages, where the bridging O atom is on the same side of one of the rings as the CH_2OH group and on the opposite side of the CH_2OH group on the second ring. The geometry of the β linkage requires that the two linked glucose units have different orientations and that the smallest repeating unit in cellulose is two glucose units with a β linkage.

The molecular weight of a polymer is an indication of the number of monomer units present. Starch, glycogen, and cellulose all have a range of molecular weights. Glycogen has the widest range of molecular weights, 5,000–5,000,000 amu, and is potentially the largest polymer. Cellulose is intermediate in size with an average molar mass of 500,000 amu.

Starch and cellulose are produced in plants, while glycogen is produced in animals and serves as an energy storage mechanism.

25.93   Both glucose and fructose contain six C atoms, so both are hexoses. Glucose contains an aldehyde group at C1, so it is an aldohexose. Fructose has a ketone at C2, so it is a ketohexose.

25.94   No. RNA cannot form a strand complementary to DNA. DNA contains guanine, cytosine, adenine and thymine and requires these same four bases in a complementary strand. RNA contains uracil in place of thymine and cannot function as a complementary strand to DNA.

Integrative Exercises

25.95 CH_3CH_2OH CH_3-O-CH_3
        ethanol   dimethyl ether

Ethanol contains $-O-H$ bonds which form strong intermolecular hydrogen bonds, while dimethyl ether experiences only weak dipole-dipole and dispersion forces.

difluoromethane   tetrafluoromethane

CH_2F_2 is a polar molecule, while CF_4 is nonpolar. CH_2F_2 experiences dipole-dipole and dispersion forces, while CF_4 experiences only dispersion forces.

In both cases, stronger intermolecular forces lead to the higher boiling point.

25.96   Determine the empirical formula of the unknown compound and its oxidation product. Use chemical properties to propose possible structures.

$$68.1\,g\,C \times \frac{1\,mol\,C}{12.01\,g\,C} = 5.6703; \ 5.6703/1.1375 = 4.98 \approx 5$$

$$13.7\,g\,H \times \frac{1\,mol\,H}{1.008\,g\,H} = 13.5913; \ 13.5913/1.1375 = 11.95 \approx 12$$

$$18.2\,g\,P \times \frac{1\,mol\,O}{16.00\,g\,O} = 1.1375; \ 1.1375/1.1375 = 1$$

The empirical formula of the unknown is $C_5H_{12}O$.

$$69.7 \text{ g C} \times \frac{1 \text{ mol C}}{12.01 \text{ g C}} = 5.8035; \ 5.8035/1.1625 = 4.99 \approx 5$$

$$11.7 \text{ g H} \times \frac{1 \text{ mol H}}{1.008 \text{ g H}} = 11.6071; \ 11.6071/1.1625 = 9.99 \approx 10$$

$$18.6 \text{ g O} \times \frac{1 \text{ mol O}}{16.00 \text{ g O}} = 1.1625; \ 1.1625/1.1625 = 1$$

The empirical formula of the oxidation product is $C_5H_{10}O$.

The compound is clearly an alcohol. Its slight solubility in water is consistent with the properties expected of a secondary alcohol with a five-carbon chain. The fact that oxidation results in a ketone, rather than an aldehyde or a carboxylic acid, tells us that it is a secondary alcohol. Some reasonable structures for the unknown secondary alcohol are:

$$\underset{\overset{|}{\text{OH}}}{CH_3CHCH_2CH_2CH_3} \quad \underset{\overset{|}{\text{OH}}}{CH_3CHCHCH_2CH_3} \quad \underset{\overset{|}{\text{OH}}}{CH_3CHCH(CH_3)_2}$$

25.98   Determine the empirical formula, molar mass, and thus molecular formula of the compound. Confirm with physical data.

$$85.7 \text{ g C} \times \frac{1 \text{ mol C}}{12.01 \text{ g C}} = 7.136 \text{ mol C}; \ 7.136/7.136 = 1$$

$$14.3 \text{ g H} \times \frac{1 \text{ mol H}}{1.008 \text{ g H}} = 14.19 \text{ mol H}; \ 14.19/7.136 \approx 2$$

Empirical formula is CH_2. Using Equation 10.11 (MM = molar mass):

$$MM = \frac{(2.21 \text{ g/L})(0.08206 \text{ L-atm/mol-K})(373K)}{(735/760) \text{ atm}} = 69.9 \text{ g/mol}$$

The molecular formula is thus C_5H_{10}. The absence of reaction with aqueous Br_2 indicates that the compound is not an alkene, so the compound is probably the cycloalkane cyclopentane. According to the *Handbook of Chemistry and Physics*, the boiling point of cyclopentane is 49°C at 760 torr. This confirms the identity of the unknown.

25.99   The reaction is: $2NH_2CH_2COOH(aq) \rightarrow NH_2CH_2CONHCH_2COOH(aq) + H_2O(l)$

$\Delta G° = (-488) + (-237.13) - 2(-369) = 12.87 = 13 \text{ kJ}$

25.100   (a)   A = adenosine = $C_{10}H_{12}O_3N_5$

$$[A\text{---}P_3O_{10}]^{4-} + H_2O \longrightarrow [A\text{---}P_2O_6(OH)]^{2-} + HPO_4^{2-}$$

(The placement of the H^+ in these reactions is somewhat arbitrary; H^+ is attracted to the strongest base, but the equilibria are complex.)

(b)   If the hydrolysis reaction is spontaneous, the sign of ΔG must be negative.

(c)   Adenosine monophosphate (AMP) + inorganic phosphate

(The placement of the H^+ in these reactions is somewhat arbitrary; H^+ is attracted to the strongest base, but the equilibria are complex.)

25.101   (a)   At low pH, the amine and carboxyl groups are protonated.   At high pH, the amine and carboxyl groups are deprotonated.

(b)

$K_a = 1.8 \times 10^{-5}$, $pK_a = -\log(1.8 \times 10^{-5}) = 4.74$

The conjugate acid of NH_3 is NH_4^+.

$NH_4^+(aq) \rightleftharpoons NH_3(aq) + H^+(aq)$

$K_a = K_w/K_b = 1.0 \times 10^{-14} / 1.8 \times 10^{-5} = 5.55 \times 10^{-10} = 5.6 \times 10^{-10}$

$pK_a = -\log(5.55 \times 10^{-10}) = 9.26$

In general, a –COOH group is stronger acid than a –NH₃⁺ group. The lower pKₐ value for amino acids is for the ionization (deprotonation) of the –COOH group and the higher pKₐ is for the deprotonation of the –NH₃⁺ group.

(c)

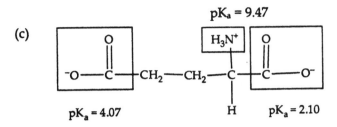

By analogy to serine, the carboxyl group near the amine will have pKₐ ~2 and the amino group will have pKa ~9. By elimination, the carboxyl group in the side chain has pKₐ ~4.

25.102 (a) Because the native form is most stable, it has a lower, more negative free energy than the denatured form. Another way to say this is that ΔG for the process of denaturing the protein is positive.

(b) ΔS is negative in going from the denatured form to the folded (native) form; the native protein is more ordered.

(c) The four S—S linkages are strong covalent links holding the chain in place in the folded structure. A folded structure without these links would be less stable (higher G) and have more motional freedom (more positive entropy).

(d) After reduction, the eight S—H groups will form hydrogen-bond-like interations with acceptors along the protein backbone, but these will be weaker and less specifically located than the S—S covalent bonds of the native protein. Overall, the tertiary structure of the reduced protein will be looser and less compact due to the loss of the S—S linkages.

(e) The amino acid cysteine must be present in order for –SH bonds to be found in ribonuclease A. (Methionine contains S, but no –SH functional group.)

25.103 $AMPOH^-(aq) \rightleftharpoons AMPO^{2-}(aq) + H^+(aq)$

$pK_a = 7.21; K_a = 10^{-pK_a} = 6.17 \times 10^{-8} = 6.2 \times 10^{-8}$

$K_a = \dfrac{[AMPO^{2-}][H^+]}{[AMPOH^-]} = 6.2 \times 10^{-8}$. When pH = 7.40, $[H^+] = 3.98 \times 10^{-8} = 4 \times 10^{-8}$.

Then $\dfrac{[AMPOH^-]}{[AMPO^{2-}]} = 3.98 \times 10^{-8} / 6.17 \times 10^{-8} = 0.6457 = 0.6$